May This book give you
pleasure !
          Sylvia Thompson
Pasadena
1988

Feasts and Friends

RECIPES FROM A LIFETIME

Sylvia Thompson

FOREWORD BY M. F. K. FISHER

NORTH POINT PRESS *San Francisco* 1988

Acknowledgments

A cookbook, fiendishly complex, does not spring full-grown from the author's head. Mine took years and the constant nurturing of many people. When the manuscript was finished, even more people gave an astonishing amount of time to producing the finished work.

I am indebted to, and wish to warmly thank . . .

Editor-in-Chief Jack Shoemaker. He is that rara avis in publishing today who not only says to an author that he wants her to be happy with her book, but then sees to it that she is.

Kathleen Moses, an editor who is a joy to work with. Kate's sensitivity and common sense smoothed out myriad conceptual, technical, and, yes, temperamental lumps and bumps.

The estimable Frances McCullough. Fran taught me considerable with her pencil, and, as is the case with Kate, I am grateful to have gained her as my friend.

My daughter Dinah Sapia. Dinah read the manuscript with a stunningly sharp eye, viewing it, to my great benefit, from the perspective of an inquiring new cook. Her contribution was invaluable.

David Bullen. After years of having a book exist only on typewritten 8 × 10 pages, to see it come to life in David's extraordinarily fine design gives me the keenest possible pleasure.

Family and friends who have contributed recipes, tested and tasted for me. Their kindness, their patience, and their palates have helped me enormously. My very special thanks to Hildegard and Fred Manley.

Philip Brown, who has been most generous in sharing his wealth of culinary knowledge.

M. F. K. Fisher, for all that she has taught me.

My mother, for her bottomless wellspring of inspiration, encouragement, and love.

My children, who have ever sustained me.

My husband, as always, who has given me everything—in my work as in the rest of my life—I could need or want or wish for.

But how can I thank Robert Lescher enough for his faith in me at a time when the sky was falling?

Or Susan Lescher. Without her, I'd probably still be pottering about in the garden instead of tap-tap-tapping away at my desk. Without her, I could not have written this book.

Sylvia Thompson
The Chimney House
Idyllwild
May Day, 1988

Contents

Foreword by M.F.K. Fisher

It is hard not to call on the good old truism about coming full circle, when I remember that the first introduction I ever wrote was for Sylvia Thompson's first book. . . . That time, when I introduced *Economy Gastronomy*, I carefully refrained from identifying Sylvia as my goddaughter. It was difficult for me, because both she and I were several years younger then, and I was very proud of her, as well as more naïve than I now am, and I honestly felt it would not be "kosher" of me to seem to woo her potential readers. This really hurt the sensitive feelings of her mother, Gloria Stuart, who was and always will be my Honey-Colored-Actress. She could not understand why I so carefully avoided any personal connotations in my obvious admiration for this book written so clearly and so well by a girl I had known since before her birth. With me, it was essential to stay impersonal, but to a proud young mother it was plainly a peculiarity of behavior and a real puzzlement.

Of course, this shy and well-meant lapse of tact has long since been forgiven and properly forgotten, and my relationship with my goddaughter has flourished over the many years since that first mistaken caution. By now I can boast, like any proud parent whether appointed by God or nature, about the talents and various excellences of this mature child.

That is why I can state without any cavil what I knew all along: She writes well. She'll write more. She may even write better. And what is perhaps even more important, my girl Sylvia understands and practices the fine art of instinctive seasoning.

Of course, she blames a lot of it on her immediate forebears. I know her mother, and I knew her father too, and I also knew her grandmother of whom she has written in this book called *Feasts and Friends*! They all contributed to her innate taste, of course. I shall always believe, though, that her skills as a superb cook are more than inherited. She is one of the few people I've ever known who understands without any nudging from past, present, or even future influences that grated fresh ginger, when added at precisely the right moment to a soupy batter, can turn plain gingerbread into a memorable happening.

So . . . *yes!* It's a good feeling finally to be able to say that I'm very proud that my girl (*my* goddaughter!) has written another book . . . and that I know she'll write more. Both of us have come full circle, and it gives courage to us as well as to the cooks we are to know this now, never saying, though, "once and for all!" We well know that there will be more circles for us . . .

A Few Notes to the Cook

The day after we moved to the mountain, I baked my fresh ginger cake (page 152) as a thank-you gift for a friend. The moment I slipped the cake into the oven was the moment I remembered that adjustments for the altitude should have been made. The oven door had a window. I watched my cake rise to a beautiful rounded billow—thank heaven!—and then, looking me dead in the eye, the cake gave a shudder and a heave and the billow collapsed into a crater.

I have been most grateful when adjustments are given in other recipes (blessings on thee, Pillsbury!) and I hope fellow cooks lucky enough to be breathing pure mountain air and using pure mountain water will find mine useful. Still, high altitude cooking can be quirky—like the time I baked a scalloped potato casserole for a guest and the potatoes weren't cooked after three hours. The moral of that story, said the Duchess, is not to use storage potatoes in a mountain scallop. (At least, I *think* that's the moral . . .)

Our house is at 5,800 feet. *At high altitude*, then, means adjustments for around 5,000 feet. *If there is no note on a recipe and an oven temperature is given, consider it implicit that the oven temperature should be 25°F higher at high altitude.*

When I call for something to be set "in a cool place," I mean somewhere between 50°F and 60°F. I request a cool place for temporarily keeping food, usually when it's between stages of preparation. The refrigerator can have a drying influence on delicate dishes and many foods too easily absorb nearby odors, a famous refrigerator problem.

My cool place is in our larder, which is built against a north-facing wall. In winter, the larder is cool enough to keep our opened jams and jellies. But in warm weather, the temperature climbs, so then my cool place becomes our cellar, which holds to about 60°F. Just as bread bakers have been creative making warm places for their bread to rise (under the bed covers, on top of the hot water heater, in a pot wrapped in a blanket), be resourceful. Perhaps it's cool beneath the kitchen sink. Perhaps you can set something up in front of a north-facing window. As a last resort, try filling the bathtub with cold water—if you elevate your pan of plumping apricot *confiture* or sautéed baby artichokes on a rack above the water, might that be cool enough? Test with a thermometer and see.

But certainly there are parts of this glorious country where even cold bath water warms up! If that's a condition of your existence, the fruit drawer of your refrigerator is the least drying and most sheltered "cool place."

Speaking of the larder, it's an invaluable old-fashioned idea that ought to be in more kitchens. I designed the house we live in and, in doing the plans, every time I'd have to juggle rooms around, my first question to myself was, "Yes, but where does my north-facing larder go?" It's a step from the kitchen (with a baking center/pantry of equal size—4½ feet wide by 3½ feet deep by 9 feet high—opposite). All foodstuffs that aren't in the refrigerator are in the larder. An exhaust fan high in the north wall constantly pulls fresh air through a pipe under the floor into the larder. A north-facing wall is the best, but if you have a place in or near your kitchen against any exterior wall (sheltered from direct sun), all a larder is, really, is an enclosed space vented to the outside with open shelves for provisions, screen shelves for vegetables and fruits, and ideally at least one marble shelf, which will be the coolest keeping place of all.

And while we're on the subject of cooling, some of us were raised with the rule that you have to cool foods before putting them in the refrigerator. Well, that rule's out (along with the one that says you have to cook pork until it's grey . . . progress!). Cover hot food loosely in small quantities so it can chill rapidly, refrigerate, and when it's cold, repack, covering tightly.

About measuring. I measure flour by spooning it lightly into the cup, then skimming off the excess with something flat like a chopstick. This method doesn't pack the flour as much as when the measuring cup is swept through the bag. And I never sift the flour unless a recipe, like my grandmother's white cake, makes me.

Check your measuring tools. I have found they are not standardized. Four tablespoons are supposed to make one-quarter cup. Some measuring tablespoons give more than that. It's a good idea, one rainy afternoon, to see if your measuring spoons and cups are compatible.

And, if you haven't one, I urge you to get a kitchen scale. Some foods are fairly standard. My "one large onion" is your one large onion. But in the matter of apples, for example, "two large apples" can be puzzling. Just *how* large? But "10 ounces apples" is a satisfying request. Especially if you have a scale.

Something else about measuring. Sometimes, especially when a chemical reaction is involved, it's essential to be precise. And sometimes, when there's leeway in the balance of flavors, a handful of this and a slosh of that are fine. Cooking your food to *your* taste, not mine, is the goal. But when I seem detailed about a procedure, it's that I would love you to taste the dish the way I've found it marvelous—*then* you can take off on your own.

About butter. Unsalted butter is the freshest tasting because it *is* the freshest. It doesn't contain the preserving ingredient of salt and once it starts to go off, there's no disguising it—the butter begins to taste like cheese. But since out of habit, most of us still reach for just plain butter in the dairy case, I have been specific in the recipes. Where I feel unsalted butter makes a critical difference in flavor, I call for it. Where I feel unsalted butter would be nicest but I don't want you to have to run out to the market just to buy it, I say it's preferable. The rest of the time, I call for "butter" and you should use unsalted if you have it. However, there are compositions in which lightly salted butter can be an enhancement—all the Breton recipes call for it because butter is salted in Brittany.

When calling for chicken or beef broth, I specify "excellent" quality. That means don't use powders or cubes as a base—they are little more than fat and salt. I rarely have time to make broths from scratch, but certainly homemade is the ideal. In its place, I use canned "ready-to-serve" (i.e., not condensed) broth, which I find remarkably close to homemade. I hesitate to give brand names because products come and go. Taste for yourself.

When I speak of "turns of the pepper mill," mills, of course, vary in how much pepper they let down with each turn, their coarseness of grind, and whatnot. So apply the number loosely to your own mills—I hope you have one for white and one for black—and to your own fondness for pepper. (You might want to see the Appendix for more about flavors in pepper.)

And although I don't say so each time, as with Parmesan or Romano cheese, nutmeg really ought to be freshly grated. A small silvery nutmeg grater is an inexpensive stocking present (ask Santa) and whole nutmegs are available from cookware shops and most shops that sell coffee and tea.

When I see a handsome rank of herbs and spices lined up by a friend's stove, I wince. Certainly they're lovely to look at and it's tempting to keep seasonings within arm's reach. But heat and light play havoc with the essential oils in these dried leaves, seeds, roots, fruits, pods, buds, stigmas, barks, and berries. A cool dark place or the refrigerator—or the freezer, if you buy in bulk or use them little—will give these pretty bits their longest possible life.

When using dried leaves of herbs, remember to rub them between your fingers as you add them to the dish. This helps release their essential oils— you'll smell their pungence. If you don't, toss the jar and buy fresh. You owe it to yourself to cook with the best possible ingredients and first-rate herbs and spices top the list. If, when you open the jar or tin, the scent doesn't make your head spin, *out*!

Finally, ever since—somewhere French—I spooned soup from a flat soup bowl (called a soup *plate* in some quarters), I've preferred it to the traditional American deepish bowl. You can plainly *see* everything to advantage, and somehow the soup seems more esthetic as you sweep your oversized spoon across it. Our stack of large flat soup bowls, celadon with a marine blue carp leaping across, came most reasonably from Chinatown—the place I've learned to look first for all sorts of cooking treasures.

More notes are in the Appendix. I wish you happy feasting.

Feasts and Friends

RECIPES FROM A LIFETIME

At Alice Vinegar's Knee

Being a child of the senses, it's not surprising that my earliest memory is of food. But it was something somebody else was eating that I remember: my grandmother's Japanese gardener sitting in the cab of his green pickup truck, the door ajar, so that, from my spying-place behind the lily pond, I could see on the seat beside him the big round basket holding his lunch. I vividly remember the ritual. He would pull a red thermos bottle from the basket, unscrew the cap, and into a little cup with no handle (that alone baffled me), pour something thin and steaming and water-green. After a deep draught of it, he'd set the cup above the dashboard and then take out another thermos bottle and spoon sticky snow-white rice from it (my grandmother's rice was always fluffy and each grain silky and separate on my spoon) into a small white bowl that looked as though it were a large china blossom. He held the bowl very close to his chin and then, wonder of wonders, swivelled the rice into his mouth with two long thin sticks. Then more green poured into his handleless cup, then more rice into his blossom bowl. When he finished, he'd screw on the caps of both thermos bottles, tuck them with cup and bowl and sticks back into the basket, pop down from the cab, and return to tending my grandmother's pansy rings on the sloping lawn.

Finally one day the gardener silently motioned me over to his truck. I can still remember feeling strange, clambering up on the running board as he bent down with a gummy heap of rice between his sticks for me to taste. He smelled sweet of the grass he'd been mowing and the toasty brew he'd been drinking and the rice he'd been swivelling into his mouth. I couldn't taste. And certainly I couldn't drink anything green even if he had offered it. I was three-and-a-half and I was used to my grandmother's wholly American food.

I lived with my grandmother during a crucial stage in my life, three going on four going on five, when the first memories are laid down. Early in 1939, my parents (my mother was a film star and my father was a screenwriter) woke up one morning and found they were both between commitments so they decided to go around the world. Happily, my grandmother's house in Santa Monica seven blocks from the Pacific Ocean—and another house she would be keeping for a friend on the beach—had room for me. So until France declared war on Germany and my parents, luckily in Marseille, caught the last American ship to slip through the Mediterranean, I was part of my mother's mother's household.

All my earliest memories are bound up in those two stuccoed California houses, the Spanish bungalow on a bluff overlooking the chaparral of Santa Monica Canyon and the Spanish beach house next to Louis B. Mayer's (painted raspberry then and painted raspberry now), where I fell asleep against the rhythmic crashing of the surf behind my pillow.

As little as I was, I sensed that my grandmother and I were kindred spirits. We were both great appreciators. She was my first teacher and I have the feeling she found me an apt pupil. I learned the names of all the flowers, bushes, birds, dogs, cats, and wild creatures that were part of our lives in Santa Monica. I was mesmerized hours each day, watching her in the kitchen and at table, absorbing unawares a sense of her culinary art. I gravely sat when she had visitors, an endless stream of friends of all ages.

Sometimes, as Patty or Pansy or Rena or Mae perched on a stool and chatted, my grandmother put together a chocolate cake she served warm from the oven. I found the recipe in her spidery hand on the inside back cover of her 1902 copy of *Mrs Rorer's New Cook Book*. Under swirls of cold whipped cream, this cake is a miracle of lightness. And it's not too sweet.

Typical of cooks of her day, my grandmother noted only the ingredients in the recipe, not how to turn them into a cake—she *knew* how! I've taken the liberty of adding a contemporary mixing method.

CHOCOLATE CAKE WARM FROM THE OVEN*
[*12 servings*]
Whipped cream keeps hours in the refrigerator and the baked cake can wait patiently up to half an hour before serving.

2 cups heavy cream, cold
1 or 2 tablespoons sugar
1 tablespoon vanilla plus about 1 teaspoon
 for the whipped cream
A little unsweetened cocoa for the pan(s),
 sifted (if you haven't any, use flour)
3 squares unsweetened chocolate
2 cups light brown sugar, firmly packed

1 ½ cups milk (low-fat or non-fat is fine),
 at room temperature
2 cups all-purpose flour
1 teaspoon baking soda
½ teaspoon salt
1 stick butter, plus a little for the pan(s),
 softened
3 extra large egg yolks, at room temperature

---

*Truth to tell, my grandmother also baked this cake in two 8-inch rounds, cooled them completely, then filled and frosted them with fluffy white frosting made with the leftover egg whites. The frosting on page 17 is ideal—make ¾ the recipe, which will be more than enough.

Whip the cream with just enough sugar and vanilla to lightly sweeten;* cover and refrigerate. For a pan, use a 10 × 2-inch square or a 13 × 9 × 2-inch rectangle. Brush with butter then dust with cocoa or flour, shaking out excess.

When ready to mix the batter, heat the oven to 350°F.

In a medium-sized vessel in the microwave at ⅔ power, or over low heat, melt the chocolate with 1 cup of the brown sugar and ½ cup of the milk, stirring occasionally; cool. Lightly stir the flour, baking soda, and salt together in a mixing bowl. Add the butter, yolks, tablespoon of vanilla, remaining brown sugar, and milk. Beat slowly until blended, then beat at medium speed or by hand 2 minutes, scraping the bowl and the beaters or spoon twice. Add the chocolate mixture and beat another minute. Smooth the batter into the pan(s) and rap gently on the counter to knock out any air bubbles.

Bake until a fine skewer thrust into the center comes out clean, about 35 minutes. Cool 10 minutes in the pan(s), then turn out right side up onto a serving plate—or, if it must wait, onto a cooling rack; then slide the cake onto the plate when ready to serve. Cover with swirls of whipped cream and carry to the table.

[*At high altitude:* Use 1⅔ cups light brown sugar and 1⅔ cups milk and bake at 375°F.]

My grandmother was born in 1884 (we think—she was of a generation of women who could never quite remember their birthdate) in the San Joaquin Valley, that hot fragrant swath down the center of California. (The Sacramento Valley is the San Joaquin's northern half—physically, it is all one valley, the Great Valley, over twenty-five thousand fertile square miles.) Even in those days, the San Joaquin was a horn of plenty heaped with tomatoes, green peppers, corn, eggplant, cucumbers, zucchini, green beans, onions, sugar beets, turnips, parsnips, carrots, potatoes, sweet potatoes, winter squashes, pumpkins, wheat, olives, and alfalfa. Only the tender crops—peas, spinach, lettuces, and artichokes—were left to the across-the-coastal-mountains Salinas Valley (cool and sea-scented, spilling into Monterey Bay); such crops would bolt in the fierce summers of the San Joaquin. But the ferocious heat made sweet the strawberries, watermelons, casabas, Crenshaws, cantaloupes, peaches, nectarines, plums, figs, apricots, mulberries, grapes, and almonds. The San Joaquin was truly God's garden.

The people of the Valley were plain people. They lived in plain houses in plain small towns with names like Sanger, Visalia, Reedley, Dinuba, Hanford, Lemoore, Turlock, and "The Raisin Capital of the World," Selma, where my grandmother was born. The Valley has been much developed these last hundred years. But the fields, where there are fields, are the same. The produce is the same, or a hybridized offspring thereof. And the people, from

---

*Page 245 has the way to whip it fastest.

everything I have learned about them over a lifetime of visiting and reading, have hardly changed at all.

Now here is the sort of thing you would have been served a hundred years ago were you a guest in the house in Selma my great-grandfather built for my great-grandmother. The house once stood next to his smithy, but after she discovered he was up in San Francisco singing and dancing with the ladies of the Barbary Coast, my great-grandmother set fire to his forge and burned it to the ground. Now the lovely Victorian house sits a spit away from Highway 99, the main trucking route that gathers all the produce down through the Great Valley. And this is the sort of thing you'd be served today in most any coffee shop or restaurant along that highway.

Raisin pie is a homely matter, looking rather unpromising when you put your fork to it. Unlike Southern versions that are gussied up with chopped pecans and dark corn syrup—and mincelike versions sploshed with apple cider—San Joaquin Valley raisin pie is just great big fat sweet raisins lit with lemon. Because of its tangy edge, I've found it's a good pie for both pie fanciers and those who fancy they don't *like* pie. (In pioneer days, this raisin pie was lit with cider vinegar because cider vinegar was the cook's lemon. Cider vinegar is still marvelous in this pie if you're out of lemons—you get its lovely tang and a whiff of apples as well.)

Old-fashioned cooks say that cutting up raisins releases their flavor (scissors are easiest). I wouldn't argue. Seeded muscats are specified because that was the only raisin my grandmother used. Sad to say, muscats have become increasingly scarce.* California monukka raisins (seedless) are a delicious alternative.

This is a very old recipe.

San Joaquin Valley Raisin Pie
[*8 to 10 servings*]
Like most pies, this is best the day it's baked, but both filling and pastry will be the better for having been prepared the day before.

1 recipe of your favorite pastry or my Perfect Pie Pastry (recipe follows)	*³/4 cup sugar*
	2 cups water, cool
1 pound† seeded muscat, monukka, or other large dark seedless raisins, half of them cut in half	*2 tablespoons cornstarch*
	¹/4 cup fresh lemon juice (1 large juicy lemon)‡

---

*Sometimes they are available in the market in boxes beside dark Thompson seedless and golden raisins. But since muscats provide only about ¹/2 percent of the annual raisin crop—in a good year—they are easier to find in shops that specialize in candied fruit. When you do find muscat raisins, buy several pounds. Well-wrapped, they'll keep in the refrigerator one year and in the freezer indefinitely.

†3 rounded cups of seeded or 2³/4 cups of seedless raisins.

‡Or use 3 tablespoons cider vinegar and omit the lemon and orange zests.

½ *stick butter, preferably unsalted, plus a*
    little for the pastry shell
The zest of 1 lemon, finely shredded
The zest of 1 orange, finely shredded
1 extra large egg, well beaten

¾ *teaspoon mace*
*3 tablespoons fine dry breadcrumbs**
A little confectioner's sugar, sifted
1 quart vanilla ice cream (optional)

First make the pastry.† Roll out the bottom and fit into a 9 × 1½-inch pie dish. Trim, then brush dough with butter. Roll out the top and cut in strips for a lattice.

In a large saucepan over medium heat, bring the raisins, sugar, and water to a simmer. Simmer just until the raisins are plumped and tender, a few minutes. Meanwhile, dissolve the cornstarch in the lemon juice (or vinegar) and add it to the plumped raisins with the butter and zests (if you are using them). Stir over medium heat until very thick and you can see the bottom when you stir. Cool slightly, then stir in the egg, mace, and crumbs. Cool till lukewarm (or cover and refrigerate overnight, if more convenient).

Heat the oven to 425°F. Stir the filling well, then smooth evenly into the shell. Lay on the lattice top.

Bake on the lowest rack of the oven 15 minutes, then set the pie on the center rack, reduce the heat to 350°F,‡ and bake until the pastry is beautifully browned and the filling bubbles in at least one spot, 20 to 30 minutes more. The filling will continue to cook as it cools. Cool on a rack. Serve warm, lightly dusted with sifted confectioner's sugar, and with or without vanilla ice cream.

After forty years (is it possible?) of baking pies, I've found the following pastry to be the best of the best—in fact, I daresay it's well nigh perfect. You know, you can tell how a crust will taste by its appearance. If the pastry is golden with an inner warmth and lustre and if it positively *looks* delectable, it will be. People who have made a study of such things have adjectives for the crust I'm describing. They call it "flaky" as opposed to "tender" and "short" as opposed to "crisp." I have always been wary of such terms. They remind me of some of the words used to describe wine—I *think* I know where the distinctions lie but do I really? What I do know about the pastry is that it bakes to tones of roasted nuts—almond, walnut, hazelnut, and, where juices have overflowed and caramelized, chestnut—that the top crust rises and falls in voluptuous mounds and valleys as it drapes itself over the filling, and that the pastry shatters on the tongue into a hundred sweet shards. It is, in fact, all of flaky, tender, short, and crisp, so there.

The right formula can make any baker look good. This one does—lard

---

*Two small slices of white or light wheat bread will make them, as on page 239.
†Detailed notes about preparing the pastry, the shell, and the lattice are on pages 253–256.
‡Baking a pie with custard filling: So the egg will have less chance of seeping into the dough and making it soggy, begin in a hot oven and place the pie close to the source of heat. This will set the bottom pastry and warm the egg so it, too, will start to set. Not all pie bakers follow this technique, but it works for me.

gives lightness,* butter flavor, egg richness, and vinegar tenderness. One caution: when the fat is firm and cold, this dough handles like a dream. When the fat is soft, this dough handles like a nightmare.

This recipe makes two crusts. I find it worthwhile, in terms of time and energy, to make two crusts even if baking only one: I freeze the second for another time.

Perfect Pie Pastry
{Makes two 9-inch crusts}

The dough may be refrigerated for a couple of days before rolling and, if well wrapped, overnight after rolling out.

2 cups all-purpose flour, plus more for the board

A slightly rounded ½ teaspoon salt

½ cup (4 ounces) lard or vegetable shortening, cold

½ stick butter, preferably unsalted, cold; plus 1 tablespoon, softened, for the shell

3 tablespoons beaten egg (less than 1 extra large)†

3 tablespoons water, iced

2 teaspoons cider vinegar

Detailed instructions for making pie pastry are on pages 253–256.

Mix the flour and salt in mixing or food processor bowl. Cut the lard and cold butter in ½-inch chips evenly over the flour. In a small bowl, blend the egg, ice water, and vinegar.

Hand method: With your fingertips, rub the flour and fat together with crisp light strokes until the largest pieces are the size of small peas. Toss the flour with a fork while drizzling the egg mixture over it, never hitting the same place twice. Press flour, fat, and liquid evenly together to make a dough.

Food processor method: Process the flour and fat until the largest pieces are the size of small peas, about 6 seconds. Pour over this the egg mixture and process until the dough masses together and revolves around the blade once.

Pat the dough into a perfect ball, then cut the ball in half (or according to the recipe) and pat into inch-thick rounds. Wrap in foil if you're going to refrigerate them, then bring to slightly cooler than room temperature before rolling.

Roll out rounds to 12½ inches in diameter, ⅛-inch thick.

Proceed according to the recipe.

The sweetness of my grandmother's cooking wasn't only in her baking. From those young years in her house to cooking with her after I was married, I can remember only delight in my grandmother's kitchen. How many friends have told me they never learned to cook as children because their mothers and

---

‡If you prefer, shortening may be substituted for the lard—it also adds lightness to pastry.
†Once, at this point, I found I had no eggs in the house, so I used 6 tablespoons of ice water altogether instead. The finished pastry was gorgeous.

grandmothers wouldn't let them in the kitchen—they might make a mess. Even though I have no recollection of actually helping her cook as a child (I did what all beginning cooks do: helped set the table, dried the dishes, and watched), I do remember how much I enjoyed the whole notion of cooking because my grandmother did it with such pleasure, it all came out so deliciously, and everything in her kitchen, as I remember it, was sweetness and light.

My grandmother was a purely American cook—she had been taught by purely American cooks. The early life of her mother, also named Alice, was hard. The elder Alice had been born in Angel's Camp, the California gold rush town, in 1854, two years after her own mother, Berilla, crossed the Great Plains from Missouri in a covered wagon. In the white frame house my great-grandfather built there were no frills. I've stood there. In the large open kitchen, I imagine that the simplest and freshest sort of cooking was done. Surely Berilla paid an occasional visit and the young Alice absorbed from her own grandmother, as I was absorbing from her, a sense of cookery from the heartland of this country. Growing up with such richness from the earth, such splendid things to eat, even though other pleasures were few, certainly would give a girl a taste for the pure and simple. One flavor, perhaps two, well married. If there was cream in, you could taste its sweetness. If coconut, it was grated fresh. If lemon, it was the very dish a lemon would have chosen for itself. Parsley was my grandmother's entire *bouquet garni*—well, there was bay for her poached salmon and sage for her turkey dressing, but those were for Occasions. Elegance born not of elaboration but of understatement.

This brief formative time with my grandmother was one of the most instructive of my cooking life. It was an intensive course of instruction, for next to nurturing her family and her prize-winning pansies, what my grandmother best loved in life was having friends in for cards. These parties, once a week at least, meant a frenzy of cooking and polishing and setting up. These were my first lessons in entertaining, from a master.

I hugely enjoyed those afternoons, the circle of soft-voiced, flower-scented, marcelled, and manicured ladies wearing green eyeshades against the California sunshine, bent over the cards with a concentration I took advantage of to cadge a fingerlength watercress sandwich or a fistful of Jordan almonds. And I adored the nights coming downstairs (in whichever house it was) for a drink of water or any excuse and finding the big round table with its bright green felt cover itself nearly covered with spangles of poker chips, fans of playing cards, cut crystal dishes of cashews and opera creams, tall glasses chockablock with tinkling ice, blue smoke of a dozen cigars and cigarettes wafting around the table over the men and women I loved.

My grandmother's favorite summer dish to make for her friends was her masterpiece: poached whole salmon in cream sauce with moments of hard-cooked eggs.

Now my grandmother poached her salmon the traditional way—in a sprightly stock pungent with tarragon vinegar, the dominant flavor in her sauce. She never wrote down her method of timing, so I use this contemporary rule: ten minutes per inch, measured at the fish's thickest part, counting from the time the stock comes to a simmer. Once I cooked a whole six-pounder, four inches thick, which took forty minutes' simmering, and once a two-and-a-half-pound chunk of salmon, three inches thick, which took thirty minutes. The girth's the thing.

However, there is an unknown element in the timing that must be taken into consideration when you're planning your schedule—it is the time the stock takes to come to a simmer before you can begin counting. It might be twenty minutes for a smallish amount of stock or thirty or forty minutes for a bigger pot. Since salmon is so costly and since you surely will be making this for a special party, best to start the poaching sooner rather than later—the cooked fish can be kept warm and happy in a low oven and the guests can be kept warm and happy in the living room.

There are other methods for cooking salmon that give a poached texture as well. A dear friend serves a sublime Silver salmon from the waters off Northern California's coast. She moistens the fish with dry vermouth, wraps it tightly in foil, and bakes it in a 350°F oven, also using the ten-minutes-per-inch rule. Another friend also tightly wraps salmon in heavy foil and plunges the packet into boiling water in her fish poacher. She keeps the water at "a gentle boil" and allows eight minutes to the pound, counting from the moment the fish hits the pot. Although received opinion has it that the water should only be tepid when the fish goes in and should never even reach boiling, she has cooked schools of salmon this way and her salmon is lovely. Both methods are for serving salmon cold, but they work equally well for serving the salmon hot.

As for which cut of salmon to choose, a whole fish is handsomest, I think. And if you can buy it boned, by all means do so.

ALICE VINEGAR'S POACHED SALMON WITH HARD COOKED EGG SAUCE
[8 servings]

THE STOCK AND THE SALMON
The stock may be prepared up to 24 hours in advance and refrigerated.

6 pounds whole, 4 pounds dressed, or 2 ½ pounds center chunk of fresh salmon*   *3 quarts or more water, cold*

---

*By the way, you know how to tell if a fish is fresh, don't you? Guidelines are on page 247.

For every 3 quarts of water
  1 tablespoon black peppercorns
  4 large scallions, coarsely chopped
  4 unpeeled carrots, coarsely chopped
  4 leafy celery stalks, coarsely chopped
  A handful of chopped parsley
  ½ cup tarragon vinegar
  1 large bay leaf
  2 tablespoons fresh tarragon leaves, or 2 teaspoons dried
  2 teaspoons salt

Lay the salmon in its poaching pot—one of enamel or stainless steel in which the fish fits snugly is ideal.* If you haven't a pot for a whole fish, cut the fish in half—you can put it back together on the platter and mask the seam with sauce. Measuring the amount, cover the fish with 2 inches of water, then remove it from the pot and return the salmon to the refrigerator. Add the peppercorns, scallions, carrots, celery, parsley, vinegar, bay, tarragon, and salt to the pot and bring to a boil over high heat. Boil the stock rapidly, uncovered, 30 minutes. Refrigerate, if desired.†

An hour before you're ready to poach, bring the stock and the fish to room temperature. Multiply the number of inches the salmon measures at its thickest part by 10 for the number of minutes of *simmering time*—remember to add to your schedule 20 to 40 minutes for bringing the stock to a simmer.

Dampen a dish towel and wrap the salmon in it, leaving slack on both ends. Let the ends of the cloth hang a little over the edge so you can handle the fish more easily. Pour the stock over the fish in the pot—if the fish isn't amply covered, add tepid water. Bring the stock to a simmer over medium-high heat, then turn the heat to its lowest, set the timer, and maintain the stock at a shudder. While the salmon is cooking, make the sauce.

THE HARD COOKED EGG SAUCE‡
You may prepare the eggs, the *roux*, and the infusion up to 8 hours in advance, but keep covered and refrigerated.

1 stick less 1 tablespoon butter for the roux   *7 tablespoons flour*
  plus a small lump of softened butter for   *2 cups milk, preferably extra-rich*§
  the surface of the sauce

  For the infusion
    1 unpeeled carrot, coarsely chopped
    1 small unpeeled onion, stuck with 2 cloves

---

*No aluminum—the vinegar would react to the metal and cause the stock to turn grey.
†A note on refrigerating hot foods is on page xviii.
‡Spooned over steamed asparagus, branches of spinach, or stalks of chard, the sauce makes a special first or vegetable course. The recipe makes 4 cups—eight servings.
§If extra-rich milk isn't at your market, pour a little heavy cream or half-and-half into the measuring pitcher before filling it to the mark with ordinary milk.

A few celery leaves
A dozen turns of the white pepper mill (1 teaspoon, medium grind)
A dash of cayenne pepper
A small pinch of nutmeg
¼ bay leaf
2 teaspoons fresh thyme leaves, or ½ teaspoon dried
4 sprigs of parsley

1 tablespoon fresh tarragon leaves, or 1
teaspoon dried
About 1 cup of the fish-poaching stock*
About 6 tablespoons tarragon vinegar
4 extra large eggs, hard cooked,† shelled,
and coarsely chopped

About ½ teaspoon salt
A few turns of the white pepper mill
(¼ teaspoon, medium grind)
A bunch of parsley

In a heavy medium-sized pot over medium heat, make a *roux* by melting the butter and whisking in the flour until smooth. Turn heat to low and cook this *roux* for a couple of minutes; whisk occasionally so it won't color. Cool. In another heavy medium-sized pot, simmer the milk with the carrot, onion, celery leaves, pepper, cayenne, nutmeg, bay, thyme, and parsley over very low heat for half an hour. (If prepared in advance and refrigerated, heat the infusion to continue.)

Strain the hot milk infusion through a fine sieve into the cold *roux*, whisking until smooth.‡ Add the tarragon and whisk over medium heat until the sauce thickens and comes to a simmer. It will be very thick. Set the pot in a deeper pot of hot water over low heat and run a lump of butter over the surface. Cover and let the sauce compose itself in this *bain marie*.

FINISHING THE SAUCE AND THE FISH

The moment the salmon is ready, remove it from the heat.§ Put a serving platter and bowl for the sauce in the oven to warm. Lift the salmon onto your work surface, leaving it wrapped. Working quickly, ladle about 1 cup of the poaching stock through a strainer into a pitcher. Whisk enough stock into the sauce to loosen it—thick but not too thick. Whisk in tarragon vinegar until the sauce has a tangy, sprightly edge—you want a certain sharpness to contrast with the suave sweetness of the eggs and fish. Stir in the eggs, taste for salt and pepper and a last time for tarragon and vinegar. The sauce should be medium-thick—you may wish to thin it with more stock. Again run butter over the surface and cover the pot in its *bain marie*.

---

*If the sauce is to cover vegetables, use chicken broth or the pot liquor from cooking a mild vegetable such as carrots.

†The easy coddling method, page 246.

‡To ensure against lumps, the rules are: whisk hot liquid into cold *roux* or cold liquid into hot *roux*.

§Should you want to serve the fish cold, at this point set the pot with its lid askew in the refrigerator and let the fish repose in its stock overnight. Next morning, drain the fish on a cooling rack for an hour or so, then observe the directions in the recipe for preparing and serving it. If you were to garland the salmon with nasturtiums, Chantilly dressing, page 19, would be a fine accompaniment. Otherwise, offer a classic cucumber sauce, as on page 66.

Unwrap the salmon, leaving the cloth beneath. Scrape away all the skin and grey fat. Use the cloth to roll the salmon over gently onto the serving platter. (Fit the 2 pieces of fish back together, if necessary.) Scrape away the skin and fat on this side. Slip parsley furls around the salmon, spoon a suggestion of sauce down the center, turn the remaining sauce into its bowl, and stagger to the table with your triumph!* Moisten each slice with sauce, then pass the bowl.

(To make a fish *fumet*—stock—worth freezing as the basis for a splendid fish sauce for another day, while you're cleaning up, simmer the salmon bones in the remaining stock with a refreshment of a handful of parsley, a sliced onion, a small handful of celery leaves, and a bay leaf for half an hour, skimming away any foam that rises. Cool and strain the stock, then freeze it, tightly sealed. Use within three months.)

With the salmon, my grandmother served whole new red potatoes steamed in their jackets and the best green vegetable in season—asparagus or lovely fresh spinach steamed in branches, its rich green a beautiful contrast in color and its bite a fine contrast in flavor to the salmon. Or fresh peas.

And now, a confession. Like most of the rest of America, I hadn't bothered with fresh market peas in the pod in years. Frozen peas are ubiquitous and growers know that few people will bother shelling peas when they can zip them out of a carton in two seconds flat. For that reason, I imagined there was no serious effort to send good peas to market even in pea season.† But I was wrong. I've rediscovered gorgeous fresh peas—pods bursting at the seams, eight or ten peas in a pod, their flavor sweet, their texture that of the peas at my grandmother's table.

As many marvelous ways as there are to cook peas, my grandmother's, I think, was the best. And very American. Just peas simmered in water that cooks down to an essence, no sugar, barely any salt, and only pepper behind her back. There are many nights now in pea season when all I want for dinner is a big bowl of buttery peas. I'm having to make up for lost time.

And what about shelling all those peas? I've found that shelling peas at drink time while watching the evening news (even when the news is terrible) is a peaceable way to wind down the day.

AMERICAN FRESH GREEN PEAS
[*For each person*]
Do not wash fresh peas, and shell them at the last possible moment. Do rinse the pods.

3/4 to 1 pound of the freshest tenderest plumpest peas in the pod you can find

A handful of their pods
A little salt

---

*Notes on boning and serving the fish are on page 247.
†January through July, with tag ends in August and September.

A few turns of the black pepper mill   *A large lump of butter, preferably unsalted*
  (*¼ teaspoon, medium grind*)

In a skillet large enough so that the peas are only a few deep, bring ½ inch of water to the boil over high heat. Add the peas and pods, cover the skillet, and when the water returns to a boil, set the timer for 8 minutes. However, start tasting the peas in a few minutes in case they're younger than you've reckoned; if the peas are older, it can take 15 or 20 minutes' cooking. Meanwhile, heat a serving bowl.

When the peas are tender, lift with a slotted spoon into the dish, discarding the pods. Cover. Boil the juices in the uncovered skillet over highest heat while you stir salt, pepper, and butter into the peas. When the juices have been reduced to a spoonful per person, stir them into the peas and run to the table!

The 1-pound per person is when they're served as a separate course, in which case I like to eat them from a shallow bowl with a big silver spoon.

Something else my grandmother did with hard cooked eggs fascinated me when I was small—she colored and pickled them with beets. I found the vibrant color of the eggs entrancing, especially when they were sliced. Depending how long they had steeped, there was a circle of scarlet, then of white, then the yolk made a sunny center.

SCARLET EGGS
Pickled eggs and beets with tarragon
[*12 servings*]
You can make these as much as two weeks in advance, but then the scarlet will steep completely through the white.

13* hard cooked† eggs, shelled
A few stems of tarragon, fresh or from the
  vinegar bottle
About 30 small fresh beets, cooked;‡ or two
  16-ounce cans of "natural pack" beets, if
  fresh are out of season

1 cup cooking juices from the fresh beets or
  juice from the cans
2¼ cups tarragon-flavored white wine
  vinegar
3 to 4 tablespoons sugar (it depends on the
  pungence of the vinegar)
½ teaspoon salt, if you're using fresh beets

Arrange the eggs in a large glass or other non-metal, non-porous bowl (whatever you have that will fit them without squeezing). Lay a stem or two of tarragon on top and then the beets. Turn the juices, vinegar, sugar, and salt into a small pot and stir over medium heat until the sugar dissolves, then pour over the bowl. Top with 2 or 3 more stems of tarragon. Cover tightly and refrigerate at least 24 hours. Drain before serving.

---

*I boil an extra egg, in case one is lost in shelling.
†Easy directions for velvety eggs, page 246.
‡How to cook fresh beets, pages 237–238.

For a Fourth of July party, arrange the eggs and beets on fresh clean grass or parsley on a white plate. Tuck cornflowers or other blue flowers here and there and top each egg with a little paper American flag on a toothpick (Stationers have them).

Salmon and scarlet eggs were summer. In winter, my grandmother's favorite treat for parties was her incomparable fresh coconut cake. (Although for my mother's Fourth of July birthday, *both* the salmon and coconut cake were jubilantly served.)

Many books have their version of the finest possible white cake. After a lifetime of trying all the others (packaged mixes included), in my opinion and in the opinion of everyone who tastes it, this really is the best. It's a stately cake—I say if you're going to bake a layer cake, then bake a mountain of one.

For years, I read about seven-minute frostings and how marvelous they were, but *I* knew better—nothing was worth standing over a hot stove beating maniacally for so long. The price I paid was a youth ill-spent making frostings that were either the quick-fix-confectioner's-sugar-stuff or frostings that sank spindly into the night. Once, just after the Birthday Child blew out the candles on The Birthday Cake, all the candles began sliding— slowly and with great dignity, mind you—off the top and down the sides of the cake. That did it. I flexed my beating arm (not really, the portable mixer does all the work), and now, heaped over and layered through Alice Vinegar's magnificent white cake, is gooey fluffy frosting that weakens the knees.

And over the frosting is a mantle of delicate fresh (or good-as-fresh) coconut. My grandmother made this cake only with fresh coconut. The flavor of the dried coconut we find on most coconut cakes is, for one thing, more concentrated—true with all dried foods: think of the difference in flavor between fresh and dried apricots, for example. More than that, processed coconut is treated with sugar, so the natural coconut flavor is off balance. Wrestling with the real thing is an adventure you owe yourself once in your life. But when there aren't coconuts at your market, or when you can't face the hassle, I've found a way of treating processed coconut flakes that rinses off the extra sugar and plumps them, making them taste wonderfully fresh.

A MOUNTAIN OF A COCONUT CAKE
[*16 servings*]
The frosted cake will keep in the refrigerator or a cool place up to a day in advance, if necessary.

Both sorts of coconut may be covered airtight and refrigerated up to 2 days. Neither freezes.

PREPARING WITH FRESH COCONUT*

Choose the heaviest sloshiest coconut—the more milk, the fresher. Poke through the "eyes" with a screwdriver, drain away the milk (sad to say, it is useless), and set the coconut in a 400°F oven for 20 minutes. Bash with a hammer. If it doesn't crack open, return it to the oven until it does. Break it apart and pry out the meat with a strong spoon and pare off the skin with a sharp knife. Shred the meat on a ⅛-inch grater.

PREPARING WITH DRIED COCONUT

8 ounces dried coconut flakes   *1½ cups water, cool*
1½ cups milk (low-fat or non-fat is fine)

Cover the flakes with the milk and water and steep for an hour or two, stirring occasionally. Drain in a sieve,† then pat the flakes moist-dry.

THE WHITE CAKE

This recipe makes three 9-inch layers. As soon as they have cooled, the layers may be wrapped in foil and kept in a cool place (not the refrigerator) up to 24 hours before frosting.

3½ cups sifted cake flour, plus a little for the pans   *¾ stick unsalted butter,‡ softened, plus a little for the pans*
1 tablespoon plus 2 teaspoons baking powder   *6 tablespoons vegetable shortening, softened*
1½ teaspoons salt   *2 teaspoons vanilla extract*
¼ teaspoon mace   *¼ teaspoon lemon extract*
1 cup (about six extra large) egg whites, at room temperature   *The zest of 1 lemon, finely grated*
2⅓ cups sugar   *1½ cups whole milk, at room temperature*
     1 recipe Fluffy White Frosting That Never Fails (recipe follows)

Brush the bottoms of three round 9-inch cake pans (1½ inches deep) with butter. Line the bottoms with waxed paper, then butter the papers and dust with flour, shaking off excess.

Sift the flour, baking powder, salt, and mace together three times.§ Set aside. In a mixing bowl, with a mixer at low speed or a rotary beater, beat the egg whites until foamy, then gradually moving to medium speed, slowly add 7 tablespoons of the sugar. Stop when the whites will just hold a peak. (If you need the bowl, slide them onto waxed paper.) Heat the oven to 350°F.

In a large mixing bowl with a mixer at medium speed or with a wooden spoon,

---

*This method, as well as the one using dried coconut, makes about 4 cups—enough to amply cover this cake.

†The sugar in this "milk" keeps it from being terribly useful, although I keep meaning to try it as the liquid in making yogurt with powdered milk.

‡Unsalted butter lends its delicate flavor and shortening its lightness. For the lightest possible cake, omit the butter and use ¾ cup shortening altogether.

§In olden times, flour was always sifted three times before being used in cakes. Even with contemporary pre-sifted flour, for this cake, the extra lightness of air is welcome.

beat the butter and shortening until very smooth and creamy. Add the vanilla and lemon extracts and lemon zest and beat while you slowly add the remaining sugar. Beat until very light, scraping the beaters or wooden spoon and the sides of the bowl twice. Slowly beat in the flour in 4 parts, alternating with the milk in 3 parts, beating just until smooth after each addition. Now, using your open flat hand, quickly but thoroughly fold in the whites. Smooth the batter into the pans—up against the sides a bit—then rap them gently on the counter to knock out any air bubbles.

Stagger the pans in the oven on the center and upper racks. After baking 20 minutes, quickly reverse their arrangement—top to center, back to front, sides to center. Bake until a fine skewer thrust in the center comes out clean, 30 to 35 minutes altogether.* Cool in the pans on racks 10 minutes. Then, removing the papers, turn out right side up on racks to cool completely; allow 2 hours.

When layering on the cake plate, spread an inch of frosting between each round and on top, then smooth the remaining frosting around the sides. Pile the coconut on top and press it firmly into the sides.

[*At high altitude:* Use 1 tablespoon plus ½ teaspoon baking powder and 2 cups plus 3 tablespoons sugar and bake at 375°F.]

FLUFFY WHITE FROSTING THAT NEVER FAILS†
[*Makes 8 generous cups*]
Although the frosting will hold its shape beautifully once on the cake, you should apply it soon after it's made.

1 ½ cups sugar	*½ teaspoon fresh cream of tartar*
½ cup light corn syrup	*¼ teaspoon salt*
¼ cup water, cool	*2 teaspoons vanilla extract*
⅔ cup (about 4 extra large) egg whites, at room temperature	*¼ teaspoon almond or lemon extract (they are equally compatible with vanilla)*

In the 2-quart top of a double boiler or a metal bowl, stir the sugar, corn syrup, water, egg whites, cream of tartar, and salt together until blended. Set over boiling water and beat at high speed with a portable mixer or rotary beater until the frosting holds a peak when you lift the beaters—a full 7 minutes.

Turn into a larger bowl, add the extracts and continue beating ferociously until the frosting has cooled, firmed up enough to hold its shape when spread, and is just so fluffy you can hardly bear it.

Sometimes, rarely, my grandmother would cook something just for herself, a solitary treat. Once I watched her melt a shocking amount of butter in a

---

*Page 242 gives other tests for finished cake.
†Wonderful with chocolate cake as well, as on page 4. Measures for the 3 egg whites left over there (passels and heaps for a two-layer 8- or 9-inch cake): 1 rounded cup sugar, 6 tablespoons corn syrup, 3 tablespoons water, scant ½ teaspoon cream of tartar, scant ¼ teaspoon salt, 1½ teaspoons vanilla, scant ¼ teaspoon almond or lemon. Makes about 6 cups.

skillet, drop in a pair of something fascinating, slithery (a dull orange I rarely saw in nature, not a child's dish in any wise), and gently burble them in the butter until firm, then squeeze over a good bit of lemon juice, twist on a little black pepper, and silently feast, a dreamy look on her pale Dutch face, on butter-poached shad roe. That, in retrospect, was a lesson, too: that cooking and dining with pleasure needs no more company at table than a delighted cook.

How came Alice Vinegar to be such a beautiful cook? I daresay heredity, to begin with. One inherits an organization of the nervous system and for a cook, one needs a palate just as a musician needs an ear. I'm convinced that my mother and I and my children, creative cooks all, are merely links in a culinary chain connected to Alice and Alice and Berilla—and Aljailina and Nancy and Ann and Susanna before them. But of course natural gifts need shaping, as mine have been shaped over a lifetime. And basic to my grandmother's education as a cook were the books she was given as a young woman and which she used her whole life long.

Her favorite was *Crumbs from Everybody's Table*, a turn-of-the-century collection of recipes from women of the Salinas Valley. Many if not most of the recipes originated in other places, as indeed most everyone had come to the Salinas Valley from somewhere else—if not in her own generation, then usually the generation before her. As my grandmother was living just over the Diablo range, pehaps a cousin or friend carried the book as a gift to our young cook.

I love eating something from a distance. The first time I thought about it, it was an Algerian blood orange. When I realized I was tasting North Africa, I shivered. Through the dishes in my grandmother's cookbook, I savor the furthest and most fascinating distance of all, our past. Let me share some of my favorites.

To begin, a poem of a summer salad from Mrs. G. S. Hamilton of Pacific Grove: nasturtiums! trumpets of gold, copper, vermilion, or cerise against circlets of chartreuse-blue. They have been eaten discreetly for years. In a French book on growing vegetables published one hundred years ago,* nasturtiums are included:

> The flowers are used for garnishing salads. The flower buds and the seeds, while young and tender, are pickled in vinegar and used for seasoning, like Capers.

(I've considered pickling nasturtium buds and seeds, but I'd rather have more blossoms this year and more volunteer nasturtiums next year . . .)

Of course, nasturtium salad is only for organic gardeners. My grand-

---

The Vegetable Garden by Mm. Vilmorin-Andrieux.

mother knew to look under the leaves and in the blossoms for the peppering of aphids that were surely there. Then she'd squinch her eyes and blow them off, spritzing away anyone who was left. For my part, I have too many times dashed into the garden while guests sipped their drinks, snatched up a passel of nasturtiums for garnish, forgotten how much aphids love them, too, and been horrified to see a few delicate green or dark black dots marching across the platter.

All the poetry in this salad isn't in the flowers. Let's call Mrs. Hamilton's creation Chantilly Dressing because it is finished with whipped cream.* The dressing has a tantalizing play of pungent and smooth, and the first time I made it, our nasturtiums being under snow, I dipped in a winter flower, cauliflower. Superb! Mayonnaise suddenly seemed heavy by comparison.

Indeed, with the exception of being a "spread," this dressing can do almost anything mayonnaise can do. Try all the variations you can think of—use fruit-flavored vinegar or lemon juice, add fresh herbs or capers or threads of orange peel. . . .

NASTURTIUM SALAD WITH CHANTILLY DRESSING
[Makes about ½ cup: 6 servings]

THE NASTURTIUMS

"Sprinkle flowers at nightfall so that every particle of dust is washed away. Early in the morning while the dew is on, gather the latest blossoms and tenderest leaves, and put in a cool place until wanted. Prepare a dressing as follows":

THE CHANTILLY DRESSING

A light cooked dressing

The dressing holds handsomely in the refrigerator for at least 4 hours before serving.

2 tablespoons cider vinegar	*1 tablespoon egg yolk*
¼ teaspoon dry mustard	*1 tablespoon unsalted butter*
¼ teaspoon salt	*2 tablespoons heavy cream, whipped*

In a small non-aluminum† saucepan, mix the vinegar, mustard, salt, yolk, and butter together. Whisk over low heat until thick. Cool, and fold in the whipped cream.

To serve, arrange about 3 nasturtium blossoms over 5 or 6 leaves (both are edible) on individual salad plates. Spoon 1 heaping tablespoon of dressing onto its own leaf and place to the side.

Lighter still and absolutely superb is

---

*Chantilly, in the argot of cuisine, indicates whipped cream is involved. Chantilly, a suburb overlooking Paris, is famous for the beauty of its whipped cream as well as for its lace.
†The vinegar would react with the metal and cause the sauce to turn grey.

ANOTHER DRESSING FOR NASTURTIUMS
[*Makes about ½ cup: 6 servings*]
This may be prepared several hours in advance, but do not refrigerate.

6 *tablespoons light olive oil*
1 *tablespoon fresh lemon juice*

2 *tablespoons fresh orange juice*
A *sprinkling of salt, preferably coarse*

Whisk everything together and taste for salt. (The nip of pepper is provided by the nasturtiums.)

Citrus juices (rather than an aromatic or fruity vinegar) allow the flavor of the flowers and leaves to snap through. Pass the dressing in a pitcher and let guests sprinkle on their own. Another day, serve it with small French marigolds heaped over chicory.

A second elegant heirloom came to Mrs. E. Williams from the South—Transparent Pie. I often find the nomenclature in old-fashioned recipes as casual as the instructions (typically, after the list of ingredients: "Mix and bake"). First, the filling is not transparent but translucent; second, having only a bottom crust, it's not a pie, it's a tart; and third, I have seen half a dozen other transparent pie recipes and all they have in common is the title.

For flavoring, Mrs. Williams calls for "white jelly (tart)." I chose quince—it's costly (if you can find it) but its perfume is part of what makes this memorable. If quince jelly isn't possible, guava is splendid, and if that isn't possible, use crab apple or the best apple jelly with a jot of lemon zest.

A friend has described it precisely: "Lordy, lordy, what a pie."

TRANSPARENT PIE
[*11 to 12 servings*]
The pie is at its best with still a hint of warmth—a long hour after it emerges from the oven. If that's impractical, try to serve it within a few hours of baking.

½ *recipe your favorite pie pastry, or my Perfect Pie Pastry, page 8*
1 *cup quince jelly, preferably light colored,* * *or guava or crab apple or apple jelly with ½ teaspoon finely grated lemon zest added*
1 ½ *sticks unsalted butter, softened, plus a little for the pastry shell*

¼ *to ½ cup sugar (it depends on the tartness of the jelly)*
4 *extra large eggs, at room temperature*
⅓ *cup heavy cream*
⅓ *cup half-and-half* †
2 *teaspoons vanilla extract*
A *sprinkling of mace*

---

*Rarely, but it happens, you'll find a quince jelly that isn't golden at all, but brown. The color of the finished pie won't be as beautifully pale as it might be but the flavor will still be superb.
†Or if you have low-fat milk on hand, pour a scant ½ cup heavy cream into a measuring pitcher and add milk to make ⅔ cup altogether—this to approximate turn-of-the-century cream.

First make the pastry.* Roll out and fit into a 9 × 1½-inch pie dish. Trim, then brush dough with butter. Partially bake it.

In a small pot over low heat or at ¾ power in the microwave, melt the jelly. Stir until smooth, then cool slightly. In a large bowl, with a mixer at medium speed or with a wooden spoon, beat the butter and sugar until very smooth and creamy. Add the eggs one at a time, beating after each until blended.

Heat the oven to 425°F. Whisk the cream, half-and-half (or milk) and vanilla into the jelly until blended, then beat the mixture into the butter until smooth. Smooth into the prepared pie shell.

Bake on the lowest rack of the oven 10 minutes, then set the pie on the center rack, reduce the heat to 350°,† lay a sheet of foil lightly on top, and bake until the tip of a knife inserted just off-center comes out with bits of filling attached—the filling in the center should jiggle a little but the filling around the edges should be firm—about 20 minutes more. Do not overcook! The filling will continue to cook as it cools. Cool on a rack, then shake a suspicion of mace over the top before serving in modest slices. It's rich.

And here is a dessert from my mother's childhood, which she remembers with special affection: Mrs. John Harvey's Dutch apple pudding with lemon sauce. Except that the page in *Crumbs from Everybody's Table* has been so much used, the incomparable lemon sauce is there but much of the apple pudding recipe has disintegrated. Which turned out to be what the Japanese call a happy accident. In looking for a replacement, I've discovered variations of Dutch apple pudding (it isn't really a pudding but a cobbler) that are treasures, and I found this exceedingly light dough in a 1911 collection from the *Los Angeles Times Cook Book No. 4*. I'll warrant it's a match for Mrs. Harvey's.

DUTCH APPLE PUDDING AFTER MRS. JOHN HARVEY'S
Warm apples on a pastry bed
[*4 to 8 servings*]
In baking, a fairly wide shallow (1½ inch) shape is important: the fruit must be evenly distributed so it will cook evenly and the dough must be about ½-inch thick so it, too, will cook evenly. Half the recipe may be made in a 7-inch glass pie dish.

THE PASTRY DOUGH AND THE APPLES
The dough should not be made more than ½ hour in advance and the dessert should be served warm, as the pastry loses its appeal when cold.

---

*Detailed notes about making pie pastry and partially baking it are on pages 253–256.
†Footnote on page 7 explains why.

1 cup all-purpose flour	*6 tablespoons heavy cream**
1 ½ teaspoons baking powder	*3 to 3 ½ medium-large (1 pound) cooking*
¼ teaspoon salt	*apples (tart or sweet†), peeled, cored,*
¼ stick butter, cold	*and sliced in eighths*
1 extra large egg	

In a mixing bowl, blend the flour, baking powder, and salt. Cut in the butter in small chips. With your fingertips, rub the flour and butter together until the butter is the size of small peas. Blend the egg and cream together in a cup and mix it into the flour, stirring just until everything holds together and all the flour is moistened. Cover while you prepare the fruit.

THE PUDDING

¼ stick butter, melted, plus a little for the	*The apple slices*
pan, softened	*3 tablespoons sugar*
The pastry dough	*¼ teaspoon nutmeg*

Heat the oven to 425°F. Generously butter an 8 × 1 ½-inch cake pan or baking dish. Pat the dough into the bottom of the pan, then arrange the apples in overlapping swirls. Sprinkle with the melted butter, sugar, and nutmeg.

Bake until the pastry is golden brown and the fruit tests tender with a fine skewer, 25 to 30 minutes. Serve at once from the dish.

While the pudding bakes, make the lemon sauce. You'll find this one of the most delectable dessert sauces you've ever tasted. The silky not-too-sweet lemon-butter-nutmeg complements the flavors of nearly every fruit, every nut, chocolate, and vanilla. The recipe is my adaptation.

HOT LEMON SAUCE
[*Makes 2 cups: 4 to 8 servings*]
The sauce can be made a little in advance, covered and held in a *bain marie*, or made a day in advance and reheated, also in a *bain marie*.‡

¾ cup sugar	*½ cup water, boiling*
1 stick butter, preferably unsalted	*1 extra large egg plus perhaps another yolk*
The juice and grated zest of 1 lemon	*or whole egg, if the sauce is reheated*
	1 teaspoon nutmeg

In a small pot, stir the sugar and butter together over low heat until the butter has melted—the sugar will still be grainy. Whisk in the lemon juice and zest and let the pot simmer over very low heat while you put the kettle on. In a small bowl, whisk the egg lightly, beat in a spoonful of the hot lemon mixture, then whisk the

---

*Lacking heavy cream, use ⅓ cup milk (non-fat is fine) and add 2 more tablespoons of butter.
†Lots of good choices described on pages 235–236.
‡Notes on *bain maries* are on page 237.

mixture back into the pot. Whisk in the nutmeg and boiling water, then whisk until the sauce has thickened.

If you're making the sauce ahead of time, note the thickness at this point, because reheated, the sauce thins out somewhat; you may want to whisk in another yolk or whole egg as above before serving. Serve hot.

This is an old-fashioned Dutch apple pudding variation that I love—apple slices on a feathery bed, brown and white swirls gliding through.

APPLE JOHN
Warm apples blanketed with pastry
{*4 to 8 servings*}
Add a little nutmeg to the dough for Dutch Apple Pudding (page 21). Arrange the apples cut sides up directly on the bottom of the buttered pan (swirled or heaped, as you like). Dot with butter, then drop the dough in spoonfuls over the apples, smooth it evenly with the back of the spoon and bake the same way.

When the fruit is tender, run a knife around the edge of the pan and invert onto a hot serving dish. Dot with more butter, sprinkle with brown sugar, and dust with cinnamon. Serve at once, passing the brown-sugar bowl and a pitcher of heavy cream.*

GRUNTS!
Warm fruit under or over pastry
{*4 to 8 servings*}
And if, instead of apples in either a Dutch Apple Pudding (page 21) or Apple John recipe (preceding), you use 3 or 4 cups of ripe berries, pitted cherries, halved apricots or plums, sliced peaches, nectarines, pears, or pineapple, cuts of rhubarb—or classic combinations like blackberries and apples, apricots and pineapple, black raspberries and gooseberries, peaches and plums, strawberries and rhubarb, and so on—you'll have a delicious colonial Grunt!

Running close in our family's affection to her poached salmon, coconut cake, and Dutch apple pudding is my grandmother's carrot pudding with hard sauce. We couldn't have Christmas dinner without it. The recipe is my grandmother's embellishment of Mrs. John Hebron's. At the Christmas table, there are Carrot Pudding People and there are Mince Pie People, and there are people, children mostly, who say they won't touch either with a ten-foot pole. For them, we have vanilla ice cream. And you know what happens—everybody has a little of everything.

Now my grandmother always made her carrot pudding with walnuts, but

---

*Two cups of cream will suffice for the dough and the pitcher.

last year, I couldn't believe it—no walnuts were to be found anywhere in the house. It was Christmas Eve night, no markets open, so I closed my eyes and used pecans instead. My mother—everyone—said it was the best carrot pudding ever.

MY GRANDMOTHER'S CARROT PUDDING
A steamed pudding
[*15 to 20 servings*]

You can make and cook the pudding any time of year if you'll enfold it in a brandy-soaked cloth, refrigerate it tightly wrapped in foil, and freshen the cloth with more brandy every few months. This way, the pudding will keep indefinitely.

Measurements are firmly packed. Grating is on the medium blade and chopping is of medium texture.

1 cup seeded muscats or the biggest darkest seedless raisins you can find
1 cup currants
1 cup grated peeled baking potatoes
1 cup grated unpeeled carrots
1 cup grated unpeeled tart apples
1 cup chopped toasted walnuts or pecans
1 cup all-purpose flour
1 teaspoon baking soda

½ teaspoon cinnamon
½ teaspoon nutmeg
½ teaspoon ground allspice
¼ teaspoon ground cloves
1 stick butter, softened, plus a little for the mold(s)
1 cup sugar, plus a little for the mold(s)
The Stuart Ladies' Hard Sauce (recipe follows)

Choose any metal, heatproof glass, or earthenware mold or molds that add up to 8 cups (coffee cans equal 4 cups to the pound). Butter the mold(s) copiously, then dust with sugar. In a pot as tall as the mold plus 2 inches, set a trivet (or a round cake rack or some canning jar rings) ½-inch high. Fill the pot with 1 inch of water. You may need more than one pot if you have more than one mold.

While preparing the other ingredients, plump the raisins and/or currants in hot water 10 to 15 minutes, if they are very dry.

Squeeze the liquid from the potato shreds, then mix them in a bowl with the carrots, apples, nuts, raisins, and currants. On waxed paper, mix the flour, soda, and spices. In a large mixing bowl at medium speed with a mixer or with a wooden spoon, beat the butter and sugar until very smooth and creamy. Stir in the carrot mixture, then the flour; blend thoroughly. Spoon the batter into the mold or molds, *filling no more than two-thirds full*. Run a knife down through the batter to collapse any air pockets. Cover with its lid (if a proper steaming mold) or with a double thickness of foil crimped tightly to the sides and secured with string.

Set the mold on the trivet, cover the pot, and set over high heat. When the steam begins to curl from beneath the lid, lower the heat to maintain the water at a boil. Add boiling water as needed to keep it 1-inch deep. Steam until the pudding springs back when lightly touched in the center (remove the lid or foil to test), about 2½ hours. Remove from the pot.

With the cover off, let the pudding breathe 5 minutes, then free the sides with a knife and unmold either onto a hot serving dish or a rack to cool. Return the pudding to the mold if it's to be reheated.

To reheat, steam the pudding as above until hot, about 1 hour. Carry to the Christmas board! and serve at once with hard sauce.

[*At high altitude:* Steam about 3 hours.]

To flame the pudding—a touch of European glamour my grandmother knew not—warm as much brandy as you please over low heat, then pour it over the pudding and set aflame, *watching carefully that your face and hair and anything else flammable are out of harm's way!*

I can't say what my grandmother used for hard sauce when she was a young thing, but this recipe evolved one Christmas, a rare time when my grandmother, mother, and I were all in the kitchen. Grandma creamed the butter and powdered sugar and then she and my mother began adding the bourbon—Grandma was a bourbon drinker and bourbon gives a lovely American nip to this sauce—occasionally tasting by dipping in the tips of their little fingers gracefully. It was exacting work and took time. The result was a hard sauce that makes other recipes seem sissy. Sets off the carrot pudding—and the company—wonderfully.

THE STUART LADIES' HARD SAUCE
[*Makes about 2 1/3 cups: 15 to 20 servings*]
This keeps forever. Wouldn't you?

1 stick unsalted butter, softened	*1/2 cup bourbon*
1 pound confectioner's sugar, unsifted	

In a mixing bowl with a mixer at medium speed or with a wooden spoon, cream the butter and sugar until light and fluffy. Slowly beat in the bourbon. Turn into a bowl, preferably crystal or glass, swirl the top, cover tightly with plastic film, and chill at least 4 hours.

The conventional amount of spirits, by the way, for this sauce would be an overflowing tablespoonful. You may wish more temperance than my ladies.

And finally from *Crumbs from Everybody's Table*, Mrs. Charles Hudson's recipe for cookies is *really* from the past—Shrewsbury cakes. "Shrowsbury Cakes" are in a collection of Elizabethan and Jacobean recipes given to Martha Washington by her first husband, Daniel Custis.* Today, English children call them Shrewsbury biscuits—"biscuits" having replaced "cakes" in England. After four centuries, the recipe remains in English cookbooks.

---

*Martha Washington's Booke of Cookery.

In Martha Washington's recipe, the venerable baker wants them rolled half-an-inch thick, but in most of the other historical recipes I've seen, the cookies are rolled thin. Thin Shrewsbury cakes melt in the mouth and seem to me English cousins of *langues de chat*, those ineffable cat's tongues the French tuck in with champagne. Roll them Jacobean thick or melting thin and see which you prefer.

SHREWSBURY CAKES

[*Makes over 100 2-inch cookies*]
Stored airtight, these will keep until eaten.

2 sticks unsalted butter, softened	*1 extra large egg*
1 cup plus 3 scant tablespoons sugar, plus a little more for the board	*1 3/4 cups flour,* plus a little more for the board*

In a mixing bowl with a mixer at medium speed or with a wooden spoon, beat the butter, sugar, and egg until light and fluffy. Stir in the flour and mix well. Wrap and chill the dough from a long hour to a week to make it easier to roll.

When ready to bake, heat the oven to 400°F. Roll out the dough† ⅛-inch thick on a work surface lightly sprinkled with flour—and a little sugar, if you like, to make the cookies extra crisp. Cut with a glass or 2-inch cutter, then set 1 inch apart on ungreased baking sheets. This dough may be rolled and re-rolled without harm.

Bake until the rims are nicely browned, from 6 to 8 minutes. Cool on racks.

About flavoring. Mrs. Hudson enjoys the native sweetness of the ingredients alone (as do the French in *langues de chat*). But earlier cooks had a penchant for embroidery: an eighteenth-century English recipe adds caraway seeds; of three nineteenth-century Virginia recipes, one adds grated nutmeg and cinnamon, one pounded coriander seeds, and one beaten mace—or the most popular flavoring of all, rose water. A scraping of vanilla seeds makes my next-to-favorite Shrewsbury cake—I confess that I add it to Mrs. Hudson's recipe. But my favorite is coriander. Its warmth seems to enhance a cup of coffee and the coffee, in turn, enhances the coriander. (A friend who is a scholar, interested in their history, is even more interested in the Shrewsbury cakes and, mouth full, declares they are the best cookies I've ever made.)

This is how I've incorporated early American flavorings in an early English cookie.

---

*Unbleached would be closer to the spirit of the original flour used, but all-purpose would be fine, too.
†A stockinette sleeve helps, page 254.

FOUR FLAVORS OF EARLY AMERICAN COOKIES
[Makes over 100 2-inch cookies]

*1 recipe Shrewsbury Cakes (recipe
   preceding)*
½ teaspoon nutmeg or mace
*⅛ teaspoon cinnamon (if you're using
   nutmeg)*
½ teaspoon caraway seeds

A generous ½ teaspoon ground coriander
*A scant ½ teaspoon rose water, orange
   flower water,* or brandy*
*Or in place of one of the above flavorings:
   seeds scraped from ¼ vanilla bean*

After beating the butter, sugar, and egg until fluffy, lay out 4 sheets of waxed paper and set ½ cup of the mixture on each of 3 sheets. To the mixture remaining in the bowl, add the nutmeg and cinnamon *or mace only* and ½ cup less 1 tablespoon of the flour. Beat until blended. Wrap airtight and chill for at least 1 hour. Repeat with another portion of the creamed mixture, taken from one of the sheets of waxed paper, using the caraway seeds and the same amount of flour. Continue, using the above order of flavorings, and you won't need to wash the bowl—just pick out any errant seeds.

Roll, cut, and bake as for Shrewsbury Cakes—and hide them, if you can.

When my parents landed in New York on their ship from Marseille, they decided to stay in the east—my father wanted to write a play. So Alice Vinegar tearfully packed me on the Super Chief and, under the eye of a blue-serged stewardess, I crossed the country by myself—just the beginning of a great adventure!

About my grandmother's nickname. It came from a close friend of my parents. On occasion, Grandma could belie her old-fashioned demeanor with a surprisingly sharp tongue. Once at one of my mother's dinner parties, she may have been too tart to a fellow whose cinematic as well as personal reputation was more than her match. He turned to her with his famous slow toothy smile and said, "Why, we should call you Alice Vinegar!" But he was always darling to me, my Uncle Bogart.

---

*The French is best.

Chéz La Bretagne

We spent much of the winter of 1940–41 in the Connecticut countryside while my father collaborated on a play with a friend from his newspaper days. Her family lived in the tranquil colonial town of Ridgefield, and we frequently went up to stay in their farmhouse.

Ridgefield was then known for a favorite dash-to-the-country dining spot of Manhattan's *fin becs*, an inn owned by a superb cook from Brittany, Mme Prigent. I was allowed to tag along when the neighborhood children ambled over to the ice cream store (where they put chocolate shot over your fresh blackberry ice cream cone, and a double scoop cost ten cents). As I licked my cone, I would gaze down the road at the three-storied Victorian frame house set behind a low stone wall and wonder who lived there. The children said it was an inn. It had a splendid name—La Bretagne.

By early summer, the play was ready for tryouts. At the same time, my mother had won the plum of playing Emily to Thornton Wilder's Stage Manager in a summer stock production of *Our Town*. What to do with Sylvia? She can stay at La Bretagne with Mme Prigent, said our friends.

I quickly came to feel part of Mme Prigent's family. There was Jacques, a little older than I (I turned six at La Bretagne) but nice about it, Yvonne, his sister, in her early teens and unfailingly dear to me, and Grand'mère, *la doyenne*, who, it seemed to me, ignored everybody. As for Madame, slight and dark with an inner tranquility such as I had never perceived in anyone, Madame was imperious, as the gifted can be.

La Bretagne was my introduction to *haute cuisine*—as it happened, the cuisine of Brittany. The name itself reminds us of its origins. Brittany is peopled with descendants of Celtic refugees who fled from the Saxons in Britain around the year 500. Nourished in that granite province surrounded on three sides by the Atlantic, Mme Prigent's mystical directness was born of generations of wresting lives of grace from an intractable land and sea. Part of my happiness at La Bretagne was that I was drawn to Madame as a budding sculptor would be to a master. I became increasingly aware of what went on in the kitchen, I watched closely, and absorbed much. I cherish Mme Prigent's lessons: the freshest ingredients, the lightest hand, absolute simplicity. But then, I'd been primed for her lessons, hadn't I? Fascinating how dissimilar my first two teachers were in their backgrounds and how similar their teachings.

An aside about two Breton ingredients. In contrast to everywhere else in France, the best butter in Brittany is lightly salted—that's why no recipe in this chapter calls for unsalted butter. And the salt used is, of course, sea salt.* Not that, in small quantities, you can discern between sea salt and salt from other sources. But since we're trying to capture unique flavors here, my feeling is, every little bit helps.

There were new tastes for me from the beginning of the day at La Bretagne. Breakfast, for example, might be savory buckwheat pancakes. When I bake them now, if I close my eyes, I am sitting with Jacques on the sunny stone wall of La Bretagne, a cup of cider at my elbow, a plate with a fan-folded *galette* in my lap.

There are two sorts of pancakes in Brittany, *crêpes* and *galettes*. *Crêpes* are comparatively thin pancakes usually made of whole wheat flour, but are sometimes half wheat and half buckwheat. They are from Lower Brittany† and, as a general rule, are filled with sweets, folded in thirds and eaten hot with sugar. In Upper Brittany, pancakes are called *galettes*. They are usually made of buckwheat, are slightly thicker than *crêpes*, filled with savories, folded in quarters, and eaten hot or cold with pepper and salt. Cider—usually sweet for *crêpes* and hard for *galettes*—is the traditional accompaniment. As much as I appreciate the delicacy of *crêpes*, I find *galettes* a gastronomic adventure.

The following traditional recipe evolved from one in *Gastronomie bretonne*, a treasure trove of Breton recipes by Simone Morand. Indeed, lacking Mme Prigent's kitchen notebook, Mme Morand's collection has been an invaluable guide. French friends, years of experimenting with classical recipes in French cookbooks, and my mother's keen palatal memory have been other inspirations for these dishes. After a considerable process of refining, refining, refining, I hope that in these pages—and at their tables—readers will have a sense of what it was like to live *chez la Bretagne.*‡

---

*Available at most health food stores.
†The names are confusing, because Lower Brittany isn't lower, it's on the west, thrust into the sea. Upper Brittany is bordered on its land side by Normandy, Anjou, and Poitou.
‡*Chez* means "at," in the sense of "in the house of."

GALETTES DE BLÉ NOIR
Savory buckwheat pancakes

[*Makes ten 9-inch* galettes: *allow 1 or 2 per person*]

The batter must have a good rest before baking, which makes *galettes* ideal for preparing in stages. The batter may be kept up to 2 days in the refrigerator. The baked cakes may be layered between waxed paper, wrapped airtight, and refrigerated 2 or 3 days, or frozen 2 or 3 months without harm.

Use your largest heaviest skillet or griddle. Cast iron, stainless steel, and heavy aluminum are recommended, nonstick fluorocarbon finishes are not.

About 3¾ cups water, or 1⅞ cups water and 1⅞ cups hard cider,* cool
1 small egg, lightly beaten
2 cups buckwheat flour
¾ teaspoon sea salt, plus a little for seasoning the top (optional)

About 2 tablespoons butter for the skillet, melted, plus more for spreading on the galettes
About 2 tablespoons light oil for the skillet
Freshly ground pepper

Add water to the egg to make 2 cups. In a mixing, food processor, or blender bowl, add the liquid to the flour and salt.† Whisk or process until smooth. Slowly add more water (or water-and-cider) until the batter is the consistency of half-and-half. Cover and set in a cool place or the refrigerator for the rest of the day or overnight. When ready to bake, whisk the batter to blend again—it should have the consistency of heavy cream.

Set a heavy 11-inch skillet over almost-high heat. Blend the melted butter and oil. When the skillet smokes, brush‡ it with the butter and oil, remove from the heat, stir the batter with a ½-cup measure, fill the measure with batter, and pour most of it into the skillet. At once dip and swirl and turn the skillet so that the batter thinly covers the bottom—it will be lacy in places, but if there are any major holes, fill with a drop or two of batter. Bake until the top is dry, the edges curl, and it has browned in places, about 1½ minutes. With a broad pancake turner, scoop around the edges to loosen the *galette*, then slip the turner under and flip it over. The cakes will come up and will flip more easily as the skillet settles into its job. Bake only about 30 seconds longer if the *galette* will be reheated. Turn out onto waxed paper.

Bake the remaining batter the same way, stirring it each time with the measure. If your skillet is not very heavy, adjust the heat so the cakes don't burn. Stack the *galettes* with waxed paper layered between them. Or serve hot.

Unless otherwise specified, brush the *galette* with butter, grind pepper over it and sprinkle with salt, then fold it in quarters—in half and then in half again, making a fan. Sometimes a square is specified—fold in thirds, then fold one end over the

*Half-cider/half-water is traditional in some parts of Upper Brittany.
†When preparing a thin batter, first blending together an equal amount of flour and liquid makes lumps easy to work out.
‡This will frizzle a fine basting brush. I have an inexpensive one, about 1½ inches wide, from the paint section of the hardware store that I keep for just such occasions.

center, lift up and turn the package over onto the plate, finishing the fold, so there's a smooth square side up: nine layers in all, with the filling woven through.

You can butter, fill (suggestions follow), fold, season, and serve the *galettes* as you go. Or you can reheat them one at a time on a dry griddle over high heat, or wrap a stack in foil and set in a moderate oven until hot. Or, as I've said, Bretons also eat *galettes* cold.

These next are my favorite: by all means, drink good cider with them for breakfast, lunch, or dinner.

GALETTES AU FROMAGE
Buckwheat pancakes with melted cheese
[*For each* galette]
While the *galette* is baking on its second side (or reheating), lay a large (4- or 5-inch square) thin slice of Gruyère, Cheddar (unFrench but delicious), or other melting cheese * on top. When the cheese has softened, fold the *galette* in a square as described above, grind black pepper over the top, and eat piping hot.

Sometimes I top the cheese with a couple of slices of tomato. And a thin sheet of ham.

Then for a big Sunday morning breakfast or a midnight snack:

GALETTES AU COQUERICO
Buckwheat pancakes with egg, ham, cheese, and mushrooms
[*For each* galette]
While the *galette* is baking on its second side (or reheating), brush with melted butter, then break an egg over it. Lightly salt and pepper the egg, then top with a thin 4- or 5-inch square of cooked ham (or smoked chicken or turkey, un Breton but splendid), a thin slice of melting cheese, and a handful of sliced mushrooms you've sautéed in a little butter separately. When the egg's white has set, about 1 ½ minutes, fold the *galette* in a square as described at the bottom of the preceding page, grind black pepper over the top, and eat piping hot.

The warmth of buckwheat embraces a lovely range of flavors. *Galettes* are also filled with small grilled fish (eaten cold), with sautéed onions (hot or cold), with chunks of *pâté* (hot or cold), and with sausage ("smoky link" sorts, best eaten with the fingers, hot). And of course there are few combinations more lyrical than buckwheat, buttery apples, and honey . . .

---

*"Melting cheese" explained, page 244.

Beyond *galettes*, I have found a fascinating Breton bread-sort-of-cake or cake-sort-of-bread that is wonderful plain or toasted, buttered or unbuttered (and it's lovely dunked in coffee). Fragrant, dense, with a superb crust, *gâteau de pain* isn't at all fragile, which makes it nice to tote along on picnics—a peach or plum in one hand and a thin wedge in the other. It's a handsome and unusual hostess gift, it's fun to make—and it can be out of the oven in less than two hours.

GÂTEAU DE PAIN
A not-too-sweet Breton cake/bread
[*At least 20 slices*]
This keeps fresh a long week in a cool place, a couple of months in the freezer. When stale, it makes marvelous toast.

¼ cup water, lukewarm
2 rounded teaspoons (1 package) active dry yeast
3 ⅓ cups all-purpose flour
1 cup sugar
1 teaspoon sea salt

½ stick butter, melted, plus more for the dough, the bowl, the baking paper, and your hands
The zest of 1 large lemon, finely shredded
3 extra large eggs, at room temperature, plus another, beaten, for the top
A generous 1 tablespoon coarse* or granulated sugar

Detailed notes on making bread are on pages 239–241.

In a medium-sized mixing bowl, stir the yeast and water together and let rest until dissolved, about 5 minutes. Turn the flour onto waxed paper. Add ⅓ cup of the flour to the yeast mixture and beat until smooth. Sprinkle your working surface with 1 tablespoon of the flour and knead the dough for 1 minute. Pat into a ball, slash a cross in the top, and drop into the mixing bowl, which you have filled with warm water. The dough—called a "sponge"—will bobble to the surface and more than double in bulk in about 10 minutes.

Hold back the sponge and empty the water, then stir in ¼ cup more flour to the dough. Beat until blended and knead again (your board sprinkled with another spoonful of the flour) for 1 minute. Brush all over with butter, cover lightly with a damp cloth, and let the sponge rise a second time at around 70°F until doubled in bulk, about 30 minutes.† Punch down and knead out bubbles.

Meanwhile, line a baking sheet with parchment or brown paper. Draw a 9-inch circle on the paper and copiously butter the paper inside and a bit outside the circle. Into a mixing bowl, turn the ball of dough, the sugar, salt, melted butter, lemon

---

*Described on page 258.
†The complete dough is so rich with butter, sugar, and eggs that it takes nearly 24 hours for it to double in bulk. I don't recommend doing it; the finished loaf is, oddly, tough. This way, the yeast rises twice on its own, giving the finished loaf its volume. It is, however, a fairly flat loaf.

zest, and eggs. Beat with a wooden spoon until well blended. Beat in the remaining flour by the ½ cupful. Let rest 5 minutes, then beat 2 minutes—the dough will be smooth and elastic.

Turn the dough into the circle on the baking sheet. With buttered hands, pat the dough flat and even within the circle. Cover and let rest at about 70°F for 30 minutes—don't expect it to rise, and further resting is not beneficial. After 20 minutes, heat the oven to 425°F.

Brush dough all over with beaten egg. Make a border: using a wine cork as guide (or something close to 2 inches), use a salad fork dipped each time in flour to indent a circle around the rim. Now randomly prick the center all over, every ½ inch or so—do not prick the border. Sprinkle the top with sugar.

Bake for 20 minutes—it will be a gorgeous deep brown. When removing bread from the oven, be careful not to touch the caramelized sugar—it burns! Run a long thin spatula beneath the loaf to free it from the paper. Cool on a rack (but then, it's *wonderful* warm from the oven).* Slice in wedges or straight across, as you like.

After breakfast, the center of La Bretagne became the kitchen, as guests were expected for luncheon. The kitchen was at the back of the house, it was huge, and my impression is that it opened to the garden on three sides with a screened-in porch that ran along the back. Dominating the sunlit room was the enormous black iron stove that filled one corner. Gothic in appearance, with ornate handles, grids, pipes and vents, ovens, warming ovens, griddles, burners, drawers, and wells, there, at her blazing stove, Madame—coaxing it as she adjusted a burner, murmuring to it as she set a rack straight, bending over it in concentration as she stirred a pot—was an artist playing upon a grand passionate instrument.

Behind the house was the vegetable garden. Particular delight for me at La Bretagne was in that garden, carved from a rocky pasture flung out like a patchwork quilt behind the old stone house. After the discreet pansy rings of my grandmother's garden, I was awed by the armies of vegetables marching across the field. Everything Madame could grow in it, she did. Early mornings were spent peaceably there. I remember how sweet the air smelled of good things growing and how deliciously still the garden was on hot June days, no sound except the occasional dull clapping of the milk goat's bell and the flick flick flicking of Madame snipping asparagus from its bed, pulling broad beans from their bushes, baby carrots, turnips, leeks, and radishes from their rows, sorrel and lettuce leaves from their stalks, and tags of early peas dangling among peasticks.

In the center of the kitchen was an immense fruitwood table that seemed

---

*On an occasional loaf, there will be a bubble on the underside. It seems to be a quirk of the dough.

forever heaped with the morning's crop of vegetables and Madame's marketing. There would be a slither of silvery fish—beautiful to me in their iridescence—a couple of legs of lamb and a prehistoric Persian-red pile of crayfish and lobsters. Madame allowed Jacques and me in the kitchen these early hours as long as we were helping, and so at odd moments I could stop to examine her amazing store.

Our main responsibility, after helping gather vegetables and fruits in the garden, was helping to set the tables. There were a dozen or so small tables ranged around what had been the drawing room. There was a fireplace at its back, for, like the kitchen, this front room looked out onto the garden on three sides. I loved my job—following behind Yvonne as she laid the blue willow china plates. I was to straighten and polish the lady with her parasol crossing a tiny arched bridge by a weeping willow. Often I would lose myself in her landscape, feeling myself in the little Japanese garden, watching the lady mince daintily across the bridge. Blue willow ware still moves me.

When cooking began in earnest, Jacques and I stationed ourselves on stools on the screened-in back porch to watch. But more than watching, I think I loved listening to the sounds of the kitchen. No one spoke. The hollow plunking of Madame's pestle pounding shallots in her mortar, the staccato of Grand'mère mincing onions on the chopping block, the thump of Yvonne rolling out pastry on a board, the rumble of the large blade fan pulling steam from cauldrons—a delicious chorus to a child who had lived with so much obedient silence.

In early summer, artichokes were a frequent beginning for luncheon at La Bretagne. The climate of coastal Brittany is ideal for artichokes and many villages are famous for them. As an hors d'oeuvre, little ones whose fuzzy chokes haven't formed yet are served *croque-au-sel*, raw, seasoned only with coarse sea salt and milled pepper and accompanied with buttered bread. Such nubbins are rare at markets far from where they grow. But if, early in the season, you ever see artichokes no bigger than walnuts, bring them home and after tasting one or two raw, sauté the rest with garlic—a traditional method. You'll find their nutty, roasted flavor a revelation.

To keep artichokes fresh, see that their stems are in water—they are a flower, remember—and keep them in the refrigerator.

PETITS ARTICHAUTS SAUTÉS
Tiny artichokes braised with garlic
[*4 to 5 servings*]
All but the final stewing may be done in advance—unless, of course, you wish to serve them at room temperature. They are very good that way.

24 *walnut-sized artichokes, stems trimmed*
   flush with the bottoms
About 3 tablespoons olive oil
2 large garlic cloves, very finely chopped
A handful of chopped parsley

The zest of 1 large lemon, finely shredded
A sprinkling of coarse sea salt
A few turns of the black pepper mill
   (*¼ teaspoon, medium grind*)

Rinse the artichokes and dry thoroughly. Find a skillet or saucepan in which they fit snugly in one layer, take them out, then add a light veil of olive oil.

Heat the oil, add the artichokes, and sauté over medium-high heat, turning often with tongs, until they are browned all over, about 10 minutes—you'll want to use an anti-spatter screen and wear an apron. Stir in the garlic and cover. The dish may be prepared to this point a few hours in advance; set on the lid askew and keep in a cool place. Reheat before continuing.

Stew the artichokes over low heat until, when pierced with a thin skewer, they are tender, 10 to 15 minutes; longer, if they've been cooled and held. Occasionally shake the skillet, holding the lid, as you would popcorn. Meanwhile, heat a serving dish. Remove to the dish, sprinkle with parsley, lemon shreds, salt, and pepper, and serve.

To eat, hold each artichoke by the *tip* and bite down at your fingertips. The soft inner leaves and heart will pop into your mouth. A memorable first course.

One of my mother's favorite luncheon dishes at La Bretagne was the cheese soufflé, which was a *spécialité de la maison*. Madame lined individual buttered soufflé dishes with leaves of ham (ham from the Lower Breton town of Morlaix is much prized), pressed leaves of cheese against them, then filled the dish with cheese soufflé preparation, a tasty notion.

Here is another country egg dish for luncheon—although I find it equally suited to late breakfast or light supper:

OEUFS POCHÉS À LA BRETONNE
Poached eggs on toast with creamy onion sauce
[*6 servings*]
The onion *fondue*, the *crème fraîche*, and the poached eggs may all be prepared in advance.

1 recipe Fondue d'oignons, *hot (recipe*
   follows)
1 cup crème fraîche, *cultured or* à la
   minute (*recipe follows*)
A pinch of nutmeg
A few turns of the white pepper mill
   (*¼ teaspoon, medium grind*)
A pinch or two of sea salt

9 thick slices of French or homestyle bread
   (*not sourdough), crusts removed, toasted*
Some butter for the toast
6 extra large poached eggs, * *hot*
A handful of chopped fresh chervil or
   parsley

---

*If you're not happy with how your poached eggs turn out, there's a lovely method on page 246–247.

For the sauce, in a heatproof bowl, blend the *fondue*, *crème fraîche*, nutmeg, pepper, and salt. Cover and set in hot water over low heat just until heated through, about 10 minutes, stirring occasionally. Meanwhile, heat individual plates.

Butter the toast. Arrange a whole piece on each plate. Set a well-drained poached egg on top, moisten with sauce, then spoon more sauce onto the plate around the edges of the toast. Cut remaining toasts in half diagonally both ways to make triangles and set 2 toast points as garnish for each serving. Sprinkle the dish with chervil and serve at once.

The *fondue d'oignons*, softened onions that are the heart of this exquisite sauce, is a delightful addition to the culinary repertory. It is the Breton version of the basis for *soubise*—in classical French cuisine either a sauce of butter-cooked finely chopped onions stirred into a *béchamel*, or a garnish of pureed onions mixed with rice. In addition to being mixed with *crème fraîche*, as in this recipe, and also *béchamel* sauce, a spoonful of *fondue d'oignons* at room temperature stirred into mayonnaise makes a delicious sauce for almost any cold cooked fowl, fish, meat, vegetable, or hard cooked egg dish. Or simply spoon over the *fondue* as a sauce on its own.

FONDUE D'OIGNONS
Butter-stewed onions
[*Makes about 1 cup*]
Tightly covered in the refrigerator, this keeps at least a month, so you might want to double the recipe and have some on hand.

½ stick butter	*¼ cup sweet cider*
2 large mild sweet onions, finely chopped	*1 tablespoon dry white wine*

Melt the butter in a large heavy skillet. Stir in the onions, cover, and stew over lowest heat, stirring frequently. When the butter has been absorbed and the onions threaten to brown, about 15 minutes, stir in the cider and wine. Continue stewing and stirring occasionally until the liquid has been absorbed and the onions are melting tender, about 30 minutes in all.

Keep the *fondue* warm—or warm it up, if out of the fridge—in a covered bowl in hot water over low heat.

This next is an invaluable formula that I learned from my friend Norah (of whom, more later). Don't think it's just thin sour cream. After a day's sitting quietly and thinking about things, the cream assumes a lightness and delicacy very much its own.

CRÈME FRAÎCHE À LA MINUTE
Crème fraîche at a moment's notice
[*Makes 1 cup*]
This keeps (refrigerated in a tightly covered jar, of course) at least a week, if you
don't devour it first.

²/₃ cup sour cream *1 or 2 egg yolks, if necessary to thicken in*
¹/₃ heavy cream *cooking*

Blend sour and heavy cream. That's it.
　　If you want a thinner consistency, use equal parts.
　　In cooking, however, this mixture must be stirred in at the last minute just to
warm up, or the cream will thin out dismayingly. If this happens and you need it
thick, whisk in an egg yolk or two over low heat until thickened.

A particularly Breton note among Mme Prigent's dishes that my mother remembers was an eel salad, but she doesn't remember details and I haven't
found a recipe that jars her memory. I've never tasted it, but they say the flesh
of eel is fine and succulent—rather like shark, than which there is no whicher.
The next time I see one at the fishmonger's, home the monster comes with me
to deal with! There is one tiny thing. Prosper Montagné, in his notes on eels
in *Larousse gastronomique*, states that ". . . they must always be kept alive until the moment of preparation." I have managed to dispatch small fish I have
caught, but I certainly couldn't whack an eel. Fortunately I don't imagine too
many American fishmen have live eels on the premises.
　　Mother remembers another of Mme Prigent's fishes that is easier to manage, *poisson à la bretonne*. In classical terms, when something is garnished *à la
bretonne*, it signifies that small white beans or a combination of leeks or onions, celery, and, optionally, mushrooms are involved. In its delicate contrast
of colors—shafts of orange-and-pale-green beneath ivory—of flavors—
sweet flesh beneath tart cream—and of textures—crisp beneath unctuous—
this dish is dazzling.
　　Did I know this and forget it or did I just learn it, that fillets are scored on
one side so they won't curl when cooking? I've poached fillets of so many fishes
over the years without scoring them, and perhaps they've been a little curly
but they've been fine. Because this is a homestyle dish, we won't bother, unless you're a purist and would like to, in which case, on the whiter side of each
fillet, use a sharp knife to make light diagonal cuts about every inch or so, the
length of the fillet. And, if you like, you can fold thin fillets in half, tip to tip,
scored side inside—folded, they take up less room in the pan and look rather
handsomer on the platter. Thicker fillets or thin steaks are, of course, poached
flat. Enough nonsense.

POISSON À LA BRETONNE
Fish with a creamy sauce of julienned vegetables
[*6 servings*]
The vegetables and the *roux* may be prepared a few hours in advance.

1 ⅓ sticks butter

4 whole slender leeks, rinsed, or 8 whole large scallions; cut in matchsticks

4 celery stalks, cut in matchsticks

4 large unpeeled carrots, cut in matchsticks

3 tablespoons flour

3 cups hard cider*

3 cups excellent beef broth

1 ½ pounds flavorful firm-fleshed not-too-fat fish—handsome fillets or thin steaks of uniform size—or shellfish,[†] at room temperature

1 cup heavy cream or half-and-half

A dozen turns of the white pepper mill (1 teaspoon, medium grind)

In a large heavy skillet, melt 1 stick of the butter. Add the leeks, celery, and carrots; cover and stew over low heat until softened but still crispy, about 15 minutes. Shake the skillet and gently turn the vegetables occasionally. At this point, the covered vegetables and their juices may be set aside in a cool place.

Meanwhile, in a small heavy saucepan, melt the remaining ⅓ stick of butter, then whisk in the flour. Cook this *roux* over lowest heat a couple of minutes, whisking occasionally so it won't color. Cool. Cover, if made in advance.

When ready to cook the fish, in a large skillet, bring the cider and broth to a simmer. Slip in the fish and reduce the heat so this stock no more than trembles. If the fish isn't covered by stock, after 2 minutes, gently turn the pieces over. The flesh of fish, when cooked, will be milky and translucent, no longer pink. For steaks, run the pointed tip of a knife between flakes. Thin fillets and delicate shellfish will be cooked in under 3 minutes; 5 minutes should be maximum for most thin steaks. Lift out the fish onto a heatproof serving platter, cover tightly with foil, and keep warm in a very low oven.

Reduce the broth to 2 cups by boiling uncovered in the skillet over highest heat, 10 to 15 minutes. While the stock is reducing, gently warm the vegetables in their buttery juices.

Off the heat, whisk the cold *roux* into the hot stock. Return to medium-high heat and whisk until the sauce bubbles and thickens. Whisk in the cream and whisk a minute or two for it to warm. Off the heat, add the vegetables and stir to distribute them evenly and to blend in their juices. Grind over the pepper (no need for salt, the broth has plenty). Spoon the vegetable sauce over the fish and serve.

Steamed potatoes in their jackets for mashing in the sauce should accompany the fish. To drink, offer more of the cider with which the sauce was made.

---

* 1 ½ cups sweet cider and 1 ½ cups inexpensive dry champagne or dry white wine may be substituted.

†A list of candidates is on pages 235–236.

The cider. One of the aspects of this dish that makes it memorable is a sauce with the tingle of dry cider at its center. Brittany, like Normandy, is said to have *une cuisine au cidre*—a cidery cuisine. And, although the great orchards of Normandy are better known, there have been apple orchards in Brittany for fifteen hundred years.

Breton cider is dry or hard cider with an alcoholic content of not less than 3.5 percent. The best-flavored cider is at least 5 percent. Of the bottles I've bought, some have 4 percent and some 7 percent. I imagine that in most cities you can buy either French or English cider. You'll find it slightly sparkly, ever so dry, and wonderfully appley.

In the classic order of things at La Bretagne, after the luncheon entrée came *une salade de saison*, lettuces from the garden dressed with a light *vinaigrette* of olive oil and white wine vinegar.* And, of course, there was cheese. Little uniquely Breton cheese has ever been exported, so as a cheese course, Madame offered *fromage blanc* (page 168) and *chèvre* from the family goat.

And for dessert, *gâteau breton aux pommes*. The dough is a rich but eminently handleable *pâte sucrée*, short sweet pastry. An aspect of its beauty is that it melts down, around, and into the filling so that the finished pastry is soft fruit centered in crispy crunchy layers, the two of equal measure. Simplicity itself and endlessly adaptable to the seasons.

GÂTEAU BRETON AUX POMMES
Breton apple pastry
[8 servings]
Although it will keep handsomely for days (warm in the oven to crispen), the pastry is best served within a few hours of baking. However, all but the preparation of the fruit may be done in advance.

THE PÂTE SUCRÉE[†]
Short sweet pastry
This may be prepared and refrigerated a day or two before baking.

1 cup all-purpose flour
½ cup less 1 tablespoon sugar
1 stick butter,[‡] cool but malleable, in
*   ½-inch chips*

2 extra large egg yolks, cold
1 tablespoon plus 1 teaspoon Calvados (rum
*   or brandy may be substituted)*

---

*One part oil to three of vinegar, with salt, pepper, and herbs to taste.

†This pastry makes an especially toothsome tart shell—up to 10 × 1 inch (alas, the finished pastry is too fragile for a large freeform shell). The pastry may be baked either with the filling or blind (page 255) and filled an hour or two before serving. Ideal with fruits in the tartish spectrum—lemon, raspberries, plums, sour cherries, and such—as the pastry contributes its own sweetness. Roll ⅛-inch thick as directed and, if using a ring, set on a well-buttered baking sheet with one end open. The recipe makes a scant 14 ounces.

‡Not Breton, but better here, is unsalted butter.

Traditional method (messy, and at some point I always think This Is Ridiculous, but it's right and it's fun and it works): Turn the flour onto your work surface. In a well in the center put the sugar, butter, and yolks. Working lightly and quickly with your fingertips, smoosh the center ingredients together into something resembling a paste, working out lumps in the butter. Gradually pull in the flour, then work lightly until all the flour has been evenly absorbed—scrape down your fingers frequently.

Sprinkle over the Calvados, never hitting the same place twice, then gather and coax and blend the moisture in. With a dough scraper or spatula, sweep in all the errant bits and then press everything together firmly.

Now with the heel of your hand (fingers up out of the way), slide a walnut-sized knob of dough across your working surface—simply straighten your arm. Do this with all the dough, then gather it up and do it a second time. This is called *fraisage* and it blends the dough beautifully.

Food processor method: Turn the flour and sugar into the work bowl and turn on/off to blend. Add the butter and process until the largest bits are the size of small peas, about 4 seconds. In a small bowl, blend the yolks and Calvados together then pour evenly over the flour mixture. Process just until the dough masses together and revolves once around the blade.

Shape the dough into a perfect ball, cut it in half,* and pat into inch-thick rounds. You can wrap and refrigerate the rounds if you wish or you can proceed directly.

THE FRUIT AND THE BAKING

A little flour for rolling
About 1 tablespoon butter, softened
About 1 tablespoon sugar
1 large sweet crisp cooking apple,† peeled, cored, and thinly sliced

1 tablespoon Calvados (a compatible spirit may be substituted)
1 or 2 tablespoons beaten egg (less than 1 egg)
The merest flick of sifted confectioner's sugar

Use an 8-inch cake or tart pan with a removable bottom or an inch-high flan ring of the same size to be set on a rimless baking sheet. Make a catch-tray of a large square of foil and center it on the oven floor.

Sprinkle a smooth dish towel and the stockinette sleeve of your rolling pin‡ with flour, or lightly flour the pastry on the cloth and cover with waxed paper. Roll out both rounds ¼-inch thick and cut out with the cake pan or flan ring. This may be done a few hours before baking, in which case wrap and refrigerate them.

When ready to bake, heat the oven to 375°F about 5 minutes before continuing.

Brush the cake pan or flan ring and baking sheet with butter and dredge with

---

*But not for a tart.
†Choices, pages 235–236.
‡About the sleeve, page 254.

sugar, knocking out excess. Fit one round of dough into the bottom. Arrange the fruit over it in a flat even layer, about ½-inch thick, and sprinkle with Calvados. Cover with the second round of dough. Brush the top with beaten egg, then pull a salad fork over it in a diamond crosshatching pattern.

Bake until a rich golden brown, a full 45 minutes. Let rest a couple of minutes, then run a thin knife around the edge and lift up the pastry from the cake pan or lift up the flan ring to reveal the pastry. Use a long thin spatula to free the pastry from the cake pan bottom or baking sheet and slide it onto a rack to cool. Just before serving, dust with a suspicion of sifted confectioner's sugar—you still want to see the gilded crosshatching beneath.

This versatile little sweet need never want for filling. In any season, all you'll need is 1½ to 2 cups (the amount depends upon how much the fruit will cook down) of sliced or whole small pieces of unsweetened fruit and a sprinkling of rum.

In spring, make a *gâteau breton* with cuts of sweetened rhubarb and sliced strawberries with a flick of finely grated orange zest. In early summer, fill the pastry with halves of apricots or pitted cherries (lightly sweetened, if tart). Midsummer, there will be raspberries or, if you're lucky, raspberries and red currants, blackberries or mulberries, blueberries, gooseberries, sliced peeled peaches, nectarines, or unpeeled plums. In the fall, instead of apples, try peeled and thinly sliced quinces or pears. And in winter? Fill the pastry with stewed pitted prunes, dried apricots, peaches, or pears.* And, easiest of all, you can always fill it with a ¼-inch layer of fine preserves. *Délicieux!*

Usually by the time dinner guests arrived, the day had been long, I was tired, and my interests lay upstairs in my tiny panelled room on the top floor under the eaves, listening to Charlie McCarthy and Easy Aces on the radio. And when there were summer thunder and lightning storms, I would hide, terrified, beneath my quilt. But from downstairs came such good smells! What was Madame serving for dinner?

To begin with, *rillettes*!†

Deliberately eating fat is something many of us Enlightened find un-

---

*Should you want to write the name of your *gâteau breton* for a menu, the fruits as listed would be: *de rhubarbe et fraises . . . aux abricots . . . cerises . . . framboises . . . framboises et groseilles . . . mûres . . . petit machins bleus* (the French have no native blueberries, so they are called "little blue things") *. . . groseilles vertes . . . pêches . . . brugnons . . . prunes . . . coings . . . poires . . . de pruneaux . . . d'abricots secs, pêches* or *poires sèches . . . aux confitures.*
†Pronounced ree-*yette* because often as not—you never know when—the double *l* in French makes a *y* sound.

thinkable. Yet there remains a world of delectables composed in another time and another place in which every scrap of the pig, lamb, ox, duck, chicken, and whatnot was used, and since a goodly portion of the beast was fat, there's pure fat in. Many of these dishes have become part of great regional culinary traditions, and fat-laced or no, once in a blue moon it's fun to succumb to their temptations. Among such pleasures are the *rillettes* of provincial France, a suave sort of potted meat spread on the proverbial crusty French bread or *croûtons* (page 44) and eaten, in the manner of *pâtés*, with *cornichons* or any small tart pickles.

As a matter of fact, the proportions of this recipe—more than three parts lean to one of fat—make *rillettes* no fatter than the conventional *pâté* or *terrine*. And, surprisingly, lard has 62 percent less cholesterol than butter.

As is often the case, what began as the means to an end—before refrigeration, a method of keeping autumn's meat and fowl until spring or longer*—became a culinary end unto itself. And, as is also so often the case, one and one add up not to two, but three and sometimes four here. As the meat lolls on its cushion of fat, the flavor smoothens, the texture silkens, and the composition gains a deep and elusive dimension it did not have when first composed. But that is true of nearly all mixes, isn't it, that everything improves after resting?

The meat in classical *rillettes* is always pork—pork on its own or combined with rabbit, goose, chicken, duck, or turkey. The meat begins as small bits, then it is poached for hours in melted lard and enough liquid to keep the fat from frying. The meat finishes as shreds, but the color and texture of *rillettes* depend upon the recipe. *Rillettes* is plural for a singular—like the Ides of March. That's because the shreds of meat in the conserve are themselves the *rillettes*.

A value beyond the good taste of *rillettes* is that once having made a batch—this recipe makes five sumptuous pounds, not a morsel too much—it is very comforting having a cache in the refrigerator. I made these *rillettes* last July, went through three pounds in summer and autumn and still managed to have two to serve for a Christmas party. As I write this in May, my one remaining pot is still sweet. (*Rillettes* do not freeze satisfactorily.) This is a classic recipe.

RILLETTES DE LAPIN
Creamy potted rabbit and pork
[*Makes 4 pints of 1 ¼ pounds each: at least 10 servings each pint*]
Make this at least a day or two before serving. See notes above about long keeping.

*The blanket of fat around meat acts as a barrier, which prevents air from reaching and spoiling it.

2²/₃ *pounds rabbit**

2¹/₂ *pounds pork cut from the blade or rib end, shoulder or Boston butt, or fresh breast*

1 *pound leaf lard (from the kidneys) or whitest pork fat*

2 *tablespoons sea salt*

2¹/₄ *cups water, cool*

³/₄ *cup Muscadet (Chablis may be substituted)*

¹/₂ *teaspoon ground thyme*

A dozen turns of the white pepper mill (1 teaspoon, medium grind)

About 1¹/₄ pounds best quality† packaged lard

Choose stoneware crocks or heatproof glass jars‡ of any size whose total adds up to 8 cups. Sterilize them,§ wrapping each in a cloth so it won't chip. Leave in the covered kettle until needed.

Cut rabbit and pork meat from the bones; save the fat but discard the bones (or make a stock and freeze for another day). Trim away any skin and fiber from the leaf lard or pork fat, then cut the meat and fat into 1-inch dice. Turn the meats, fat, salt, and water into a large heavy saucepan. Over lowest heat, bring to a simmer, cover and simmer gently, taking care the first half hour to stir frequently so nothing sticks. After that, stir whenever you think of it and keep pushing the cubes of meat beneath the liquid. When most of the cubes of meat have fallen apart, in 4 to 4¹/₂ hours, remove from the heat and stir in the Muscadet.

Now, use a table fork against the side of the pot to break up all the remaining blocks of fat into small flakes and the remaining bits of meat into shreds. Blobs of fat are unappetizing and must be broken up. I prefer not to shred every last scrap of meat but to leave some bits for texture—however, the classic *rillettes* are thoroughly shredded. Blend in the thyme and pepper, set on the cover askew, and cool.

Stir the *rillettes* with a fork to evenly distribute the meat in the liquid, then lift out one crock or jar with tongs, being careful not to touch the sterilized interior. Shake out excess water, then ladle in the mixture to ¹/₂ inch below the rim. Tamp the meat down with the ladle, then gently cut down through the crock several times with a table knife to force out air pockets. Fill the remaining vessels the same way. Wipe the rims clean with a damp cloth, then set in a cool place for the fat to set a bit.

Melt the packaged lard,‖ set a soup spoon on top of the *rillettes*, and pour the melted lard into the spoon (so you don't make a crater in the meat), dribbling it over the surface until the crock is filled to the rim. Set in a cool place or in the refrigerator. When the first layer of fat has set, top it off with a second layer the same way, to

---

*If the rabbit has been frozen, tonight make a little *pâté* of the liver and tomorrow sauté the kidneys with mushrooms to flavor a risotto. If the rabbit is fresh, you may prefer to freeze these bits for another day.

†The only way to know which of the brands available to you is best is by buying and tasting them.

‡Pottery crocks, however picturesque, are not suitable for keeping because they are more porous than stoneware and fired at a lower temperature, thus they might crack or crumble in the sterilization process.

§How-to, page 242.

‖Of course you could use your own rendered lard, but it isn't an improvement, as this lard won't be eaten, it only acts as a seal.

make it smooth. Cover airtight with plastic wrap, then cover with two layers of foil, tying a string or snapping a heavy rubber band around the top of the crock. Store at 32°F to 50°F. *

To serve, bring the *rillettes* to a little cooler than room temperature. Discard the cover of lard. Offer slices of French bread or *croûtons* and *cornichons* or small domestic sour gherkins.

Once opened, the *rillettes* will keep about one week.

By *"croûtons,"* I don't mean the sorts of cubes you float in soup, I mean crisp golden toasts so easily made that it's criminal to buy them. Melba toast is made the same way.

CROÛTONS / MELBA TOASTS
Stored in a tin, they'll keep.

For *croûtons*, use an unsliced loaf of sweet French or Italian bread no more than 2½ or 3 inches wide. Let it get stale enough to slice easily. Leave the crust on and, with a serrated knife, slice about ⅜-inch thick. Lay on your oven rack (spacing doesn't matter) and toast at 300°F until golden golden. If they are not golden golden on the bottom, turn them over until they are. Turn off the oven, open the door, and let cool.

For Melba toasts, use an unsliced loaf of dense homemade quality white, wheat, or rye bread. Follow the directions above, except trim off the crusts and slice less than ¼-inch thick. Cut large pieces into more attractive and manageable triangles or fingers.

In early summer at La Bretagne, following the hors d'oeuvres at dinner was surely something of asparagus (there are towns such as Cherrueix, on the bay of Mont-Saint-Michel, known all over Brittany for their asparagus). Perhaps a soup? This one is pure rapture.

POTAGE AUX ASPERGES
Puree of fresh asparagus soup
[*6 first-course servings*]

Some of the preparation may be done a few hours in advance and all but the finishing touches an hour or so before serving.

---

*The refrigerator is usually around 37°F; if the meat drawer has its own dial and you can spare the room, turn it to coldest. If you're lucky enough to have a spare refrigerator, 32°F is perfect for the long-keeping of apples, page 235, and *rillettes*.

1 *pound fresh asparagus*

2 *cups excellent chicken or veal broth*

2 *cups water, cool, plus 2 quarts of ice water*

½ *stick butter, softened*

4 *smallish (1 ounce) shallots,* very finely chopped*

3 *tablespoons flour*

2 *egg yolks*

½ *cup* crème fraîche, *cultured or* à la minute, *page 37*

A dozen turns of the white pepper mill (1 teaspoon, medium grind)

About ¼ *teaspoon sea salt*

A sprinkling of chopped fresh chervil or parsley

Until ready to cook, keep the asparagus stems in a vessel of water in the refrigerator—like artichokes, they are a flower.

Cut off the asparagus tips at about 2 inches; cut the stalks in 1-inch pieces (no need to trim the ends). In a large skillet over high heat, bring the broth[†] and cool water to a boil, add the tips only, return to a boil, and cook briskly until they test barely tender with a thin skewer—it can be only 2 minutes. Lift out and plunge them into ice water to stop cooking. Wrap in plastic film and refrigerate.

Cook the stalks in the same broth the same way until tender, about 10 minutes after the broth returns to a boil. Puree the stalks with the broth through the medium blade of the food mill[‡] into a heavy pot—keep with it until only a small bundle of asparagus strings remain.

In a small heavy skillet over medium heat, melt half the butter. Add the shallots and sauté until very soft, stirring frequently, about 5 minutes—they must not brown. Remove from the heat, whisk in the flour, then moisten with some of the puree, whisking until smooth. Whisk the shallot mixture into the puree. The soup may be prepared up to this point a few hours in advance and set in a cool place, lid askew.

About 15 minutes before serving, over medium heat, bring the puree to a simmer and simmer 10 minutes, stirring frequently—do not cook longer or it will turn grey.

Off heat, whisk the egg yolks and cultured *crème fraîche* into the puree—*crème fraîche à la minute* must be added at the last moment. Grind in the pepper, then taste for salt. Add the reserved tips. Set the saucepan in a pot of hot water over low heat for the tips to warm up; cover, but stir occasionally. If you won't be serving from the pot, heat a tureen or serving bowl.

When the soup is hot, stir in an enrichment of the remaining ¼ stick of butter and, if you're using it, the *crème fraîche à la minute*. Serve at once, garnished with a few lacy leaves of chervil or parsley.

---

*When I am out of shallots, I substitute a combination of equal parts onion and whole scallions with a bit of garlic.

[†]A very light chicken (or veal, should you have it) broth in the background of a fresh vegetable soup gives subtle richness without intruding upon the vegetable's flavor.

[‡]Lacking a food mill, you can puree the soup in the blender, but the texture won't be as good.

In the French manner *chez* La Bretagne, after the soup comes seafood. Perhaps *coquilles Saint-Jacques à la bretonne*, a gratin of scallops and buttery onions. Bay scallops the size of a thumbnail are ideal for this superb dish, which owes its inspiration to M. Metayer's, from *Cuisine et vins de France*.

COQUILLES SAINT-JACQUES À LA BRETONNE
Gratin of scallops and buttery onions
[*8 first-course servings*]

The onion *fondue* may be prepared well in advance, and all may be in readiness hours ahead for the final browning.

A scant 1 stick butter	*A dozen turns of the white pepper mill*
1 pound fresh scallops, preferably the small	*(1 teaspoon, medium grind)*
bay size; if large, cut into ¹/₂-inch dice	*About ¹/₄ teaspoon sea salt, if necessary*
2 ¹/₂ tablespoons flour	*About 3 tablespoons dried breadcrumbs*
¹/₂ cup Muscadet, cold (Chablis may be	*About ¹/₄ cup chopped parsley, preferably*
substituted)	*Italian*
1 cup Fondue d'oignons, *page 36*	
¹/₄ cup crème fraîche, *cultured or* à la	
minute, *page 37*	

In a large heavy skillet over medium-high heat, melt ¹/₂ stick of the butter. Add the scallops and sauté while you stir with a wooden spatula and shake the skillet until the scallops are opaque, 2 to 3 minutes—they must be a shade less than cooked. Turn the scallops and their juices into a bowl; cover.

In the same skillet (without washing it), make a *roux* by melting half the remaining butter and then whisking in the flour. Cook over low heat for a couple of minutes without coloring, stirring often. Off heat, whisk in the Muscadet and, when the mixture is smooth, the broth from the scallops. Next whisk in the *fondue d'oignons*, then the *crème fraîche* and the pepper. Taste for salt. Stir in the scallops.

Scoop up ¹/₃ cup of the composition and spread unevenly about ¹/₂-inch thick in 8 scallop baking shells or shallow ramekins (or all together in a buttered 9-inch glass pie dish). At this point, you may cover the dish(es) tightly with plastic film and refrigerate several hours.

When ready to serve, preheat the oven to 450°F or heat the broiler. Sprinkle the dish(es) with a veil of breadcrumbs and top with the remaining butter in thin flakes. Bake or broil until the sauce is sizzling and the crumbs are crisp and brown, 10 to 15 minutes (perhaps 5 minutes longer for the pie dish). The dishes can wait a few minutes before serving because they will be HOT. Set on salad-size plates, sprinkle with parsley, and serve.

This is such a useful first course that it's a shame scallops aren't always available—and when they are, their price can pull them off-limits. So I've made the dish with bay shrimps—it even makes those handy-and-affordable-but-blah frozen darlings tasty, imagine.

BAY SHRIMPS À LA BRETONNE
Gratin of bay shrimps and buttery onions
[*8 first-course servings*]

1 recipe Coquilles Saint-Jacques à la
bretonne *(recipe preceding)*,
substituting frozen bay shrimps for the
scallops*

Turn the frozen shrimps into the skillet with the ½ stick of melted butter. Stir over medium-high heat until the shrimps have completely thawed. Lift them out into a bowl and simmer the broth in the skillet briskly until reduced by half. Add it to the shrimps and proceed as directed. You'll need no further salt.

And, of course, offer the wine with which you made the sauce.

About the Muscadet. This tingling white wine, whether as part of a dish or accompanying it, is one of the elements that makes Breton cuisine admirable. Muscadet grapes were originally named *Melon de Bourgogne*. A Gamay *blanc*, the vines were brought from Burgundy at the turn of the eighteenth century when frost destroyed ancient vineyards at the mouth of the Loire. The grapes were renamed and now Muscadet is one of the few French wines called by the name of the grape and not the name of the vineyard's district.

Pale yellow to leaf green, Muscadet is light and dry with an assertive acidity, yet at the same time it is fruity and fresh. Indeed, freshness is one of Muscadet's charms, and it is best drunk under two years old. By happy coincidence, its grapes are grown on the banks of rivers not far from the sea, and Muscadet is considered the ideal wine for both freshwater fish and seafood. I also find it an engaging companion on picnics.

There are three Muscadet *appellations controlées*. The first growths (the most superior vineyards) producing the fruitiest wines with the finest bouquet are from Sèvre-et-Maine—southeast of Nantes along the Sèvre Nantaise river. If you find a Muscadet de Sèvre-et-Maine labelled *"mis en bouteilles sur lie,"* buy it. It won't be much more expensive and it is considered the quintessential Muscadet because it is fruitier, fuller-bodied, and slightly sparkly. (However, if it is suspiciously cheap, *don't* buy it. It may be doctored with carbon dioxide and sugar.)

Second in quality, dry and full-bodied but slightly greener and more acid, is Muscadet from Coteaux de la Loire. These vineyards are northeast of Nantes, planted on hillocks (*coteaux*) bordering the Loire. Some recommend the extra tartness of Coteaux de la Loire with raw oysters and clams as well as "fishy" dishes that want a wine of pronounced acidity.

---

*Buy them frozen—they'll have a better chance of tasting fresh than those that have already been thawed whoknowswhen?

Third in quality is simply Muscadet, grown in villages south of the district of Sèvre-et-Maine. I've never tasted this, but I understand it can sometimes verge on being *too* sharp.

All Muscadets must be served very cold.

Mme Prigent would not have been able to offer Muscadet during the forties at La Bretagne. For more than the first hundred years of its existence, Muscadet was drunk only where it was produced. It must have galled her to have to serve wines from Burgundy, Bordeaux, the Loire, or the Rhone when she knew delicious Muscadets existed.

There is one evening at La Bretagne I remember indelibly, Bastille Day. Madame told me an important French lady was coming—excitement in the house was tangible. I was given marvelous flourishes to wear: Yvonne made me a garland of marguerites for my neck, a *tricolore* ribbon for my dark brown hair, and a crisp organdy apron for my new broomstick skirt.

Yvonne had also made the skirt for me, under Grand'mère's guidance. It was a length of calico simply seamed, gathered, waistbanded, and hemmed, dipped in thick starch, pleated tightly and evenly by hand around a broomstick, and tied in half a dozen places. The broom had rested against a sunny wall on the open-air rooftop porch outside Yvonne's room for a couple of days. When the fabric dried, the skirt pulled out in wonderfully rustic puckers. Stiff and simple reminiscence of the country pleats the women of Brittany still wear on feast days.

At nightfall, the great lady arrived—I knew it was she!—all silken and sleek, surrounded by a chattering entourage. I had hidden myself, out of shyness, in a bush by the front steps. She turned, smiling, and the late summer light lit her long neck and lyrical face. It was Lily Pons.

And what did Mme Prigent offer the elegant French diva and her friends for dinner that festive night? *Gigot à la bretonne*, considered one of France's great provincial dishes. Simplicity itself, *gigot à la bretonne* consists of slices of roast leg of mutton or lamb on a bed of white beans simmered with onions, shallots, and tomato. I have cooked more complicated versions—dishes that, at the time, I thought authentic, but which in fact were some non-Breton's notion of a Breton *cassoulet*. But lamb, beans, onions, shallots, and tomatoes are it, and all it needs to be. The dish has enormous charm.

In Brittany, *gigot à la bretonne* is made with *gigot de pré-salé*—*pré-salé* means "meadow-salted." As Breton rivers empty into the ocean, sweet and salt waters mingle. In their ebbing and flowing, these waters flood vast ocean-bordering meadows. With their roots in the salty marsh, wild herbs and grasses upon which the sheep graze are slightly salty, hence, so becomes the sheep's flesh.

Rich red mutton meat is prized in France, England, the Middle East, and many other parts of the world. Americans have never developed a palate for it. I imagine that's because there's very little mutton on the market. There's very little mutton on the market because there's no demand for it and there's no demand for it because there's so little mutton on the market that Americans haven't had a chance to taste it!

But even in Brittany lamb is often substituted for mutton in this dish. The distinction between mutton and lamb is that mutton is between one and two years old and lamb is under one year old. Then how old is the leg of lamb you're buying for your *gigot*? How much does it weigh? The more it weighs, the older it is. Few answers in life are so simple. A five-pound leg is young lamb. Age also tells in the color of the flesh (the darker, the older) and in the fat (the thicker the layer, the older).

All lamb, of course, must be cooked to the most succulent degree. I've heard there are people (none would admit it to me) who want their lamb well done. That makes me weep. There are no circumstances under which lamb should be cooked more than medium-rare. To my taste, a rosy-pink 120°F to 125°F on the meat thermometer is perfect. A medium-pink 135°F is absolute max!* Most French cooks roast leg of lamb at high temperature, for example Raymond Oliver's 400°F / 12 minutes per pound, and Escoffier's 440°F / 9 minutes per pound. The degree of doneness is unspecified, so you can be sure it's rare. Paula Wolfert, in her masterwork, *The Cooking of South-West France*, directs a 5½-pound leg of lamb be roasted "in the style of Bordeaux" at 500°F for 25 minutes. There are good meat cooks (Americans) who feel that lamb should not be roasted over 325°F. Still others combine the methods by roasting lamb at 450°F for 15 minutes then lowering the heat to 350°F until it reaches the desired degree of doneness.

For my part, although I well know the virtues of slow-roasted meat (I roast beef, for example, at 300°F / 20 minutes per pound to 115°F, and it's poetry), meats differ, and I prefer the French high temperature for lamb. One thing: I don't rely on the minutes-per-pound formula one hundred percent. The shape of the leg must be taken into consideration: how large, how small, how chunky, how thin.

The ideal way to prepare lamb for *gigot à la bretonne*, however, is not to roast it in an oven but on a spit over wood or non-petroleum-based charcoal. If you can do this, please do. After preparing the lamb, balance the spit by running it close to the bone. Roast over a medium-hot fire (details in the recipe). A five-pound leg of lamb might take less than an hour to come to 135°F—but there are many indeterminates in this form of cooking.

---

*Once, I wrote 145°F, but I was still a child.

Whichever method of roasting you choose, do check with a meat thermometer* after about three-fourths of the calculated roasting time and then every five minutes until the meat reaches the desired degree of doneness. When the lamb has cooked, it is crucial that it be allowed to rest before carving—the juices need to settle and the tissues need to compose themselves.

Finally, unlike beef, American lamb comes to the market without aging. The French insist it must be aged at least a little in order to be tender and have full flavor. So three or four days before your party, buy the meat. Ask the butcher when it came in—a leg of lamb will age to advantage up to a week before cooking. Once home, wrap it loosely in foil and refrigerate.

GIGOT À LA BRETONNE CLASSIQUE
Breton roast leg of lamb or mutton with white beans
[*At least 10 servings*]
The dish will profit if the beans are cooked the day before, but the meat must be roasted and the composition put together just before serving.

THE BEANS

5 cups (2 pounds) Great Northern or other medium-sized dried white beans	*11½ quarts water*

Herb Bouquet
8 or 10 stalks of parsley
4 or 5 sprigs of fresh thyme, or 1 teaspoon dried leaves
1 bay leaf

4 medium-large peeled onions	*A dozen or more turns of the white pepper*
2 large peeled shallots	*mill (1 teaspoon plus, medium grind)*
3 large ripe tomatoes, peeled†	*A little sea salt*

Pick over the beans, rinse well, then turn into 4 quarts of water in a large pot. Bring the uncovered pot to a boil over medium heat, boil the beans a few minutes, and pour off the water.‡ Add 4 quarts of *boiling*§ water and soak an hour or two. Then pour off this water and add 3½ quarts water at the same temperature.

Tie the parsley, thyme, and bay together with string or in a square of dampened cheesecloth. Add the herb bouquet, the onions, shallots, tomatoes (the vegetables whole) and pepper to the beans.‖ Bring to a simmer over medium heat, uncovered.

*The best sort is described on page 250.
†Peeling directions, page 259.
‡When you pour off the water in the early stages of simmering beans, much of the gas that can be a misery seems to go down the drain, too.
§Dried beans can be temperamental: I've found they behave if, when changing or adding water, the temperature of the water remains constant.
‖Salt comes after simmering as it tends to toughen things by drawing out their juices.

Set on the cover askew and simmer the pot over lowest heat until the beans are tender but before they begin to break up, about 1½ hours. Keep the vegetables covered with liquid and stir a few times with a wooden spatula so nothing will stick. Taste for salt, then set the beans in a cool place or the refrigerator, the lid askew, overnight or until needed.

THE LAMB OR MUTTON

One 5- to 6-pound leg of lamb or mutton   *A dozen or more turns of the black pepper*
2 large garlic cloves, in thin slivers   *mill (1 teaspoon plus, medium grind)*
A little olive oil, if spit roasting   *A little sea salt*

Cut away any papery membrane and purple ink on the meat. *If you're spit roasting* over coals or in the oven, trim away all but a veil of fat around the roast. *If you're oven roasting in a pan*, trim away all fat on the bottom and sides and all but a veil of fat on top. With the thin tip of a knife, make incisions in the meat evenly all over and push in the garlic slivers.

Roasting on a spit over coals: * Make a drip pan of heavy foil measuring 6 to 8 inches wide and 4 inches longer than the meat. Lengthwise, center the foil beneath the spit where the meat will be; widthwise, set it off-center, with 2 inches toward the back and 4 inches toward the front of the grill. Lay a solid rectangular bed of coals beside the drip pan toward the back:† 6 inches wide and 4 inches longer at each end than the meat.‡ Set the coals (or wood) so that the thickest part of the meat will be 5 to 6 inches above the source of heat.

Allow about 45 minutes for the coals to be ready: you can hold your hand at spit level for only about 3 seconds. Allow up to 1¼ hours for the lamb to roast to 135°F (pink). Brush the leg with olive oil, balance it on a spit, and flick on the motor. Baste the meat occasionally with oil. Every half-hour, add 5 or 6 coals, evenly spaced, to the bed. Test with a good meat thermometer.

Roasting in the oven: Set the meat rounded side up in a large shallow baking dish or pan. (You're supposed to set the meat on a rack so the bottom won't fry in the fat, but I never do and it never seems fried.) Set the uncovered pan in the center of the preheated oven.§ More options: you can turn the joint once or twice or roast it without turning and you can baste it every 10 minutes or not baste it. I do not turn and I do not baste because no matter what I do or don't do, a leg of lamb has never failed to roast beautifully. Test with a good meat thermometer.

---

*This is the rule for spit roasting any big cut of meat or fowl.

†If you've had experience roasting over a wood fire, by all means use wood here. But the varieties, thicknesses, and burning properties of wood make definite instructions for keeping a fire at the correct temperature 1¼ hours almost impossible. If you've never roasted over wood, you might enjoy beginning with a simple tenderloin of pork, page 233.

‡This is predicated on the theory that your spit revolves with the top of the meat turning away from you and the bottom of the meat turning toward you—fat drips from the ascending side. If, for some reason, your spit revolves in the reverse direction and you can't change it, build your bed of coals at the front and set the drip pan 4 inches toward the back.

§Page 49 gives temperatures and times.

When the lamb is ready, remove it from the spit or oven and wrap in foil to let the juices settle for at least 15, and up to 30, minutes while you finish the beans. Pepper and salt just before slicing.

PUTTING IT TOGETHER

The beans and vegetables	*A little sea salt*
½ stick butter	*The lamb*
2 large shallots, finely chopped	*A bunch of parsley*
About 24 turns of the white pepper mill	
(2 teaspoons, medium grind)	

When the lamb goes on to roast, set the pot of beans over medium heat and stir occasionally with a wooden spatula until beans are hot. Lift out and set aside the tomatoes, onions, and shallots. Discard the bouquet of herbs and drain the beans (save the broth for soup). Cover and keep the beans hot. Heat a large gratin dish— something about 3 inches deep with a 4- to 5-quart capacity.

Melt the butter in a large heavy skillet and stew the raw shallots over medium-high heat until tender, stirring occasionally. Meanwhile, break up the tomatoes into smallish pieces with your fingers, slice the onions in eighths (like an apple), and coarsely chop the reserved cooked shallots. Add these to the shallot skillet and cook over medium-low heat, stirring and slightly crushing the vegetables. When all is a tender amalgam, about 5 minutes, stir back into the beans. Taste for pepper and salt, cover, and keep hot.

Carve the lamb.* For this country dish, I like the slices meaty, but you might prefer them thin.

Quickly smooth the beans into the dish. Moisten the top with some of the lamb drippings. Arrange the scragglier pieces of lamb directly over the beans, then overlap the handsomest slices on top of them. Pour the remaining drippings over the dish and garnish with furls of parsley. Grind pepper over and sprinkle with a little salt. Serve at once on hot plates.

I would imagine Mme Prigent kept the setting for this rough jewel of a Breton dish simple. First a basket of baby carrots, peppery radishes, and spring onions newly pulled from the earth. Afterwards, a salad of watercress from a moist corner of the garden to follow, accompanied by one of Grand'mère's fresh cream cheeses (page 168) wrapped in apple leaves.

And for a Bastille Day dessert, *fraises à la Cardinal*: strawberries in a cardinal's robes of pureed fresh raspberries. (Strawberries are grown to perfection in Brittany. The town of Plougastel-Daoulas, on the Plougastel peninsula, is famous in France for the quality of its berries.) I find this one of the most sensuous desserts imaginable. Ruby and garnet reds shimmer, sweet/

---

*How-to, page 249.

tart flavors tingle, and sleek strawberries with a nap of raspberries melt in the mouth. The classic *Cardinal* is finished with slivers of toasted almonds. I don't understand the almonds and I omit them—they have nothing to do with the berries and I have the feeling some chef thought he ought to throw something over the top and reached for a nearby bowl of nuts. In terms of color, texture, and sensuality, if anything were to go on top, I would think it might be candied violets. But they aren't needed either. However, a single-petaled rose of vivid pink would be wonderfully Matisse.

Theoretically, this sauce may be made with frozen raspberries. But frozen raspberries no longer have the plush texture of summer. A puree is a puree, you say, and plush velvet no longer applies. Not so. There is a sumptuous quality in a puree of fresh raspberries that is not found in one of frozen berries. Past texture, there's a philosophical problem. It's my feeling that one of the rewards of self-discipline in this world of instant-everything is the arrival of the seasons—the strawberry season, the raspberry season, the sweet corn season, and so on.

SAUCE CARDINAL*
Puree of fresh raspberries
[*Makes 2 heaping cups: 8 servings*]
The sauce may be prepared up to 5 or 6 hours in advance—give it at least an hour or two to temper the sugar.

1 heaping pint fresh raspberries of the finest quality
2 cups unsifted confectioner's sugar

2 teaspoons fresh lemon juice
2 teaspoons fresh orange juice
8 pink roses (optional)

Do not wash the raspberries unless they are gritty. Coarsely puree the berries, then pass the puree through the finest blade of the food mill or a coarse sieve into a large bowl to cull most of the seeds. Whisk in the confectioner's sugar and lemon and orange juices, then pass the sauce through a fine sieve to catch any lingering imperfections. Turn into a pretty vessel, cover, and set in a cool place.

For FRAISES À LA CARDINAL for 8: If the berries are sandy, lightly spray 2 quarts (2 pounds) of large firm sweet ripe strawberries with cool water, then pat them thoroughly dry. Hull them.† Turn into a colander, cover lightly, and refrigerate for up to 8 hours. A couple of hours before serving, heap the berries into a serving bowl, cover, and return to the refrigerator. Also chill the dessert bowls.

At the table, spoon strawberries into the bowls and splash with sauce. Set a perfect rose on top, if you can. Pass the sauce for extra helpings.

---

*For a FRESH STRAWBERRY SAUCE, use the same proportions of ingredients, substituting hulled strawberries. Don't bother putting them through the finest sieve—the seeds are too small and will drive you crazy.
†I've seen some who lop off the graceful shoulders of the berries with a knife just to take out the stem. A thumbnail nips out the stem tidily, leaving the berry intact.

As summer advanced, Mme Prigent spooned the pureed raspberries over fresh peeled peach halves poached until tender in vanilla-scented syrup (equal measure sugar and water and as much vanilla bean as you can muster, stirred until the sugar has dissolved and the syrup comes to a boil)—PÊCHES À LA CARDINAL. She served poached and sauced summer pears the same way—POIRES À LA CARDINAL.

(Some city chefs set the fruit on vanilla ice cream before napping with raspberry puree. They're the ones who garnish with slivered almonds . . .)

Then after coffee for La Pons, Madame served a sip of Calvados to finish so fine an evening.

I really never cared for brandy until Calvados. Now at the end of a day when I've worked particularly hard or well or both, I pour myself half an inch of what I call My Treat in a big warm bell glass. Calvados against my pillow, apples beneath my nose, heady reward indeed for a good girl.

Not because I am partial to it, but because Norman Calvados is a natural and traditional companion to an appley Breton cuisine, I'd like you to understand Calvados so you'll buy a bottle and not substitute decent but unappled stuff.

Just as Cognac and Armagnac are made from the fermented juice of grapes, Calvados is made from the fermented juice of apples. After crushing—a process carried out in most particularly traditional ways—the apples are left in an unadulterated mash (no chemicals) to ferment for at least one month. The hard cider that emerges must have at least four percent alcohol. No sugar may be added, which accounts for Calvados' characteristic dryness. The cider is then twice distilled in old-fashioned pot stills: it finishes with an alcohol content of up to seventy-two percent.

Fine Calvados is then aged in oak casks—sometimes the shells of hazelnuts are added. Cider poured into the casks is clear as water. Calvados drawn years later is golden as the oak. But of the twelve types of Calvados permitted by French law, not all are well aged. And like Cognac and Armagnac, Calvados, when young, can be hot and rough as youth itself. No matter how old the bottle you may find, Calvados ages only in the barrel. The key to aging is this: three stars or three apples on the label mean two years in the cask; *Vieux* or *Réserve* means three years; *Vieille Réserve* means four years; *V.S.O.P.* means five years.

The Vallée d'Auge has the reputation for producing the finest Calvados. The valley, between two small rivers, is a land of exceptionally chalky soil, which also renders remarkable Pont-l'Evêque and Camembert cheeses.

As Alexis Lichine says, "At its best, a well-aged 'Calva' will combine the fleeting sappiness and tang of apples with a dry oakiness gained from the bar-

rel. It is not for the faint-hearted, but in nuance and depth of taste it is sur-
passed only by the best of Cognac and Armagnac. . . ."*

Now I have before me two bottles of Calvados. Both are *"Appellation Calvados pays d'Auge controlée."* My Treat is labelled "V.S.O.P." Smooth smooth
smooth. It is also depressingly costly. I wouldn't dream of using it for cooking. The other bottle has no letters but *"Fine"* above the vintner's name. It's
fine for cooking—for drinking, it's like swallowing little licks of flame. It's
not inexpensive but much cheaper than the V.S.O.P. Calvados prices, in
terms of quality, are comparable to those of Cognac.

Alice B. Toklas gives a warming recipe using Calvados in her enchanting
Cook Book, and I quote:

HOT TODDY FOR COLD NIGHTS†
(Attributed to Flaubert)

2 jiggers Calvados
1 jigger apricot brandy

Warm over flame. Slowly pour in a jigger cream. Do not stir.

This comes from the *Auberge de vieux puits*, a charming Norman inn in Pont
Audemer, an afternoon's carriage ride from Croisset, where Flaubert wrote
Madame Bovary. The author was clearly a valued guest because in my *Guide
Michelin* a specialty of the restaurant is *Truite Bovary au champagne*. I wonder if
they still make his toddy. I know I do, warming it in a snifter, although I use
equal parts of Calvados and apricot brandy—I find two parts of apples bury
one part of apricots.

If Calvados would demolish your budget, then buy a bottle of Apple Jack,
American apple brandy, for Breton recipes. The differences between French
and American apple brandy is aging—ours are sent out younger—and
proof—ours are sent out stronger, up to one hundred proof compared to
eighty proof of the French.

Summer and my stay at La Bretagne came to an end. After hugs from Madame, Grand'mère, Yvonne, and Jacques—and a pat for the goat—I was
trundled off to New York City. Alas, in time it became clear that the muses
wanted my father to work not in the theater in New York but in the movies in
Hollywood, and so again I crossed the country on the Super Chief, this time
with my parents, back to California and a delicious new life.

---

*Alexis Lichine's Guide to the Wines and Vineyards of France.
†The recipe ought to warm two people.

My Mother's Apprentice at the Garden of Allah and Afterward

Early in 1943, M. F. K. Fisher wrote in *The Gastronomical Me:*

> I know a beautiful honey-colored actress who is a gourmande, in a pleasant way. She loves to cook rich hot lavish meals. She does it well, too.
>
> She is slender, fragile, with a mute other-worldly pathos in her large azure eyes, and she likes to invite a lot of oddly assorted and usually famous people to a long table crowded with flowers, glasses, dishes of nuts, bowls of Armenian jelly and Russian relishes and Indian chutney, and beer and wine and even water, and then bring in a huge bowl of oxtail stew with dumplings. She has spent days making it, with special spices she found in Bombay or Soho or Honolulu, and she sits watching happily while it disappears. Then she disappears herself, and in a few minutes staggers to the table with a baked Alaska as big as a washtub, a thing of beauty, and a joy for about fifteen minutes.
>
> But this star-eyed slender gourmande has a daughter about eight or nine, and the daughter hates her mother's sensuous dishes. In fact, she grows spindly on them. The only way to put meat on her bones is to send her to stay for a week or two with her grandmother, where she eats store ice cream for lunch, mashed potatoes for supper, hot white pap for breakfast.
>
> "My daughter!" the actress cries in despair and horror. I tell her there is still hope, with the passage of time. But she, perhaps because of her beauty, pretends Time is not.

My mother's hostess book for January 30, 1943 notes:

> Groucho
> Nunnally Johnsons
> Dalton Trumbos
> M.F.K.
>
> Braised oxtails and dumplings(!)
> Peas carrots onions
> Baked Alaska

Yes, I didn't like oxtail stew.

We had moved back to Hollywood and were installed in villa 12 at the bottom of The Garden of Allah. In those days, "The Garden" was the home or home-away-from-home of some of the most brilliant, amusing, glamorous, and naughty people in the entertainment world, and sometimes it seemed that all of them came to my mother's parties. What my mother cooked was often as exotic as the guests. Groucho Marx once said, "When I come to the Sheekmans, I never know what I'm eating but I always love it."

As a young man, my father had been a columnist and theater critic on the *Chicago Times*. In 1930, when the Marx Brothers came to town in *Animal Crackers*, my father went by the theater to interview them. He also made a few suggestions on how to turn the show into a movie. Groucho wanted not only my father's ideas but my father as well. When their train left, he was on it with them, en route to Hollywood. My father and Groucho became best friends and remained so the rest of their lives.

After collaborating on *Monkey Business*, *Horse Feathers*, and *Duck Soup*, Daddy was working on *Roman Scandals* for Eddie Cantor. The leading lady was Gloria Stuart, who had already made two classics, *The Old Dark House* and *The Invisible Man*, and whose beauty Groucho once described as "legendary." His first day on the set, my father saw Miss Stuart reclining on a silk chaise longue, reading a Chinese newspaper. He went up to her and said, "You're holding that thing upside down." She stared at him. But a few months later, she proposed to him. My father went to Tiffany's to buy her an engagement gift. There on the counter in a silver frame was a photograph of Gloria Stuart. A shy man, he asked a busy clerk for help.

"What does she look like?"

My father pointed at the photograph. "Like that."

Although most of creative Hollywood had passed through The Garden of Allah at one time or another, in some ways it was its own best self during the war. The Garden of Allah was something of a club—the writers making it the Algonquin Round Table West—and I was its happy mascot.

The Garden had begun in the late twenties, when an "h" was added to the Russian actress Alla Nazimova's name and her Spanish-style mansion on the

Sunset Strip became a hotel. Around her huge swimming pool shaped like the Black Sea were then built dozens of bungalows over several acres. The bungalows, all stucco and terra-cotta tile, were each attached on at least two walls, wonderfully conducive to Hollywood gossip.

The "villas" were apartments in the bungalows. Each had a small but functional kitchen and dining alcove, a living room, and one or two bedrooms and bath. Everything was provided for the guests, from the Spanish-style dark-wood-and-gold-tapestried furniture (ghastly) to maids (indifferent) and Ben, the middle-aged bellboy (drunk or sober, Ben could procure anything for anybody anytime). Bougainvillea, oleander, hibiscus, fern, and bamboo flourished around the bungalows, and banana, loquat, date palm, pittosporum, myoporum, magnolia, native oak, and deodar studded the paths. The paths and steps were paved in random stones by a mason who had tippled on the job, which meant I couldn't roller skate in The Garden.

Walking through The Garden of Allah in the early forties was like finding oneself on the movie set of a village in Mexico or Morocco or the Florida Keys, and one half-expected Humphrey Bogart and Lauren Bacall to come strolling arm-in-arm down the path. Which, in fact, they often did.

Each villa had its own character and its own stamp of guests. For example, Bogart's villa, 8, was in the center of The Garden next to the pool, and when he wasn't in town, it was Errol Flynn's. Across from villa 8 was Natalie Schafer's, in the process of a friendly divorce from Louis Calhern, who lived next door with Dorothy Gish. Mr. Calhern was my best grown-up friend. He often took me to Schwab's Pharmacy, across the street, and bought me bubble gum (impossible to get during the war) and ice cream. Richard Dix (with whom my mother made one of *The Whistler* movies) was on that side of The Garden, as was *Topper*'s Roland Young and a beginning nightclub comic, Jackie Gleason.

Miscellaneous talents had another corner on the other side of the pool—the stars of *Duffy's Tavern*, Ed Gardner and his wife, actress Shirley Booth, Broadway playwright/actor/director Elliot Nugent, and longtime disc jockey Al Jarvis (whose Girl Friday was a bouncy Betty White).

Kay Thompson (then designing musical numbers for Judy Garland and her own nightclub act with The Williams Brothers) and her husband, *Suspense* producer William Spier, lived on that side, too. They were also special friends. Later Kay wrote about another little girl who lived in a hotel, Eloise.

Across from the Spiers, in villa 16 at the bottom of The Garden, lived the cherubic humorist Robert Benchley (to many nowadays best known as Nathaniel's father and Peter's grandfather). Mr. Benchley was at our end of The

Garden—the writers' corner—with neighbors like William Faulkner, Clifford Odets, Edwin Justis Mayer, and my father, Arthur Sheekman. There were actors in our corner, too—my mother, of course, and Charlie Butterworth and John Carradine.

John Carradine and his wife, Sonia, lived next door to us for a time. The Carradines also had children, and despite the fact that I was at a stage when I didn't like boys, occasionally David and I had great shoot-'em-up battles through Mr. Benchley's banana trees.

Villa 17, kitty-corner to us, was one of two villas reserved for musicians: Frank Sinatra, Woody Herman, Artie Shaw, and Benny Goodman stayed there. Georgia Gibbs warbled in and out. Villa 1, at the top of The Garden bordering Sunset Boulevard, was for Paul Whiteman, Xavier Cugat, José Iturbi, and the guitarist Tito Guizar.

One of the things I loved best about life at The Garden was the constant procession of parties my parents gave. As much as I'd thrived on the Gallic order of the day's rounds at La Bretagne, I now loved watching my mother cook. I knew in my heart of hearts that this was Important Cooking even though it didn't appeal to me.

Here is one dinner my mother served friends, among them the writers Frances Goodrich (who once answered a hostess's question about the guests of honor, "How did you like the Korngolds?" with "They were delicious—"), and Albert Hackett. Later, their play, *The Diary of Anne Frank*, was to win the Pulitzer Prize.

> *Bouquet de la mer*
> Beaten biscuits
> *Pigeonneau aux petits pois, champignons*
> Parsley stuffing
> Cornbread loaf
> Fennel & celery sticks
> White radishes
> *Poires flambées*

The splendid entrée on my mother's menu that night, *Pigeonneau aux petits pois*, is a classic French recipe for small game birds—squab, quail, woodcock, and Cornish game hen (the latter, a fraction of the cost of squab and I think just as tasty). Not only is this a recipe that enhances the flavor and succulence of game fowl's lean meat but it's also wonderfully simple.

Gauging braising time for game birds can be tricky. An 11-ounce squab and a 15-ounce Cornish game hen—weighed after their tidbits went into the broth pot—both took 45 minutes. Assume that 45 minutes is average for birds 1 pound and under; 1½-pound Cornish hens, which ought to serve two, would take about 1 hour. To preserve their juices, cut them in half lengthwise *after* braising.

PIGEONNEAU AUX PETITS POIS
Squab braised with fresh peas
(Also for Cornish game hens and other small game birds)
[*6 servings*]
All but the final cooking of the birds and peas may be done in advance.

Six ¾- to 1-pound game birds (squab are around ¾ pound, Cornish game hens from 1 to 1½ pounds), at room temperature
4½ cups excellent chicken broth
A very scant 8 ounces lean salt pork, trimmed of rind

6 large egg-shaped boiling onions
3 tablespoons butter, if necessary
⅓ cup flour
4¼ pounds peas in the pod
Lots of freshly ground black pepper (1 teaspoon plus, medium grind)
Watercress, parsley, or celery tops

In a pot over low heat, simmer the birds' livers, giblets, necks, wing tips, and fat deposits in the chicken broth. Remove the livers when tender—a matter of minutes. Wrap and refrigerate. Simmer until the giblets are tender, about an hour. Remove and discard everything in the pot (for kitty?) but the giblets, including the fat. Return the livers to the pot, cover loosely, and refrigerate.*

Cut the salt pork into ⅛-inch dice—you'll want about 1 cup. In a heavy skillet that just holds the birds and peas (there will be about 4 cups of shelled peas), cook the salt pork over medium heat until golden brown, stirring frequently. Lift out the dice, leaving the fat, cover the dice, and set aside.

Meanwhile, cut an X in the root ends of the onions and cook uncovered in boiling water 5 minutes, drain, and peel. Rinse the birds and pat dry. Tuck an onion inside each and truss.† In the fat in the skillet, brown the birds on all sides over medium-high heat. Lift out the birds, cover, and set aside.

If necessary, melt butter to make about 3 tablespoons of fat in the skillet. Off heat, whisk in the flour, then whisk over high heat until the *roux* is a rich deep brown. Remove the broth from the refrigerator, ladle up 3 cups of lean broth, and whisk it into the *roux* over low heat. When smooth, whisk in the salt pork and some pepper, then lay the birds in the skillet, breast down.

At this point, you may cover the skillet and set it in a cool place for a few hours. Just how many hours depends on how cool is cool: at 55°F or less, up to 6 hours. Otherwise, refrigerate.

As close to cooking time as possible (see timing notes above), shell the peas without rinsing and distribute them around the birds with a few pea pods. Grind lots of

---

*Note on refrigerating hot food, page xviii.
†Trussing notes are on pages 244–245.

pepper over the dish (the pork gives ample salt) and cover. Braise the birds over medium-medium-high heat (the sauce should bubble merrily) breast down for half the time, then use tongs to turn the birds breast up. Meanwhile, warm the reserved livers and giblets in the remaining broth, then lift out and chop them medium-fine, wrap in foil, and keep warm. Heat a serving platter.

When the birds test done—a thin skewer poked in the thigh close to the body produces juices that run *clear* (no hint of pink)*—remove their strings, arrange them on the platter, and spoon the peas around them, discarding the pods. Taste the sauce for seasoning (chances are it's perfect), pour it over the birds, sprinkle the livers and giblets over the dish, tuck some greenery here and there, and serve. (My mother also garnished the birds with sautéed mushrooms, but I feel the peas and smoky undertaste of pork need nothing more.)

When I first copied out the recipe from Mother's file, I thought, Cook fresh peas forty-five minutes? But on tasting them, I found that one of the pleasures of the dish is that the peas are well cooked—they lend a melting plushness to the braise. That's why I suggest it isn't the same dish with frozen peas and why I ask that you wait to make this sometime from January to June (or whenever you see peas at the market). Do it right.

I especially loved our villa because my room was only a few feet down the hall from the living room. When I was in bed, I could share in the hush when Marc Connelly, Julius Epstein, or Nunnally Johnson told stories, the shouts when Dalton Trumbo, Hy Kraft, or Kyle Crichton argued politics, the joy when Harry Ruby, Arthur Schwartz, or Abe Burrows sang their songs, the snap when Groucho Marx, Dorothy Parker, or my father zinged zingers, and the clamor when everyone joined in.

Once, when Groucho was telling a story, he lowered his voice to deliver the punchline. I couldn't hear it. The living room roared with laughter. To my astonishment (I was a docile child), I found myself in the living room in my pajamas asking Uncle Groucho please to tell me the end of his story. Now Groucho was uncommonly fond of children and probably much too liberal with them, but this time he said, "I'll tell you the punchline next year when you're ten, Sylvia, now go back to bed!" A year later, when he took me to a ball game, I asked him for the punchline. He didn't remember. "I waited," I said. I was crushed. Instead he gave me a kiss and bought me another hot dog.

At one of those games, I crossed paths with a certain young man for the first of several times. Then twenty, he was one of the writers on Groucho's radio show, and Groucho often took him to the ball game as well. My parents had a box next to Groucho's. The young man and I both remember being at the game watching the Hollywood Stars play the Sunday afternoon Babe Ruth, in a huge camel's hair coat, threw out the first ball and then spoke a few croak-

---

*This is the test for doneness for all poultry.

ing words from home plate. We must have sat near one another but we don't remember meeting. All we can remember was seeing Babe Ruth.

From those years on, my parents' friends were my friends and I was part of the parties because I had helped—from the moment we landed at The Garden of Allah, I was, and in some respects still am, my mother's apprentice in the kitchen.

Yet our styles could not be more dissimilar. Style in cookery reflects the spirit of the artist as much as style in architecture or landscaping. My style has evolved over the years from an interest in the complex to a passion for simplicity. My mother has never made Just Roast Beef in her life. It wouldn't interest her. Her style is based on the intricacies of composition. It borders on the baroque. Everyone adores it.

For example, after tasting Mother's goose in Kirschwasser aspic, the poet Samuel Hoffenstein composed the following:

> You know the story of Jason
> Who hunted the Golden Fleece
> When the Goose with the Kirschwasser Aspic
> Rose from among the Geese.
> "The hell with the Fleece" said Jason.
> "We'll roam and hunt no more.
> The Goose with the Kirschwasser Aspic
> Is what I've been hunting for."
> Sam Hoffenstein
> On hearing the wings of all the poets
> brush thro' Gloria's kitchen

Goose is delectable, but an extravagance. Oven-poached this way and enrobed in aspic, the meat is uncommonly succulent. But if the purse is thin, turkey or chicken would be as handsome. The aspic shimmers and its honeygold combined with the green of cool roasted peppers (page 105) and the cream and red of barley salad (page 147) makes a gorgeous buffet for the holidays. All prepared in advance.

The aspic, by the way, is a stiff formal aspic, one that holds itself nobly. Whereas aspics for more casual matters—salads and desserts—want only one tablespoon of gelatin for every two cups of liquid, this calls for one tablespoon per cup. I find it exciting to work with.

THE GOOSE IN THE KIRSCHWASSER ASPIC

[12 servings]

The stock is made and the goose poached the day before molding, and the mold may be prepared a day before serving.

THE GOOSE

For the stock
 The neck, heart, and trimmings from the goose
 1 large unpeeled onion, coarsely chopped
 2 unpeeled carrots, coarsely chopped
 1 large leafy celery stalk, coarsely chopped
 A good handful of parsley
 6 cups water, cool

One 9½- to 10-pound goose; if not frozen, *About 2 cups dry white wine*
 ask the butcher to cut it in half   *About 1 cup dry vermouth*
 lengthwise   *Another good handful of parsley*
About 6 cups excellent beef broth   *A small handful of black peppercorns*
About 6 cups excellent chicken broth

Into your soup pot, turn neck, heart, trimmings, onion, carrots, celery, parsley, and water. Bring to a simmer, set the lid on askew, and simmer over lower heat. (It will keep simmering until the goose has been cooked.) Heat the oven to 425°F.

Rinse the goose and pat dry. If the butcher hasn't done it, cut in half lengthwise with poultry shears or cleaver. Remove the fat deposits, wing tips, and excess neck skin, and add to the soup pot. Fit the pieces cavity-sides-up in a roasting pan. Add beef and chicken broths, white wine, and vermouth to come two-thirds the way up over the pieces. The amount of liquid depends on the shape of your pan; when adding, just keep roughly to the listed proportions or whatever combination of broths and spirits pleases you. Distribute parsley and peppercorns around. Cover and roast on the lowest rack 15 minutes, then reduce the oven heat to 325°F.

In 45 minutes, use tongs to turn the pieces of goose over. Roast until the legs move slightly in their sockets and, when pricked with a thin skewer in the fleshiest part of the upper thigh, the juices run clear—180°F on the meat thermometer. Allow about 2 hours altogether.

Turn the pieces over again in the pan. Pour the contents of the soup pot over the goose, piling on the vegetables to cover it. Set with the lid askew in a very cool place or the refrigerator overnight.

Next morning, lift the goose from the broth onto your work surface. As you work, be meticulous about wiping away fat—you don't want a speck of fat in the aspic. And always keep all the meat covered with a damp towel so edges won't dry.

Skin the legs and wings, then pull off all meat. Make a slit in the skin down the goose's back and pull off the skin. With a small sharp knife and your fingers (with your fingers, you can best keep the meat intact—you'll want to cut up the meat in special shapes later), pull off all the meat from the carcass. Be sure to get the meat underneath the breast clinging to the bone, and meat tucked beneath the long thin bones lying next to the neck—nose around for every morsel. Scrape all fat and gristle from the meat.

Cut the breast pieces lengthwise in half, then in half widthwise, to make pieces no more than ½-inch thick. Cut these pieces on the bias twice to create 8 diamond-shaped lozenges about 3 inches long. Cut the remaining meat into similar shapes, always with at least one point. You should have 6 cups of pure meat. Turn into a bowl and cover.

(About the trimmed fat—you'll be wanting it for cooking during the year.* Cut it into even chunks, slowly bring to a simmer in a heavy pot with about ¼ cup cold water. Simmer uncovered until the pot sizzles—all the water has evaporated. Strain into a jar, cover tightly, and refrigerate. It will keep.

And goose liver, as you know, is a Treat and should be made, at the earliest opportunity, into a fine little *pâté*.)

The aspic can be in the works while you're cutting up the meat.

THE ASPIC AND GARNISH

The poaching broth from the goose
4 egg whites
The shells of 6 eggs
9 envelopes of unflavored gelatin
¾ cup 90-proof Kirschwasser liqueur

2 bunches of small skinny carrots, trimmed
   and peeled
Watercress or whatever greens and/or flowers
   you fancy

Strain the broth into a transparent vessel and let it set at least 10 or 15 minutes so all the fat will rise. Ladle off the fat,† removing every speck with strips of paper towels. Turn the broth into a large pot, whisk in the egg whites and crumble in the shells. Bring to a boil over medium heat, turn heat to low, and simmer very gently 10 minutes. Turn off the heat and cool 10 minutes, undisturbed.

Line a large sieve with one thickness of a wrung-out tightly woven towel. Set over a large bowl and, gently pushing aside the clump of egg whites, ladle in the clarified broth. You'll want 8½ cups. Cool.

Ladle a couple of cups of the broth into a small pot and sprinkle the gelatin over it. Stir to blend, then soak 5 minutes. Set over medium heat and stir while the gelatin dissolves and the mixture comes to a simmer (or do this in the microwave). Stir back into the clarified broth, then pass through the sieve lined with two layers of fresh damp towels once more for good measure. Stir in the Kirschwasser.

At some point, simmer the whole carrots until tender but still slightly crisp when pierced with a thin skewer, 10 to 12 minutes. Drain, pat dry, and wrap tightly.

THE MOLD

These directions are based on a round 13-cup mold, 8 inches wide and 4 inches deep—I use a copper saucepan. Your mold must hold at least 13 cups. A round shape twice as wide as it is deep is ideal, but use what you have that comes close. Metal is the easiest to work with, but glass will do. Thick ceramic is making it hard on yourself, as the mold must chill thoroughly for the aspic lining to set and if, in

---

*Goose fat is incomparable in flavoring robust country dishes—and in browning meats, frying potatoes, and braising turnips (page 161). The fat doesn't burn as quickly as oil and butter.
†For cooking, keep this fat separate from the pure rendered fat, as this will be adulterated with broth.

unmolding, the aspic doesn't slip out, it's harder to heat the mold to get it to do so. But of course if you have the perfect mold and it's ceramic, use it.

Rinse the mold with cold water (do not dry) and add half the aspic. Turn the rest into a metal bowl set in ice. Also, fill a big vessel with ice. Set your mold in the ice, then keep rolling it over the ice until a thin layer of the aspic completely coats the sides—use a pastry brush to help smooth the aspic along. When the mold is coated, add the unset aspic left in the mold to the aspic in the metal bowl. Push your mold deep into the big vessel of ice, level and upright.

To build the mold, the consistency of the aspic when added must be syrupy—like unbeaten egg white. If the reserved aspic has started to set, heat the metal bowl briefly to melt the aspic a little, then vigorously whisk both melted and set aspic together to make all of it syrupy.

On the bottom of the mold, use the nicest diamonds of meat, best sides down, to make a tight star—or any design you wish. Between the tips, set whole baby carrots or skinny carrot tips, tips pointed out. Wrap and refrigerate the remaining carrots. Spoon over just enough aspic to cover this first layer and let set. Make another star with the next-best pieces of meat, staggering them slightly so the tips of the previous layer can be seen through them (or continue your own design). Between the tips on the outside, fit smaller pieces of meat, tips pointed out, and set scraps in the center. Cover with a thin layer of aspic and let it set. Continue layering in this manner until all the meat has been used and the mold is filled, finishing with a layer of aspic. Let it set.

Lay plastic film on top and over the sides of the mold—press tightly. On top, set a flat plate or round of heavy cardboard that just fits inside the mold. Weight evenly with three 1-pound cans. Refrigerate at least 8 hours for the aspic to firmly set and up to 24 hours before unmolding.

If any aspic is left over (it's unlikely), chill it, then mash it with a fork and use around the base of the mold as garnish.

When ready to unmold, run a knife around the edge. Lay your serving platter on top of the mold, then invert it, giving the mold a little shake to ease the aspic down. (If you use a pot for a mold, as I did, the handle will get in the way of the dish. Nevermind, just get someone to steady the dish while you shake the pot—the aspic is firm enough that it won't come apart while gliding through the air a little distance.) If it doesn't come out, lay a hot towel on top of the mold until it does. Set the reserved carrots around the aspic at intervals, tips out, and flourish between the carrots with greenery. Keep in a cool place until serving.

For a buffet, you'll want someone to slice and serve the aspic (using a very sharp knife and a pie server or pancake turner), because the effect would be ruined if the aspic was pre-sliced, and it's impossible to hold a plate with one hand and cut down through all those layers with the other.

(For the record, I have doubled this recipe for a gala occasion, and it worked beautifully.)

Robert Benchley was a guest at that dinner party with Sam Hoffenstein. Benchley was a frequent guest, being everybody's favorite. Although the twinkle in Benchley's eye was known to flicker with sadness, from my child's view he had a mischievous air about him—confirmed when my mother told me years later that occasionally the two of them sat on camp stools beneath the banana tree at the back of a certain actor's villa, sipping martinis, nibbling almonds, and listening to the man trying to get a new girlfriend into bed.

Next to the framed Hoffenstein poem on my mother's kitchen wall is a *billet doux* from Benchley—typed in elite with black and red ribbon—which came floating over from villa 16 after one of my mother's parties. It was the favor of a recipe in kind.

NEW ENGLAND BOILED DRESSING FOR
BOILED NEW ENGLANDERS

¼ tbs. salt
3 teaspoons mustard (this is for jaded palates. The rule calls for 1
    teaspoon)
1 ½ tbs. sugar
Few grains cayenne
2 tbsp. flour
1 egg or yolk of 2 eggs
1 ½ tbsp. melted butter
¾ cup of milk
¼ cup vinegar

Mix dry ingredients, add yolks of eggs slightly beaten, butter, milk and vinegar *very slowly*. Cook over boiling water till mixture thickens—strain—add pepper from peppermill, and cool.

MOULDED SALMON

Use same rule as for boiled dressing. When cooked, add ¾ tbsp. granulated gelatine soaked in 2 tbsp. cold water. Pour over contents of one can of salmon (rinsed in hot water and separated in flakes). Fill mould and chill.

SERVE WITH

Cucumber Sauce. Beat ½ cup heavy cream (ha-ha) until stiff (ha-ha-ha). Add ¼ teasp. salt, few grains pepper, and gradually 2 tbls. vinegar. Then add 1 cucumber, pared, chopped and drained through cheese cloth.

Then take off all your clothes and call

Villa 16

The boiled dressing (delightfully pungent) makes 1¼ cups. I only use a pinch of salt . . . the mustard is *dry* . . . whisk constantly until the sauce is thick as mayonnaise then whisk a minute more to ensure the flour is cooked . . . I use white pepper in a white sauce.

The moulded salmon (very New England) makes 5 to 6 servings and you can prepare it a day in advance. Discard any fat, vertebrae, and skin from the salmon . . . a fork is helpful in separating flakes . . . use a 3-cup mold, lightly oiling it before filling . . . to unmold, set in place, lay a hot cloth on top and the salmon will slip down. (I unmold it onto fresh spinach leaves and garnish it with black olives, wedges of tomatoes, and hard cooked eggs. Lovely colors.)

The cucumber sauce (elegant and delicious) makes 2½ cups—surprisingly, it may be prepared well in advance and it keeps for days: just tilt the bowl to let any whey/cucumber juice run out. The chopped cucumber should measure about 2 cups . . . squeeze it nearly dry in the cloth.

During that insouciant period, my mother practiced some subliminal culinary consciousness-raising on me. My bedroom had twin beds and occasionally we would have an overnight guest. The light kept me awake, so my mother bought a tall grey cardboard screen and on it in her artist's hand with half a dozen colored pens wrote quotations about food and stood the screen between the beds.

A quotation just above my head, which I stared at nightly, was, "I'm a meat and potatoes boy . . ."—Groucho Marx. Among others, still indelibly scripted in my mind's eye after all these years were:

> "Soup of the evening, beautiful soup . . ."—Lewis Carroll. "The way to a man's heart is through his stomach . . ."—Fanny Fern. "Fate cannot harm me,—I have dined to-day . . ."—The Reverend Sydney Smith. "Doubtless God could have made a better berry, but doubtless God never did . . ."—William Butler, of strawberries. "An apple is an excellent thing—till you have tried a peach!"—George du Maurier. "He was a bold man that first eat an oyster . . ."—Dean Swift. "Four persons are wanted to make a good salad: a spendthrift for oil, a miser for vinegar, a counsellor for salt, and a madman to stir all up . . ."—Spanish proverb. ". . . a dinner of meats without the company of a friend is like the life of a lion or a wolf . . ."—Epicurus. "Better is a dinner of herbs where love is, than a stalled ox and hatred therewith . . ."—Proverbs. And

If you wish to grow thinner, diminish your dinner,
And take to light claret instead of pale ale;

> Look down with an utter contempt upon butter,
> And never touch bread till it's toasted—or stale.
> —Henry Leigh

While my father was at the studio and my mother rehearsing the show she took to hospitals and army camps all over the country, my own days were spent across the street at the Eunice Knight Saunders School, run for Hollywood children by a dippy but shrewd pair of Southerners. School across the street was wonderfully convenient. I'd get up fifteen minutes before it started and scramble an egg for myself and my father. He taught me how: He called them Mashed Eggs and as I was stirring, he'd lean across me and into the pan drop bits of sautéed chopped salami or crumbled bacon or chopped red onion or chives or lumps of cream cheese or bits of lox or some or all of these things (mostly all of them) while I *very* softly scrambled—he liked his eggs soft as velvet. Daddy always made thick fresh orange juice with a big silvery pull-down squeezer that looked like a car jack. My father and I cooked breakfast for one another because my mother never ate breakfast and liked to sleep late. After breakfast, I'd give them both a kiss and slide through the side bars of the wrought iron gate on Havenhurst Avenue (I was very thin) and dash across the street in time for the Pledge of Allegiance.

The Saunders School property was owned by a director from silent screen days, Irvin V. Willat. Mr. Willat lived next door to the school, behind a tall plank fence covered with purple passion flowers. He had pale blue eyes, wavy strawberry blond hair, a beautiful waxed strawberry blond moustache. Sometimes he wore stiff strawberry blond riding boots to the knee which made him look just like the photographs of him on his wall standing next to slinky women in satin gowns with marcelled hair, pencilled eyebrows, and beestung lips. He was a darling man and he was fond of the children in the school, especially me. Sometimes, bored with a Spanish lesson, I'd sneak next door and Mr. Willat would give me tea. He made me feel so grown up. We'd sit in the garden under his apricot tree and I'd listen to him reminisce about his life on the set.

One June day I found Mr. Willat making jam from his apricots. He invited me to cook with him. He gave me a basket of ripe fruit and told me to make apricot jam of my own. It was the first time I cooked anything from start to finish more complicated than an egg. Mr. Willat showed me how to smash the pits with a hammer and take out the kernels inside, he got a chair for me to stand on so I could stir the pot to keep the jam from scorching, then he let me pour the beautiful translucent paraffin over the jars to seal the preserves, finally he wrapped three warm jars in a tea cloth and tucked them in my arms to take home. For once, chatterbox Sylvia could not speak. The rapturous scent of his kitchen, the mysterious transmutation from plump gold fruit to melting burnished essence, the enormous pride I felt left me dazed. Mr. Willat couldn't know that whenever I have stood over a preserving kettle the forty years since, I think of him and that afternoon.

Lacking his recipe, this is how I make apricot jam in June. Only it isn't jam. It's *confiture*, the French preserve, whose texture lies between jam's I-am-an-essence-of-my-former-self and preserve's I-am-almost-as-I-was. I find friends especially like the fact that the apricots are cut in halves—this makes the texture luxurious. The method is French, although our apricots (and my citrus additions) are pure California sunshine. Of all the preserves from my kitchen, this is my favorite, and given fine apricots, I promise yours will rival any *confiture* you've ever eaten.

The recipe takes time, but I figure it's not a sacrifice to give a few hours to a year's supply of apricot *confitures* for ourselves and our friends. It's made in three stages rather than one exhausting sprint, so that helps.

Note for the harassed cook: apricot *confitures* with slivers of apricot kernels have that exquisite bitter almond undertaste and an ultra-luxe look. (Yes, you can eat one or two kernels at a time, but not by the fistful or you'll get sick—they yield prussic acid. M. F. tells me that, when they were little girls, she and her sister Anne once ate a whole pile of them to see if it was true that they would die. They were soundly thrashed for it.) If you're pressed for time, you can skip the kernels and just vow you'll do it properly next year. *Or* buy a tiny vial of bitter almond flavoring from a European food shop and stir in a few drops when the finished preserves are cool.

This is an excellent method for all preserves and marmalades—the English do it this way, too.

CALIFORNIA CONFITURE OF APRICOTS
[Makes 27 or more 8-ounce jars]
Because the jars are vacuum sealed, if you store them in a cool dark dry place, the *confiture* will keep for years. Ha.

1 lug* (20 to 22 pounds) fully ripe but firm apricots (I use Royal Blenheims, but I understand Tiltons and Wenatchees are also excellent)

About one 10-pound bag plus 1 cup sugar

The juice of about 4 juicy oranges
The juice of about 4 juicy lemons
8 to 10 drops bitter almond extract (optional)

---

*To make less (or more) of the recipe, simply weigh the culled and pitted fruit and use ¾ that weight in sugar. For every 5 pounds of fruit—purchased weight—use the juice of 1 orange and 1 lemon and, lacking the apricot kernels, 2 drops of bitter almond extract.

You can use an assortment of sizes of canning jars, as long as they all have new sealing caps and good rings.

The first day, pick over the fruit—use overripe but not underripe fruit (tinged with green)—and wash only if grimy (it's going to be boiled plenty, so don't worry about germs). Pull apricots apart or cut in half on the seam line; remove and set aside the pits. Weigh your biggest roasting pan, turn the fruit into it and weigh again, deducting the pot's weight from the total. Weigh out sugar equal to three-fourths the weight of the fruit. (A bathroom scale will serve, if you haven't a kitchen scale.)

Layer the apricots and sugar in the pan (or use two big pans). Cover and set in a cool place.* In an hour or two, the sugar will begin dissolving; stir with your hands carefully to blend. Leave to macerate overnight or up to 36 hours, so long as the temperature is 60°F or less, else the fruit could start to ferment. Stir gently whenever you think of it.

Lay the pits in a towel and whack with the side of a hammer. You want the kernels inside the shells, 72 perfect ones, so don't whack with abandon. Pour boiling water over them, then slip off their skins. Cover (no need to dry) and set in a cool place.

When you're ready to cook, thoroughly stir the fruit and sugar together. Balancing the sugary syrup and fruit, ladle 2 quarts of the mixture into your preserving kettle (the heavier the metal, the less chance of scorching). Set the kettle over medium-low heat. Mix the orange and lemon juices. Add a generous ¾ cup juice and 36 unbroken halves of kernels to the fruit. You'll be making four batches in all.†

Simmer uncovered until a bit of cooled syrup held between thumb and index finger still stays connected by peaky threads when the fingers are opened. Allow at least 1 hour. Stir frequently, especially toward the end, so the preserves won't scorch on the bottom.

Remove from the heat. Let settle a bit, then skim off any foam. Pour into a large shallow pan, not aluminum—the acid in the fruit might react with it and the fruit would be discolored. Add each batch as it is finished. Stir to blend. Cool. If you're using the bitter almond extract instead of apricot kernels, stir it in—8 to 10 drops *for this entire recipe.* Cover and return to your cool place up to 24 hours. This steeping in the syrup plumps the fruit. (Don't forget the water baffle for the ants. They are watching and waiting.)

The next day, pack, seal, and store according to directions on pages 243–244.

After Mr. Willat's apricot jam, the first recipes I learned to follow, like most children, were cookies. About this time, my mother received a postcard from M. F. It was addressed to:

---

*Preserving season is ant season, so, lacking room in the refrigerator, I set the pan in the bathtub, with cold water up the sides—ant baffle and cooler at the same time.
†Should you be the lucky owner of one of the big (14½ inches wide by 5½ inches deep and a capacity of 3 gallons) French copper preserving kettles, you can make this recipe in two batches, adding the juice of 2 oranges and 2 lemons to each batch. The pans are available in many fancy cookware shops and from Williams-Sonoma, Box 7456, San Francisco, California 94120-7456.

Mrs. Arthur Grant Sheekman
Garden of Allah
Sunset Boulevard
HOLLYWOOD
California

The date is October 28, 1944. Was Los Angeles ever so small a village that such an address could have reached her? Typed on the back was*:

<u>Lace Cookies (Otamela)</u> (or, to put it in English, Oatmeal)

1 egg, 1 cup sugar, 1 tablespoon flour, 1 cup oat meal (Quick Quaker Oats), 1 teaspoon vanilla, 1 pinch salt, ½ cup melted butter. Beat egg. Mix with sugar. Add flour, oatmeal, seasoning, and finally melted butter. Drop by teaspoonfuls on greased pan . . . 6 to a pan is enough. Bake at 400-until brown, remove from oven, let cool perhaps 50 seconds, and remove with spatula before they stick and break into 1000 pieces. Serve when cool. Tricky but beautiful . .

MFKF *for* GSS, with apologies for typing—

The moment I read the card, I begged my mother to make them—they sounded heavenly. She did. They were. Then one day when she was out, I made them by myself. 1000 1000 pieces! But they were so mysteriously exotic (a pale dab of batter unfolding into the most delicate wafer imaginable, and "*Otamela*"—such a mellifluous word!), and even though for ages they met with disaster at my young hands, these cookies have charmed me.

Today when I bake them, I use the "old-fashioned" oats in our larder, whizzing them 2 to 3 seconds in the food processor or blender until the flakes are half their former size. And after my maiden run, I boldly place 9 dabs on a large sheet. I bake the cookies on the top rack of the oven until the entire cookie is toffee brown, about 6 minutes. I've found that a long narrow spatula run sideways underneath the cookie is the surest means of retrieval, and if they harden too soon, I return the sheet to the oven a few moments till they're soft again. Sometimes I roll the warm cookies on the buttered handle of a wooden spoon to make "snaps." Stored airtight, they keep and keep. Beautiful indeed!

[*At high altitude:* Bake for 7 minutes.]

As time passed, my native fascination with cookery was sparked, in large measure because I was maturing and my mother's projects were becoming ir-

---

*The recipe makes about three dozen cookies.

resistible. *Sept fruits*, for example. In those years, I can't remember a summer when my mother didn't have a crock of seven fruits succumbing to the blisses of brandy tucked away for Christmas, when the thick dark mysterious syrup and plump shimmering ghosts were ladled up for giving. My mother has no idea where she learned the rule (although Irma Rombauer has a recipe for "Tutti-Frutti" that comes close), but scarcely a spring has gone by that the first sight of strawberries hasn't stirred the juices and we know it's time to pull out the crock.

 Sept fruits is fabulous heated and ladled over vanilla ice cream. I'm sure it has other uses, but that's what we've done in our family. But more than the eating, making the conserve adds a delightful dimension to summer.

SEPT FRUITS
Seven summer fruits conserved in sugar and brandy.
As with the brandy that makes it, *sept fruits* will keep indefinitely.

Fresh fruits as they come into season; our
 choices:
Strawberries, hulled
Apricots, in halves
Sweet cherries, pitted
Peaches, thickly sliced
Plums, in halves

Raspberries
Nectarines . . . blueberries . . . red
 currants . . . gooseberries . . .
 mangos . . . . or . . .
An equal weight of sugar
Brandy (a decent grade), to cover, as needed

Scald and scrub a stoneware crock that holds at least 3 gallons. Set it in the coldest place you have—my *sept fruits* has fermented only once, but once was once too many. Find a place to keep the crock for the summer—once you begin filling it, it's impossible to move.

 Lightly rinse the fruit, pit, and peel it only when absolutely necessary. Weigh. Ideally, you should have an equal measure of each fruit in the composition, but that's unrealistic because a flat of strawberries can cost the same as four pints of raspberries. Leave the fruit in the largest possible pieces—they will shrink considerably.

 In a large bowl, use your hands to mix the fruit and sugar; mix until the sugar liquefies. Turn into the crock, cover with brandy, then stir the brandy in. Devise some means of keeping the fruit beneath the brandy—I use a pot lid weighted with a jar. Cover closely. If ants threaten, seal securely with tape.*

 I usually launch my crock with a flat of strawberries (about 9 pounds—they are cheap and contribute more than their share of rich color and flavor), 9 pounds of sugar, and a half-gallon of brandy—I don't need to add more brandy until well along in summer. Along about August, our last fruit is added—always a windfall.

---

*Setting the crock in a vessel of water, our usual ant-baffle, isn't recommended here. The clay is so porous, water seeps into the *sept fruits* and fruited brandy seeps into the water. Ask how I know.

I used pineapple once, but it overpowered everything, so I won't again. Last year, I tried mangos for the first time and they were lovely.*

After the last fruit has been added, tape the lid down and forget about the crock till time to ladle it into sterilized canning jars† for Christmas giving. Be sure the tag lists all the lovely ingredients and what to do with it. A glorious tradition.

As I advanced to rinsing, buttering, smoothing, folding, arranging, and serving in my mother's kitchen, even the inevitable washing and drying had its place in teaching me how a dish is put together, how a dinner is presented, how a successful party is composed and launched.

One of the parties I remember best was a twenty-six-boy *rijsttafel* that would have made a Dutch colonial blink. *Rijsttafel* (literally "rice table") is a Dutch concoction of any number of Indonesian (strongly influenced by Indian and Chinese) delicacies. Traditionally, each dish is carried in and served by an Indonesian lad, thus the genesis for calling it a "twenty-six-boy" menu. (My father and mother were served their first *rijsttafel* in the legendary Raffles Hotel in Singapore during their trip around the world.) I was a good number of my mother's twenty-six boys myself, for I had peeled, chopped, sliced, spiced, whisked, and stirred many of the dishes into being, then helped serve from the buffet. From her tiny kitchen with her four-burner-hotplate-one-oven stove—on rationing—my mother sent this forth:

Rijsttafel

Chicken curry with rice	Pimiento strips
Filet of sole & oyster mold	Chopped eggs
Fried shrimps	Chopped onions
Chinese vegetables	Chopped green peppers
Indonesian bean sprouts	Crushed peanuts
Shish kebabs	Garlic almonds
Butterfly fritters	Chopped raisins
Lentils Omar Khayyám	Shredded coconut
Bieten met Appelen	Major Grey's chutney
Broiled tomatoes cinnamon	Red pepper relish
Broiled bananas ginger	Pickled mushrooms
Creamed radishes	Mustard pickles
Chilied eggs	Preserved kumquats

Beer   Gamay Rosé
Fresh pineapple sticks   Almond paste cookies
Coffee Grog

---

*Any fruit not mentioned, beware of—it would probably be too soft, too stringy, too seedy, or too tough.
†Notes on the jars and how to sterilize them are on pages 242–243.

This *rijsttafel* was served the end of May 1945. My mother cooked it again two months later for fourteen more guests to celebrate her and my father's eleventh wedding anniversary. (That was the night a guest arrived, looked around, and asked, "Where's Gloria?" and Groucho answered, "In the kitchen, where she belongs.")

Here is the recipe for a darkly handsome, wowie-zowie way with hard cooked eggs. Served over yellow rice (page 214) with Indonesian bean sprouts on the side (page 75), these make a superb and unusual vegetarian dinner.

CHILIED EGGS
Hard cooked eggs in a spicy sauce
[*4 to 6 servings*]
The sauce and eggs may be prepared several hours in advance.

¼ cup peanut or other light oil
2 rounded tablespoons chili powder
1 large onion, thinly sliced
A knob of fresh ginger the size of a large egg (about 2 ounces), unpeeled* and finely shredded
2 garlic cloves, finely chopped

4 ripe tomatoes, peeled, seeded,† and chopped
¾ cup excellent chicken broth or broth from cooking a mild vegetable
6 extra large eggs, hard cooked‡ and shelled
A scant ½ teaspoon salt

In a large heavy skillet over medium heat, heat the oil. Stir in the chili powder—take care it doesn't burn—then the onion and ginger. Cover and cook until the onions have softened, 5 to 6 minutes, stirring frequently. Add the garlic, tomatoes, and broth. Bring to a simmer, turn heat to low, cover and simmer 5 minutes, shaking the skillet frequently. Turn into a deep saucepan (so the sauce will cover the eggs). The sauce may be prepared in advance to this point. Cover and refrigerate.

When ready to serve, return the sauce to a simmer over medium heat, and add the eggs. Cover and warm the eggs over low heat another 5 minutes, shaking the pot occasionally. Taste for salt. Heat a shallow serving bowl.

Remove the eggs, cut them in half lengthwise, and set in the bowl. Pour over the sauce and serve with a good rich chutney (pear, for example, as on page 163) and yellow rice.

These bean sprouts are addictive. Six servings by no means serve six people. Some nights, I can eat four. They are crunchy, delicate yet flavorful, a versatile vegetable accompaniment—don't limit them to accompanying Dishes Oriental.

---

*Please see footnote about peeling ginger on page 152.
†How-to on page 259; save the strained juice for cooking.
‡An easy method is on page 246.

INDONESIAN BEAN SPROUTS
Bean sprouts quickly sautéed
[*Up to 6 servings*]

2 tablespoons peanut or other light oil
6 large whole scallions, cut in matchsticks
A splash of chicken broth

1 pound perky, crisp, very fresh bean sprouts
1 to 2 teaspoons soy sauce

Heat your serving bowl. Then, in a wok or large heavy skillet over high heat, heat the oil. Add the scallions, broth, and bean sprouts (don't worry, they'll cook down!) and sauté, stirring constantly, till the vegetables are warmed through, 2 to 3 minutes. Sprinkle lightly with soy sauce and serve at once.

Soon after the last *rijsttafel* triumph, my father's sister, Edith, came from Chicago for a visit. A special part of what Edith brought with her were tastes of my father's childhood, Jewish dishes that she learned from my Granny Sheekman. My grandmother came from Rostov-on-the-Don in Russia and consequently her cooking bore a Russian influence. I have before me a sheet of canary typing paper—singed in places, blotched with oil, dog-eared and scribbled on in pencil and three colors of ink—on which Edith wrote in her schoolteacher's hand one of my father's favorite recipes, *holodna*: cold chicken in a lemony custard.

Aunt Edith notes that *holodna* is best after the second or third day and that it will keep four to five days (I wouldn't know because ours has always disappeared sooner). Great for summer entertaining. In fact, this is such a beautiful looking, delicious, light, and unusual dish, it would be ideal for something like a wedding feast—it could be made comfortably in advance of all the dither.

Notice the absence of herbs in Edith's recipe. If Edith had been raised in France, there would certainly be thyme in her broth. The Jewish cuisine I know—from cooks whose families were born in Russia, Poland, and Hungary—calls for seasonings common to the cuisines of those countries. They are restrained. Herbs are parsley, dill, and bay, with celery leaves added occasionally. Spices rarely venture past peppercorns, paprika, nutmeg, cinnamon, and ginger—once in awhile, cayenne. Seeds are caraway, poppy, celery, and mustard. Once a friend's mother got upset when she saw me putting garlic in my chicken soup. "Sylvia," she said, "you can't put garlic in chicken soup!" I'll bet Jewish chicken soup in southern Italy has garlic in it.

Speaking of origins, the closest kin to the flavors of *holodna* I know is the Greek *avgolemono*—egg and lemon sauce (page 178). Except *avgolemono*'s a thinnish sauce—not set, as is this splendid custard. I can't imagine how it got to Chicago.

HOLODNA
Cold poached chicken in lemony custard
[*8 servings**]
Holodna wants at least 4 hours in the refrigerator before serving—you can make it
2 or 3 days in advance.

THE CHICKEN AND THE BROTH[†]

One 5-pound excellent whole roasting or
    young stewing chicken or 4 pounds meaty
    fryer parts, rinsed, and trimmed of fat
2 pounds chicken backs and/or necks—3
    pounds, if you're poaching fryer parts
1 large unpeeled onion, cut up

1 large leafy celery stalk, cut up
1 large peeled carrot
A good handful of parsley plus about ¹/₃ cup
    chopped, for garnish
3 quarts cool water

Cut the chicken into serving pieces—the French method (page 244) is nicest and
fairest, but French or American, divide the two breast pieces crosswise instead of
down the center. Turn the backs/necks, trimmings, onion, celery, carrot, handful
of parsley, and water into your soup pot. Set on the cover askew and bring to a simmer over medium-high heat. Skim off the grey scum, turn the heat to low, set on
the cover askew again, and simmer gently 1 to 2 hours.

Drop in the chicken pieces, pushing them beneath the broth. Cover again and
listen for the first simmering bubbles, then turn the heat to its lowest to maintain
the simmer. Poach the chicken until the meat tests tender and the juices run clear
when a fine skewer is thrust into the thickest part, 35 to 40 minutes. Do not overcook! As each piece is ready, remove it to a bowl and cover with a plate.

Strain the broth into another large vessel and let it set about 10 minutes. Pull out
and reserve the carrot. Rinse the pot. Ladle off as much fat as you can from the broth,
then pull strips of paper towels over the surface to absorb the last dibbles. Slowly
pour the broth through a fine sieve back into the pot, leaving any grey sediment behind. Boil the broth down until it is well flavored, about 7 ³/₄ cups.

Remove the skin from all the chicken except the wings,[‡] and trim gristle from
the drumsticks. Cut the breast pieces in half lengthwise. Arrange the pieces in a
single layer in a fairly deep, wide serving bowl. Slice the carrot into rounds a scant
¹/₄-inch thick and set over the chicken. Sprinkle with parsley. Keep covered while
you make:

---

*Four meaty breast pieces, two meaty second joints and two meaty drumsticks—the two
chicken wings can't be counted as a serving for company, but if you're a wing person, make that
9 servings.
†For an Occasion, I would use only chicken breasts and simply poach them with 2 to 3 young
carrots in excellent ready-to-serve chicken broth, to save time and energy.
‡Leaving the skin on while cooking not only adds flavor to the broth, but helps protect the delicate meat from drying out.

THE LEMONY CUSTARD SAUCE

6 extra large eggs, beaten
1 teaspoon sugar
½ teaspoon salt
About 8 turns of the white pepper mill
(²⁄₃ teaspoon, medium grind)

A pinch of nutmeg
¼ cup fresh lemon juice (1 large juicy
lemon)
3 cups of the chicken poaching broth

In a large heavy non-aluminum saucepan, blend eggs, sugar, salt, pepper, and nutmeg. Whisk in the lemon juice, then the broth. Taste for seasoning—it should be lemony but subtle. Stir constantly over medium-low heat until the sauce noticeably thickens and coats the spoon—do not let it send up even one bubble! Pour at once over the chicken and carrots, cover loosely with plastic film, and refrigerate until cold. Cover tightly. Spoon the custard over any exposed pieces from time to time. Serve at your leisure.

In her turn for Aunt Edith, my mother cooked the sublime classic, fillets of sole, Marguery.

Marguery's in Paris was a celebrated restaurant of the *Belle Epoque*, noted for its lavish decor, lively clientele, and fillets of sole. All the great chefs of Europe and America and cookbooks of the period offered their versions of the dish, but Marguery kept his a secret. It is said that Claude Monet charmed the recipe from him. I suspect the artist in Monet, not the gourmet, wanted the ivory-napped fillets speckled with pink and flecked with green to adorn his yellow and blue dishes in his yellow dining room at Giverny.

This recipe, in Marguery's own words, is from George Rector—Rector had apprenticed with Marguery in Paris long enough to be given the recipe. Later he owned a fashionable restaurant of his own in New York City. Like many great chefs, Marguery glosses over mundane but critical details of execution, so I have taken the liberty of adding my cooking notes in brackets.

FILLETS OF SOLE, MARGUERY
Poached fillets sauced with oysters and shrimps
[*4 servings*]
Have eight fillets removed from two sole or flounders [or buy 1 pound fillets]. Place bones, skin and heads in a stewpan. Add one pound of cut-up fish (flounder, haddock or cod) [lacking sole trimmings, buy 1²⁄₃ pounds "chowder fish"], ½ cup of sliced carrots, ½ leek, 2 sprigs of parsley, 10 peppercorns, ½ bay leaf and 1 quart of cold water. Bring to boiling point and simmer until fish stock is reduced to 1 pint [30 to 35 minutes; this may be done in advance]. Strain, pour fish stock over fillets which have been seasoned with salt and a few grains of cayenne and arranged in a buttered baking pan. Cover fillets with buttered paper and place in a moderate oven [350°F] to poach for 15 to 20 minutes. Carefully lift fillets out of pan and arrange

them on a hot [heat proof] platter (do not overlap or put one fillet on top of another) [cover tightly with foil and set aside; heat the broiler]. Strain fish stock into a small saucepan [a skillet has more surface] and reduce it by boiling to one cup [about 18 minutes], remove from fire [turn into a fresh small saucepan] and add 4 tablespoons of dry white wine (Hock type) [Rhine wine]. Thicken sauce with 3 egg yolks which have been slightly beaten [whisk them in, then set over hot water and whisk until creamy] and add, bit by bit, ¼ pound of fresh [softened] butter, whipping constantly until the sauce is perfectly smooth. Then add 1 teaspoon of finely chopped parsley. Pour sauce over fillets which have been garnished with 1 dozen small steamed oysters and 1 dozen small boiled shrimp. Place platter under moderate flame until lightly browned.

I confess to being greedy and wanting a more generous garnish, so I buy 8 ounces small shucked oysters and 8 ounces medium-sized raw unshelled shrimps (twice what the recipe suggests). I drop the oysters into the stock while it's reducing to 1 cup; when their edges curl, in about 1 minute, I lift them out. I drop the shrimps into 1 cup salted boiling water until they turn coral, then I shell them and add them to the oysters.

Nights when I long for such elegance but can't manage the ritual, I toss together a delicious but

FAUX MARGUERY

For each person: lay 4 to 5 ounces fillets (any fish) in a skillet that just accommodates them. Barely cover with a stock of something like 3 parts dry vermouth or white wine, 2 parts water, and 1 part oyster liquor* or clam juice. Lift out and reserve the fillets. To the stock, add ¼ onion, finely chopped, and ¼ carrot, finely shredded. Cover and simmer over medium-high heat until the vegetables soften, about 5 minutes. Heat a serving platter.

Lay the fillets in the skillet, cover, and poach at a bare simmer until the flesh between flakes is milky, not pink, 3 to 5 minutes, depending upon thickness. Lift the fish onto the platter, cover with foil, and keep warm. For every scant cup of stock in the skillet, rub together 1 rounded tablespoon *each* of softened butter and flour (called *beurre manié*). Whisk this paste into the stock over medium-high heat. When the sauce is smooth and thickened, drop in a handful of shellfish—small shelled shrimps, tiny scallops, fresh crab, and/or little oysters. Stir until cooked or warmed through, a matter of moments. Point up the sauce with a squeeze of lemon juice, a pinch of cayenne pepper, and enrich with a drizzle of cream (not essential). Spoon over the fillets, color with chopped tarragon or parsley, and serve.

Marguery's or *faux*, offer potatoes for mashing in the sauce.

---

*Desperate and miles from anything resembling fresh, I've been known to use the liquor and a few small oysters from a can, sea-salty but sweet, from oriental waters.

When I was eleven, we moved from The Garden to a house in the Hollywood hills. Soon I was going to Bancroft Junior High School on a big yellow school bus (more fun than just crossing the street). I loved it. Except for home economics. My mother laughed at my first D—in sewing—but my father looked grave. I was stricken but I knew I would redeem myself in the next semester's cooking class. I hadn't counted on the teacher, Mrs. Ethel Somebody, a small grey owl of a woman. Her big thing was Washing Dishes. From Left to Right. She couldn't be serious. I'd been washing dishes forever, but in The Garden's kitchen, from Right to Left. Mrs. Somebody was not amused. I got my second D.

When finally we were allowed to cook, we had to use margarine in the cream sauce. She couldn't be serious. In those days, margarine came uncolored with a little capsule of coloring, and you put it in a plastic bag and kneaded it till the pale white stuff turned sunshine yellow. Not only did we have to put margarine in the cream sauce, but we had to measure out diddly amounts of things. By then I could make cream sauce with my eyes closed, and Mrs. Somebody caught me flicking in the flour and sloshing in the milk. Another D, a big one, for my final grade.

I've remembered something else Mrs. Somebody made us do. Cut marshmallows into a perfectly reasonable Waldorf salad ("Now, girls, wet your scissors so the marshmallows won't stick"). I told Abby about it and Abby hooted. Abby was the first in a line of housekeepers my mother hired. Abby introduced me to the music of Pearl Bailey (whom she closely resembled), and when my parents went out, Abby made us our own private dinner: hamburgers, mashed potatoes, baby peas, Waldorf salad, Graham Torte, and Dr. Pepper. There were no marshmallows in Abby's Waldorf salad.

Abby's graham torte was a dense buttery cake made with graham cracker crumbs, walnuts, and dates—wonderful toasty flavor—and garnished with slathers of whipped cream. We don't have her recipe because Abby was one of those cooks who will not share their cooking triumphs. For years, my mother and I chased through cookbooks in search of a Graham Torte that might be Abby's. I found a hint of it in my first copy of *The Joy of Cooking* and after refining it over the years, my mother and I both agree I've got it.

(I remember when Mae and Kyle Crichton gave my mother *The Joy of Cooking*—the third edition, 1941. For some reason, Mother turned her nose up at it, has no idea what happened to that copy, and only recently bought one because I said she had to. So I grew up without *The Joy of Cooking*. But in 1955, I received a copy as a gift, and Mrs. Rombauer taught me worlds those early years. Her style of American plainsong embellished with echoes of European richness is particularly to my taste, and I still enjoy her homely old-fashioned asides. I urge any reader interested to ask a rare cookbook dealer to keep an eye out for an early copy of *The Joy of Cooking*, which is pure Irma Rombauer.)

My mother had bought an electric mixer. Remembering my grandmother sitting stolidly on a stool beating beating beating batter, I thought the Mixmaster a miraculous machine and loved watching its beaters whirl around the white glass bowl while the bowl spun on its pedestal beneath. I think my fascination with the Sunbeam was the genesis of my interest in baking—I loved feeding it creamy things to beat.

GRAHAM TORTE, AFTER ABBY'S

[*12 servings*]

This torte may be made 3 or 4 days in advance. Cool thoroughly, then wrap tightly in foil and keep in a cool place.

1 stick butter, softened, plus a little for the mold	*1 cup milk, at room temperature*
1 cup sugar, plus more for the mold	*1 ¼ cups (5 ounces) toasted walnuts*
2 teaspoons vanilla extract	*(although I've come to prefer pecans),*
3 extra large eggs, at room temperature	*chopped medium-fine*
2 cups fine graham cracker crumbs*	*1 cup (7 ounces unpitted) pitted dates,*
2 teaspoons baking powder	*chopped medium-fine,† firmly packed*
½ teaspoon cinnamon	*A little confectioner's sugar, sifted*
	1 ½ cups heavy cream, whipped (optional)

Brush a ring mold or tube pan of about 8 ½ cups capacity (mine fits this recipe perfectly: it's fluted, 9 × 3 inches with a 3-inch hole) with softened butter. Dredge with sugar,‡ knocking out excess.

Heat the oven to 350°F. In a bowl with a mixer at medium speed or with a wooden spoon, cream the butter, sugar, and vanilla until you have soft, fluffy, butter-sugar crumbs—the mixture won't be creamy because there's too much sugar and not enough liquid. Scrape the beaters or spoon and bowl, then add the eggs one at a time, beating after each until blended—*now* it's creamy! Again scrape the beaters and bowl.

On waxed paper, blend the graham crackers, baking powder, and cinnamon. Add this mixture to the bowl in 4 parts alternating with the milk in 3 parts. Once again, it will not be homogenized—in other words, it will look odd. Stir in the nuts and dates, breaking up any clumps of dates that have stuck together. Smooth into the mold and rap lightly on the counter to knock out any air bubbles.

Bake until the top springs back when tapped lightly with a finger and the sides have begun to pull away from the mold, 40 to 45 minutes. Cool 10 minutes on a rack upright then turn out gently—right or wrong side up—onto the rack. Serve

---

*About 26 squares, crushed to a powder beneath the rolling pin.

†Don't fall for the package of "chopped dates," which are little squiggly sugar-sprinkled extrusions of date *paste*. Dates taste most like themselves if you buy them unpitted—that way, they have been processed as little as possible, and anyway, pitting dates only takes moments.

‡The sugar makes it possible for the baked torte to slip out of the mold and also gives it a light glaze.

warm or cooled with confectioner's sugar sifted over the top at the last moment. Pass whipped cream on the side—unsweetened, the torte's sweet enough. Or wrap it and take it on its own to a picnic!

After Abby left to get married, my mother found more good cooks to tend her kitchen. The best was a quiet Dane named Ellen. I'll never forget the first dinner she cooked for us. It was roast chicken, and when my mother slipped the spoon into the cavity for the dressing, out came fragrant apples and prunes. I was entranced. Ellen's Danish soups, roasts, desserts, and cookies were simple and glorious and the first taste of Europe I'd had since La Bretagne (my mother's cooking was international, of course, but became her own through her own native whimsy).

When Ellen left to get married, Mother hired a German couple, Anna and Frank. Anna made fine spicy *Sauerbraten mit Spätzle* and a divine *Rotkraut mit Apfeln*—red cabbage with apples. My father adored it and before they moved to Sebastopol to grow Gravensteins, Anna told my mother how she made it so that Mr. Sheekman would not go without. The color is a beautiful magenta, the texture is nicely crisp, and the taste is one of my favorite plays of flavors, sweet-tart. This cabbage keeps and keeps when tightly covered in the refrigerator, and my father was caught more than a few times eating it straight from the jar, cold.

ROTKRAUT MIT APFELN, AFTER ANNA'S
Sweet-tart red cabbage with apples
[*8 servings*]
This may be prepared a day or two in advance and warmed up.

11 *fluid ounces dry red wine*	2 *tablespoons cornstarch*
½ *large red cabbage, finely shredded*	*A pinch of cinnamon*
1 *red onion, finely shredded*	*A pinch of allspice*
2 *unpeeled tart green apples, cored and medium-shredded*	*About* ½ *tablespoon salt*
2 *cups water, boiling*	*About 6 turns of the pepper mill*
3 *tablespoons cider vinegar*	(½ *teaspoon, medium grind*)
2 *tablespoons dark brown sugar*	1 *tablespoon butter*

Reserve 2 tablespoons of the wine and turn the rest into a large non-aluminum* skillet with the cabbage, onion, apples, water, vinegar, and brown sugar. Cover and simmer over medium-low heat until the cabbage turns magenta yet is still crispy, about 30 minutes. Stir occasionally. Heat a serving bowl.

---

*Aluminum would react with the wine and turn everything grey.

Dissolve the cornstarch in the reserved wine and blend it into the skillet, then stir until thickened. Add the cinnamon, allspice, salt, pepper, and butter. Serve now or later.

The older I got and the more I cooked—my mother still pressed me into service for her dinner parties—the more I grew to enjoy it. By the time I was in high school, I was making dinner for the three of us on cook's nights off. In the beginning, most everything came out of *America's Cook Book*, compiled by the New York Herald Tribune Home Institute, with THIS COVER IS WASHABLE printed in yellow across the shiny black front. I made dishes like Italian Hamburg Loaf, Spanish Lamb Stew, and Finnan Haddie Rarebit (my father adored finnan haddie), which, in spite of myself, smacked awfully of Mrs. Somebody's idea of cooking. Finally I gave up *America's Cook Book* in favor of my mother's files.

My parents had bought a wonderful turn-of-the-century house in Brentwood, not two miles from my grandmother's in Santa Monica—except that by then, Alice Vinegar had moved to New York. The garden my mother inherited was the fruit of forty years' labor by one of Southern California's finest horticulturists. The acre (a wall at the back separated it from a convent's cloister) was studded with specimen deodars, Australian tea trees, apricots, avocados, cherimoyas, guavas, and sapote trees, as well as a venerable bed of old roses, which I loved. My mother took up landscaping and gardening the way she had taken up acting, cooking, and just before this period, *découpage* and interior design for the shop she ran for several years—the way she was to take up painting, bonsai, silkscreening, and handset printing in the future. She had built a little greenhouse, lath house, and aviary, and connected them with sweeping paths of used brick. Guess who got to chip old mortar off the old bricks. Guess who was expected to give the rest of every Saturday to watering and weeding. Guess who loathed, hated, and abhorred gardening.

Giving onto the garden was a large open kitchen with a skylit breakfast room, papered in a lifesize French railway station drawn by Saul Steinberg. There, my best friend and I cooked and served our first dinner party.

Diane and I were sixteen. We invited our boyfriends. The menu was asparagus vinaigrette, tomato aspic, Chinese honeyed duckling, whipped sweet potatoes in orange cups, broiled pineapple, and Indian pudding with vanilla ice cream. I find it unimaginable but Diane has kept the menu we wrote in bastard French ("*Pudding au tom tom . . .*"). Everything—*everything*—failed. The boys (a football hero—hers—and a dolt—mine) had never been next to fresh asparagus in their lives and pushed the spears around on their plates. The aspic unmolded splat. The duck roasted to charcoal and, of course, had scarcely enough meat on it for one football player, much less four ravenous teenagers. The sweet potatoes were too sweet and the pineapple was too sour. My boyfriend finally popped a stick of gum into his mouth (the way he met every crisis). By the time we opened the oven and found the Indian pudding was soup, we laughed so hard we had to bolt from the room to save our dignity.

It was the Indian pudding that hurt. I'd promised Diane it would be fabulous. My mother had made it often at The Garden and I'd adored it, but at the last minute, she couldn't find her recipe. The one we unwittingly baked that night was from the faction that likes its Indian Pudding *soft*. The custard is slowly baked for hours and hours, then halfway through, milk is poured over the dish so the pudding finishes soupy as a Cape Cod fog. My mother's, on the other hand, was from those who like their Indian Pudding *set*. Finally, after years of wrestling, I've evolved an Indian Pudding I think perfect.*

The elements of cornmeal, eggs, and spices make this a wonderfully versatile dessert. Indian pudding can follow anything from a sedate New England boiled dinner to the searingest Tex-Mex chili. It isn't too sweet, it isn't too rich, and the hot gingery custard with cold vanilla ice cream is *so* good. If, like some Yankees, you like yours cold, cut down on the spices—they are too forceful when cooled.

FINALLY, INDIAN PUDDING!

[*12 or more servings (depends on what precedes it)*]
May be prepared in advance, although I think it best an hour or so out of the oven.

1 quart extra-rich milk†	*5 extra large eggs*
²⁄₃ cup light molasses	*1 tablespoon cinnamon*
¹⁄₃ cup dark brown sugar	*1 tablespoon ginger*
¹⁄₃ cup yellow cornmeal	*1 tablespoon mace*
¹⁄₂ teaspoon salt	*1 ¹⁄₂ quarts vanilla ice cream*
³⁄₄ stick unsalted butter, plus a little for the dish, softened	

Brush a round 9 × 1⅝-inch glass baking dish‡ with butter. In a large heavy saucepan, whisk together the milk, molasses, brown sugar, cornmeal, and salt. Set over medium heat and whisk until the mixture thickens and comes to a simmer, about 15 minutes. Lower the heat and continue whisking while it simmers briskly 5 minutes. Take the pot off the heat, cut in the butter, and stir until it melts. Set a lid on

*Cornmeal was called Indian meal in the days when the pudding was a Yankee institution. It began life as Hasty Pudding, an ancient English porridge made with wheat flour. In the Colonies, cornmeal was cheaper than wheat and so it was renamed Indian Pudding.

†If extra-rich milk isn't available at the market, slosh a little heavy cream or half-and-half into the measuring pitcher before filling it to the mark with ordinary milk.

‡Or any dish at least that deep with a 7- to 12-cup capacity. The custard must be at least 1¼ inches deep to bake properly.

askew and cool 20 to 30 minutes, stirring occasionally. Heat the oven to 325°F. In a bowl, beat the eggs, cinnamon, ginger, and mace together until blended, then whisk into the cornmeal mixture. Smooth into the dish, then set in a larger pan; pour hot water into the pan up to two-thirds the height of the dish.

Bake until a knife slipped into the center comes out clean, about 50 minutes. Remove from the water bath, cover, and set out of a draft. To serve, spoon warm or cold from the baking dish into dessert bowls and top with vanilla ice cream.

Then, after seventeen years of being Mommy's and Daddy's good little girl, I had an appetite to be my own. I had been accepted at the University of California at Berkeley, my mother's alma mater. The day I left, for auld lang syne, my father made me breakfast. Fresh orange juice from the old car jack device, fried Golden Delicious apples with maple syrup—my favorite of his newer *spécialités de la maison*—and, of course, mashed eggs. I had great difficulty swallowing, partly because I was so eager to go and partly because it was all I could do to keep from weeping.

Paris, Imagine!

Of course, Berkeley was an education for me in more ways than the university. My world opened up. Wide. I loved my life there, I loved my classes, I loved studying hard and getting good grades, I loved the bay and the art and the music and the food in San Francisco. (This was, of course, in the early fifties, decades before Berkeley became a gastronomical mecca. In those days, we thought Kip's Charburgers were the best food in town.) I loved working on the *Daily Cal* and I especially loved all the bright young men I was suddenly—miraculously! inexplicably!—attracting. I flung myself from one delicious moment to the next.

So that, in the fall of my sophomore year, when a once-best friend told me she was off in the spring with two sorority sisters to the Sorbonne, I begged to go along. It took delicate negotiating with my parents, the sorority sisters, and the university—none of whom was enthusiastic—but at last everyone caved in.

We sailed in early February on the French liner *Liberté* and all the four of us did for five days was feast by day and dance by night. Dancing aboard ship is make-believe. All those beautiful young men do not exist in the real world—especially Basque sailors, with whom one of our number fell hopelessly in love. Dining aboard ship is quite the same—essence of this, *fumé* of that, nothing anyone in the real world has ever seen before or will ever see again, spooned from silver cups, plucked from silver baskets, served from silver trays.

Except that there was a most esthetic and delectable apple composition, right up my alley, which I inquired about and have re-created many times since:

POMMES DE NUIT
Hot buttered rum-flamed apples and cold whipped cream
[*6 servings*]
These really must be done at the last minute.

1 stick unsalted butter
6 fine sweet firm cooking apples* peeled,
  cored, and quartered†
A generous 3 fluid ounces dark rum
  (Calvados or other good brandy may be
  substituted)

3 tablespoons sugar, preferably vanilla
  sugar‡
1 cup heavy cream, cold, unsweetened, and
  whipped

Melt the butter in a large heavy skillet, preferably cast iron, over medium-low heat. Gently lay in the apples, cut sides down. Cover and cook the apples, turning them as necessary with a wooden spatula or spoon, until they are very tender and richly browned all over, 30 to 40 minutes. When they test nearly tender with a fine skewer, carefully warm the rum in a small pot over low heat (or in the microwave).

When the apples are tender, sprinkle them with sugar, shaking the skillet gently to distribute the sugar and being careful not to break up the quarters. Turn off the heat, pour over the rum, and set it aflame—watch out for what's overhead! Serve at once (in glass bowls, if you have them), passing the whipped cream on the side. Serve with delicate crisp cookies.

It was midnight by the time our boat train arrived in Paris. We found the Hôtel de l'Avenir—my French professor had recommended it—and fell into bed. But I couldn't sleep. At dawn, I began to dress, my heart pounding. I shook my friend and asked if she didn't want to get up and come with me to see Paris. Pharumph. By six I could stand it no longer and called the concièrge—my professor had said that as soon as I woke up, *petit déjeuner* would be brought to my room. When the tray arrived, my knees grew weak as I took it from the plump pink *bonne* who smiled and gave a flick of a curtsey at the door.

On my tray, service for one: a ceramic pitcher of hot milk, a thick brown pitcher of dark-roasted coffee (I had come to love its bitter flavor on the ship), a flute of bread faintly warm from the oven, a saucer with pats of sweet butter, another saucer with bright red cherry preserves, and another saucer with cubes of brown sugar. Nothing, not the sumptuous breakfasts on the *Liberté*, not the French books I had read nor the French movies I had seen, nothing prepared me for that tray. In its Gallic simplicity (what the French regard as

---

*Some excellent choices are on pages 235–236.
†If you haven't an apple corer, quarter the apples and slice out the core. Then a recommendation for a corer is on page 237.
‡Vanilla sugar notes, page 258.

essentials for starting the day), tearing hunks from the slim shiny loaf, spreading every crevice with butter and spooning over tart cherries, pouring milk with one hand and coffee with the other into the enormous white bowl of a cup (a lesson learned on the ship), plopping in cubes of brown sugar, stirring until I could feel the sugar dissolve, then sipping and chewing as I looked down from my perch and saw the early morning bustle of the Left Bank—Paris, imagine!—it was one of the dearest meals of my life.

The three sisters were sleeping soundly, so I closed the door and climbed down the creaking old stairs to the street.

Outside the hotel, I turned right on the rue Madame and began walking, no notion of where I was going. At the first street I came to, I turned right again, onto the rue de Vaugirard. In a few minutes, I came to the corner of what I could see was a vast formal garden. A plaque said the *Conseil de la République*—the French Senate—met there, in the *Palais du Luxembourg*. The Luxembourg Gardens! I remembered my father saying he wanted to see them, as Bernard and Olivier met there often in *The Counterfeiters*.

A block later, the rue de Vaugirard ended at my first Parisian boulevard. The Boulevard St. Michel was wonderfully alive at seven in the morning, lots of kids my age tooling along on bicycles, swinging arm in arm down the broad tree-dappled sidewalks, squatting on their haunches against closed shops, smoking cigarettes, and taking the morning sun. I smiled to myself. It was just like Berkeley.

For the next nine hours, I wandered. It was as though Paris had taken me by the hand. Just as I had stumbled on the Luxembourg Gardens, I walked straight into the Sorbonne, crossed the Seine, looked up and I was in front of Nôtre Dame, then down an avenue and there was the Place de la Bastille, then around a corner, the Place des Vosges and the Musée Victor Hugo. I recrossed the river, made a wrong turn and landed in the Gare d'Austerlitz, a grey industrial part of Paris. Famished, I bravely entered a café and, in the company of stolid workmen in overalls, ate my first *omelette aux fines herbes*. Heaven.

Afterwards, walking along the Seine, hoping it was the right direction, I remembered the girls at the hotel. I should call. No, first I'd phone the two Maibelles. Maibelle Junior and Senior. They were expecting me. Californians, both mother and daughter had married Frenchmen—Senior's an artist, Junior's a count. Junior had tousled chestnut hair (my mother called it Maibelle's Mixmaster Hairdo) and wore tweed culottes. Senior had gorgeous cheekbones and lavender-blue hair. Maibelle Jr.'s apartment, where they both lived, was on the Seine, next door to the Ecole des Beaux-Arts. I was shown into the drawing room, all gilded, tapestried, and deep-piled elegance, sunny windows with geraniums on the sills, window seats giving onto the Louvre across the way.

The two Maibelles swept me up in their warmth and announced it was time for tea, the first of many I would take in that magnificent room. Maibelle Jr. served tea every afternoon at four and often friends dropped in. Soon we were joined by an artist, an elegant white-haired man in his seventies who brought a gift of heather honey. Everyone began to chatter in French and I tried to behave as though I was used to all this but I had difficulty keeping my head from tipping back in rapture.

Maibelle Sr. poured. The tea was pale in my cup and richly scented. I noticed there was no milk and sugar on the tray. My mother, I think, hadn't brewed a pot of tea in all my years of growing up, and I may have had three teabag cups at the dorm during three sets of finals. I sipped it. There nearly went my head again! The tea was smoky-sweet, sensuous, ephemeral. When I asked what it was, Maibelle wrote it out for me in her large round script, Lapsang Souchong, *Compagnie Coloniale.*

Louise, the cook, carried in a sugar-dusted cake, a *quatre-quarts*. With restraint, I ate only two pieces then went back into the kitchen and asked how she had made it. Louise laughed. Any ninny could make *quatre-quarts*—the "four quarters" are equal weights of eggs, butter, sugar, and flour, *Mademoiselle*. So my first cake in Paris was an English pound cake!

Quatre-quarts is considered homely when compared with *génoise*, the classic French cake-of-all-work. Yet I note in *Larousse gastronomique* that the only difference between the two is that *génoise* has twice the weight of eggs; the technique is the same. There's an aura around *génoise* that has always made me a little nervous, but whipping up a *quatre-quarts* is simple. Shows you what a little mystique can do.

I have been fascinated by the recipe and have tried many variations over the years. How can there be variations when it's so straightforward? Aha. Do you begin by creaming the butter and sugar or do you fold the butter in at the end? Do you, in fact, cream the butter or melt it? Do you separate the eggs or add them whole? Do you use granulated or powdered sugar? And when and where do you add the flour?

I found this best of all possible *quatre-quarts* in *La cuisine moderne*—moderne being 1907. It's an especially buttery cake with a close old-fashioned texture. How can it be more buttery than other pound cakes? Its secret is that it uses confectioner's sugar—the amount of confectioner's sugar for its weight takes up less space in the cake than granulated sugar would do and thus butter is predominant. Louise would love it.

Flavoring *quatre-quarts* is a matter of whim. You can add nutmeg, mace, or something spicier, caraway or poppy seeds (these, more English), vanilla, almond, lemon, orange, orange flower water, or any spirits you like. But do try it first plain with just the sweet flavors of the basics.

About whether to flour or sugar the pan. Flour has little effect on the outside crumb and is the choice if you're going to do something more to the cake than dust it with sugar; granulated sugar over the butter in the pan gives the finished exterior a slight but lovely glaze.

This cake has been made since at least the eighteenth century, so obviously an electric mixer isn't essential, but if you use one, the cake will be lighter than if you don't.

QUATRE-QUARTS
French four-part butter cake
[*Up to 16 servings*]
Wrapped airtight in plastic film and set in a cool place, the cake keeps moist 2 or 3 days. *Quatre-quarts* also freezes beautifully so you can bake one for now, another for later.

A *little granulated sugar for the pan(s)*
   (optional)
4 *extra large eggs*
1 3/4 *cups confectioner's sugar*
1 3/4 *cups all-purpose flour, plus a little for*
   the pan(s) (optional)

2 1/4 *sticks unsalted butter, melted and*
   cooled, plus a little for the pan(s),
   softened
Added flavoring to taste (suggestions
   above), such as 1 1/4 teaspoons French
   orange flower water (optional)
Sifted confectioner's sugar for the top

Choose two round 9 × 1½-inch cake pans or one 9- to 10-cup tube pan.* Brush well with butter, then dust with flour or sugar, knocking out the excess.

In a large mixing bowl, whisk the eggs and sugar until just combined. Set the bowl into a pot of hot water, taking care the water doesn't touch the bottom of the bowl. Whisking almost constantly, set the arrangement over low heat until the eggs are bright yellow and a little warmer than lukewarm, about 5 minutes.† Heat the oven to 300°F. Remove the bowl from the water and beat the eggs on a mixer at medium to high speed or with a whisk until the mixture is cool, light, and has tripled in volume, 5 to 10 minutes.

Shake the flour through a sieve over the bowl while you gently fold it in with a large rubber spatula. Blend butter with any flavoring. Drizzle the butter over the batter, folding it in—keep sweeping down and bringing batter up from the bottom of the bowl to be sure no butter is hiding there. Fold until blended, but don't overmix. Smooth the batter into the pan(s), slightly pushing the batter up against the sides. Rap gently on the counter to knock out any air bubbles.

Set the pan(s) on a baking sheet and bake until light brown, slightly pulled away from the edges, and a thin skewer thrust into the center comes out clean, about 45 minutes for most sizes. Cool right side up on a rack for 5 minutes, then run a table

*A larger pan would also be fine—the cake will just be shallower.
†*Or* you can put the eggs and sugar in a heavy stainless mixing bowl directly on the burner at medium heat for 30 seconds while you whisk constantly and hold your breath.

knife around the rim and turn the cake out onto the rack—right or wrong side up, as you choose. Cool. Serve dusted with confectioner's sugar. Best in slices about ½-inch thick.

[*At high altitude:* If baked in a flat pan and you don't want the cake to dip slightly in the center, use 1¾ sticks butter; if baked in a tube pan, you can use the full amount of butter. Bake at 325°F.]

I don't think filling suits a *quatre-quarts*, unless it's a tart preserve such as apricot, plum, or cherry—although the English make this sort of thing into a Sandwich Cake by halving it through the center and filling it with jam.

An elegant variation of *quatre-quarts* from the past is called *Trois frères* ("Three Brothers"), created in the nineteenth century by the three Julien brothers. The *trois frères* mold is a round fluted-in-swirls shallow tube pan about 8 inches wide. The cake was originally made with rice flour, flavored with maraschino liqueur,* and served on a round of sweet pastry. Wonderfully crunchy finish.

TROIS FRÈRES
Apricot-and-almond-covered butter cake
[*Up to 16 servings*]

1 recipe Quatre-quarts *(recipe preceding)*
About ½ cup best apricot preserves, warmed
About ½ cup toasted almonds, coarsely chopped

1 tablespoon coarse sugar†
A handful of diced angelica (optional)

Bake the cake in a tube pan and unmold as directed, widest side down. While still warm, set the cake on its rack over waxed paper.

Generously brush all over with apricot preserves, then smother with chopped almonds. Sprinkle the top with coarse sugar. Some add diced angelica as well. Slide onto its serving plate. Best sliced about ½-inch thick.

Quatre-quarts, being pure of heart, is susceptible of many moods. Don't be taken in by the little drift of confectioner's sugar or the dignified fall of apricot and almonds. Given a bittersweet chocolate glaze—rich dark dramatic sleek and shiny—and *Je t'aime* swept across in chocolate, the *i* dotted with one perfect candied violet, who knows what might happen . . .

To me, this is the ultimate in chocolate finishing:

*Maraschino notes, pages 121–122.
†Described on page 258.

GLAÇAGE AU CHOCOLAT
Bittersweet chocolate glaze
[Makes 1 ½ cups: ample for glazing any shape of quatre-quarts]

4 ounces semi-sweet chocolate   1 stick unsalted butter, at room temperature
4 ounces unsweetened chocolate

Heat the chocolates together (in the microwave at ⅔ power or in a double boiler over medium heat) until almost melted, stirring occasionally. Remove from the heat and add the butter in about 6 slices, stirring with a wooden spoon after each addition. When the glaze is thoroughly blended, set in a cool place until tepid, 20 to 30 minutes, stirring occasionally. Now stir until the glaze thickens to the consistency of thin mayonnaise.

Brush the crumbs off your cake and set it on a rack over waxed paper. Evenly pour over the chocolate, then use a table knife to smooth it out—if it's a chilly day, work quickly so the glaze doesn't set before you've finished. Lift up the cake with two pancake turners and set onto a doilied serving plate.

If you want to pipe a message (fervent or otherwise) on the cake, and decorate it a bit, make this:

CHOCOLATE DECORATIVE ICING
[Makes a generous ¼ cup]

2 ounces semi-sweet chocolate   A scant tablespoon unsalted butter, at room
                                                                                    temperature

Follow directions for the glaze above. The icing won't need much cooling to be thick enough to pipe through a paper cone.

A couple of days later when the sisters decided they would rather study French in Majorca, I found a place for myself with a family on the rue de l'Université. He was an American newsman, avuncular, adorable, who had made newsreels when there were still newsreels in movie theaters. She was French—FRENCH!—and their young son was French, too. Their eldest son was in school in America and I was given his room.

Madame set a fine table. The family's *bonne*, Jacqueline, a wiry blonde from the provinces, was a simple but superb cook. I tasted my first *potage santé* at her hands—pale green, the consistency of thick cream, with little croutons floating on top of the beautiful flat soup dish. It appeared more emerald than pea soup, and pea soup is what I expected when I lifted my spoon. But oh, that herbal zing! I had three helpings and was sorrel-struck forever.

Jacqueline's way with Health Soup was to wilt some sorrel in butter, moisten it with broth (whatever was on hand, but light), thicken it with a few spoonfuls of potato puree and a couple of egg yolks, flavor it with a pinch of chervil, and simmer it about 25 minutes. That is the classic *potage santé* and the soup I made for years. But I now make a soup that is, if possible, even more satisfying. The recipe, literally "Soup of Health," is from *La cuisine moderne*.

A friend, who has been passionate about the classic version, on the first spoonful of this silky matter said, "It's lovely, but I prefer the other." On the second spoonful, said, "Delicious." On the third spoonful there was silence and halfway through the bowl, he said, "I feel like a traitor. I like this better."

POTAGE DE SANTÉ
Soup of pureed sorrel and other greens
[*2 servings*]
The soup may be made several hours or even a day in advance, then reheated gently.

½ *stick butter, preferably unsalted*
2 *whole leeks, rinsed* and thinly sliced*
(8 whole scallions may be substituted)
A good handful of sorrel leaves, finely chopped
The leaves from 2 stalks of fresh chervil, finely chopped
2 *middling-sized leaves of romaine or Cos type lettuce, finely chopped*

1 ½ *cups excellent beef† broth; if at all salty, dilute with water*
2 *egg yolks*
A splash of cream or milk
About ¼ teaspoon salt, if the broth is unsalted
A few turns of the white pepper mill (¼ teaspoon, medium grind)

Reserve 1 tablespoon of the butter. In a heavy saucepan over medium heat, soften the leeks in the remaining butter for about 4 minutes, stirring frequently. Add the sorrel, chervil, and lettuce and stew about 3 minutes, continuing to stir frequently. Stir in the broth, turn heat to low, set the lid on askew, and simmer 30 minutes, stirring occasionally. Remove from the heat. Heat your soup bowls, preferably shallow and flat.

Beat the yolks and cream in a bowl, whisk in a little of the hot soup, then whisk this mixture back into the pot. Whisk over low heat just until the soup sends up one tentative bubble, then remove from the heat. Enrich with the reserved butter, taste for salt, grind over the pepper, and serve.

Although half-an-hour's simmering seemed too much when I read the recipe, after tasting it, I found that the leek or scallion slivers reduced to a puree give the soup its body. And even though cooks today respect chervil's distinctive flavor by simmering it as little as possible, I find it blends into part of the whole just perfectly in the simmering. But if you feel strongly about the mat-

*The method, page 249.
†Beef gives the soup a certain dimension, but you may substitute chicken or a light vegetable broth, if you prefer.

ter, add it at the last, and only a few leaves. Lacking fresh chervil, use parsley and, if you have it, a flick of powdered fennel or two or three crushed fennel seeds—chervil's flavor is just that, mild parsley overlaid with fennel. And don't worry about how much is a handful and how big are the bulbs, sprigs, and leaves. The beauty of these soups lies not in precision but in the fresh green glories of the garden.

(Myself, I think dried chervil has as much relation to the flavor of fresh as dried parsley does to its fresh leaves—zip. Worse. It tastes like new-mown hay—lovely scent, but not in soup! Chervil is an easy-to-grow annual, beautiful in the garden—its leaves are delicate and fernlike, and it sails through frosts, should that apply, so wherever you live, you can have it the year around. Grow some under a deciduous tree next to your sorrel. Chervil's also a good pot-in-a-sunny-windowsill plant.)

There were many firsts for me at Madame's table, but after the sorrel soup I most fondly remember her cheese tray. When Jacqueline brought in the cheese tray that first evening, my eyes popped. My father was a cheese man and I grew up with his favorites, Camembert, Liederkranz, and cream cheese. Sometimes Daddy brought home fresh cream cheese in a folded paper carton from Nate 'n Al's (the Beverly Hills deli where Groucho and my father and all the Hollywood funny men met for lunch) and I loved it, but usually we ate cream cheese from Philadelphia and it was pleasant but not thrilling on rye toast. When I tasted the light, sweet, un-Arabic-gummed *Petit-suisse* the first time, I was agog.

Then her husband urged me to taste a cheese that was square and golden-crusted: Pont-l'Evêque. It at once became my favorite—Camembert with even more character. Pont-l'Evêque is a Norman cheese, as is Camembert, and has been made since the thirteenth century. It is eaten from October to June. It is molded in small squares in pretty boxes, or sometimes in larger wheels. But be careful when you buy it from a wheel. Once, in March, in a fancy cheese shop, I ordered some. The young man asked if I wanted a taste. Surprised, I said, Sure. That was lucky, because the cheese had an aftertaste that would rouse the dead. It had been kept too long. (I suspect the young man knew that, and that's why he offered me a taste.)

And then! At my second dinner, the cheese tray was presented again. I thought the first had been the special occasion of my arrival. Now I remember all those evenings during dinner, waiting impatiently for everyone to finish so we could get to the cheese. There were triple-cream cheeses from the Ile-de-France, sprightly Bleus from the Auvergne, and chalet-made Vacherins from the Franche-Comté. (I wish I'd known then the lesson I read too many years later about How to Help Yourself to Cheese.* The rule is so obvious, but it has eluded so many of us: preserve its shape! How many noses have I lopped off wedges of Brie? How many wedges have I cut from squares of Gjetost? How many slices on the side instead of wedges have I taken from rounds of Reblochon? Heaven knows how I mangled the magnificent cheeses at Madame's table.)

I hugely enjoyed the neighborhood of our apartment. It was in the dignified seventh *arrondissement*, very quiet, very family. Usually after school from my autobus stop on the Seine, I would walk down the rue Jean Nicot to the big open air market on the rue St. Dominique. I would buy a treat of some cheese or sausage or pastry to hold me until dinner (I was still a growing girl). It was there at the *confiserie* I discovered *pain d'épice*. Then, it was exotica. Now, it seems I've seen long thin cellophane-wrapped loaves of the Burgundian honey bread on the counters of grocery stores everywhere.

But none have tasted the same as that *pain d'épice* from the rue St. Dominique. I always kept some in my school bag and snitched hunks to give me moral support while the sleek brunette geography professor sat on the edge of the long dais in the ancient Sorbonne amphitheater, slim legs crossed, chalk bouncing in one hand, rattling off elevations of the Alpes Cotiennes and the depths of the Plaine d'Aquitaine in her high-pitched voice, no notes in sight. One morning's lecture, in fact, I ate an entire *pain d'épice* out of nervousness trying desperately to copy down all her facts, and it was a couple of months before I could face *pain d'épice* again.

Pain d'épice has been a tradition in Burgundy since the fourteenth century. Traditional recipes call for rye flour. But just because something is traditional doesn't make it matchless. A whole lot of indifferent cooks can get something going for a very long time and make you believe it's marvelous just because they say so. I have been making *pain d'épice* on and off for more than thirty years, and I have come to believe that the lovely light tang of rye flour clouds the delicate flavor of the spices and honey, so I use untraditional white flour. And finally, after all these years, I've made a bread that tastes the way those little loaves did out of my school bag in the *Salle Richelieu*.

I might add that *pain d'épice* is not to everyone's taste. If you are a honey fancier, you'll like it. *Perhaps* you'll like it, it's a bit of an acquired taste. But there are those of us who think one or two thin slices of *pain d'épice* in the afternoon, slathered with sweet butter, sipped with black China tea, can cure all the ills to which flesh is heir.

From Julia Child's Kitchen.

PAIN D'ÉPICE FROM THE RUE ST. DOMINIQUE
Burgundian spiced honey bread
[At least 24 slices]

Make this at least 2 or 3 days before serving so that the flavors may ripen. Tightly wrapped in foil in the fruit drawer of the refrigerator (the least drying place), it will keep for months.

Softened butter for the pan and paper
²/₃ cup fresh anise seeds
½ teaspoon cinnamon
1 ³/₄ cups unbleached flour
2 teaspoons baking soda

¹/₃ cup pungent dark honey, warmed until liquid
The zest of 1 large orange, finely shredded
1 tablespoon sugar
½ cup water, hot

Brush a 7 ½ × 3 ½ × 2 ¼-inch loaf pan* with butter, then line it with brown paper. Brush another piece of brown paper a little larger than the top of the mold with butter.

Heat the oven to 275°F. In the blender, with a coffee mill, or with mortar and pestle, grind the anise seeds to a powder—you'll want 2 tablespoons. On waxed paper, mix the anise, cinnamon, flour, and soda. In a mixing bowl, blend the honey, orange zest, sugar, and water. Add the flour and stir just until blended.

Smooth the batter into the pan, then rap gently on the counter to knock out any air bubbles. Set the buttered paper on top and bake until a fine skewer thrust in the center comes out clean and the bread has begun to pull away from the sides of the pan, about 1 hour. Cool 5 minutes, turn out of the pan, and remove the paper. Set right side up on the rack, cover with a dish towel—to retain as much moisture as possible—and cool thoroughly.

Tightly wrap the *pain d'épice* in heavy foil and keep in a cool place (the bread is on the dry side, so airtight wrapping is essential). Slice very thin and spread with unsalted butter.

Also on top of the counter at the *confiserie* was a white oval box that contained more exotica, *calissons d'Aix*. The confections inside, small shuttle-shaped lozenges, are simply equal weights of sugar and ground almonds bound with apricot preserves and covered with royal icing. But! The woman behind the counter once offered me a *calisson* to taste. I was hooked for life. This is the sort of candy you'd make for your daughter's wedding feast or would take as a birthday gift to an elegant spoiled friend.

When you have no plans to go to Paris or to Aix-en-Provence, you can make *calissons* yourself. A recipe from the classic *La cuisinière Provençale*.

---

*Or anything with a 3 ½ cup capacity.

CALISSONS D'AIX
Iced confections of almond and apricot paste
[*Makes a scant 2 pounds*: 48 pieces*]
The candies keep in a tightly closed tin box in a cool dry place almost indefinitely.
See note about rice paper on page 256.

2 rounded cups (9 ounces, lightly packed)   1 cup (8 ounces) best-quality apricot
   ground blanched almonds   preserves
1 rounded cup sugar   Glace royale (recipe follows)

Traditionally, *calissons* are shaped like lace shuttles, but that wastes some of the
candy, so I cut them into diamonds; you'll have scraps left from the 48 good pieces.

In a bowl, mix the ground almonds and sugar, then blend in the preserves. Either
put this mixture through a $\frac{1}{16}$-inch sieve or whiz in the food processor until it
makes a fine paste. Line two 7 × 11-inch baking sheets† with rice paper. Turn the
mixture into a heavy pot and cook over low heat until warm, about 20 minutes, stirring occasionally. Turn the paste into the pans—it's important to have the paste
warm so it will bond to the paper. With moistened fingers, smooth the paste evenly,
then lay waxed paper on top and roll a glass or mug over the surface to give it a sleek
finish.

When cool, spread the top thinly and smoothly with *glace royale*. Dry thoroughly, lightly covered, for a day or two, then with a long sharp knife, carefully (the
icing can shatter) cut down through the rice paper into 1 $\frac{1}{2}$-inch diamonds (ovals,
if you're a purist).

This is a slightly thinner royal icing than usual, which makes it easier to
spread evenly. It is just the right finish for *calissons* and other iceable confections. The method is English and uncommonly fine.

GLACE ROYALE
Royal icing
[*Makes a scant 1 cup*]
The icing is best made a day before using, to ripen the rawness of the sugar. It keeps
nicely several days.

1 extra large egg white, at room temperature $\frac{1}{4}$ teaspoon water, cool
1 cup confectioner's sugar

In a non-plastic bowl, stir the egg white with a wooden spoon just enough to loosen.
Add $\frac{1}{2}$ cup of the sugar and beat until blended, then beat briskly 5 minutes. Cover
with a damp cloth and leave about 15 minutes, then slowly beat in $\frac{1}{2}$ cup more

---

*This is half M. Reboul's recipe. Certainly you can double the amounts.
†If these aren't in your cupboard, line any large baking sheet with rice paper then simply spread
the paste $\frac{1}{4}$-inch thick.

sugar. Refrigerate in an airtight jar. When ready to use, add the water and beat with a wooden spoon until blended. Spread thinly, keeping the bowl covered with a damp cloth while working, as it dries quickly.

Maibelle Jr.'s household was my second family and home. They were extraordinarily generous and dear. Often Maibelle Sr., after a visit to her hairdresser in St. Germain des Prés, would meet me and take me to lunch. She treated me to my first veal kidneys at Le Grand Véfour, my first *cassoulet* at Brasserie Lipp (still engaging, still one of my favorite restaurants, and it amuses me no end that, at last look, it was still not listed in *Michelin*), my first *zuppa inglese* at San Francisco (English soup indeed!), and my first *petit filet* of beef at a café with a country Portuguese feeling, a stone's throw from St. Germain. That steak— darkly, silkily sauced and pungent with mushrooms—was, for me, the quintessential piece of meat.

The *petit filet* is part of a French *filet* of beef, which corresponds roughly to the American tenderloin. In American terms, the broad end of this four- to six-pound piece is in the sirloin (toward the rump) and the balance is in the short loin (toward the ribs). This spot in the middle of the back on cattle anywhere in the world will always be the tenderest of the tender—it gets very little exercise.

Everything, in bringing home this exquisite meat, depends not only on the age of your butcher's beef but also on his skill in cutting, his willingness to give you exactly what you want, and on your making it crystal clear what it is you want. Price has a lot to do with neighborhood. I, a country mouse, pay half what my mother, a city mouse, pays for tenderloin and both our meats are superb. However, you'll get just what you want and pay less for it if you cut the steaks yourself. It isn't difficult. Page 237 tells how.

After thinking about it for years and years, I finally set about re-creating that *petit filet* I dined on with Maibelle Sr. in Paris. The cooking was most satisfying, very *haute cuisine*, and when I sat down to dinner with our guests and tasted the first bite, I gave a whoop of joy.

And for a special dinner party, all you have to do at the last moment is sauté the steaks, a matter of minutes.

PETIT FILET, THE QUINTESSENTIAL PIECE OF MEAT
[*4 servings*]

THE SAUCE AFTER ESPAGNOLE
The sauce is smoother if made a day in advance.

1 large onion, finely chopped
1 large leek, white part, finely chopped
2 large shallots, finely chopped

1 leafy celery heart, finely chopped
3 medium-large unpeeled carrots, finely chopped

*1 medium-sized unpeeled turnip, finely
   chopped*
4 ounces lean salt pork, in ¼-inch dice
*1 pound veal or beef marrow bones, in
   2-inch lengths*
*1 pound chicken backs, necks, or other bony
   bits*
7 cups excellent beef broth
3 tablespoons tomato paste
1 × 2-inch strip of orange zest
A good handful of chopped parsley
*½ tablespoon fresh thyme leaves, or
   ½ teaspoon dried*

*1 tablespoon fresh marjoram leaves, or
   1 teaspoon dried*
½ bay leaf
*12 to 24 turns of the black pepper mill
   (1 to 2 teaspoons, medium grind)*
½ stick butter, preferably unsalted
6 tablespoons flour
½ cup bone-dry vermouth
½ cup bone-dry white wine*
12 juniper berries†
*¾ cup dried mushrooms, preferably cap
   pieces*
½ cup Madeira
1 teaspoon fresh lemon juice, if necessary

In a large shallow roasting pan, arrange the onion, leek, shallots, celery, carrots, turnip, salt pork, bones, and chicken parts. Set on the top rack of the oven and heat to 425°F. Stir the vegetables, turn the bones, and scrape the pan every 10 minutes until everything is caramelized, a long hour. Turn into your soup pot.

Deglaze the pan with a little of the broth, whisk in the tomato paste, then turn this mixture into the soup pot. Add the remaining broth, orange zest, parsley, thyme, marjoram, bay, and pepper. Set over medium heat with the cover askew and bring to a simmer (no need to skim, as the stock will become a sauce, not a clear soup, and the things that rise to the top give flavor). Turn heat to lowest and simmer until reduced to 4 cups. Check in about 2 hours by ladling the stock into a clear measure; don't count the fat.

When the stock has reduced, melt the butter in a small heavy skillet and whisk in the flour. Cook over medium-low heat until chestnut brown, about 15 minutes; whisk occasionally. (This *roux*, together with the browned vegetables and bones, adds deep color and flavor to the sauce.) Whisk into the pot. Also stir in the vermouth, wine, and juniper berries, pinching each berry as you drop it in. Turn heat to low, set the lid on askew, and simmer another hour, stirring frequently—at this point, things can stick to the bottom and burn. Meanwhile, soak the mushrooms in the Madeira.

From the pot, pull out and discard the bones. Line a colander with two layers of damp cloth and set over a big bowl. Pour the contents of the pot through it. When cool enough to handle, gather up and squeeze the bundle to glean every drop of stock. In case any tidbit has escaped, pour the stock through a sieve into a glass vessel. Let the stock settle, then siphon up the lean from the bottom, leaving the fat behind. You'll have about 3 cups.

---

*Don't be tempted to use red wine. One would think it would be the wine of choice, but I've tried it and although the sauce becomes more deeply colored, it is also sweeter than it ought to be. A dry white wine, such as the ubiquitous Chablis, is best.
†Since they are used so seldom, it's possible yours are past their prime—you'll want them to be piney-fresh for this sauce.

Turn the stock into a smaller heavy pot. Add the mushrooms and pour the Madeira through a damp cloth into the pot to filter out any sand. Whisk to blend, then bring to a simmer over medium heat, turn heat to lowest, set the lid on askew and simmer. Whisk frequently and this time pull a fine sieve across the top to skim off any froth. Simmer until reduced to 2½ cups, a long half-hour. To measure, let the sauce settle and again siphon up the lean with a bulb baster, leaving any fat behind. Pull strips of paper towels across the top to finish the degreasing. Taste. Pepper people will add more pepper now. If your mushrooms are a particularly rich variety, you might want to balance their sweetness with a little lemon juice.* Cover loosely and refrigerate; when cold, cover tightly.

About 30 minutes before serving, turn the sauce into a heatproof vessel, cover, and set in hot water over low heat; whisk occasionally.

THE MEAT AND GARNISH
The meat may be prepared for sautéing in the morning.

4 wide strips of lean bacon
1 quart water, simmering
Four 5- to 7-ounce beef fillet steaks, 3 inches
*   wide and 1½ inches thick, trimmed of*
*   all fat and outside membrane*
About 2 tablespoons olive oil

8 ounces perfect medium-sized fresh
*   mushrooms, rubbed with a towel, the*
*   ends trimmed*
3 tablespoons butter, preferably unsalted
Watercress or parsley and/or your chosen
*   vegetable garnish (see recipe following)*

And you'll need some good cotton string.

In a skillet over medium heat, simmer the bacon in the water a couple of minutes, then turn off the heat (the bacon does not have to be blanched officially, just rinsed of some of its salt—its function is to moisten the edge of the steaks while cooking). When cool, snugly pull one strip of bacon around the outside of each steak; secure it with string, making the steak as evenly round as possible.† Pat the steaks dry and lightly brush the tops and bottoms with olive oil. Wrap loosely in plastic film and set in the coldest part of the refrigerator, if this is being done much in advance.

One hour before cooking, bring the steaks to room temperature and slice each mushroom in about 4 slices.‡

In a medium-sized heavy skillet (preferably cast iron) over medium-high heat, melt 1 tablespoon of the butter. Sauté the mushrooms in it, stirring almost constantly, until they are nicely browned. Turn mushrooms and juices into a bowl, cover, and keep warm. Heat a serving platter and sauce boat or bowl.

Add 1 tablespoon oil and 2 tablespoons butter to the skillet and melt over medium-high heat. When the foam has subsided, lay in the steaks. After 4 minutes, tip the steaks up with a pancake turner to be sure they are seared underneath—

---

*When I use less expensive South American dried mushrooms, I find this isn't necessary—for this sauce, I prefer them.

†Remember to make a double loop the first time and it will hold that way while you tie another knot or bow.

‡Do this at the last minute, otherwise the mushrooms will darken—there aren't that many to do.

it may take a minute more. Then with the turner (never a fork, you'd lose juices from the tine holes), turn the steaks—they should be a beautiful rich brown.

For rare beef, cook the steaks 2 to 3 minutes on the second side. For medium-rare, 4 to 5 minutes. Much depends on the metal of your skillet and the efficiency of your heat—the surest way to tell when the meat is right is to nip into the center of your own steak with a small sharp knife and squint. Clip and discard the strings, leaving the bacon in place (unless you'd rather not). Arrange the steaks on the platter, spoon over the mushrooms and their juices and surround with garnish. Turn the sauce into the sauce boat and rush to the table!

The ideal garnish, in season, is

SAUTÉED CHERRY TOMATOES
[4 servings]
All the elements may be prepared in advance.

About 4 quarts water, boiling
2 pounds cherry tomatoes, ripe but firm,
  stemmed
Ice water
1/2 stick unsalted butter

*1/4 cup dry breadcrumbs**
A handful of chopped fresh parsley, sweet
  basil, dill, lovage, marjoram, oregano,
  rosemary, thyme, or . . .

Pour the boiling water over the cherry tomatoes in a bowl, time 1 minute, then lift out the tomatoes and turn into a bowl of ice water. When cool, drain and peel the tomatoes (a nuisance, but worth it). You can cover them and keep them in a cool place for a few hours.

In a large heavy skillet or wok over medium heat, melt the butter, then brown the breadcrumbs, stirring frequently. Cover and refrigerate until needed.

A few minutes before serving, heat a serving bowl, then add the tomatoes to the buttery crumbs in their skillet and stir gently with a wooden spatula over medium-high heat until the tomatoes are just warmed through. Turn into the bowl and sprinkle with chopped herbs. Serve at once.

When cherry tomatoes aren't available, I like halves of tomatoes sprinkled with buttered breadcrumbs, slipped under the broiler just enough to warm them and sprinkled with chopped parsley or other herb, for color.

With the fillets, the dessert I serve is the one Maibelle Sr. ordered for us that day, tawny baked pears that seemed Portuguese. Choose your favorite flavor of port to make the dessert, as each will lend its distinctive quality.

---

*Toast 2 large slices of white or light wheat bread at 300°F until crisp dry. Crush finely beneath a rolling pin.

POIRES À LA PORTUGAISE
Pears baked in port with almonds and raisins
[*4 servings*]
The pears will keep several days in a cool place.

A heaping ½ cup golden raisins   *4 medium-sized sweet but firm pears,*
About 1 cup port   *peeled, cored, and halved*
About ½ cup roasted almonds,* chopped *A sprinkling of cinnamon*
The zest of ½ lemon, finely shredded

Cover the raisins with port and soak as long in advance as possible.† Heat the oven to 350°F. Mix the nuts and lemon zest together. Set the pears cut side up in a shallow baking dish in which they just fit. Sprinkle with the raisins, nuts, and cinnamon, then sprinkle the port over the pears.

Bake uncovered, basting a couple of times, until a fine skewer pierces them easily, 15 to 20 minutes. Serve warm or at room temperature, basting with the syrup just before serving.

At school, I was part of a lively circle. I made my first friend at our first lecture. When I sat down next to her in the ancient amphitheatre, she gave me a glittering smile and I noticed her mascara was Delft blue (I hadn't known mascara came in blue). With her white skin, blue eyes, long dangling blue earrings, and high heels (I'd never seen high heels in class), I was fascinated. She said, *"Bon jour,"* with so perfect an accent I couldn't guess her nationality and when the professor began his lecture, she took notes in French as fast as she could write. For my part, having had countless French lessons as a child and being able to read and write the language to some extent, I felt as though someone was playing a bad joke on me—the professor could have been rattling off facts and figures about Gothic cathedrals in Urdu for all I understood. I saw an entire semester going down the drain. Maybe it wasn't too late to join the ladies in Majorca.

When the class was over, I just sat there. Then I heard the girl with the blue mascara laughing, and in a charming English accent she said, "You need help!" Her name was Leila, she was living with French cousins, her French was fluent and she said she would do what she could to pull me through. Her first move was to make me promise to speak only French. It was love at first sight.

Leila and I quickly made friends with other students, and we all did our

---

*Less Portuguese, but equally delicious another time, are roasted hazelnuts or walnuts.
†Mine come from a jar of raisins and prunes in port that I keep the year round for just such occasions—but overnight or just a few hours will suffice.

best to live our Sorbonne lives to the fullest. Our version of the legendary writers' *Aux Deux Magots* was on the corner of "Boul'Mich" and rue des Ecoles: the red canvas awning over the sprawling student indoor-outdoor café proclaimed, *"Chez Dupont, Où Tout Est Bon."* One of our band didn't agree that everything was good there and occasionally composed poetry on Chez Dupont napkins in green ink. Everyone carried notebooks and frequently we sat for an hour or more without talking while we wrote poetry or our impressions or philosophical essays, then read aloud what we had written for criticism. Sad to say, Chez Dupont no longer exists—and there is no plaque on that corner to mark the fact that Albaum, Goodman, Sheekman, et Cie. sat there and wrote when they were young.

One afternoon, I recited a few lines about life on the rue de l'Université. Apart from my poem's literary merits, Leila was furious that I spoke English with my American host, Mel said I should be living with other students, and Françoise knew of a pension three blocks down the rue des Ecoles run by a Madame Galetti. I must move. And so I did.

Life was heaven in the Galettis' rabbit warren of an apartment. My room was on the outside (street singers and peddlers were forever calling to me from the tiny rue Jean-de-Beauvais beneath my window), wedged in the corner between the Galettis' bedroom and the bathtub. Each guest got one tub a week—six inches of lukewarm water for forty-five minutes—and often I was stranded inside or outside my room until the bather had finished his ablutions.

Monsieur Galetti, grey-goateed, tall, thin, sallow, was the image of Don Quixote. Madame Galetti was short, zaftig, and German, had lived in Paris for forty years and thought of herself as very nearly French. But she was not French in her view of life. Forced into her position by economics—she did not at all approve of coeducational pensions—Madame was forever sighing in the midst of a sentence and gazing off into the distance.

But their guests made a splendid table. There was bright and quarrelsome Jacques from Brooklyn (Jacques was Jack, as Sylvie was me), the only other American and also the only other student at the Sorbonne. Gorgeous raven-haired Jhamid from Karachi. Warm worldly Ismail (who fell in love with me and begged me to marry him and follow him to the banks of the Tigris— where are you now, Ismail Mirza?) and pudgy sweet Bakhir from Baghdad. The three were serious men in their thirties studying law at the *Faculté de Droit.* Everyone else was polishing his or her French at the *Alliance Française.* Unrufflable blonde Suzanne from Hamburg, mother hen to us all. Plump laughing Lilo from Copenhagen. Sloe-eyed Anne-Marie from Stockholm. Intelligent ambitious Maryse from Amsterdam. Dear blue-eyed Reinhardt from the Black Forest, our handsome resourceful student prince. And two special friends, Elena and Noretta, fair-haired soft-spoken twins from Milan, studying to be translators. (As Elena was writing down my home address in her book she asked, "Is this permanent?" I said of course, and she remarked with bewilderment, "The addresses of my American friends have so many lines crossed out—they seem to move so much, I don't understand it—we live in the house my great-grandmother was born in . . .") There was constant laughter at the Galetti table, with everybody chattering in heavily accented French, enormous warmth and interest and generosity among all the boarders. We were a family.

Pension meals were breakfast every day and luncheon, the main French meal, every day except Sunday. Madame's food was classic, simple, fresh, and I adored it, every single crumb.

Breakfast was as much as you wanted of warm baguettes of bread—the bakery was three doors away—cherry preserves, sweet butter, and scented tea. The bread was the most tempting I'd ever eaten and one day I realized I'd worked up to most of a loaf for myself every morning. So for luncheon on my birthday in the middle of June, I found my "birthday cake" at my place: an enormous baguette wrapped with white gypsophilia, tied with pink ribbon and set with a long pink taper!

(As a birthday present to myself, I went to see von Weber's *Oberon* at the Paris Opera, delicious music and fairies flying high across the stage. It was the only performance of *Oberon* given that season, and although neither of us knew it, the young man who had been at the ball game the day Babe Ruth was there was also in the audience.)

Madame Galetti's luncheon, as in most of Europe, began with soup. Two of her vegetable soups I was especially fond of, simple yet special—one made with red wine and another with white wine. My re-creations, I hope, do hers justice. There was never a want of wine chez Galetti.

Hot, this soup is light but deeply strengthening, and cold, with *crème fraîche*, it is sublime.

SOUPE AU VIN ROUGE
Vegetable soup flavored with red wine
[*4 to 6 servings*]
This may be completely prepared in advance and is even better, of course, the next day.

1 large whole leek, trimmed and rinsed*
1 medium-large onion
1 large peeled turnip
1 large unpeeled carrot
1 medium-sized leafy celery stalk

1 large strip of lean bacon (if served warm)
A generous 1 tablespoon butter (olive oil, if served cold)
4½ cups excellent beef broth
2 cups dry red wine

---

*Method, page 249.

2 tablespoons instant tapioca
Perhaps ¼ cup water, cool
2 ounces smallish mushrooms, thinly sliced
6 or 8 turns of the black pepper mill
   (½ teaspoon or more, medium grind)

A handful of chopped parsley
Crème fraîche, cultured or à la minute
   (page 37), if the soup is served cold

Cut the leek, onion, turnip, carrot, celery, and bacon, if you're using it, into ½-inch dice. In a large heavy pot (not aluminum*) over medium-high heat, melt the butter (or heat the oil). Sauté the diced vegetables and bacon over high heat stirring frequently until a few leek bits have browned, 6 to 7 minutes. Add the broth and wine, bring to a simmer, turn the heat to low, set the lid on askew, and simmer gently a short hour.

Stir while you sprinkle in the tapioca, then cover again and simmer 20 minutes more. Now taste: if the soup is on the verge of being salty, add a little water. Add the mushrooms, cover, and simmer until they are tender and the soup is dark and lustrous, about 20 minutes more. (Meanwhile, if you're not serving from the pot, heat a tureen or bowl.) Grind over the pepper and serve garnished with parsley.

Or let the soup cool, chill it, and serve with *crème fraîche*. And don't forget thick slices of French bread for sopping up the last drops from your bowl.

This next is an elegant soup.

Soupe au vin blanc
Vegetable soup flavored with white wine
[*6 to 8 servings*]
Also even better the next day.

2 tablespoons olive oil
1 large whole leek, trimmed, rinsed,[†] and
   cut in thin rounds
1 medium-sized sweet pepper, preferably
   red, in small dice
1 large garlic clove, finely chopped
8 ounces fresh mushrooms, preferably
   button-size, rubbed with a towel,
   quartered

4 medium-sized unpeeled carrots, finely
   shredded
3 medium-sized tomatoes, in small dice
   (peel and seed them, if you have time)[‡]
1 bunch fresh spinach, well-rinsed,[§] in
   thin strips
5 ½ cups excellent chicken broth
1 cup dry white wine
12 turns of the white pepper mill
   (1 teaspoon, medium grind)

Over medium-high heat in a heavy pot (not aluminum‖), heat the oil and add the leek, sweet pepper, and garlic. Sauté, stirring frequently, 10 minutes. Remove

---

*The metal would react with the wine and discolor the soup.
†The method is on page 249.
‡How-to, page 259.
§Page 258 gives an easy way to do this.
‖The metal would react with the wine and discolor the soup.

from the heat and stir in the mushrooms, carrots, tomatoes, spinach, broth, wine, and pepper. Set the lid on askew and return to the heat. Bring to a simmer; cook until the vegetables are tender-crisp, about 20 minutes. (If you're not serving from the pot, heat a tureen or bowl.) Raise the heat and cook briskly until the vegetables are to your taste, 5 or 10 minutes more, then serve.

Madame Galetti had a special way with vegetables and there are a couple of salads she made that I fondly remember, none of which could be simpler. Years later, I was amused to find this first one at the fashionable Left Bank restaurant Closerie de Lilas. They called it

CRÈME AUX TOMATES
Creamy tomato salad
[For each person]
Last-minute.

1 large firm ripe tomato, peeled* and thinly sliced

A little chopped parsley or other favorite herb

A drizzle of red wine vinegar

A pinch of coarse salt

A few turns of the white pepper mill

A dollop of crème fraîche, *cultured, or* à la minute *(page 37)*

Arrange the tomato in a swirl on a handsome chilled salad plate. Sprinkle with parsley, vinegar, and salt, mill the pepper over it, and top with *crème fraîche*. Serve at once.

And here are roasted sweet peppers. Their delicate charred border lends a dramatic touch, and their color, texture, flavor, temperature, and ease of preparation make them a useful accompaniment for almost any meat, fowl, or fish.

SALADE DE PIMENTS DOUX RÔTIS
Salad of roasted sweet peppers
The peppers may be prepared a couple of hours in advance—but not much more, or else they'll begin to lose their shape.

Often in recipes for roasted peppers, you are directed to peel them. But part of the charm of this dish is its simplicity, so don't.

[For each person]

½ large or 1 small sweet pepper

About 1 teaspoon olive oil, plus more for the dish

About ⅓ teaspoon of your favorite vinegar

A dash of salt

A few turns of the black pepper mill

---

*How-to, page 259.

Choose firm sweet green peppers of the same size, preferably tinged with red—in season, use red or yellow sweet peppers or a mix of three colors (the best). Cut in half lengthwise, cut out the ribs, and discard the seeds.

Heat the oven to 350°F. Brush the bottom of a shallow baking dish with olive oil and arrange the peppers on it, cut sides up. Drizzle about 1 teaspoon of oil over each half, then brush the oil all over the inside of the pepper. Sprinkle very lightly with vinegar.

Bake uncovered until the edges have browned but the peppers are still a bit crisp when pierced with a fine skewer, 25 to 30 minutes. Transfer to a serving platter, sprinkle lightly with salt and pepper, and set in a cool place. Serve at room temperature.

Madame Galetti's main course was usually something French and classic and poached. She had only a tiny oven and anything for fifteen people was almost impossible in two skillets, whereas one good-sized poacher fits comfortably over two burners. There were *oeufs à la florentine*, one of my favorite combinations of foods in the world: poached eggs on a bed of buttered spinach, blanketed with Mornay sauce (*béchamel* flavored with Gruyère and Parmesan cheese) and sprinkled with more cheese. And there was poached turbot with *hollandaise*, poached ham with braised lettuces, poached leg of lamb—Madame called it *gigot à l'anglaise*, English-style—simmered with carrots, turnips, and onions, the vegetables served with the meat and a caper sauce (*béchamel* heightened with lemon juice and capers).

For my birthday luncheon, Madame poached and sauced a chicken *au blanc*—pure white, without benefit of browning—in a heavenly creamy sauce over rice. The flavors were splendid—sprightly lemon, smoky bacon, and nippy tarragon woven through sweet chicken and cream. The chicken was especially succulent, the rice especially flavorful. (The rice is *au gras*, cooked in broth with a little fat exuded from the bacon, which makes it particularly moist.) I first found a recipe for this dish in Elizabeth David's *French Provincial Cooking* (one of the cookbooks that has influenced me most). The incomparable Mrs. David's *La poule au riz à la crème* is close in spirit to Madame Galetti's chicken, but not in technique—Mrs. David's chicken is cooked in the oven and the rice is cooked separately. Over the years, I have combined hers with other recipes into one that I think is the dish Madame served on the rue des Ecoles.

I am amused because Mrs. David calls this "a mild and soothing dish." English understatement? I call it a minor masterpiece, and not so minor at that. An example of what, for my part, is cuisine at its best: simple and perfect. And easy.

POULET AU BLANC À LA CRÈME
Poached chicken with rice and creamy sauce
[*6 servings*]
Last minute, but once finished, everything may be held up to half-an-hour before serving.

THE CHICKEN AND THE RIZ AU GRAS

7 cups excellent chicken broth
One whole 3 ½- to 4-pound plump prime chicken, rinsed and trimmed of fat and wingtips, at room temperature

6 or 7 strips of lean bacon
1 ½ cups long grain rice
A dozen turns of the white pepper mill (1 teaspoon, medium grind)

In your soup pot, bring the broth to a simmer. Meanwhile, cover the chicken's breast with 4 or 5 strips of bacon, then truss,* securing the bacon in place. Lower the chicken, bacon side up, into the pot. Lay a folded strip of bacon over each leg. Return the broth to a simmer, turn the heat to its lowest, cover, and simmer 30 minutes.

Lift out the chicken and pour the broth into a pitcher. Smooth the rice into the pot. With a bulb baster or ladle, pull up 3 ½ cups of lean broth and pour over the rice. Set the chicken breast-down on the rice and lay the two free bacon strips down its back. Grind pepper over, cover the pot, bring to a simmer, turn heat to its lowest, and simmer until juices from the chicken run clear (when stuck with a fine skewer in a thigh) and the rice is cooked, 25 to 35 minutes. Meanwhile, make the sauce.

THE SAUCE

1 large juicy lemon
½ stick butter, preferably unsalted, plus a lump for the top
A scant ½ cup flour
1 ½ cups half-and-half, cold
1 ½ cups chicken-poaching broth

A 2-inch sprig of fresh tarragon, chopped, or ¼ teaspoon dried leaves
3 egg yolks
1 ½ tablespoons dry white wine
About ⅛ teaspoon salt
About 6 turns of the white pepper mill (½ teaspoon, medium grind)
A small bunch of parsley, chopped

This sauce is most efficiently put together with a flat whisk.

Cut off about ¼ of the lemon and ream it: you'll need 1 ½ tablespoons of juice. Reserve the rest of the lemon for garnish.

In a large heavy saucepan over medium-low heat, melt 3 tablespoons of the butter. Blend in the flour then let this *roux* cook a couple of minutes without coloring, whisking once or twice. Whisk in the half-and-half, and when it has been incorporated, blend in the broth and tarragon. Bring to a simmer, then turn heat to its lowest. In a small bowl, mix the yolks, lemon juice, and white wine together, then

---

*Instructions, should you need them, page 244.

slowly whisk into the sauce. Stir until it bubbles, then remove from the heat and add the remaining tablespoon of butter, cut in bits, and salt and pepper to taste. Run a lump of butter over the top to keep a skin from forming. Cover and set in a larger pot of hot water over low heat to keep warm. Heat a serving platter and sauce bowl.

When the rice and chicken are cooked, lift out the chicken with a cooking fork thrust into the cavity. Stir the rice, then make a bed of it on the platter. Discard bacon and string and set the chicken on the rice to be carved at table. Nap the chicken with a little of the sauce and sprinkle chopped parsley over it. Slice the rest of the lemon in thin rounds and garnish the dish. Turn the sauce into its bowl and serve.

And once, Madame Galetti poached a rabbit. I had difficulty—eating bunnies was unthinkable. But the rabbit was a breeze compared to what I discovered was the *pièce de résistance* at a dinner party given for me by a Monagasque count and countess, friends of Hollywood friends. The apartment was in Neuilly-sur-Seine overlooking the Bois de Boulogne. As I floated onto the terrace, I was astonished and dismayed to see my host GRILLING A WHOLE BABY GOAT ON A SPIT! To my surprise, after I took my first polite mouthful, I found I enjoyed the kid enormously, but (unusual for me) my palate memory of the flavor was vague for years. I wanted to taste kid again to refresh that memory. The time came.

Like the gypsy recipe that begins, "First, steal a chicken . . . ," first I had to find a baby goat. Second, I had not to think about it being a baby goat. (Kid is baby goat that has not yet been weaned, just as milk-fed veal is calf that has only been nourished on milk.) I learned that spring is the time to buy fresh kid (fortunately, it was spring) and that Italian butchers are the most likely to have them. I was lucky enough to find not only the meat but also a knowledgeable butcher who instructed me on its cooking.

Then the surprise. Joe, the butcher, said it's not a good idea to grill the animal whole. The midsection—the loin and ribs—he said, would cook much faster than the legs and shoulders (although my dear friend Philip Brown, my ultimate authority on all things about meat, told me that if you wrap the midsection in heavy foil, shiny side in, the beast will cook evenly). Joe said he always separates the kid into shoulder/foreshank, rib/loin, and leg sections for his customers (he also cracks the bones wherever they will be carved, a great help). In fear and trembling, I ordered the kid. I could have bought a small pearl for the price. I don't know if the same is true elsewhere, but in this part of the world, one is obliged to buy the whole animal. Kid is a luxury item and butchers take no chances of being stuck with cuts they can't sell. When I saw the meat, I appreciated Joe's point. None of the joints was thicker than my fist, and when I held the midsection up to the light, the layer of flesh on the ribs was translucent.

The kid weighed fourteen pounds. We would be eight at table, so I chose the two rib/loin sections, one leg, and one shoulder/foreleg, to see the difference in texture and flavor between the cuts. These four pieces came to eight and three-quarter pounds; including the wasty shank and breast bones, that would be ample for eight. I froze the remaining two meaty joints, which would serve five at another party.

Joe urged me to marinate the kid in olive oil and lemon juice. I wasn't sure why, but I figured it couldn't hurt, so I did. But I didn't add salt or pepper to the marinade. Salt draws out juices and I wanted to serve the kid with very little seasoning. Being Italian, he suggested I also add oregano. I thought oregano a shade on the emphatic side for so delicate a meat and chose its warm but lighter cousin, marjoram, instead. It was lovely. The marjoram should be fresh—I had just bought a pot of it to set out in the garden. (I find I'm using marjoram more and more.)

The flavor of the meat? Remarkably subtle. The first taste is an impression of lamb's sweetness, then comes an undertaste, faint and pungent all at once, of that wild gamy whiff so appealing in goat cheese. There is no fat on the meat so it isn't rich except in the way baby lamb and veal are rich in their intense purity.

Now, if you have a tried and true method for grilling, by all means, use it. For the record, here's what we did.

Our grilling surface is twelve by twenty-six inches and we used an entire eight-pound sack of mesquite charcoal for our fire. Calculate how much charcoal you'll need by comparing your surface area with ours. Joe said it would take an hour to cook the shoulders and legs and half an hour to cook the loin/rib sections—I found that just a little too long for each.

Mesquite shoots out sparks when it's hot. Watch it.

GRILLED KID
[For 8 people]

6½ to 8¾ pounds kid, depending on the meatiness of the selections, cut up as described above
About ½ cup olive oil, plus more for the rack

½ cup fresh lemon juice (2 large juicy lemons)
2 good handfuls of fresh marjoram leaves, or a generous 2 tablespoons dried
Fresh flowers or greenery, for garnish

Bring the meat home about 24 hours before serving. Find a pan or pans in which the pieces of meat will fit in a single layer. Blend the oil and lemon juice and moisten the bottom of the pans. Lay in the kid, meaty sides down, and pour the rest of the marinade evenly over the pieces. Sprinkle with one handful (or tablespoonful) of marjoram. Cover and set in a cool place (60°F or less—at that temperature, the marinade will preserve it; if you haven't a cool place, then cover with foil and set on the lowest shelf of the refrigerator). In the morning, turn only the leg pieces over. Brush all the meat with marinade and cover again. Brush the meat two or three times during the day.

Bring the meat to room temperature an hour before serving.

Plan to use enough non-petroleum-based coals to make a solid bed on your rack.* Set the meat rack about 6 inches above the source of heat. About 45 minutes before you plan to start the meat, ignite the coals. You want to start the meat over a hot fire, then let the coals cool down as the meat cooks. When the coals are red— you can only hold your hand at the meat rack level 2 seconds—liberally brush the rack with oil. Arrange the leg and shoulder sections on it. Spread out the coals evenly beneath them, extending 1 to 2 inches further on all sides, cover meat lightly with a big tent of aluminum foil, shiny side in, and set the timer for 30 minutes.

Throughout the grilling, baste with the marinade every 10 minutes.

After 30 minutes, turn the joints over with tongs and move them away from the center of the fire. Brush the rack again with oil and fit the loin/rib sections, meaty sides down, on the rack in the center. If necessary (to replace pieces that are wearing thin), add new coals, up to 6, evenly spaced directly on hot coals. In 15 more minutes, turn the midsections over. In 5 more minutes, test the leg and shoulder pieces with a good meat thermometer† in their fleshiest parts—it should register 135°F (medium-medium-rare).‡ When ready, remove the pieces to a carving board and cover with the tent of foil. In 5 more minutes, test the midsections; when ready, remove them to the board and cover with foil. If not serving on the carving board, heat a big platter.

Let the meat set for about 15 minutes (the pieces that settle longer will not suffer), then carve. I prefer to cut the slender pieces into a meaty chunk or two for each person, but another might prefer carving in slices as for lamb. However you do it, sprinkle with the second handful of marjoram leaves, flourish festively with flowers, and carry to the table.

And what to serve with the kid?

On the Left Bank, close to the Seine and not far from the Sorbonne, is a fascinating twisting street, the rue de la Huchette. In the fourteenth and fifteenth centuries, it was called rue de Rôtisseurs. It is once again a street of roasters, now being lined with small Greek *tavernas* and Middle Eastern cafés whose windows display extraordinarily rich and brilliant arrangements—

---

*Or use wood, if you know how.
†If you haven't one, notes are on page 250.
‡Unlike lamb, I don't think I would like the delicate but gamy meat of kid much rarer—nor more done: I've since cooked kid to 140°F and it was, for me, terrible, but those who like their meat well-done were happy.

vegetables and fish and shellfish and meats and fruits and cheeses and pastries and confections of shimmering freshness set in patterns that rival the beauty of the mosaics in Ravenna—the centerpieces of the living mosaics are nearly always a startling whole pig or lamb revolving slowly on a spit, the animal's skin gleaming copper and gold in the soft light of coals from below.

From the window display at one such restaurant, I chose a salad of green peppers, tomatoes, and green olives called *salade Meconia*. I was mad about it—familiar ingredients that, to my Western palate, were given a beguilingly fresh treatment. It is a perfect accompaniment to anything grilled, and it is especially delicious on the plate next to roasted or steamed potatoes, both for color and flavor—the juices mixed into the potato are divine.

SALADE MECONIA
A Middle Eastern salad of sweet peppers, tomatoes, and green olives
[*8 to 10 servings*]
Make this in the cool of the morning.

3 large firm *ripe tomatoes, peeled* and cut in ½-inch-thick crescents*

9 large garlic cloves, very finely chopped

3 large sweet peppers, peeled† and sliced into ⅜-inch-wide strips

1½ cups small to medium-sized unpitted green olives

A scant ½ cup fruity olive oil

18 or more turns of the black pepper mill (1½ teaspoons, medium grind)

A little salt (the olives provide most of the salt)

Heat the broiler. Lay the tomatoes on a rimmed baking sheet, sprinkle the garlic over them and slip under a hot broiler until the tomatoes have warmed and some of the garlic has lightly browned, about 5 minutes. Turn the tomatoes, garlic, and pan juices into a shallow serving bowl. Add the peppers.

Gently crush the olives with the flat blade of a cleaver or chopping knife, releasing their juices. Pull out the pits if you feel strongly about it, but the restaurant didn't and I don't. Add the olives and their juices to the bowl.

Drizzle over the oil, grind over the pepper, then gently toss the salad until the garlic is blended in. Taste for salt. Cover tightly and set in a cool place. Serve at room temperature. If the tomatoes prove very juicy, drain off excess juices to make a superb dressing for another salad.

Roasted potatoes are the classic accompaniment with kid. Instead, I chose to steam some and serve them at room temperature because they go so well with the salad. And, as a counterpoint to the bite of the salad, serve pear chutney flavored with coriander (page 163).

---

*Peeling tomatoes, page 259.
†How-to on page 259.

In late June, my semester at the Sorbonne was over (after the most grueling and minusculely detailed examinations I'd ever faced). Leila and I sat with everybody enrolled in the *Cours de civilisation et langue française* in the Salle Richelieu, as one by one our names were called. Did we pass? Would we receive our diplomas? The highest grade was, as I recall, *Avec grand mention*: all the German students went bounding up. Next came *Avec bon mention*: all the Scandinavian and English students went—Leila, too, of course. Next came *Avec mention* and the Middle Eastern students went up. Last came *Sans mention*—you'll get credit for the courses at your universities, kiddies, but utterly without distinction—and up slogged all the Americans. But Leila had pulled me through it. My diploma is gorgeous, engraved and poster-sized, signed in big round script by all ten of my extraordinary professors.

I would have been desolate to leave Paris were it not for the prospect of a summer in Italy. My parents had decided to join me abroad and had taken a house on the Italian Riviera. So I said good-bye to the Galettis and all my dear friends at 40, rue des Ecoles, to the *Chez Dupont* gang, to my friends on the rue de l'Université, and the two Maibelles, and boarded the night train to Rapallo.

Tina's Cucina and Other Italian Beauties

Villa Glicini is in San Michele di Pagana, a bend in the road along the Gulf of Genoa between Rapallo and Santa Margherita Ligure. The province is Liguria, on the eastern end of the Italian Riviera. Overlooking the sea, the small stucco cottage dripped with purple clusters from leafy vines—*glicini*, I learned, means wisteria. Scarlet bougainvillea spilled over railings of tiny balconies facing the Ligurian Sea and wild oregano warmed the air from bluffs below. The rooms were butter yellow, the staircase connecting the four stories was white marble. My room was on the top floor. It was dormered and my bed was hung with a canopy of cream-colored mosquito netting, very Sleeping Beauty. And down in the kitchen, my mother told me, was the best cook she had ever known. Clearly, my reward for behaving myself in Paris was that I had died and gone to San Michele!

The kitchen of the Villa Glicini was the exception to its beauty. A below-grade dungeon of grey stone walls, it held an ancient small stove with gas rings, an old-fashioned ice box (block of ice on top, food beneath), a small narrow marble-topped table and a sink with cold running water beneath windows that looked *up* to the garden.

"Ch'è bella cucina, Signora!" Tina exclaimed to my mother, smiling broadly when she first saw her "beautiful kitchen."

Tina was a short dumpy woman from Trieste. She was in her forties and wore the uniform of so many in her position—an unchangeable place in the European social order assigned to women without education and without hope or even thought of one—women whose life is service, whether to strangers or to family, who have metamorphosed from gay laughing girls in bright colors hugging laughing boys whizzing around on the backs of Vespas to greying women trudging along the road lugging string bags and wearing long-sleeved black cotton dresses to their shins. But Tina's hair and eyes were shiny black, her voice was melting soft, and her smile was radiant. Piccolo, her small grey and white cat, came with her.

Tina set to work, polishing her *mezzaluna*, that arched steel master of the chopping board. As she rubbed the blade back and forth gently with a sponge dipped in salt and vinegar, she and my mother worked on the marketing list, Tina dictating in firm, low tones and my mother frantically thumbing through her Italian/English dictionary to find the meaning. Tina didn't ask whether or not my mother wanted something, she simply ordered it.

By the time the *mezzaluna* sparkled like plantinum, the shopping list was finished and the two women, string bags and baskets in hand, went off to the open-air markets of Santa Margherita just down the road, driving in the marvelous black Citroën saloon car my father had bought in Paris. They came back hours later loaded with newspaper packages of golden cherries, white peaches, yellow peppers, tiny zucchini, enormous eggplants, feathery fennel, hard-crusted sesame-seeded rolls, rounds of creamy Bel Paese, six or eight sorts of sea creatures, a leg of veal, a fat fowl, sweetbreads, armloads of sweet basil, lemons, pine nuts, and a gallon of the superb Ligurian olive oil. (Later, my mother reported that Tina had been surprised on their first expedition to learn that she would eat everything we ate. In Italy, Tina explained, the lady of the house ordered three grades of meat: one for the family, one for the servants, and one for the dogs.) And, finally, they would lug through the door a couple of *fiaschi*—enormous glass jugs—of the local *vin ordinaire*, Portofino *bianco*. Straw-colored, dry and quenching, Portofino *bianco* was not ordinary to us. Although it was plentiful and almost as cheap as bottled water, we were taken with its sunny charm.

Tina was given her own *fiasco*. Soon my mother noticed that Tina finished off her *fiasco* more than twice as fast as the three of us finished ours. And the food seemed to disappear in more than generous double portions in the kitchen. When my mother discovered Julio, Tina's balding, baby-faced, unemployed lover wolfing down prosciutto, melon, and Portofino *bianco*, he stood with dignity, swallowed a mouthful half-chewed, and pronounced that he was very grateful indeed for *la signora's* hospitality.

We discovered Tina was crazy about film stars. A glimpse of "Spencher Trachy" in the Santa Margherita fish market kept her on the ceiling all day. When my mother told her that Groucho and his good friend Eden (later his wife) were coming to visit, Tina was beside herself. The morning they were due to arrive, having brooded for a couple of days over what to cook, Tina told my mother she had planned the most beautiful luncheon she could possibly make and she wanted to go shopping for it right away. An hour later, in she breezed, a basket of neatly wrapped packages in one hand and two small brown dead rabbits swinging by their ears in the other. My father blanched, my mother swallowed, and Tina was sent back to the market. She was furious, and no amount of explaining about sensitive middle-aged stomachs could soothe her. She ended by huffily serving her *crespolini*—delicate *crêpes* curled around prosciutto and mozzarella and covered with *béchamel* sauce—followed by *fritto misto di mare*, a crispy heap of mixed fried fishes followed by a *granita di melone*, ephemeral water ice made of cantaloupe. Groucho, who had dined at La Réserve the night before, told Tina her cooking was the best he had eaten in all of Europe. She wasn't surprised.

This *crespolini* is as light a composition of paste as it is possible to conjure. I have the feeling Tina tasted the dish on a visit to the south, where mozzarella, once made exclusively of buffalo's milk, is used abundantly and with affection—mozzarella is not indigenous to northern Italian cooking. The only dish like it I've tasted was served fifty miles south of Naples, in the shadow of the ochre marble Greek temple at Paestum.

Crespelle are Italian *crêpes* (and these are incomparable). *Crespolini* are *crespelle* rolled and stuffed then cut in various shapes before saucing. *Crespelle* are also called *cannelloni* when the *cannelloni* are not made of pasta dough. *Capisci?*

A couple of caveats. I've found that flavor and saltiness in both prosciutto and mozzarella vary enormously. The *crespolini* can be too salty if you should happen to come up with both ham and cheese that are on the salty side. Once I made the *crespolini* with four ounces of domestic prosciutto and the supermarket's brand of mozzarella and I was astonished to realize I could taste neither in the dish. And once I used three ounces of Italian prosciutto and a very good mozzarella and the dish was disconcertingly salty. So ask the deli person for a small taste of the ham before you buy—and don't buy it unless the prosciutto is flavorful and not so salty you wince.

CRESPOLINI ALLA TINA
Ultra-delicate rolls of *crêpes* with prosciutto and mozzarella
[*8 servings*]
The dish of *crespolini* may be prepared for baking a few hours in advance.

THE CRESPELLE*
Italian *crêpes*
The batter may be prepared up to 2 days in advance and refrigerated in a tightly covered jar. The *crespelle* may be baked, wrapped airtight, and refrigerated up to 24 hours, or layered between waxed paper, wrapped airtight in a plastic bag, and frozen a month or two.†

---

*The recipe makes 2 ¼ cups batter: eleven 9-inch *crêpes*.
†In fact, it's a good idea to double the recipe and freeze extra *crespelle* for what-on-earth-can-I-cook? insurance. Sautéed thinly sliced mushrooms, a passel of bay shrimps (also from the freezer, tasteless but nourishing) bound with cream sauce flavored with a splash of dry vermouth fills them nicely, then covered with mild cheese and baked until bubbling: our last-minute supper last night.

½ cup all-purpose flour
4 extra large eggs, at room temperature
1 cup milk (non-fat is fine)
2 tablespoons unsalted butter, plus 2 more
for the skillet, all melted

Perhaps 1 or 2 tablespoons of water, cool
1 tablespoon olive oil or other light oil, for
the skillet*

Hand method: In a bowl, whisk the flour and 2 of the eggs together until perfectly smooth,† then whisk in the remaining eggs, the milk, and the melted butter until blended. You may bake the batter at once but it will profit from resting.

Food processor or blender method: Put the flour, eggs, milk, and melted butter into the work bowl or jar and process by turning on/off until the batter is smooth, about 3 times. Cover and set in a cool place for at least an hour.‡

If the batter has rested any length of time, you may need to whisk in a little water until the batter again has the consistency of half-and-half.

To bake, set a 9½-inch§ skillet (stainless steel or heavy aluminum are recommended, nonstick fluorocarbon finishes are not) over almost-high heat and brush very lightly with a mixture of melted butter and oil. Each time, use your measuring cup to mix the batter: When the butter sizzles, take up a scant ¼ cup (scant 3 tablespoons for an 8-inch skillet, scant 2 tablespoons for a 7-inch skillet).

Off the heat, drop in the batter on one side of the skillet, at once tilting the skillet downward so the batter covers the skillet as thinly and evenly as possible—the thinner the coating, the finer the cake. Tip to fill any holes or add a drop or two more batter. On the other hand, if there's too much batter in the pan, turn the skillet upside down and dump the extra batter back into the bowl; later, you can trim that edge of the cake. Return to the heat. When you can see through the cake that it's browned underneath—in about 45 seconds (as little as 20 seconds for a 7-inch skillet)—turn the skillet upside down, rap it on the counter and dump the cake out onto waxed paper.

Bake the rest of the batter the same way, stacking the *crespelle* and keeping them covered. You may need to add a splash of water to thin the batter at the end.

THE FILLING‖

A generous ½ stick unsalted butter
A rounded ½ cup all-purpose flour

2 cups milk, cold#
4 ounces finest mozzarella cheese, grated

---

*I find *crêpes* drop from the pan with a good deal more certainty when baked with half melted unsalted butter and half olive oil than when baked with butter alone.

†In putting together a batter, you will have no lumps if you first whisk-until-smooth the flour with an equal amount of liquid; then the balance of liquid ingredients may be whisked in; we saw this in the Breton *galettes*.

‡The fervent action of the blades develops the gluten in the flour, which tends to make the *crespelle* tough; the rest gives the gluten a chance to relax.

§If you'll be using a different size skillet, then choose a baking dish with one side having the same measurement so it will accommodate the filled *crespelle*.

‖The recipe makes about 3½ cups.

#Remember, there are two traditional ways of adding liquid to a *roux* to ensure there will be no lumps: whisk hot liquid into cold *roux* or cold liquid into hot *roux*.

1 *extra large egg*
1 *extra large egg yolk*
A few turns of the white pepper mill
  (*½ teaspoon medium-grind*)

⅛ teaspoon nutmeg
About 4 ounces lean, flavorful, not-too-
  salty imported prosciutto, cut in short
  thin strips

In a large heavy saucepan over low heat, melt the butter, whisk in the flour, and cook 2 minutes, whisking occasionally so the *roux* won't color. Whisk in the milk, raise the heat to medium, and whisk until thickened—you've just made a binding of *besciamella*. Add the cheese and stir frequently until it melts. Off heat, whisk in the egg, additional yolk, pepper, and nutmeg. Add half the prosciutto, then stir and taste as you add the remaining strips—don't let the sauce get too salty. Return to the heat and whisk until one bubble pops up. Remove from the heat and cool, stirring often.

SALSA BESCIAMELLA*
Béchamel or cream sauce

⅔ stick unsalted butter
A rounded ⅓ cup all-purpose flour
4 cups milk, cold

16 turns of the white pepper mill
  (*1⅓ teaspoons, medium grind*)
A scant ¼ teaspoon nutmeg

Prepare as you did the sauce above; after it has thickened, remove from heat and add the pepper and nutmeg. It will be a light sauce.

PUTTING IT TOGETHER

The besciamella
The crespelle
The filling

½ cup grated (about 2 ounces) Parmesan
  cheese
About ½ teaspoon nutmeg
¼ stick unsalted butter, melted

A 9½ × 13½ × 2¼-inch baking dish is perfect for this dish, but any broad flattish 4-quart dish would do.

Spread the bottom with ¼ inch (about 1 cup) of the *besciamella*. Have the stack of *crespelle* pale sides up. Spread cakes evenly to the edges with a rounded ¼ cup of filling (for *crespelle* of another size, divide the filling in as many cakes as you have). Roll up snugly and lay seam side down at one narrow end of the dish. Continue in this manner, using all the *crespelle* and all the filling (when the dish seems to be full, tip it and the rolls will slide down, making room for more.) If you plan to bake at once, heat the oven to 375°F when half the cakes have been filled.

Run a sharp knife lengthwise down the dish, cutting the *crespelle* into rows of inch-wide *crespolini*. Whisk the remaining sauce and spread it evenly over the top, then shake the dish gently to level everything. Sprinkle with Parmesan and nutmeg and drizzle with melted butter. If you're preparing this in advance, cover with plas-

---

*The recipe makes 4 cups.

tic film and refrigerate, bringing the dish to room temperature an hour before baking. When ready to bake, heat the oven to 375°F.

Bake on the upper rack of the oven until sizzling and beautifully browned, about 30 minutes. Cool a few minutes, then serve with a pancake turner.

Had Tina not made *crespolini*, she might have served Groucho her exquisite green *gnocchi*—spinach and ricotta dumplings much prized in Liguria. Tina's are more delicate than any I have tasted. The paste is bound with lots of eggs and little flour, and the shape—fingerlings—means they cook very evenly. Tina never finished her *gnocchi* with anything so vulgar as tomato sauce—just a gilding of sweet butter and a veil of cheese. These dumplings are also delectable floating in a soup plate of good broth, sprinkled with any freshly grated dry cheese. Poach them first in their own pot of simmering water, however, lest they cloud the broth.

GNOCCHI VERDI SQUISITI
Delicate spinach and ricotta dumplings
[*Makes about 60: 8 to 10 first-course servings*]
The paste may be prepared up to a day in advance and the poached *gnocchi* ready in their dish a few hours before heating. (Truth to tell, any left over are almost even better warmed up the next day.)

2 1/2 pounds fresh spinach	1/8 teaspoon nutmeg
1 pound* ricotta cheese	1/4 teaspoon salt
5 ounces block Parmesan cheese, finely shredded	6 turns of the white pepper mill (1/4 teaspoon, medium grind)
3 extra large eggs	Boiling water for poaching
1/4 cup all-purpose flour, plus more for the board	About 3/4 stick unsalted butter, melted†
1 tablespoon chopped fresh sweet basil leaves, or 1 teaspoon dried	A few turns of the black pepper mill (a pinch)

Rinse, cook,‡ squeeze dry, and very finely chop the leaves of the spinach. You'll need 1 cup. In a mixing bowl, whisk the ricotta, 3 ounces (about 3/4 cup) of the Parmesan, and the eggs together until smooth. Add the spinach and whisk until blended, then add the flour, basil, nutmeg, salt, and white pepper and again whisk until smooth. The mixture will be moist and light. Cover with plastic film and refrigerate, if desired. Chilling will help the fragile paste hold together.

In your spaghetti pot, bring about 4 inches of unsalted water to a boil, then turn down the heat so one bubble at a time barely breaks the surface. Meanwhile, liber-

*Some brands are packaged as 15 ounces; that's fine.
†I read that in Milan, the butter is browned—a tasty notion.
‡Rinsing and cooking fresh spinach, page 258.

ally dust your work surface with flour. Scoop up 1 rounded teaspoonful of the paste and drop onto the flour. Stiffen your hand and with the flat of your palm, roll back and forth, back and forth, ever so lightly, making a dumpling the size and shape of your little finger. Roll onto a sheet of waxed paper.

When 12 *gnocchi* are shaped, drop them from the paper into the water. Set the timer for 4 minutes and let them poach uncovered. Roll 12 more *gnocchi* as before. When the timer rings, lift out 1 dumpling and test—it should be firm but almost translucent. Lift the dumplings with a slotted spoon onto a thick towel to drain. Continue in this manner with the remaining paste.

Brush a medium-sized shallow baking dish—anything with a 7-cup capacity about 1½ inches deep—with some of the melted butter. Lift the *gnocchi* from the towel with a pancake turner and arrange a layer in the dish, all going in the same direction and touching but not crowded. Drizzle with melted butter and sprinkle with shredded Parmesan. Layer this way until all are used, keeping the layers parallel. Cover and keep in a cool place until ready.

Heat the oven to 350°F, then bake the *gnocchi* uncovered until the butter is bubbling like crazy and the top is just beginning to turn gold, about 30 minutes. Do not overbake. Serve with a pancake turner. Some may break up, but they'll still be sublime. A grinding of black pepper on top is not amiss.

For dessert, Tina made a delectable water ice of cantaloupe. Nothing is more heavenly on hot summer nights. Over the years, I've tried three things with this ice that have taught me interesting lessons. First, knowing that the Sicilians, patrons of all ices, often add pieces of fresh or candied fruit to their mixtures, once I stirred in a handful of chopped candied orange peel. That was a mistake because the peel always turned up as an annoying distraction from the clean clear flavor of the melon. Second, I folded in whipped cream, a quarter of the volume of the ice, turning it into sherbet. That was a mistake because the cream blunted, again, the clean clear flavor of the melon. And third, I put the puree through a hair sieve. That was a mistake because just an edge of pulpiness makes the texture more interesting and the flavor more intense because there are more surfaces to flick about the tongue.

Tina did not boil the sugar and water syrup as is usually directed—uncooked sugar makes the fruit taste fresher and it doesn't materially affect the freezing of the ice.

For a little drama and to provoke delighted anticipation, Tina presented the ice in its melon shell (classically served on a white napkin on a silver salver, but my mother was fresh out of silver salvers at the villa) in a glass bowl filled with ice. And, for Groucho, somehow Tina came up with a great golden melon blossom (whose patch had she plundered?) pinned on top of the lid. Any orange-gold blossom will do.

Use the orange-fleshed melons the first time you make this, then you may later want to experiment with the pale-fleshed melons such as honeydew and casaba.* All should have rind of a warm color with a perceptible melon scent, and the blossom end should give a little when pressed.

This water ice is meant to be smoother than the traditional coarse-crystalled coffee or lemon *granita*.

Granita di melone
Melon water ice
[Makes 2 quarts: about 16 servings]
Three or four days before serving, bring the melons home and let them rest at room temperature so the flesh will become juicier. Do not cut; melons don't ripen well after cutting.

The *granita* preparation is best made the day before freezing.

3 cantaloupes or 2 Persians or 1 Crenshaw; choose large handsome ripe melons†
1²/₃ cups less 1 tablespoon sugar‡
3¼ cups less 1 tablespoon cold water

7 tablespoons fresh lemon juice (two large juicy lemons)
7 tablespoons fresh orange juice (1 juicy orange)
A melon blossom or other suitable flower (optional)

Ideally, the day before serving, cut lids off the melons in a decorative zigzag pattern about one-fourth the way down; discard the seeds. Taking care not to pierce the rind, scoop out the flesh from lids and bottoms, turning the flesh into a bowl. Scrape out and discard the greener flesh to make the largest possible shells for serving. Cover the shells and set in a cool place.

Coarsely puree the flesh, then put it through the finest blade of the food mill or a ¹/₁₆-inch sieve (the food processor would turn it to Instant Soup, not what you want). You'll need 4 cups puree. Stir the sugar in the water until dissolved, then add it with the lemon and orange juices to the puree. Blend thoroughly, cover tightly, and refrigerate 12 to 24 hours so the flavors will ripen. If you're rushed, it may be frozen at once. Follow manufacturer's directions for making ice cream in an ice cream maker.

Or turn the freezer to its coldest setting and pour the mixture into a shallow 9-inch square metal pan. Cover and freeze until the ice is firm around the edges and the center slushy, from 2 to 6 hours. Working in two batches, use the food processor, blender, mixer, or a rotary beater to smooth the slush—but do not let it melt. Pack into a tightly covered container and let firm up in the freezer an hour or two

---

*I made a watermelon ice with great expectations, but to our surprise, it was both odd and disappointing because it was like eating the watermelon itself, whereas an ice of muskmelon gives its perfumed flavor a sparkling new dimension.
†Cantaloupes should be football-shaped and have a pronounced cavity where the stem was, Persian melons should be round, and Cranshaws pointed at the stem end.
‡Superfine sugar dissolves fastest but it isn't necessary.

before serving. If more time passes and the ice becomes hard, let it soften a little at room temperature. Chill your dessert bowls.

Pack the melon ice into the shell(s), mounding it high on top. Fit on the lid(s) and set one shell in a serving bowl of ice. Top with a blossom, if you can. Set any other shell(s) in the freezer until needed. Serve, scooping the melon ice from the melon shell into the bowls. One large cantaloupe will hold about 3 cups of ice, which will serve 6 people.

If you would like to invent your own fresh ices, Tina's rule, which is classic, comes to this:

YOUR OWN ITALIAN WATER ICES
[*Each quart makes 8 servings*]

Using fresh raw fruit, the proportions are equal measures of finely pureed fruit or juice and sugar syrup—granulated sugar dissolved in twice its volume of cold water.

To calculate the syrup, divide the cups of syrup you'll need by 2 ½; that will give you the amount of sugar. Double that for the amount of water.*

For every 8 cups mixture from fruit that is orange, red, or blue, add 7 tablespoons fresh lemon juice and 7 tablespoons fresh orange juice. For every 8 cups mixture from fruit that is blonde, add 14 tablespoons fresh lemon juice. If it's lemon ice, omit this extra lemon. Freeze as in the preceding recipe.

When practicable, carve serving shells of the fruit itself—ices in oranges, lemons, and tangerines may be a bit overdone these days, but they weren't always and the time will come again when lemon ice from lemon shells seems delightful. Meantime, there will be pineapple and melon shells until they are overdone, too. Don't forget the flower!

Tina did beautiful things with fresh fruit. My first breakfast in Italy, my father joined me on the little terrace overlooking the gulf (my mother had taken up painting and was already at her easel—the days of sleeping late were long past). Tina brought out two small bowls of *macedonia di frutta al maraschino*, prisms of summer fruit soaked in cherry liqueur. For breakfast!

If you haven't met it, maraschino is a clear liqueur of silvery sweet, cherry almond intensity. Its touch of almond comes from crushed cherry stones and some of its warmth comes from honey. Less a sipping cordial than a flavoring for sweets and drinks, of all spirits with fruit, maraschino is my favorite. Native to Dalmatia, the cherries for maraschino are black and called *marasca* by the Italians. In all the world, *marascas* are grown only in the Friuli-Venezia Giulia district of Italy and a couple of hundred miles down the Dalmatian

---
*Sugar, when dissolved, is reduced to half its dry volume.

coast around Zadar, née Zara. It is in Zara/Zadar, a city surrounded on three sides by the Adriatic, that the finest *marascas* are grown. There, maraschino has been made for four hundred years. (I find it is curious that a taste for maraschino has so kept to northern Italy. The further south one dines, the less one finds maraschino in sweets and the more marsala and rum.)

The growing season in Liguria is so long it provides for three successive crops, thus there is never a want of fresh fruit for a *macedonia*.

MACEDONIA DI FRUTTA AL MARASCHINO
Mixed fresh fruit with maraschino liqueur
[*Allow about ²/₃ cup per serving*]
Although it's still a treat hours (even a day or two) later, for the fruit to be at its prime, serve as soon as possible.

Choose the finest fresh fruit of the season with an eye to a lively palette of colors, a sweet/tart contrast of flavors, and textures with a play of soft and crisp. For example, you wouldn't want a mix of pears, bananas, and honeydew melon—all pale, all soft, all sweet. Each fruit should be distinguishable—don't cut them so small and mix so many that it's a mishmosh. Tina's summer basics were:

Freestone peaches, yellow or white, in crescents
Purple-meated figs, halved or quartered
Sweet cherries, yellow or red, pitted
Crimson plums, quartered

Oranges, sectioned
Bananas, not too thinly sliced
Red apples (when not mealy), diced
Maraschino liqueur

Peel only the fruit you would normally peel to eat, viz., the oranges and bananas, and, another time, pineapple. Little is less aesthetic than fruit that's been fussed with—peeled, pitted, cut up—too much. Turn into a bowl and sprinkle with maraschino to taste. No other sweetening. Blend gently and serve.

Now my father's idea of heaven for breakfast was a bowl of figs. Occasionally, my mother bought them at the market, but mostly figs came through the door as gifts from friends who knew my father's passion—Liguria is famous for its figs. That summer, our favorite bearer of figs was Elisabeth Jungmann, a tall stately greying painfully shy woman who lived with a friend at the Villino Chiaro near Zoagli, on the other side of Rapallo. It was no great distance from town, but she used it as an excuse not to venture forth much. Actually, she worried always about her friend: "—he is so frail, you know—." One day, she telephoned, saying she had some figs for my father, could someone kindly come and fetch them? My mother asked me to take the Citroën and pick them up.

I rang the bell and Elisabeth (she had asked me to call her by her first name) greeted me warmly. She handed me the figs in a leaf-lined basket "for dear Arthur," then asked if I would like to meet her friend.

It was noon and he was sitting in the shade of an arbor of grapes at the back of the villino. He was in his eighties but looked a delicious dandy. A straw boater atilt his wispy white hair, a cornflower in the lapel of his vanilla linen jacket, and an open book upon his lap, his skin was baby pink and his eyes, his eyes! so round, the lids beneath them drooped alarmingly (the rims were bright red and my father, who was squeamish, told me he couldn't look at him directly), but his eyes were a riveting blue. He was indeed too frail to move easily from his chair. Seated, he pressed the hand I offered in greeting, then asked whether I knew that the stones I was standing on were part of a Roman road.* I swallowed. I hadn't. Then Elisabeth glided out with an orange and white Penguin book in her hand. He asked if I would like a copy of his book. I murmured that I would be most grateful. He opened the book, took a pen from his pocket, and, in the manner of crossing out one's name on one's calling card, on the title page after *Zuleika Dobson, Or An Oxford Love Story*, crossed out the author's name and wrote:

> For
> Miss Sylvia Sheekman
> with all best wishes from
> Max Beerbohm
> Rapallo
> 1954

Everybody we knew seemed to come through Rapallo. After Groucho left, S. N. Behrman came to interview Sir Max and his friends for a biography. Sam Behrman came to dinner. Tina made her *burrida* for him, a seafood soup native to Genoa. Behrman was rhapsodic.

Lacking Tina's recipe, my guide for *burrida* was Ada Boni's recipe from *Italian Regional Cooking*. The Mediterranean fish, molluscs, and crustaceans—and their American counterparts—commonly used in *burrida* are noted on pages 241 to 242.

For my *burrida*, I buy a complement of sweet-meated lean, dark-meated fat fish, and a goodly element of crustaceans and molluscs—mussels are essential. Mussels are available the year around in the east, and from November to April in the west.

---

*The Via Aemilia Scaurus, which connected with the Via Aurelia, the "Great Coast Road" linking Rome to Pisae, Genua, Nicaea, and ultimately, Arelate (Arles), probably built before the second century B.C. Today's highway closely follows the same route, only today it runs in front, rather than in back of, the Villino Chiaro.

One of the beauties of this soup is its ease of preparation. There's no stock to make beforehand, yet the broth is fabulous. The secret, an amalgam that will surprise you. It's very subtle and the proportions are not to be tampered with. I ruined a couple of *burridas* in the early days when I made the common mistake: if a little is good, more will be better.

By the way, *burrida* is not to be confused with the Provençal *bourride*, also a special fish soup, but of vastly different character.

BURRIDA
Genoese fish soup
[*8 servings*]
The base may be prepared a few hours in advance, but the fish should be cooked just before serving.

Thick fish steaks are ideal, but thickish fillets of the great soup fish are better than generous steaks of lackluster fishes. Consider the *shelled* weight of molluscs and crustaceans in your calculations.

3 pounds boned and shelled weight of freshest fish or fish and shellfish. For example, buy:	*²⁄₃ cup fruity olive oil (makes the soup silky)*
12 ounces angler, monk, or rockfish steaks	*1 onion, chopped medium-fine*
	1 garlic clove
12 ounces tuna or mackerel steaks (or eel, if you can find it)	*2 anchovy fillets, finely chopped*
	A small handful of parsley, finely chopped
12 ounces shark steaks	*2 large (1 pound) meaty ripe tomatoes, peeled, seeded,§ and chopped medium-fine*
2 or more pounds mussels in the shell (buying none that are open and won't close when prodded), well cleaned*	*¹⁄₃ cup finely chopped toasted walnuts*
1 pound squid, cleaned, hoods cut in ¹⁄₄-inch rings and tentacles chopped (or octopus, precooked† and cut into ¹⁄₂-inch slices or strips)	*1 bay leaf*
	1 ¹⁄₄ cups dry white wine
	A few turns of the white pepper mill (¹⁄₄ teaspoon, medium grind)
A few handfuls of raw shrimps, shelled and cleaned‡	*Perhaps a little salt*

Trim steaks of skin and fat and cut into 1½-inch chunks. Cut any fillets into medium-sized pieces. If you use eel, skin it, then cut it into pieces to match the rest of the fish. Cover and keep all seafood in the refrigerator.

In a flameproof casserole or heavy pot (in Genoa, *burrida* is cooked and served in the same vessel), heat the oil. Sauté the onion and garlic over medium heat until the

---

*How-to, page 251.
†Preparation notes for squid, page 258; octopus, page 251.
‡Why to clean shrimps, page 257. Save their shells for shrimp butter, same page.
§The method for peeling and seeding, on page 259.

onions are golden and the garlic has browned, about 15 minutes; stir frequently. Discard the garlic and add the anchovy, parsley, tomatoes, walnuts, and bay leaf to the pot. Stir until this forms a good amalgam, 2 or 3 minutes. Blend in the wine. You may prepare the soup to this point a few hours in advance. Bring to a simmer before continuing.

Simmer the base gently about 5 minutes until the wine has reduced a bit, then add all the fish except the mussels. Return to a simmer, cover, and simmer very gently and stir occasionally and carefully with a wooden spatula or spoon while the fish cooks. Meanwhile, if you are using them, cook the mussels in a large skillet (page 133). Heat soup bowls, preferably shallow ones.

When the chunks of fish are translucent and the rings of squid (or strips of octopus) are tender, 20 to 30 minutes, add the mussels in their shells to the *burrida*, then pass their broth through a damp cloth into the pot. Grind over the pepper. Taste for salt. Serve at once, accompanied by slices of toasted Italian or French bread.

For a first course with the *burrida*, Tina made a salad of raw mushrooms—I had never eaten mushrooms raw before, and I was entranced. Although a rule in composing menus is not to repeat any element of one dish in another, anchovies are perceptible in the salad but imperceptible in the soup. And having a salty touch of the sea in the salad before the seafood soup is a graceful prelude.

I find this an uncommonly useful first course that complements all sorts of entrées.

INSALATA DI FUNGHI ALLA GENOVESE
Raw mushroom salad with anchovies
[*8 servings*]
Begin this about 45 minutes before serving.

⅓ cup fresh lemon juice (2 juicy lemons)	*12 turns of the white pepper mill*
⅓ cup olive oil	*(1 teaspoon, medium grind)*
8 medium-sized anchovy fillets, finely	*1 ⅓ pounds firm, medium-sized mushrooms,*
chopped	*fairly thinly sliced*
A handful of finely chopped parsley	*About 24 baby lettuce leaves*

Mix a dressing of lemon juice, olive oil, anchovies, parsley, and pepper. Pour over the mushrooms in a bowl and toss with your hands until the mushrooms are evenly dressed. Serve at once or let rest half an hour, then spoon onto baby lettuce leaves and serve.

Of course I appreciated everything Tina did, but I confess I spent little time in the kitchen watching her cook. I let my mother take notes. I was too busy with my new friends. The morning after I arrived, the doorbell rang and Tina came to tell me there was someone asking for me. It was a tawny young blonde with a face from a Roman coin.

"*Ciao, Sil*-via," she said with that singing Italian inflection. "I am Orsina. . . . Go get your bathing suit. You must come with me." Orsina looped her arm through mine and we strolled down the road to the beach at San Michele, laughing and chattering. Orsina, who lived in Rapallo, had been sent by one of my mother's friends.

The summer flew. I had the beguiling company of Orsina, her bubbling sister Noretta, their shy younger brother Federico, Nore's bear of a boyfriend Giancarlo, Giancarlo's skinny best friend Fabrizio, scholarly Francesco from Rome, and now and then Gioia, Nona, Massimo, and half a dozen others from half a dozen other parts of Italy. After months in Paris of being made ever so subtly to feel The American, with my Italian friends, I simply felt *Sil*-via!

We'd all meet late in the morning and take our accustomed places on the sand. For lunch, we brought basics that could be tucked into a towel with a bathing suit, then everybody shared. Noretta once brought something I particularly remember. "What is that?" I asked.

"A tomato," she shrugged.

"But it's GREEN, Nore."

"*Sil*-via, have you never eaten a green tomato?" She gave me one. It was crisp and tart and sweet and splendid. I had found a whole new fruit.

One of the favorites for lunch was a flattish bread Tina made called *focaccia*. It was an inch or two high,* chewy, crusty, pure. Commonly, the *focaccia* that came out of the bakers' ovens around eleven o'clock every morning in town were sprinkled with coarse salt and olive oil before baking. Some bakers blended chopped fresh sage or rosemary into their dough and that was lovely. All over town, you'd see people strolling down the street or riding bicycles munching *focaccia*. Tina's bread was absolute plainsong because she liked to eat it with *pesto*, gorgeous notion. Just before I'd leave for the beach, she'd give me a small rectangle of *focaccia* warm from the oven and a jar of *pesto*.

I've since read that *focaccia* is one of the oldest forms of bread—the French also have their *fougasse/fouace/fouasse*. The words derive from *focus*, Latin for "hearth" or "fireplace," because originally the bread was baked directly on the hearth. For the most part, community bakers have baked their bread in ovens since the Egyptians, so clearly *focaccia* has its origins in the home. Usually it was baked in the ashes on the hearth but sometimes a pot was set over the dough to shelter it from the ashes. I can't imagine the bread itself has

---

*Depending on how Tina finished the top before baking. The recipe will explain.

changed much since its beginning. *Focaccia* is simply flour, water, yeast, salt, and olive oil.

In Tina's *focaccia*, there is just enough olive oil woven through to give the bread that subtle but sensual olive-warmth. And I'll tell you something: when it has cooled, a slice finely drizzled with olive oil, covered with fresh tomatoes, and sprinkled with coarse salt is *maraviglioso*. And if there's any left over the next morning (it keeps beautifully), it will make sensational crisp toast. I've tried other recipes for *focaccia*, but Tina's old-fashioned sponge method results in a crustier crust, richer flavor, and denser crumb.

FOCACCIA
Flattish Italian bread
[At least 12 servings]
Focaccia is at its best hot or warm. It reheats beautifully. Keep any leftover wrapped airtight in a cool place or at room temperature—not in the refrigerator.

1 rounded teaspoon active dry yeast*	*Some optional flavorings for* focaccia
1 3/4 cups water, warm	2 tablespoons fresh chopped sage or
3 cups unbleached flour	rosemary leaves, or 2 teaspoons dried
1 1/2 teaspoons salt	A scant tablespoon coarse salt
3 tablespoons fruity olive oil, plus more for the bowl and the baking	

Detailed instructions for making bread are on pages 239 to 241.

In your mixer bowl—or a small bowl, if you'll be using the food processor—sprinkle the yeast over 1/4 cup of the water, stir, then let stand until it dissolves, about 5 minutes.

Hand or mixer method: Add 1 1/2 cups of the flour and beat 2 minutes. Beat in the remaining flour by the 1/2 cupful. Let rest 5 minutes, then knead on a lightly floured board or with the dough hook 10 minutes. The dough will be silky and smooth.

Food processor method: Turn the flour and the yeast mixture into the work bowl. Whiz until the dough comes together and masses around the blade, then count 25 turns around the blade. Turn the dough over and process another 25 turns. The dough will be silky and smooth.

Mark 6 cups in a vessel, oil it, drop in the dough, then turn the dough over. Flatten the top and cover with plastic film and a damp towel. Set in a sheltered spot around 70°F and let rise until the shoulders of the dough hit the mark, 1 to 1 1/2 hours. Punch down.

On your lightly floured surface, press out the dough 1/4-inch thick and dimple it all over with your fingertips. Sprinkle over the salt and olive oil then smooth it even with your hand. (Also, if you're using it, sprinkle over an herb: sage gives you FO-

---

*If you're in a hurry, you can use twice as much yeast. The crumb will be a little coarser but you'll save about an hour and a half.

CACCIA ALLA SALVIA and rosemary gives you FOCACCIA AL ROSMARINO.) Fold the dough in thirds, then in thirds again in the opposite direction. Knead (wear a thick apron—the oil can spurt) until the oil has been absorbed and the dough is once again silky and smooth, 2 to 3 minutes. Mark 7 cups in your vessel, oil it, and let the dough rise as before, about 2 hours. Punch down, knead out bubbles, cover, and let rest a few minutes.*

Roll out the dough between ¼-inch and a scant ½-inch thick into any shape you like—I usually make an 8 × 12-inch rectangle. Lay on an oiled baking sheet, preferably of black carbon steel, or on parchment or brown paper generously sprinkled with flour.† Brush with olive oil. Cover with a damp cloth and let rise until puffy and the shape has increased a couple of inches (my rectangle becomes 10 × 12 inches), about 1½ hours. After about 1 hour (for the tiles or stone) or 1 hour and 10 minutes (for the baking sheet), heat the oven to 400°F.

When ready to bake, you can prick the *focaccia* with a fork about 2 inches apart or dimple it every inch or so with your fingertips.‡ (If you're making FOCACCIA COL SALE, this is the time to lightly drizzle the top with olive oil and lightly sprinkle with coarse salt.) Bake on the top rack of the oven, spraying the *focaccia* and the oven (ceiling, floor, and walls) with cold water three times in the first 6 minutes of baking. Bake until crusty and hollow-sounding when lightly smacked, 25 to 30 minutes in all. Serve hot or warm cut in squares or slices and spread with *pesto* (recipe follows) or other good things. Remove to a cooling rack (pulling off the paper, if used), if not served at once.

As for *pesto*, Liguria's gift to mankind, despite all the carrying on from Genoa that *pesto* can only be made perfectly there (sweet basil sprung from Ligurian soil grown beneath Ligurian sun blended with Ligurian olive oil, that sort of thing), of course *pesto* can be glorious anywhere in the world, given first-class ingredients. But don't look to Tina's recipe for the last word. Proportions of sweet basil to Parmesan to olive oil to pine nuts to garlic vary wildly from cook to cook. Tina doesn't even add garlic to her *pesto*, some days I'm moved to use twice as much sweet basil, and pine nuts, I understand, are a modern addition. So feel free to experiment with *pesto* until you find what makes your own particular bliss. The only unbreakable rule in making *pesto* is that the basil must be garden fresh.

Tina made *pesto* with a marble mortar and pestle, but I lazily use a machine most of the time. The mortar and pestle makes a fluffier, finer *pesto*.

And following my own style, I add garlic.

---

*Or, if it helps your schedule, after punching it down, turn into a large plastic bag, seal, and refrigerate. Check it now and then and punch the dough down when it has doubled in size. You can keep the dough a day this way. Return to room temperature an hour before continuing.
†The paper, to slide onto unglazed quarry tiles or a baking stone on the oven rack: the dough finishes closer to that of *focaccia* from a baker's oven.
‡The tines result in a flatter, chewier bread and the dimpled bread is higher and lighter. I like different textures on different days.

TINA'S PESTO
Fresh sweet basil paste
[Makes a scant ¹/₂ cup]

In the freezer, *pesto* will keep the winter. To freeze, simply omit the Parmesan, then blend it in when the *pesto* has thawed. In the refrigerator, thawed or fresh, *pesto* keeps at least a week.

A good handful (about ¹/₂ cup, firmly packed) of fresh medium-sized sweet basil leaves	*¹/₂ cup grated (about 2 ounces) Parmesan cheese*
A pinch of salt	*¹/₄ cup pine nuts*
	(1 garlic clove)
	¹/₄ cup olive oil

Mortar and pestle method: Crush the basil, salt, and Parmesan. Gradually pound in the pine nuts (and garlic). When the nuts are paste, slowly blend in the olive oil.

Food processor or blender method: Turn the basil, salt, pine nuts, (garlic), and olive oil into the work bowl. Process until a fine paste, then turn into a bowl and stir in the Parmesan.

A spoonful of *pesto* stirred into a bowlful of broth lifts that broth into a new dimension—and many say that, of all the sauces in Italy, none surpasses

PESTO AS SAUCE FOR PASTA
{3 to 4 first-course servings}

1 tablespoon salt	*1 tablespoon butter, preferably unsalted, melted*
A glug of olive oil	
*3 quarts water, boiling**	*About ¹/₄ cup pasta-cooking water*
Around 12 ounces pasta, preferably thin†	
1 recipe pesto (recipe preceding)	

In your spaghetti pot, add salt and oil to water boiling over highest heat. Stir in the pasta and boil, stirring often, until tender-chewy, but with no graininess in the center. Drain over your serving bowl to heat it, saving some of the water. Dump out the rest and turn the pasta into the bowl. To the *pesto* in a mixing bowl, whisk in the melted butter and enough of the pasta-water to make a loose sauce. Toss with the pasta and serve at once.

In Liguria, the term *focaccia* can also refer to what we think of as pizza. In fact, it's the same dough, just rolled thinner and covered with good things. If you've never made bread, either *focaccia* or pizza is a simple and satisfying beginning.

---

*Detailed pasta cooking notes are on page 252.

†Sauces made with olive oil seem to show off to best advantage over skinny pasta. *Trenette* is classic, but *spaghettini* and its ilk are equally suitable. However, if you only have basic spaghetti in the house, it will be fine.

Along the Italian Riviera, pizzas are generally shaped in rectangles—convenient for our rectangular ovens. The classic *pizza alla Liguria* has three elements. The heart of the matter is onions melted in olive oil. The onions are either cut in very thin rings or finely chopped—rings give you the succulence of the onion, chopped onions give you their essence. Then, according to the temperament of the baker, the onions are topped with either a decorative lattice of, or simply strewn with, flat fillets of anchovies—I find a lattice irresistible. The top is studded with tiny black olives, the sort we know as "Niçoise"—except that Ligurian olives are preserved in olive oil, not brine, which contributes to the sweetness of their flavor. To be perfectly honest, what's special about Niçoise-style olives is their size and venue. Larger California olives are quite as tasty, and being pitted, easier to eat in pizza.

Pizza alla Liguria is kissing cousin to *pissaladière*, not far across the border in Provence. Amusingly, in both cuisines, the temptation to think that if three elements are good, four will be better is such that in some quarters, tomato sauce is first laid down and regarded by their advocates as "classic." It is certainly striking to look at—rouge red shining through pale onions with glints of gleaming black—and I can't say it isn't delicious. If you use a light hand, the sauce will tempt those who would be wary of pizza that hasn't any tomato (or cheese!). For them, I've included a quick, easy, and fresh-tasting sauce. But for the marriage of flavors, do try just the purer onions-anchovies-olives.

Uncommonly light and tasty, this pizza has been declared by more than one friend the best they've ever eaten.

PIZZA ALLA LIGURIA
Onion, anchovy, and black olive pizza
[At least 9 servings]

Elements for the topping may be prepared in advance, but they must be no more than warm when arranged on the dough. The pizza really should be served straight from the oven. There's plenty of give in terms of time along the way, but if you must have it made in advance, this crispy crust and filling reheat beautifully.

1 recipe focaccia *dough; the optional rosemary makes this pizza even more special (page 127)*

3 tablespoons olive oil, plus more for the pan

3 large onions, very thinly sliced

Rough Tomato Sauce for Pizza (optional, recipe follows)

Three 2-ounce cans of flat anchovy fillets; reserve the oil from 1 can

About 28 "medium" pitted black olives

About 12 turns of the black pepper mill (1 teaspoon, medium grind)

3 tablespoons chopped fresh sweet basil leaves, or 1 tablespoon dried

While the dough is rising, in a large heavy skillet over medium-low heat, heat the olive oil, then add the onions. Break up the slices into rings (before the skillet gets too hot, fingers are the best tool) and mix so that all rings are glistening with oil. Sauté, stirring frequently, until golden but still crisp, 12 to 15 minutes. Do not brown. Remove from the heat and cool. (If you're using it, make the tomato sauce and cool.) Cut the anchovy fillets in half lengthwise.

After the dough's second rising and rest, roll it out ¼-inch thick on a floured surface according to the shape of your baking sheet. A sheet around 15-inches square is ideal, and black carbon steel is preferable.* Generously brush the sheet with oil, lay the dough upon it, and brush the dough with oil. Cover and let rest 15 minutes to an hour.

(If you're using it, lightly but evenly spread the tomato sauce over the dough.)

Spread the onions evenly over the surface, then make a diamond lattice of the thin strips of anchovies: Run the lines corner to corner first, then in rows parallel to them about 3 inches apart. Press an olive into the dough in the center of each diamond. Drizzle the oil from one of the anchovy cans evenly over the surface, grind pepper over, and sprinkle with basil. Heat the oven to 450°F, then let the pizza rest another 15 to 20 minutes—30 minutes to heat tiles or baking stone.

Bake until the edges and bottom crust are browned and crisp, 25 to 30 minutes. Serve at once, or cool, then reheat at 375°F until crisp and hot.

Even with canned tomatoes, this sauce tastes remarkably fresh.

Rough Tomato Sauce for Pizza
[For one 15-inch square pizza: at least 9 servings]
This may be made several hours in advance.

¼ cup olive oil
Generous 2 pounds fresh ripe peeled plum or
  other sauce tomatoes (seeding is
  optional†) or a 28-ounce can of best-
  quality plum (Italian-style) tomatoes,
  drained (no need to seed)

1 tablespoon chopped fresh sweet basil or
  oregano leaves, or 1 teaspoon dried; if
  rosemary is in the pizza dough, omit this
12 to 15 turns of the black pepper mill
  (rounded 1 teaspoon, medium grind)
2 large garlic cloves, finely chopped
About ¼ teaspoon salt, for fresh tomatoes
  only

In a large heavy skillet over high heat, add the olive oil, then the tomatoes, breaking them up with your fingers. Stir in the herb, if you're using it, and the pepper. Simmer briskly until most of the juice in the skillet has been reduced and the mixture has become a rough but light sauce, about 10 minutes. Stir frequently, using the edge of your spoon to break up the tomatoes until they are small bits. Turn the sauce into a bowl to cool. Add the garlic to the unwashed skillet and stir about 1 minute over high heat—do not brown. Stir into the sauce. Taste for salt.

---

*If you have tiles or a baking stone, bake the sheet on top; if you have a baker's peel and practice, slip the pizza risen on floured parchment paper directly onto the tiles/stone to bake.
†How to peel and seed, page 259.

On weekends, we'd go dancing. At Paraggi, a little bay around the bend from Santa Margherita, a wide-bowed sailing ship had been transformed into an outdoor café. In the Italian custom, lights twinkled in swags down from the mast and in rows along the bow. Our nights there were affordable for students—a glass or two of wine could last an evening, and records were the orchestra. That summer, Orsina and I memorized every lyric of every song of Henri Salvador's.

(And that summer, the young man from the Hollywood Stars baseball game and the Paris Opera, driving to Rome from his Army job in Heidelberg late one night, rounded a corner and nearly drove into a car filled with screaming teenagers. He swerved and missed them by a hair's breadth. The next sign he saw was Santa Margherita Ligure; he turned off and spent the night there, before driving on, past the Villa Glicini and the beach at San Michele di Pagana. He was gaining on me.)

One memorable night, my friends and I all met early. It was Giancarlo's birthday and we'd planned a feast. My sense of geography in the dark failed me and to this day, I haven't any idea where we went, just that we took a motorboat from Santa Margherita briefly and had to climb a rope ladder vertically up a cliff to get to the restaurant. At the top, everyone was sitting country fashion out of doors on benches drawn up to plank tables. We sat down, Giancarlo pounded the table with a beefy hand and bellowed, "*Muscoli!*" The waiter smiled and disappeared. I asked Orsina what *muscoli* was. She told me, but I didn't know the word. Nevermind, it had a lovely swing to it. We broke bread, drank wine, toasted Giancarlo, the moon, and one another, and then it came. A bowl the size of a small washtub heaped with *mussels*! Being my squeamish father's daughter, a perfect evening was ruined.

Everybody else dived in with both hands. They would grab a mussel, pull off one shell, nip out the plump tidbit with their teeth (rather the way one tackles an artichoke leaf), tip up the shell and drain the broth, then, the wine having taken effect, most of them threw the shell over their shoulder onto the earth while they grabbed another. They ate rapidly, rhythmically, and silently. I watched, fascinated, miserable. It was a long few minutes until Fabrizio paused and looked at me across the table, then asked, "*Ah, Silvia, che fai?*" The trouble was, I wasn't doing anything. My plate was empty, my hands were in my lap. I gave Fabrizio a thin smile.

Well, damned if I was going to give in to this thing. Plunging my hand into the tangle of others, I grabbed at a mussel, pulled off the lid, put the shell to my mouth and tugged out the morsel with my teeth. Then. Was I really going to bite down? I closed my eyes and bit. I could taste a heady Mediterranean blending of warm garlic, white wine, grassy parsley, pungent pepper, and, best of all, the sweet sea taste of the mussel. It was a moment. I have been a passionate—*passionate!*—mytilophile ever since.

Now what we ate that night, *muscoli alla marinara*, is, exchanging butter for olive oil and shallots for garlic, what the French call *moules marinières*. You'd think the recipe would be standard, classic, but it's not. Some people, otherwise reasonable, want you to put in chopped carrots and celery. Others mention finishing with cream sauce! Still others . . . Well, mussels are heavenly a hundred ways, but they will never be better than this:

MUSCOLI ALLA MARINARA/MOULES MARINIÈRES
Mussels, Italian or French sailors' style
[*For each person*]
This is the sort of soup to make in the kitchen with friends gathered 'round kibbitzing. In other words, it's very last minute.

1 ½ pounds mussels: don't buy any that are open and won't close on prodding

A small handful of chopped parsley

1 large garlic clove (a small shallot, for the French), finely chopped

2 tablespoons olive oil (¼ stick butter, for the French)

½ cup dry white wine

2 or 3 turns of the black pepper mill (¼ teaspoon, medium grind)

1 fresh plum tomato, peeled, seeded,* and chopped (optional)

Pick over and clean the mussels.† Place them in a large shallow skillet in as few layers as possible. Evenly distribute over them the parsley, garlic or shallot, oil or butter (the butter in small chips), wine, and pepper; in Italy, the tomato might also be added if the sailor is in port. Heat a serving bowl.

Cover the pan and set over high heat. Shake like popcorn until the mussels open, a matter of minutes. If any remain closed and you cook them a minute or two longer and they still won't open, discard them. Serve at once, distributing the broth left at the bottom of the bowl at the end. Flat soup bowls are ideal.

Much too soon, it was the end of August and time to return to California. But first, brilliant Francesco had an idea. Why didn't Orsina and I visit him in Rome? I was dizzy with the prospect. It was arranged. Then somehow, there appeared a gap of a few days before Francesco would be home and before Orsina could leave Rapallo. Mother said, "Sylvia, go to Venice." What a woman! And so once again I kissed everybody good-bye, and got on the train marked *Venezia*.

It would be silly to say I had a favorite anything in Venice, but I adored Tor-

---

*How-to, page 259.
†Method, page 251.

cello, the island that was the first settlement in the lagoon. I had read about its history, of the refugees fleeing there in the fifth century from invading barbarians. In a grassy clearing curiously strewn with massives pieces of carved stone—half a basin here, chunk of a capital there—I found a cathedral from the seventh century. Inside, in the curved wall of an apse, in Byzantine mosaic was a tall slender Madonna draped in azure, poised in a sea of gold, her gaze level, pensive. I had difficulty freeing myself from her.

Near the cathedral was a restaurant, the Locanda Cipriani. I was surprised to find it crowded. I didn't know it set one of the finest tables in Italy. While I waited to be seated, I strolled in the garden, which was between the restaurant and the cathedral. The garden was ridiculously lush, chockablock with poles of beans and bushes of squashes and bursts of eggplants, their red and gold and purple blossoms waving at me in the summer air. A gardener with a heaped basket over his arm saluted me. I told him I'd never seen such abundance, what did he feed everything? He laughed and looked at me sideways, then tilted his head toward the cathedral. It was all in the soil, he said, and what for centuries had lain beneath it.

For lunch, I chose a *risotto alla torcellana*, *risotto* with glints of half a dozen vegetables from the garden. It was superb. But another dish that afternoon, not on the menu, captured my fancy. Seated nearby, an elegant older woman, vivaciously Italian and clearly an intimate of the establishment, was nibbling on blossoms. They were fat golden squash blossoms encased in batter and deep-fried, a little *capriccio* from the chef.

It was years before I'd have blossoms of my own and a superb dipping batter, which, I learned, is called *la pastella*. The batter I use is essentially one dictated to me by that Sicilian magician, Chico Bucaro (more of Chico later). It is extraordinary and meant for every vegetable from the blossoms of squashes and pumpkins to slices of those same squashes to eggplant and, Chico's favorite, cardoons.* All fleshy vegetables make lovely fritters, but eating a light-as-air fritter of blossom is fantasy, poetry, magic.

Janet Ross, in her exquisite collection of Italian recipes for vegetables, *Leaves from Our Tuscan Kitchen*, fills her blossoms before frittering with saffroned rice (yellow rice, page 214, would be as good). And by delightful coincidence, a dear friend has just returned from Locanda Cipriani, where he is well known. He was given zucchini blossom fritters with a small square of anchovy tucked in the throat of each flower, a charming conceit.

This is, I know, wretched reading if you're not sitting in the country with

---

*Chico thought of *cardune* (his dialect) as wild artichokes. Actually, cardoons are closely related to artichokes—in Italy, "wild artichokes" or "edible thistles" are called *cardone*. In this country, when cardoons are described in seed catalogues and books about vegetable gardening, most often only the leaves and leaf midribs are described as being edible. But Chico—and other Italians—stripped off the leaves and cut the celery-like stalks into pieces for fritters.

squashes sprawling beneath your window. For that, my apologies. But you'll
have them, one day, just make sure of it. In the meantime, this is a dash-to-
the-kitchen matter: have the dinner ready, the batter risen (Chico's batter is
yeast-risen, part of its appeal), and everybody hungry. Blossoms, whether
open or closed, whether female or male—you can use them all—begin to
wither the moment they're plucked.

One day I'll try other flowers with fleshy petals in fritters—nasturtiums,
daylilies (not the buds—they're said to be bitter), and hollyhocks come to
mind. Some flowers *not* to eat are on page 248. And of course, eat no blossom
that's been sprayed.

CAPRICCIO OF BLOSSOMS AND OTHER VEGETABLE FRITTERS
[*At least 4 first-course servings*]
The batter and those good things to be dipped in it should be prepared just before
frying.

LA PASTELLA

1 ½ teaspoons (½ package) active dry yeast
About 1 ¾ cups water, warm
2 extra large eggs, at room temperature,
*   lightly beaten*
2 cups all-purpose flour
¼ cup plus 1 tablespoon grated (a generous
*   1 ounce) Romano cheese (Parmesan may*
*   be substituted)*

A small handful of chopped parsley
3 large garlic cloves, finely chopped
12 turns of the white pepper mill
*   (1 teaspoon, medium grind)*
¼ teaspoon salt

In a medium bowl, stir the yeast into ¼ cup of the water and let rest until frothy, 5
minutes. Beat in the eggs. On waxed paper, blend the flour, cheese, parsley, garlic,
pepper, and salt together. Stir them into the yeast mixture. Whisk in warm water
to make the batter the consistency of thick cream, 1 ½ to 1 ⅔ cups. Cover and set in
a warm place (in summer, that should be easy) until doubled in volume, about 6
cups, around 1 hour. Do not whisk down.

THE FRITTERS

12 large squash or pumpkin or other edible
*   blossoms, unsprayed; or 1 generous*
*   pound vegetables in ½-inch-thick slices*

Light olive oil about ¾-inch deep in your
*   skillet; a lighter vegetable oil may be*
*   blended with or substituted for olive oil*
A cube of bread (optional)

Do not rinse the blossoms unless they are dusty. Squashes and eggplant should be
unpared and raw,* cardoons should be cooked tender.

Heat the oil in a large heavy skillet or wok over high heat. When a thermometer
registers 375°F or when a cube of bread browns in 1 minute, the oil is ready.

---

*Chico first salted his squash and eggplant slices, but I don't. Notes on salting are on page 245,
under Eggplant.

Quickly dip the blossoms or slices into the airy batter and slip into the skillet—do not crowd. Turn when the undersides are golden and let "golden" on the other side—most will take about 6 minutes. Drain on brown paper, then serve at once. Eat with fingers and pass hot moist towels.

In Rome, Orsina and Francesco met me at the train in Francesco's tiny Fiat station wagon. We had a week in Rome, seeing churches, temples, tombs, museums, palaces, piazzas, villas, fountains, gardens, baths, nearly getting our hands bitten off in the *Bocca della Verità*,* nearly getting lost in the catacombs, eating ice cream in the Piazza Navona, and, with friends of Francesco's, dining and dancing every night in Trastevere. After dinner our last evening, there was a full moon, and so we walked the length of the Tiber. Around two in the morning when I could walk no longer, Francesco said he had one last thing he wanted to show me and drove us to the top of a hill, to an elegant neighborhood. He parked, then put a finger to his lips—we had to be quiet. We followed him toward an immense carved wooden gate so tall I couldn't see behind it. Francesco motioned us to bend down. Now he's playing a trick on us! I thought. He pointed at the keyhole and whispered that we should look through it. Orsie pushed me to go first. Too tired to argue, I bent down and looked. Perfectly framed in the keyhole, sublime in miniature and shimmering in the moonlight, was the piazza and basilica of St. Peter's.

The next day, the three of us drove to Naples. My first view of that fascinating city was from the back of Francesco's Fiat station wagon, bouncing through side streets, with a hunk of fresh mozzarella dripping buffalo's milk down my chin. In that little car, I was at everyone else's waist level. It was late on a workday afternoon and the traffic moved at a snail's pace. I had more intimate glimpses into rooms bordering the street than I was prepared for—much more than were I to have walked next to them along the sidewalk, keeping custody of the eyes. Always, always, the rooms were lit with one flickering candle, usually warm red in a red glass cup before a statue of the Madonna in a grotto in the wall. These rooms were flush with the sidewalk, with young children playing on the floor inside the open door or young mothers sitting on small cots nursing babies, guarded by old women—each in one of Tina's black cotton dresses—propped up on cane chairs on the sidewalk. The sidewalk was their living room.

Francesco said this was the Spacca, the heart of old Naples. We parked the

---

*The Mouth of Truth is a marble face with an open mouth hung on a wall of Santa Maria in Cosmedin, a medieval Roman church. Legend has it that if you are truthful and slip your hand into the mouth, nothing will happen. But if you are a liar, the mouth will close on it . . .

car and strolled. Laundry hung high above us in swags over the narrow streets, everything was cheek by jowl and open-air—a vegetable or fish stand was often no more than a stall crammed into the narrowest possible opening between two buildings. It was more poverty than I had ever seen but also more life. Once Orsie and I wanted to turn down one street when Francesco insisted on going down another. I suggested we meet somewhere in twenty minutes and he blanched. Two girls on their own would not be safe in the Spacca, he said. I said that was ridiculous and argued but he won.

That evening, we had dinner in the Spacca under a string of lights out of doors in a tiny *trattoria, con specialità napoletane*. It was there I learned the trick of floating a slice of apple in a glass of peasant wine—its sweetness helps smooth the edges of a rough grape. Try it. The apple is not only esthetic but it works. And it was there, that melting August night, I ate a dish of thin pasta sauced with fresh tomatoes, eggplant, and yellow sweet peppers that forever after has evoked Naples in my mouth and in my heart. When my mother handed on her copy of *Il Talismano della Felicità*, I found a recipe that became the inspiration for bringing that evening—and Spacca-Napoli— back to life.

Although it is a simple recipe, a couple of steps in the preparation are steps with which most of us don't bother—peeling and seeding the sweet peppers and tomatoes. My mother's response, when I was describing the recipe, was, "I'm not going to do that. Why do they want you to peel and seed tomatoes anyway?" In this case, it has to do with texture. This sauce is unctuous, silky, slipping sleekly down the gullet. Tough seeds and cellophane curls of skin would be distracting. When a dish is pure beauty, take a few minutes and peel the damn things! says I to Mum. She ignored me.

But the eggplant is not peeled. Esthetics again—this time visual, not tactile. Flashes of shiny black eggplant with slivers of matte black olives are gorgeous against the bright red of tomatoes and dull green of capers and peppers. It couldn't be more Italianate.

One step in preparation I don't take is steeping eggplant in salt for an hour. Most European and Middle Eastern cooks recommend it to overcome a certain bitterness in the vegetable and to help prevent excess absorption of oil. Well, I have salted in Turkish, Greek, French, and Italian recipes and not salted in the same and the eggplants haven't shown a whit of difference, one way or the other. But then our California eggplants may be sisters to the Sicilian, which, I understand, are also sweet-meated. If yours are from cooler climes, you may choose to salt them.*

---

*Eggplant-salting notes, page 245.

The absence of onion and the discreet use of garlic in this very southern sauce interests me. If I were putting it together on my own, the first thing I would toss into the pot—so comforting, so promising, so scented—is a handful of chopped onion and garlic. The onion isn't missed at all—on the contrary, the delicate flavors of the eggplant, tomatoes, and peppers shine through. As for how the garlic is used, after a generation of Italian cooking, I have suddenly become aware that recipe after recipe in Italian books read, "Heat the oil in a skillet and sauté the garlic clove until brown. Discard it. . . ." (it's like learning a new word, suddenly you hear it again and again). Perhaps because it's my inclination to be generous with flavors I like, that bit of subtlety hadn't altogether sunk in . . .

The ideal vessel for cooking the sauce is a flameproof earthenware casserole of at least 8 quarts' capacity and at least a 12-inch sloping base. I found when I simmered the vegetables in my Mexican *cazuela*, the eggplant took nearly three times as long to cook to tenderness as it had in my large stainless steel skillet another day, but the vegetables lost none of their juices. The original recipe suggests adding a little water if necessary at the end of the simmering period. In the earthenware, the sauce was wonderfully saucy and couldn't use another drop. But if you haven't such a vessel, I recommend using a Dutch oven rather than a skillet so the vegetables won't cook dry.

This is for a day when you feel like cooking. It's ideal for a party—everything except the pasta is done ahead—thus the generous amounts. You can halve or third the recipe, if you like, but since it's irresistible, you will want to eat it soon again. It keeps for days in the refrigerator (it's too tender to freeze well).

An Italian friend, after dining on this composition, remarked: "Often a pasta is very good, but somehow you keep wishing there were more to it. This couldn't have more—it's perfect."

SPAGHETTINI ALLA SPACCA-NAPOLI
Thin spaghetti sauced with tomatoes, eggplant, sweet peppers, and black olives
[*10 servings*]
I make the sauce early in the morning, then set the pot in a cool place and reheat it for serving. Like all mixtures, the whole becomes greater than the sum of its parts for the time spent together. But do not hold the *reheated* sauce too long—mushy, it is robbed of its fresh, lusty character. Ask how I know.

3 large heavy yellow or green sweet peppers,   *6- to 7-ounces oil- or salt-cured (page 220)*
    peeled* and seeded   *unpitted black olives*

---

*Peeling method is on page 259.

1 ½ cups (yes) finest fruity olive oil, plus a
    good splash for the pasta water
6 large garlic cloves, peeled
12 large (6 pounds) fat meaty ripe
    tomatoes, peeled, seeded,* and roughly
    chopped; save the strained juice
1 large (about 1 ½ pounds) plump solid
    unwrinkled unblemished unpeeled
    eggplant, in ⅝-inch dice†
One 2-ounce can of flat anchovy fillets,
    drained and chopped

½ cup capers, drained
2 handfuls of fresh sweet basil or oregano
    leaves, chopped, or 2 tablespoons dried
About 20 turns of the black pepper mill
    (1 ⅔ teaspoons, medium grind)
Very little salt, plus a rounded 2
    tablespoons for the pasta water
6 quarts water, boiling
1 ½ pounds best quality spaghettini
1 ½ cups grated (about 6 ounces) Parmesan
    cheese

Pat the peppers dry; slice in ¼-inch strips, then cut across in half. Lightly crush the olives with the flat blade of a chef's knife, then slice in half, discarding the pits. (Please refer to notes about the cooking vessel above.)

In a large *cazuela* or Dutch oven over medium heat, heat the olive oil and sauté the garlic, turning occasionally; when the cloves begin to brown, discard them. Stir in the tomatoes and peppers, and when they have been mixed with the oil, stir in the eggplant. Turn the heat to medium-low (low for the Dutch oven), set a sheet of heavy foil or the lid on askew and simmer gently until the eggplant is tender, 10 to 30 minutes, depending on your pot. Stir frequently.

Mix the olives and anchovies together, breaking up the bits of anchovies, then stir them in to the sauce with the capers, basil or oregano, and pepper. Blend thoroughly. Set the cover on askew again and simmer gently until the sauce has softened, 5 to 15 minutes. If at all dry, loosen with the juice from the tomatoes. Taste for salt.

Set the pot with its cover askew in a cool place. When ready to serve, warm up over medium-low heat for 12 to 15 minutes, stirring frequently. Be very careful not to overcook.

In your spaghetti pot, add salt and oil to water boiling over highest heat. Stir in the pasta and boil, stirring often, until tender-chewy, but with no graininess in the center; drain.‡

Gently stir the sauce well to incorporate any oil on top (this is part of what makes the sauce so silky), then turn the *spaghettini* into the center. Or you can turn the pasta into a big hot serving bowl and pour the sauce over it. Pass Parmesan on the side.

Orsina, my lifelong friend, and dear Francesco and I had another week together, scuffling through the dust of Pompeii with ice cream cones, lopping

---

*How to peel and seed, on page 259.
†Dice the eggplant after all the other vegetables have been prepared for the pot.
‡Pasta cooking and draining notes are on page 252.

off legs of boiled octopus on a terrace in Positano, nibbling on *calzoni* at the top of Capri, and devouring delicate shell-shaped puff pastries filled with ricotta on the ferry back from Capri to Naples.

And then, after a magical winter, spring, and summer, after eating my way through Paris and a splendid amount of Italy, Cinderella had to turn back into a real person. Had to get on a plane and come home. To the same young man who, unbeknownst to me, was now waiting for me in Berkeley.

Cooking in Love

When I arrived in Berkeley that first autumn, M. F., now living an hour away in the Napa Valley, called to invite me to join her in San Francisco for luncheon with her sister, Norah. I had seen Norah the year before at a gathering of the Kennedy clan for a celebration of their father Rex Kennedy's seventy-fifth birthday. It was a dinner in the back room of a restaurant in Los Angeles's Old Chinatown. Irrelevantly, I remember my mother wearing a movie star pouf of a white fox stole and M. F. wearing Chinese embroidered black silk slippers.

Ladies' luncheons have been few in my life. Mine with M. F. and Norah was at the Cliff House, a San Francisco institution—coral pink service, banquettes curving against bay windows above the sea, murmuring of cultivated voices. I was crazy about Norah. Junoesque, with great reserve and a sensuously sculpted face, Norah seemed very Virginia Woolf and I'd been gulping billows of Virginia Woolf. Norah lived in Berkeley and I so looked forward to seeing her again. But time slipped by and it wasn't until the January after I'd returned from Europe that Norah called. She had a young man she wanted me to meet. Her timing was excellent because I'd just given up on an aristocratic fellow from South Carolina with whom I'd sailed home on the *Liberté*.

Norah's house on Panoramic Way, all dark wood and small paned windows, was set at the bottom of a bosky terraced garden balanced on one shoulder of Strawberry Canyon in the Berkeley hills. Norah's luncheon was superb but her matchmaking was a disaster. A couple of weeks later, she called again, inviting me to dinner to meet another young man. Never able to lie, I couldn't think of an excuse fast enough to get off the hook. So that Saturday night, I found myself unhappily walking to the drawing room of our dormitory to meet a Mr. Tompkins.

An extraordinarily handsome young man—barrel-chested with dark hair

and piercing dark eyes under thick dark brows—wearing what even to my un-
practiced eye was clearly a hand-tailored suit—strode toward me. I smiled at
him politely and looked around for my date. My young men were always brilliant but never able to afford more than to have their jeans patched, much less
own a suit. The drawing room was empty. The extraordinarily handsome
young man was at my side, holding out his hand. "Miss Sheekman?" he
asked. His voice, like Pinza speaking, went through me. Oh good! I heard in
my head.

His name wasn't Tompkins. It was Thompson, Gene Thompson. He escorted me to his car, then opened the door and helped me into it—a black MG
TD with the top down. He was an older man, maybe even thirty. Something
sizzled inside me.

On the way to Norah's, I asked how she had happened to tell him about
me. Gene explained that he was renting an apartment from her. He had returned to Berkeley the previous fall after five years of working and studying
in Europe. He entered graduate school, then after a semester, withdrew to
write. In six months, he and Norah had only nodded to one another, but the
week before, the sewer backed up, and while a plumber worked on the pipes,
Gene and Norah ended up on the garden steps talking.

Norah discovered that Gene had worked in Hollywood. So had her sister,
M. F. K. Fisher. Had he known her? Gene hadn't. Then by any chance had he
met her sister's good friends, Gloria and Arthur Sheekman? Gene said of
course—they were close friends of Groucho's, for whom he'd written.

Norah asked, "Did you ever meet their daughter, Sylvia?" He didn't think
so. Norah said, "May I introduce you?"

Groucho, meeting his daughter Miriam's friend, discovered Gene had
written short stories and asked to see them. Impressed, Groucho sent the
stories to Harold Ross, the editor of *The New Yorker*, who wrote back an en-
couraging letter. Groucho hired eighteen-year-old Gene as one of the writers
on his radio show. When the show went off the air, Gene spent the next few
years writing other classic shows, among them *Duffy's Tavern*. When MGM
offered him a contract as a screenwriter, Gene accepted, but Groucho called
up the studio and declined on Gene's behalf. When Gene asked him why,
Groucho answered, "You belong in school. Get out of here and go to college."
So Gene left Hollywood for the university.

I said, "Will you go back? I mean, to Hollywood?"

"If the time comes."

At Norah's table—a beautiful Provençal dinner—Gene and I found that
only the week before, at a poetry reading given by W. H. Auden, we had both
sat in the front row and both nearly fallen asleep (as had, I'm afraid, a tipsy Mr.
Auden). As we talked, we discovered that for many years, our paths had
crossed and recrossed, as if fate had been taking practice swings.

Cooking in love is not like cooking under any other circumstances. Cooking in an apartment you could put in your eye makes cooking in love the more delicate. A few days later, on our third date (Gene had begun to propose on our second date, a picnic, but I asked him to wait), I made him spaghetti in his apartment. It was one room big enough for a bed, a desk, a phonograph, and a gas heater. Up three steps was a closet converted to an alcove with a two-burner hotplate on the left and a refrigerator on the right. Beyond that was the bathroom.

I suppose I've never cooked anything I wanted so much to be sublime nor ended up laughing so much in the making as that spaghetti. I chopped the onions, carrots, celery, parsley, and garlic on a plate on my lap sitting on the bed—the only free surface was a corner of Gene's desk, which is where he usually ate, but I was afraid of scattering onions and carrots through his papers. Then I simmered the ground beef, vegetables, and tomatoes on one burner of the hotplate, brought the pasta water to a boil on the other burner, and sautéed mushrooms for the sauce on top of the heater (it was February, thank heaven). When the pasta was ready, Gene drained the pot in the tub while I grated Parmesan into a bowl in the sink. I'd already tossed lettuce with olive oil and vinegar, and dinner was served. Gene meanwhile had taken his typewriter and papers off his desk and set two places for dinner. Which was marvelous. Except he kept staring at me.

I said to him finally, "Now you can ask me."

"Ask you what?"

"To marry you!"

He did and I accepted. We went upstairs to tell Norah. We rapped on the kitchen door and she opened it. "We're going to be married," Gene said.

She stared at us. "Um," she said, and closed the door. We stood there for a moment, then walked silently down the outside stairs to Gene's apartment. Five minutes later, there was a knock on the door. It was Norah, with a bottle of champagne. She had been too stunned to react.

In June, Norah and her boys joined M. F. and her girls in Provence and, as a wedding present, gave us her house for the summer. My parents were still abroad—Daddy was writing a movie in London and couldn't be home until August. We were all unhappy about their not being with us at our small wedding, but Gene and I couldn't bear to live a summer apart and in those days, in our world, the only way to live together was to be married. I took my last exam in the morning and married Gene in the afternoon. (I somehow got an A on the final in Masterpieces of Twentieth-Century Literature, few of which I'd read, since Gene and I spent most of every waking hour together.)

On our honeymoon in Carmel, I began to think about Norah's kitchen and what I would make in it when we got back. The first thing would be the frothy Ramos Gin Fizzes we drank at the big curved bar in Big Sur's Nepenthe—a glassed-in pavilion of redwood floating eight hundred feet above the sea designed by a pupil of Frank Lloyd Wright's. I've since served the fizzes many times as festive openers for Sunday breakfast parties.

Nepenthe's Ramos Fizz*
[*1 tall glass*]
Make just before serving.

½ cup crushed ice
1 teaspoon sugar
1 whole egg
1 tablespoon Sweet-and-Sour syrup (2 teaspoons lime or lemon juice and an additional 2 teaspoons sugar may be substituted)

½ tablespoon Grand Marnier
1½ ounces gin
2 to 3 ounces half-and-half

Whiz all ingredients in the blender until frothy. Pour into a 14-ounce glass. Sprinkle with nutmeg. Serve.

My very first kitchen, Norah's, was all wood, large and sunny, with built-in everything and windows opening onto copper-leaved red currant bushes. Feeling deliciously wifely, I took to baking bread. My first try surprised me. It worked! It was a brown soda bread that had the flavor and close-to-the-texture of yeast-risen bread, but involved none of the worry. My quick brown bread can be put together in the time it takes to heat the oven and is ready to slice an hour later.

But what is there about baking bread that makes one triumphant?

Quick Brown Bread
[*At least 12 slices*]
This keeps at least a week if well wrapped and refrigerated.

A little butter for the mold, softened
2 cups whole wheat flour
1 teaspoon baking soda
½ teaspoon salt
1 cup buttermilk or soured milk,† at room temperature
1 extra large egg, at room temperature

1 tablespoon light oil
1 tablespoon honey
Sweet additions (optional)
  1 cup chopped dates, plumped dark raisins or currants, or chopped toasted walnuts or pecans

---

*Ramos Gin Fizzes were invented by Henry C. Ramos in New Orleans around 1888—apparently the term "Ramos Gin Fizz" still belongs to a hotel there. That's why when Nepenthe's Holly Fassett generously sent me the recipe, she left the "Gin" out of the title.
†To sour sweet milk, put 1 tablespoon lemon juice or cider vinegar or white vinegar in the bottom of a 1-cup measure, then fill with milk (non-fat or low-fat is fine).

Heat the oven to 375 °F. Generously butter a 1-pound coffee can, an 8 ½ × 4 ½ × 2 ½-inch loaf pan, or other 4- to 5 ½-cup mold. In a large bowl, blend the flour, soda, and salt. Measure the milk in a 1-quart measuring pitcher, then add the egg, oil, and honey and beat until blended. Turn the wets and the fruit and/or nuts, if used, into the dries and stir just until mixed. Turn into the mold, smoothing the top flat. Gently rap on the counter to knock out any air bubbles.

Bake until a fine skewer thrust in the center comes out clean and the bottom, when rapped, sounds hollow, usually 35 minutes. Run a knife around the edges, gently bang the sides of the upside-down mold against your counter until the bread slides out—catch it! Cool completely on a rack before slicing thinly.

[*At high altitude:* Use only ⅔ teaspoon baking soda and bake at 400 °F.]

A heady summer passed. I had always wanted to live in New York when I was married, Gene was willing, so we flew to the big city to see what we could see. Back from Europe, Mother and Daddy were in New York to greet us and to renew the acquaintance of the young man who had become their only child's husband. The first thing my father did for his new son-in-law was make him a late afternoon lunch of mashed eggs. We were home free.

Gene and I found a small furnished railroad flat (the bathroom connected with the bedroom connected with the kitchen connected with the dining room connected with the living room which had a fireplace) on East 88th Street, a block from the Mayor's mansion at Gracie Square. Mother and Daddy warmed our house with two magnums of Mumm's and, of course, bread and salt. A friendly young couple across the hall invited us to dinner and told us that Craig Claiborne, an editor on *Gourmet* magazine, lived downstairs, and the poet Muriel Rukeyser lived above us. I went to the dime store and bought a bag of DIRT! shaking my head all the way, and potted half a dozen herbs in a tub on the fire escape. We were in business.

We took the Fifth Avenue bus to work, watching Central Park change in its seasons—Gene was writing copy at a marvelous advertising agency on Madison Avenue and I was thrilled to be a copywriter at Lord & Taylor. We often met for lunch at Sacher's on Madison Avenue (that chocolate/apricot torte still haunts me). Saturdays, we'd shop on First Avenue. Ours was the part of New York called Yorkville, traditionally a German neighborhood, so the quality of food available was serious and splendid. We made happy rounds of the German poulterer's, the German pork butcher's (a new world, shops that sold only one sort of meat), the German delicatessen, and the Italian greengrocer's, finishing up our marketing at the big Grand Union on 86th Street, picking up our laundry at the laundromat, then coming home, building a fire in the living room, and sipping cups of hot chocolate while we were propped on our elbows, lying before the hearth.

We passed a quiet winter, Gene working on his novel nights and weekends and I busily unraveling the mysteries of the kitchen. I began to create. My first real invention was a veal stew golden with saffron. I was pleased. Still am, having refined it over the years. For those occasions when I want to make something really luxe for my guests, it's this. The vegetables are classic, the veal delicate, the shapes and colors lovely, and the sauce—!

Try to find veal from calves raised in green meadows on milk straight from the cow without medication, hormones, or additives. That meat will be butter-rose rather than white for its healthier childhood.*

SAFFRON VEAL STEW
[*6 to 8 servings*]

As with any stew, all but the finishing touches may be put together the night or morning before serving.

2 tablespoons olive oil	*About eighteen ¹/₂-inch-thick unpeeled*
¹/₂ stick butter	*young carrots, cut on the bias in inch-*
1 large onion, in ¹/₂-inch pieces	*long pieces*
2 pounds best veal stew meat or boneless	*12 ounces inch-wide peeled fresh boiling*
shoulder, cut in cubes around 1 ¹/₂ inches	*onions*
8 (1 pound) fresh plum tomatoes, peeled,	*A big pot of water, boiling*
seeded,† and cut in ¹/₂-inch pieces; save	*12 ounces button mushrooms, stems cut flush*
the juice	*with caps (save stems for another day)*
3 cups excellent chicken broth	*3 tablespoons cornstarch*
¹/₂ cup excellent beef broth	*3 tablespoons dry vermouth*
¹/₂ teaspoon saffron‡	*About ¹/₂ teaspoon salt*
About 6 turns of the white pepper mill	*A bunch of parsley, chopped*
(¹/₂ teaspoon, medium grind)	
1 large garlic clove, stuck on a toothpick	

In a large top-of-the-stove-proof casserole or heavy skillet over medium heat, warm the olive oil and half the butter. Sauté the onion till softened, stirring frequently. Pat the meat dry and add to the onion. Sauté, turning the cubes frequently with a wooden spatula or spoon, just until all edges are sealed—do not brown. Heat the oven to 325°F.

Stir the tomatoes, their juice, the chicken and beef broths, saffron, pepper, and garlic into the veal. Bring to a simmer. If you've been using a skillet, turn the stew

---

*One source is Summerfield Farm, SR 4, Box 195A, Brightwood, Virginia 22715. You must buy several pounds, but even with the expense of sending *fresh* "veal for stew" to your door, the cost is still a little more than half what my mother pays (I can't buy veal, good, bad, or indifferent, within a hundred miles), and Summerfield's meat is incomparable.

†How to peel and seed, on page 259.

‡Measuring crocus stamens by the half-teaspoonful is tricky: pile them on the measuring spoon and lightly press them in.

into a warmed casserole. Cover with foil and the lid (or two sheets of foil tightly crimped around the rim, shiny sides down) and set on the bottom rack of the oven. Set the timer for 45 minutes.

Meanwhile, drop the carrots and onions into boiling water to cover, return to a boil over high heat, and boil uncovered 5 minutes; drain at once. When the timer rings, stir the carrots and onions into the stew. Cover again and bake until the veal is just tender and the vegetables are tender-crisp, another 25 to 30 minutes. Set the lid on askew and refrigerate for the day or the night.* Bring to room temperature about 2 hours before serving, and proceed.

In a wide heavy skillet over high heat, sauté the mushroom caps in ¼ stick of butter until lightly browned, stirring constantly. Add the mushrooms and juices to the stew. Drain the liquid from the stew into the skillet and set over high heat. Dissolve the cornstarch in the vermouth and whisk into the sauce. Whisk constantly until the sauce has thickened nicely and is a blither of bubbles. Taste for salt and stir the sauce back into the stew. Retrieve the garlic.

About 50 minutes before serving, heat the oven to 325°F. Set the covered casserole on the lowest rack of the oven and heat the stew, stirring once or twice, until bubbling around the edges, 35 to 40 minutes.

Sprinkle generously with chopped parsley and serve over rice or egg noodles.

When I learned that my husband loved barley, I created another modest invention, a barley salad for a picnic with friends in East Hampton. We went crabbing, chasing after small blue-green soft-shell crabs along the beach, then grilled and ate them, shells and all, dripping with lemon butter. A rare treat for Californians whose crabs are all hard-shelled.

Barley salad's chewy nutty texture, not-sweet taste, and muted colors make it excellent for difficult-to-accompany meat, fowl, and fish dishes. This is a large recipe because it is a good choice for a potluck supper or big buffet when you want to serve something special but it must be compatible with all sorts of other foods.

BARLEY SALAD
[*About 12 servings*]
With the exception of adding the tomatoes, this may be made a day or two before serving.

A handful (½ ounce) of dried mushrooms
3 ²/₃ cups excellent chicken broth
1 ⅓ cups excellent beef broth; more, if needed

Scant ¾ cup olive oil
1 large onion, finely chopped
1 large garlic clove, finely chopped
2 cups pearl barley
¼ teaspoon turmeric

*Notes on refrigerating hot food are on page xviii.

A *dash of cinnamon*

3 *tablespoons fresh lemon juice (1 juicy lemon)*

About 2 dozen turns of the black pepper mill (2 teaspoons, medium grind)

3 *medium-large fresh ripe tomatoes, peeled, seeded,* * *and chopped*

Perhaps a little salt

A bunch of parsley, chopped, or a garnish of watercress

Set the mushrooms to steep in some of the broth to cover before you prepare the other ingredients.

In a large heavy saucepan over medium-high heat, heat 3 tablespoons of the olive oil and sauté the onion until golden, stirring frequently, about 10 minutes. After 7 or 8 minutes, add the garlic.

Drain the mushroom-soaking broth into the saucepan, leaving any sediment behind. Cut the mushrooms into ½-inch pieces and add them to the saucepan. Stir in the barley, the rest of the chicken and beef broth, the turmeric, and the cinnamon. Bring to a simmer, set the lid on askew, turn the heat to low, and simmer gently until the barley is tender but still slightly chewy, 50 minutes to 1 hour, stirring frequently. Add more beef broth if it looks as though the barley's going to stick.

Remove from the heat and add ½ cup of the olive oil, the lemon juice, and the pepper, tossing with a fork to blend. Toss occasionally as the barley cools. Cover tightly and set in a cool place or the refrigerator.

Bring to room temperature. Just before serving, fold in the tomatoes and taste for salt—if the broth has been salted, it shouldn't need any. Turn into a serving bowl—glass is especially handsome. Sprinkle with chopped parsley or flourish with watercress, and serve.

Mother and Daddy had long since gone back to Los Angeles—my father was working on the screenplay of *Some Came Running*—when dear friends came to town and we decided to given them a dinner party. New Englanders, he had been Gene's professor of philosophy (as he had also been my mother's) and she was a Berkeley legend, amusing herself by saying to acquaintances, "Did I ever tell you that before I married Stevie I was a Hore?" We invited two other old friends, a girlfriend of Gene's from college days and her surgeon husband. And one new friend, Muriel Rukeyser—we had come to know and like her enormously. I thought of venturing to ask Craig Claiborne as her dinner partner, but he was out of town.

It was our first official dinner party and I looked through my wedding-present cookbooks for menu ideas. I found two dishes I thought perfect: lobster absinthe for the main course (which, of course, instantly became lobster Pernod since the only thing the League of Nations ever agreed upon was to outlaw absinthe) and for the dessert, *colettes*, thin chocolate shells filled with pastry cream.

The morning arrived. I went up to First Avenue to buy the wine. I chose

---

*How to peel and seed, page 259.

two fine slim bottles of Chablis, but then I remembered that I had to cook the lobsters in it—for six people, the recipe said to cover three lobsters in a large saucepan with cold dry white wine. The fish man had said that was crazy. He said for seven people, I needed seven of his most succulent small lobsters. So we ordered seven lobsters.

"I'd better have two more bottles of Chablis," I said to the liquor man.

When I got back to the apartment, I suddenly realized I didn't want to kill the lobsters in a saucepan of cold dry anything. But I got out our largest vessel, a wedding present of a soup pot that held two gallons. I put it on the stove and, remembering what the fish man had said when I ordered the lobsters, grabbed one lobster "behind the ears" and dropped him gingerly into the pot.

"My God, he barely fits!" And there were six to go.

My mind raced, ruling out suitably sized receptacles like the bathtub (couldn't light a fire under it), and the great tin tub full of herbs on the fire escape (it had drainage holes in the bottom). I had it. A garbage can! Ours was plastic.

Ah, but it was garbage day. The super had emptied all the cans and they were sitting outside everybody's door. The landlord's can downstairs was also plastic. Of course there was no can in front of Craig Claiborne's door. I ran up the stairs past our apartment, saw that our friends' across the hall was also plastic, raced up to the top floor and there, in front of Muriel Rukeyser's door, was the most beautiful galvanized tin garbage can I'd ever seen. And it was new! I grabbed it and ran tippytoe back downstairs.

We jammed Muriel's garbage can into the sink, gave it a triple-thorough scrubbing and set it on the stove.

I said, "You think she'll mind?"

"It's either that or she goes without dinner."

Catching each behind the ears, I put in the lobsters. I emptied the two bottles of Chablis over them. Their toes were barely moistened. "Cover them with cold dry white wine" indeed!

We poured in the three bottles we had planned for the table. The lobster on the bottom was now afloat. Desperately, reluctantly, I threw in Cellini's ring: the two magnums of Mumm's. The lobsters were settling down. All business now, I turned on the flame. The lobsters floated lazily in the lukewarm wine. I tried to remember who had met his end in a butt of malmsey.

All was in readiness. Except for one thing. The front door opened directly into the kitchen of our railroad apartment. By the time Muriel arrived, presumably she would have discovered her garbage can missing and it would be difficult, even for a bemused poetess, to walk into a kitchen and not notice the large new galvanized tin garbage can sitting on the stove (there was no room for it anywhere else).

So when the bell rang each time, Gene opened the door to greet guests and

I threw open my arms in a gesture of welcome, standing spread-eagled in my caftan in front of the can camouflaged with dish towels, taking up as much room as I possibly could, while Gene led the guests quickly into the front room. I intended to sprint upstairs with the can and put it back in front of Muriel's door the moment we had her safely seated with a drink, but I soon discovered it was going to take a lot of lemon juice to get the lobster smell out of the metal. Muriel was the last to arrive, saw nothing, and, escorted by Gene, sailed into the living room, where Gene tethered her to an armchair, gave her a drink, and handed her over to our friends. From the kitchen, I heard the happy sounds of conversation and laughter. I told myself it was going to be all right.

The lobster was delicious. My husband poured the wine, which he'd had to dash out and buy after the lobster debacle. He was a handsome host. And helpful. He cleared away all the empty plates—and they were empty!—from the living room, had taken in coffee and everyone was chatting amiably when I swept in with the tray of *colettes*, caught my heel on the edge of the dun-colored carpet and went sprawling. The *colettes* shot forward off the tray and plopped face down on the fuzzy carpet. I fled to the kitchen.

Gene came after me. "Ruined!" I cried into Muriel's garbage can as I scrubbed away.

"Not at all," he said. The guests had dived after the *colettes*, skimmed off the dun-colored fuzz and wolfed them down. They were asking for me. I went back into the front room. Gene followed a few moments later.

Around eleven-thirty, Muriel rose to leave. I leaped to my feet, remembering. Gene caught my eye, shot a glance at the ceiling, and smiled.

"Thank you, my dear," she said at the door.

"Thank *you*, Muriel," I answered. "For . . . everything."

We stayed in New York a glorious year. When I learned that I was pregnant, Gene told me he was taking me back to Berkeley so that the child would be a fifth-generation Californian, and that Norah had already found us a house around the corner from her on Panoramic. I burst into tears.

The turn-of-the-century white frame house had, as the name of the road declared, a view of the bay from Marin County across the straits to San Francisco and on down the peninsula. My kitchen window gave onto a forest of cedars next door and on the slope in the back was a fine old garden waiting to be untangled. Guess who found she adored gardening, having learned more than she realized from her mother.

After a merry Christmas with Alice Vinegar and both sets of parents (that was the Christmas the Stuart ladies' hard sauce was created), mid-January our Theseus, David Oxley, was born. Those were pristine days, in a Berkeley as serene as the chimes from the Campanile below that caroled out the hour.

M. F. was popping in and out of Berkeley then, and occasionally she would come by on her way to Norah's with extraordinary treats. I especially remember enormous artichokes stuffed with olive-scented breadcrumbs, perhaps Parmesan, perhaps anchovies, certainly lots of parsley and garlic. And there were small brown glazed Provençal pots, rounded across the top with *pâtés* of bay shrimp, tiny curls of coral suspended in cayenned sweet butter, oh my. And once there was the most mysterious dark confection of whole figs that had simmered for days and days in an *agrodolce* of sugar and red wine vinegar. More than thoughtful remembrances, I had the sense that these were meant to be little pricks for my cooking conscience.

Gastronomically speaking, what Berkeley was to us then was the Co-op. A non-profit cooperative supermarket, it was run by an avant-garde health-conscious membership, and the quality of food in the market was excellent. Berkeley was a glorious melting pot. The produce section provided all the usual fruits and vegetables as well as most every unusual plant known to Oriental, Mexican, southern black, and native American cuisines. The legumes section stocked mung beans, and in the grains section were the first millet and soy flour I'd seen. The meat counter offered pig's ears and calf's stomachs and all the cuts from nearly any beast and sea creature that was conventionally cooked—and some not so conventionally. The atmosphere and approach, the sensibilities and openmindedness of the Co-op almost from the beginning of my serious cooking life, instilled in me my sense of freedom experimenting with cuisines and my habit of using the freshest and best-quality ingredients in their seasons.

Fresh, for example, as in ginger. The Co-op was the first market I'd seen outside Chinatown that stocked fresh ginger. The knobby look of the rhizomes was intriguing but I hadn't the vaguest idea what to do with them. Then one day I thought to replace ground ginger with grated fresh in our favorite ginger cake. The cake has become perhaps the most valued in my repertory. It's easy and foolproof and can be handed round in not much more than three-quarters of an hour after I've thought to make it.* Once I even got the cake into the oven *during* a party, causing a friend who happened into the kitchen to stare, saying, "Sylvia, you're making a cake *now?*" I serve my ginger cake warm or at room temperature with only a drift of confectioner's sugar and a flower on top—but there are times when a plop of whipped cream and just a few slivers of candied ginger are lovely. (Past that, toppings such as ice cream or fruit sauces seem to me to distract from the cake's fineness.)

---

*Knobs of peeled ginger covered with dry sherry, madeira, or rice wine keep succulent six months in the refrigerator. Good to have for spur-of-the-moment cakes, curries, stir-fries, *tagines*, and other gingery treats.

These days I also flavor the cake with a sprinkling of *quatre épices*, a French conceit of finely ground white pepper, nutmeg, ginger or cinnamon, and cloves.* M. F. has been stirring up batches and packing off jars of *quatre épices* as Christmas remembrances for years. In France, the mix is used in sausages, terrines, *pâtés*, marinades, sauces, and dried bean and potato dishes. I use it mostly in sweets—a few nights ago in the streusel over apple crisp, for example. To ginger cake, it adds peppery depth.

But why has this cake an almost mystical quality? I invariably find myself baking it to celebrate significant occasions in my life. I think it is the deep-down comfort of the dark sweeteners and knowing instinctively that ginger's heat has had a pull on cultures universally. Ancient Greeks, among others, valued ginger for its restorative properties. Chinese tacked ginger over doorways of houses of the newborn to absorb any harmful qualities of guests. And one traveled Frenchman assured his readers that ginger "confers on those who use it absolute power over any tigers they may happen to meet . . ."†

FRESH GINGER CAKE
[*At least 8 servings*]
At its best fresh, this cake keeps in the refrigerator until eaten, but do warm it up if you can before serving.

1 stick butter, plus a little softened for the mold	1 ½ cups all-purpose flour, plus a little more for the pan
½ cup water, cool	1 teaspoon baking soda
½ cup (firmly packed) light brown sugar	1 teaspoon quatre épices‖
¼ cup light molasses	¼ teaspoon salt
¼ cup dark corn syrup	Sifted confectioner's sugar for the top and
1 extra large egg	perhaps a fresh flower
Fresh unpeeled‡ ginger the size of an egg, grated medium-fine§	

*As with curry powder, every concocter has his/her favorite formula. Traditional proportions by weight are—and these numbers are queer but faithful: 25 parts white pepper, 7 parts nutmeg, 6 parts ginger, and 2 parts cloves. A blend I have from France contains white pepper, cinnamon, nutmeg, and cloves, in *that* order. I prefer ginger to cinnamon in the mix—it's warmer and drier.
†Waverly Root's *Food*.
‡If the rhizome is fresh and firm, the skin will be thin and there's no need to remove it—just trim any scarred ends. If the rhizome has shriveled and the skin thickened, use more ginger to make up for its weakened strength, and peel it.
§If you are hungry for ginger cake but haven't any rhizomes, 2 tablespoons of the spice approximates the gingeriness here. Add with the dry ingredients.
‖Lacking the blend, use a well-rounded ½ teaspoon white pepper, a scant ¼ teaspoon nutmeg, a scanter ¼ teaspoon ginger or cinnamon, and a good pinch of cloves, all finely ground.

Choose any mold with a 6- to 8-cup capacity (I use an 8-inch square). Brush with butter and dust with flour. Heat the oven to 350°F.

Melt the butter in the water either in a largish saucepan over medium heat or in a glass mixing bowl in the microwave. Do not let the water boil (and thus evaporate).

To the butter/water, whisk in the brown sugar, molasses, corn syrup, and then the egg. Whisk in the ginger, discarding any long strings the whisk brings up. Add the flour, baking soda, *quatre épices*, and salt. Whisk a minute or two until lumps dissolve. Pour into the pan. Rap gently on the counter to knock out any air bubbles.

Bake until a fine skewer thrust in the center comes out clean and the top, when tapped, springs back—about 35 minutes for a square (or ring or round), less for a shallower rectangle, more for a deeper loaf. Gently turn out onto a doilied dish to serve warm or onto a rack to cool. Finish with sifted confectioner's sugar and a posy.

[*At high altitude:* Use ½ teaspoon baking soda and bake at 375°F.]

A double recipe may be handsomely baked in a 10-inch square pan at 375°F for 35 to 40 minutes.

While I took care of David and wrote magazine articles about cookery, Gene commuted to an advertising agency in San Francisco and gave his nights and weekends to writing. He wanted to take a year off to finish his novel. We decided that we'd spend the year in Europe, where our savings would go furthest. To manage this, we resolved to live on half our income. That meant I really had to cook on the cheap.

So we were very big on soup. I went through a borsch period: my Aunt Edith's borsch with beef shanks, my mother-in-law Rose's borsch with sweet vegetables, and an unknown Russian cook's with fish. Spenger's Fish Grotto was just at the bottom of University Avenue—still is—and I could buy beautiful fish for a song. This was our favorite, inspired by a recipe I found in an old Russian cookbook in the UC library. The broth is of surpassing delicacy, the preparation is easy, and one's bowl is a feast to the eye. Every element is separate and each color bright—the black jewel of caviar (added when the purse got plumper and caviar got cheaper) set in white sour cream is especially handsome—until you stir, when the soup turns Russian pink.

RYBNYI BORSCH*
Russian fish soup
[*6 to 8 servings*]
The broth, potatoes, beets, greens, scallions, and fish may all be prepared in advance. Wrap everything well and refrigerate while it waits to be put together.

Rib-nyee borsh.

THE BROTH*

1 ½ pounds lean white-fleshed chowder fish†
4 whole scallions, chopped
2 unpeeled carrots, chopped
1 leafy celery stalk, chopped
6 parsley stalks
½ tablespoon black peppercorns

½ bay leaf
10 cups water, cold
½ cup fresh lemon juice (2 large juicy
*   lemons)*
About 1 ½ teaspoons salt
About 12 turns of the white pepper mill
*   (1 teaspoon, medium grind)*

In your soup pot over medium heat, bring the fish, scallions, carrots, celery, parsley, peppercorns, bay, and water to a boil. Set the lid on askew and boil gently 30 minutes. Strain, discarding the solids. To the broth, add the lemon juice, then salt and white pepper to taste. Cover loosely and refrigerate, if made in advance.‡

THE BORSCH

12 small unpeeled boiling potatoes
6 medium-sized beets
About 20 of the tenderest leaves from the
*   beets§ in thin strips*
6 whole young scallions, in thin rings
A handful of fresh chopped dill leaves, or
*   2 tablespoons dried dill weed*
1 pint sour cream
A 2-ounce jar of whitefish or other modest
*   black caviar (optional)*

The broth
1 stick butter, preferably unsalted; add
*   ¼ stick more if reheating the potatoes*
*   and beets*
2 pounds lean succulent white fish; angler is
*   my choice,‖ in 1 ½-inch dice*
About 12 turns of the white pepper mill
*   (1 teaspoon, medium grind)*

I recommend working in rubber gloves to handle the beets, or else you'll have pink palms for a couple of days.

Separately boil the potatoes and beets until tender.# Cut the peeled beets in matchsticks. Keep both warm—or refrigerate, and when ready to serve, reheat them gently, separately, in butter in covered skillets.

Set the greens, scallions, dill, sour cream, and caviar in separate serving bowls near your place at the table. Over medium heat, bring the broth to a simmer. Heat a soup tureen or serving bowl and bowls for the potatoes and beets.

In a large heavy skillet over medium heat, melt 1 stick of butter and stew the fish until opaque, stirring gently and shaking the pan frequently—a matter of minutes. Stir the fish and buttery juices into the broth. Turn the soup into the tureen and bring to the table with the potatoes and beets in their bowls.

*The recipe makes 10 cups.
†Buy the least expensive fish such as cod, haddock, or whiting.
‡About refrigerating hot foods, page xviii.
§Another time, use tender leaves of sorrel or spinach or chard.
‖Other good choices are on pages 241–242, under Burrida.
#20 to 25 minutes' boiling for the potatoes; cook the beets as on page 237.

To serve, place a potato or two in each person's bowl (preferably, a wide shallow soup bowl), a heap of beets beside the potato, next a portion of fish, then between the fish and the potatoes, a heap of raw greens (they will cook *à point* in the hot broth). Lightly sprinkle with scallions, gently add a couple of ladlefuls of broth, then a dollop of sour cream in the center, a dot of caviar in the sour cream, and then a flick of dill over all.

A note on the *borsch* recipe reminds me that for dessert, from the same book, I made *Vozdushni pirog*,* a dramatic pouf of egg whites and preserves. In Russia, berry, currant, cherry, apricot, apple, quince, or plum jam are favorite flavors. Traditionally, the soufflé is served with cream, but Russians, when they were Francophiles, were fond of *sabayon*, so I made that pale cloud of a sauce with the leftover yolks. (Decent California sherry, Madeira, and port have never been expensive.) For something Italo-Russian, I used Marsala and spooned *zabaglione* over the pouf. Same difference. If you prefer a teetotaler's sauce, use milk in place of spirits, and add the finely shredded zest of half a lemon.

Vozdushni pirog is especially nice baked in individual dishes because it puffs up remarkably, but then gives way at the touch of a spoon. Sugar lining the dish caramelizes the outside of the soufflé, part of its appeal.

VOZDUSHNI PIROG
Russian preserves soufflé
{5 to 6 servings}
Last minute, but made in a trice.

Butter for the dishes, softened
About ¼ cup sugar, depending on the tartness of the jam, plus more for the dishes
Generous ½ cup raspberry (or other) preserves

6 extra large egg whites, at room temperature
Sabayon/Zabaglione (optional; recipe follows)

Heat the oven to 400°F. Set the rack on the lowest rung. Butter and sugar 6 deep ovenproof bowls with 1¾ cups capacity; or a soufflé sort of dish with a 10-cup capacity; or a 7- to 8-cup dish with a 2-inch foil collar.† Reserve about 1 tablespoon of the sugar and stir the rest into the preserves in a small bowl. In a large non-plastic bowl, beat the whites until they hold soft peaks. With a rubber spatula, stir and

*Voz-*dush*-ni. Literally, Air Cake.
†Except you can't remove the collar before serving as you can do with a standard soufflé.

fold the preserves evenly into the whites. Divide among the bowls or turn into one big dish, making a swirl in the top. Sprinkle with the reserved sugar.

Bake until taller than you'd imagined it could be and nicely caramelized, about 15 minutes, then rush to the table. (Remove the collar gingerly.) Serve with or without a delicate sauce.

SABAYON/ZABAIÒNE
A frothy spirited custard
[*5 to 6 servings*]
Begin about 8 minutes before serving.

6 extra large egg yolks
6 tablespoons sugar

³/₄ cup dry sherry, Madeira, port, or Marsala*

In the 2-quart top of a double boiler or a stainless steel bowl, beat the yolks and sugar together with a mixer at medium speed or a rotary beater until pale and creamy. Blend in the spirits.

If using a double boiler, set the top over, but not touching, hot water on *low* heat. For my part, I use a stainless bowl and perch it on top of a 2-quart saucepan with 2 inches of hot water beneath it and set it on almost-high heat.

With a portable mixer on low speed or a rotary beater (if you're dressed up, wear an apron—it spatters), beat until light and pale as buttered air and the beaters make deep tracks in the sauce. Immediately remove from the heat and turn into a pretty bowl—or goblets, if a dessert on its own—and serve.

Back to soup. Also from Spenger's, I got wonderful shark to make an elegant soup (shrimp used to be cheaper than it is), the recipe for which came from a Chinese friend in San Francisco. The soup has the look of silk brocade.

SHANGHAI SHARK SOUP
[*4 servings*]
The ingredients may be prepared an hour or two in advance.

¼ cup dried mushrooms (Chinese, if you have them)
12 ounces raw unshelled medium shrimps
A good sprinkling of salt
3 ounces raw boneless chicken breast, skinned

2 whole scallions, bulbs cut in fine strips, stalks cut in thin rings
6 tender radishes, sliced into paper-thin rounds; discard the opaque top and bottom cuts

---

*Or beat this much dry champagne or white wine into the yolks and fold in a drizzle of kirsch or maraschino just before serving.

1 teaspoon sesame oil*
3 ounces cellophane noodles (also called bean
threads and saifun)
5 ½ cups excellent chicken broth
2 tablespoons tamari or other soy sauce

Silver-dollar-sized slice of fresh ginger,
finely shredded
8 ounces shark steaks, cut in ½-inch cubes
(angler or another moist fish may be
substituted†)

One to two hours before serving, plump the mushrooms by soaking in cold water (if in a hurry, 15 minutes in hot water will do). In a wide skillet,‡ cover the shrimps with cold water, add the salt, and set uncovered over medium-high heat. The moment the shrimps turn pink, remove from the heat and drain; cool until you can shell and devein them.§

Working lengthwise with the grain, cut the chicken into very thin slices, then cut the slices into fine strips. Turn the scallion rings and the radishes into small bowls for the table. Mix the sesame oil into the scallion strips. Drain the mushrooms (save the liquor for another dish) and slice them also into very fine strips. Follow directions on the noodle package for soaking, or cover with boiling water and let stand until thoroughly transparent, 5 to 10 minutes.

Cover all the above ingredients with plastic film and refrigerate.

Fifteen or twenty minutes before serving, set a big pot of unsalted water over high heat to boil for the noodles. In another largish pot over high heat, bring the chicken broth to a simmer—and call your guests to the table. If not serving from the pot, heat a soup tureen or bowl; also heat a bowl for the noodles. Into the broth, stir the *tamari*, ginger, scallions, and soaked mushrooms, then, gently, the shark, chicken, and shrimps. Set the timer for 5 minutes and let the soup compose itself; it shouldn't simmer, so adjust the heat accordingly. At the same time, boil the noodles uncovered 4 minutes, then drain, rinse with cold water, and turn into a serving bowl.

Serve in flat soup bowls thus: a portion of noodles, soup ladled over, then a light wafting of scallion rings and radish moons. Green tea is lovely with this.

We soon learned we were not alone in loving soup. Most of our friends were professors with modest means and dinners for one another were often as not a pot of great soup and a loaf of homemade bread. Once, when I was planning to make lentil soup for company, the Co-op had a special on mushrooms, so I put this together. Served with Peppery Peasant Bread, page 164, poets and kings could not wish for more.

---

*Available from an oriental market or health food store. A bottle keeps a year in the refrigerator.

†More suggestions for soup fish are on page 242, under Burrida.

‡Things simmered in a wide shallow skillet cook more rapidly and more evenly than in the traditional saucepan—the more surface, the less crowding.

§Shelling and deveining notes, pages 257–258. Save the shells for shrimp butter, page 257.

SUPERB LENTIL AND MUSHROOM SOUP*
[8 servings]

Like all soups composed of many flavors, this improves on keeping.

1 pound lentils, well-rinsed and carefully
  picked over for small stones
3 medium-large fresh tomatoes, coarsely
  chopped
1 large unpeeled carrot, chopped medium-
  fine
1 whole large fat leek, rinsed,† or if leeks
  aren't in season, 6 whole scallions; in
  thin rounds
A handful of celery leaves, chopped
A big handful of fresh summer savory,
  marjoram, or sweet basil leaves,
  chopped, or 3 tablespoons dried

2 large garlic cloves, finely chopped
One 46-ounce can of tomato juice
Water to fill the tomato juice can,
  plus a splash
2 tablespoons fresh lemon juice
2 dozen turns of the black pepper mill
  (2 teaspoons, medium grind)
1 pound mushrooms, thinly sliced
8 large plump sausages: Polish, Italian,
  Mexican, Jewish, or . . . (optional)
A handful of chopped parsley
About 1 ½ pints plain yogurt

In your soup pot, mix lentils, tomatoes, carrot, leek, celery leaves, herbs, garlic, tomato juice, water to fill the juice can, lemon juice, and pepper. Over medium heat, bring to a simmer, stirring occasionally. Set the lid on askew, turn heat to lowest, and simmer 1 hour, stirring occasionally.

In a heavy (preferably cast iron) dry skillet over medium-high heat, sauté the mushrooms until browned, stirring frequently (you won't need any fat). Blend them into the soup. Rinse out the skillet with a splash of water and add this essence to the pot. Simmer until the lentils are cooked, another 15 minutes, although another hour's simmering won't hurt.

If you're adding the sausages, cook them separately in simmering water to cover until plump and hot, then cut into half-inch rounds and turn into a hot serving bowl.

At table, ladle the soup into large bowls (preferably shallow). If you're using them, arrange rounds of hot sausage in a ring on top. Dust the bowl with parsley and add a plop of yogurt—its cool creamy sourness gives a splendid contrast to the hot sweet vegetables.

I loved learning new ways with vegetables. A neighbor, a good friend, often sautéed a late lunch of potatoes with rosemary and garlic for the two of us while our small sons flailed away in the sand pile. Ever since, I've made

---

*Rich in protein, fiber, vitamins, and minerals, without the sausage, this is a no-meat, no-fat, no-salt soup.
†How-to, page 249.

DIANA'S ROSEMARY AND GARLIC POTATOES
[2 large servings]

¼ cup olive oil
4 medium-large peeled Russet potatoes, in
1-inch dice
6 large garlic cloves, finely chopped

Leaves from six 4-inch sprigs of fresh
rosemary, or 3 tablespoons dried
About ½ teaspoon salt
About 6 turns of the black pepper mill
(½ teaspoon, medium grind)

In a large heavy skillet over low heat, heat the olive oil and add the potatoes. Stir with a wooden spatula or spoon until the pieces are coated with oil, then cover and sauté a long 15 minutes, shaking the skillet and stirring the potatoes frequently so they won't stick. Stir in the garlic and rosemary, cover again, and sauté until the potatoes are tender and some are beginning to brown, about 15 minutes more. Season with salt and pepper and serve.

Dear Norah taught me a great deal about cooking vegetables. She has a special way with them, and as we sat at the counter of her open kitchen sipping wine before dinner, I loved watching her shake mushrooms over the heat or frizzle fine shreds of zucchini in her wok. One evening, Norah braised fennel with roast lamb. I had eaten raw fennel in Italy but never imagined it could be cooked—and would be gorgeous.

NORAH'S BRAISED FENNEL
[For each serving]
The fennel may be prepared for braising in advance.

Allow one medium-sized bunch of fennel. Cut off the individual top branches close to where they join the bulb and trim the root end. Each serving should be 2 to 2½ inches in diameter—cut large bulbs in quarters lengthwise.

In a heavy skillet, cover the fennel with good rich broth; its nature depends upon what the vegetable will accompany—as a first course on its own, use beef broth. Simmer until tender-crisp when pierced with a fine skewer, usually about 10 minutes. Drain. This may be done in advance.

The last half-hour of roasting your lamb or chicken, set the fennel beside it and let braise, occasionally turning the pieces with tongs so they are coated with juices; they will glaze handsomely. Serve hot.

Norah also dresses braised fennel with *vinaigrette**—it might be served hot or at room temperature—a delicious first course.

---

*For 2 or 3 servings, 3 tablespoons oil blended with 1 tablespoon vinegar, plus a little salt and pepper to taste.

Braised celery hearts are also excellent as an accompaniment or first course when you're roasting poultry or meat. Celery hearts seem to have an air of another age about them. This and the following elegant vegetables are from J.-B. Reboul's classic, *La cuisinière Provençale*—which both M. F. and Norah independently gave me when I became a bride.

CÉLERIS AU JUS
Braised celery hearts
[4 servings]

The celery may be prepared for braising in advance, but the braising is last-minute. You don't want grey celery.

*4 tender young celery hearts (a bunch about
   2 ½ inches in diameter)**
About 4 quarts water, boiling
1 ½ tablespoons salt, and perhaps more for
   the sauce
3 strips of lean bacon
½ onion, thinly sliced
1 unpeeled carrot, thinly sliced
1 bay leaf*

*2 garlic cloves, coarsely chopped
6 turns of the white pepper mill
   (½ teaspoon, medium grind)
¾ cup dry white wine
About ¾ cup lean juices of what you're
   roasting†
A scant 1 tablespoon butter, preferably
   unsalted, softened
2 teaspoons flour
⅛ teaspoon Marmite,‡ if you have some*

Cut the celery hearts about 6 inches long, trim the root ends, remove any tough leaves, and flush the stalks under cold running water to remove any sand. Over highest heat, bring a big pot of water to the boil. Add the salt and the celery, return to a boil, and boil uncovered 10 minutes. Drain at once and pat dry. This may be done in advance.

About 20 minutes before serving, heat a serving dish. Then in the bottom of a heavy skillet just large enough to accommodate the celery, arrange the bacon, onion, carrot, bay, and garlic. Lay the celery on top and sprinkle with pepper. Cover and cook over medium heat until the onion and carrot begin to color and wilt, about 5 minutes. Add the wine and ¼ cup of the roasting juices, cover again, and cook until the celery is tender but still a bit crisp, 4 to 5 minutes more. Lift out the hearts onto the platter and keep warm. Meanwhile, blend the butter and flour together (*beurre manié*).

Strain the skillet's broth into a smaller skillet (save the bacon and vegetables for

---

*You can remove stalks of larger bunches to get down to the tender hearts.
†You can also braise the celery using excellent chicken or beef broth, depending on your menu.
‡M. Reboul calls for a *coulis*—a thickened sauce based on one of those complex glazes (veal, beef, ham, onion, carrot, tomato, white wine, garlic, thyme, and bay) taken for granted in grand French kitchens. There are no substitutes, but Marmite will give the sauce a certain depth. Marmite is an intensely flavored concentrated natural seasoning of yeast extract, salt, carrots, onions, and spices. It is also intensely colored, rather like melted chocolate. Marmite is made by Bovril in Canada, comes in a jar, and keeps forever.

Fido). Whisk in the *beurre manié* and when smooth, the Marmite, if you have it. Whisk over medium heat until the sauce thickens, adding more roasting juices until the sauce is the consistency you like. Let simmer 2 to 3 minutes, taste for salt, then spoon over the celery and serve.

And this is how I came to love turnips, teeny ones, in particular. When you see them in the market in spring, creamy mauve buds in leafy branches, remember this dish. They are particularly suited to roast chicken and pork.

Browning vegetables in lard or goose fat is very country French.

NAVETS AU JUS
Braised young turnips
{ *3 to 4 servings* }
Using leftover roasting juices or good broth, you can prepare this dish several hours in advance.

About 4 quarts water, boiling	*A few turns of the white pepper mill*
1 1/2 tablespoons salt	*(1/4 teaspoon, medium grind)*
*12 small turnips, peeled and quartered**	*A pinch of nutmeg*
1/4 cup (2 ounces) good lard†	*About 1 cup lean roasting juices,‡ cooled*
A sprinkling of sugar	*2 teaspoons flour*

Add the salt to the water boiling in a big pot over high heat. Drop in the turnips, cover the pot, then uncover the moment the water returns to a boil, about 2 minutes. Drain at once and pat dry. Meanwhile melt the lard in a large heavy skillet over medium-high heat. Add the turnips and sprinkle with sugar, pepper, and nutmeg. Sauté, turning almost constantly, until they are nicely golden.

Meanwhile, add a little of the roasting juices to the flour in a cup and stir until smooth. Turn the heat to medium and add remaining roasting juices to the skillet just to cover the turnips. Blend in the flour mixture. Whisk until the sauce thickens and bubbles, then cover the skillet and let the turnips finish cooking. Shake the skillet and stir from time to time. Test the turnips with a thin skewer—they should be tender in no more than 13 to 15 minutes. The sauce will have cooked to an essence. Serve at once or cover loosely and refrigerate, warming in a *bain marie*§ before serving.

Once, in junior high school, I was ceremoniously invited to a new friend's house for lunch. I couldn't wait to see what we'd eat. The poor girl's grandmother gave us creamed carrots and canned spaghetti. I've shuddered at the mere thought of creamed carrots ever since, until this recipe whispered *try me*

---

*The smaller the better. If they are walnut size, halve them only.
†Or goose fat, should you have some from the goose in aspic, page 62.
‡Or use excellent chicken, beef, or vegetable broth and 1/8 teaspoon Marmite, if you have it.
§As described on page 237.

from M. Reboul's page. I did. I have finally exorcized Mrs. Bixby's carrots from my mind.

Especially for spring and for those who grow their own Baby-Fingers, Sukos, and Planets.

CAROTTES À LA CRÈME
Baby carrots in a creamy sauce
[*3 to 4 servings*]
The dish may be put together a few hours in advance then warmed up in a *bain marie.* *

A good handful of unpeeled tiny new† carrots per serving (about 1 pound all together), topped and tailed
4 quarts water, boiling, plus ⅓ cup for the pan, cool
1½ tablespoons salt, plus a pinch for the pan

3 turns of the white pepper mill (a good pinch)
A pinch of nutmeg
¼ stick unsalted butter, plus a little more for the top, melted (optional)

For the béchamel sauce
Generous 1 tablespoon unsalted butter
Generous 1 tablespoon flour
½ cup milk, cold
2 tablespoons half-and-half or heavy cream

If the carrots are larger than the tip of your little finger, pare them to that size. Add the salt to the water boiling in a big pot over highest heat. Drop in the carrots, cover the pot, then uncover the moment the water returns to a boil, about 5 minutes. Drain at once and turn the carrots into a medium-sized heavy skillet with ⅓ cup water and a pinch each of salt, white pepper, and nutmeg. Cover and simmer over medium-high heat until most of the water has evaporated, 5 minutes at most. The carrots should be tender crisp.

Meanwhile, make the *béchamel*: In a small heavy saucepan over low heat, melt the butter, whisk in the flour, and cook a couple of minutes, whisking occasionally so the *roux* won't color. Blend in the milk, raise the heat to medium and whisk until thickened, then enrich with the half-and-half or cream.

Turn the carrots into the sauce and stew gently a few minutes before serving. If you're going to keep the carrots any length of time, spoon melted butter over the top so a skin won't form.

Such innocent days. Everything was new. A friend came to dinner, bringing a jar of plum chutney. *Plum* chutney? How extraordinary! I'd always thought

---

*As described on page 237.
†Or cut off the tips—½-inch-wide maximum—of larger carrots to make instant babies.

chutney was the exclusive domain of Major Grey and mangos. Her plum chutney was marvelous. And so I went on a binge of trying all sorts of fruits in all sorts of chutneys, everything from wincingly tart lemon to searingly hot ginger to something of black figs from India that couldn't be eaten for three months. Presently, second only to a certain tomato chutney whose creator will not divulge her recipe, I consider this of pears the best.

Don't pull out the chutney only on curry nights. Once its sweet tang has lifted roast lamb and pork, you'll never want them without it.

A FINE PEAR CHUTNEY
[Makes five 1-pint jars]

Vinegar and sugar preserve this. I have some five years old that is even better now than when it was new. But once a jar has been opened, it must be refrigerated—and it can keep there another five years! Be sure all your spices are spanking fresh.

2 1/2 cups cider vinegar

4 2/3 cups (2 pounds) dark brown sugar

The juice and zest of 6 oranges, the zest in long fine shreds (from a zester)

About 3 tablespoons ground coriander

2 tablespoons mustard seeds

4 cinnamon sticks, broken into 1-inch pieces

One 3-inch dried red chili, including seeds, crumbled in

1/2 teaspoon ground cloves

1/2 teaspoon salt

4 pounds underripe* flavorful pears

1 pound ripe tomatoes, peeled, seeded,† and chopped

A heaping 2 cups (12 ounces) dark raisins

A heaping 2 cups (12 ounces) golden raisins

1 large onion, very finely chopped

A piece of fresh ginger the size of a large egg (2 ounces), unpeeled and finely shredded

4 large garlic cloves, finely chopped

1 cup frozen concentrated apple juice, preferably "natural style"

1 cup water, cool

In your largest pot (and the wider the base, the more evenly the chutney will simmer), blend the vinegar, sugar, orange juice and zest, 2 tablespoons of the ground coriander, the mustard seeds, cinnamon sticks, chili, cloves, and salt. Peel, core, and cut the pears in 1/2-inch slices straight into the pot, stirring them to coat them with the syrup.‡ Add the tomatoes, dark and golden raisins, the onion, ginger, and garlic. Stir to blend thoroughly and set over high heat. When the pot simmers, turn the heat to lowest and simmer gently, uncovered, stirring every 10 minutes and ending by pushing the pears beneath the syrup.

After an hour and a half or so, blend in the concentrated apple juice and the

---

*Were they ripe, they'd end in a moosh, and one of the appeals of this chutney is its pieces of pear.

†Tomato notes are on page 259.

‡The vinegar will keep them from turning brown.

water. Simmer until the chutney is thick, dark, and syrupy and the pears are translucent, another hour and a half. Refresh the coriander by adding another tablespoon, if that's your taste (it's mine). Pack, seal, and store the chutney.*

Another of my pleasures was that I had again set my hand to making bread
(Berkeley seems to be a place where one is moved to bake bread), this time
with increasing success. The vagaries of baking with yeast were still unfolding themselves to me. Here is a loaf of which I'm proud, one of my first free
flights. The seasoning is pungent, the crumb tender, the crust crunchy, and
it slices ever so thinly.

PEPPERY PEASANT BREAD
[*At least 16 slices*]
The bread makes fine toast and keeps at least a week.

2 rounded teaspoons (1 package) active dry yeast	Rounded 1 tablespoon fennel or caraway seeds
2 cups milk, warm (non-fat or low-fat is fine)	1 tablespoon fresh chopped dill leaves, or 1 teaspoon dried dill weed
2 teaspoons salt	2 teaspoons freshly ground black pepper
1½ tablespoons olive oil, plus more for the bowl and loaf	⅛ teaspoon nutmeg
	⅛ teaspoon ginger
2⅓ cups unbleached flour, plus more for the board, if kneading by hand	1½ cups rye meal (preferable) or rye flour
⅔ cup whole wheat flour	Cornmeal for the baking sheet

Detailed instructions for making bread are on pages 239–241. In addition to the
baking sheet, you'll also need a single-edged razor blade or sharp knife and a spray
bottle.

In a mixing bowl, stir the yeast into the milk and let proof until dissolved, about
5 minutes. Stir in the salt, oil, and unbleached flour. Beat with a wooden spoon or
with a mixer at medium speed 2 minutes. Blend in the whole wheat flour, seeds,
dill, pepper, nutmeg, and ginger, then blend in the rye meal or flour by the half-
cupful. Let the dough rest 5 minutes, then knead, preferably by food processor or
mixer. Because the dough is so sticky (inevitable, with rye in it), you'll need to add
more flour if working with your hands (and more flour means heavier bread).

Hand or mixer method (mixer with a dough hook attachment): Knead 10 minutes.

Food processor method: Process until the dough pulls together and revolves around
the blade; count 25 turns. Turn out the dough, let it rest 1 to 2 minutes, then return
it to the bowl, being sure the top of the ball is now at the bottom. Process again,
counting 25 turns around the blade.

Mark 10 cups in a vessel, oil it well, add the dough, then turn it over so the top

*Complete canning instructions are on pages 242–244.

is oiled. Pat the top flat and cover with plastic film and a damp cloth. Let rise at around 70°F until the shoulders of the dough hit the mark, 1½ to 1¾ hours.

Punch down and knead out all bubbles. Oil the bowl again, add the dough, turn it over, and let it rise as before (it will usually take as long). Again punch it down and knead out the bubbles; as you knead, shape the dough into a ball. When the air is out and the dough well rounded, tightly pinch the bottom seam together. Oil a heavy baking sheet, sprinkle with cornmeal, and set the ball upon it. Brush the dough with oil, dust rather thickly with flour, cover with a dry towel, and let rise as before. Meantime, fill a spray bottle with cool water.*

When the dough is close to doubled in bulk, about 50 minutes, heat the oven to 450°F. In 10 to 15 minutes more, when the dough has doubled, use a razor blade or very sharp knife to cut a half-inch-deep cross (or any design you fancy) in the top of the loaf. Spritz the oven—ceiling, floor, and all three walls—set in the baking sheet, spritz the dough and the whole oven again, and close the door. Set the timer for 15 minutes. After 2 or 3 minutes, spray the dough and the oven, then spray every 2 or 3 minutes 3 more times.

When the timer rings, reduce the heat to 350°F and bake until the bread sounds hollow when you rap it, about 15 minutes more. Remove from the oven and cool at least a little on a rack before slicing.

As I had success baking bread, I grew bolder. I happened to buy a package of *lavash* (Armenian flat bread—crackers, really) from a delicatessen in Oakland. I was entranced. Besides its wonderful country look—enormous, thin, fragile, bubbled, sesame-seeded wheels—*lavash* has a simple grain-sweetness that enhances anything spread upon it. If there's an Armenian baker around, he probably sends his *lavash* to delicatessens to sell. But it's easy and amusing and cheaper, and the crackers are thinner, if you make them yourself. I did. If I could do it, you can, too.

You can double the recipe. *Lavash* don't get stale† and it's comforting to have them in all their toasty beauty ready for guests. *Lavash* are very breakable, however, so I hang them in a big paper shopping bag on a line strung high across the larder.

LAVASH
Armenian flat bread
[*Four 15-inch round crackers: up to 24 servings*]
These keep.

1½ teaspoons active dry yeast   ½ stick butter, melted and cooled
1¼ cups water, warm

---

*Spritzing the oven and the dough itself with water creates a moist atmosphere which, in the early stage of baking, contributes to a crusty crust. If you prefer a soft crust, don't spritz.
†Although if you live in a humid part of the world, you might have to crispen them in a moderate oven before serving.

*4 cups unbleached flour, plus more for the
board
1 ½ teaspoons salt*

*Olive oil for the bowl
About 1 cup toasted sesame seeds*

Detailed instructions on making bread are on pages 239–241. You'll also need about 5 ½ feet of heavy duty foil. *

In a bowl, stir the yeast into the water and let proof until dissolved, about 5 minutes. Stir in the butter. Turn the flour and salt into a mixing bowl, add the yeast mixture, and beat with a wooden spoon to blend as much as possible. Let rest 5 minutes, then turn onto a lightly floured work surface and knead forcefully (whacking and slamming and cursing) 5 minutes.

Mark 6 cups in a vessel, oil it, add the dough, then turn it over so the top is oiled. Pat the top flat, cover with plastic film and a damp cloth. Let rise at around 70°F until the shoulders of the dough hit the mark, about 3 hours. Punch down and knead out all bubbles. Cut the dough into 4 equal parts and pinch the pieces into balls. Set on a lightly floured work surface, cover with plastic film, and let rest 10 or 15 minutes.

On the work surface, roll out each ball of dough 16 inches in diameter—rolling back and forth over the dough is fine, as long as you turn the circle to keep the thickness even. A little irregularity in the circle won't hurt, but the dough must be translucent. Prick the round with a fork every inch or so all over, then carefully lift it up onto a large piece of unoiled heavy foil, shiny side up. If the circle messes up in places, just lift up the dough again and smooth it out.

Heat the oven to 375°F, removing the lowest rack and putting the other rack in the highest slot. (If you're doubling the recipe, heat the oven just before you roll out the last 2 balls of dough.)

To bake, lay a sheet of foil with its round of dough on the oven floor. Set the timer for 5 minutes, but keep an eye on it. Bake until the underside is nicely toasted and don't worry about a burned bubble here and there. Then pull the foil toward you, turn the round over, brush quickly with cold water, and sprinkle generously with sesame seeds. Give the foil a half-turn and slide it back into the oven. Set the timer for 4 minutes but again, watch it. The cracker must be thoroughly baked, but as the oven heats up, it may take less time on both sides.

The tendency is to turn up the heat—don't. A lower temperature longer is correct; otherwise, some parts will burn while others won't quite crispen. If you find a cracker is toasted mostly but underbaked in spots, lay it directly on the upper rack a few minutes while another is baking on the oven floor.

Cool thoroughly on a rack and then store in a big paper bag in a high dry place.

If you have an electric oven with the element on the floor, you can try a couple of things. Line the rack with unglazed tiles or thin bricks or use a baking stone. Set the rack

*Candid housekeeping note: If your oven floor, like mine, is strewn with blackened bits of this and that, best take a scrubber and clean it up. *Lavash* bake on foil on the oven floor and the subtle flavor of smoke is not one of their charms. But for heaven's sake, don't clean with an oven cleaner! The crackers would have a deadly overtaste.

on its lowest level and preheat the oven for about 30 minutes. Or bake smaller rounds of dough on foil on top of the stove on a hot griddle over medium-high heat. The intensity of the heat source and the thickness and heat-conducting properties of the tiles/bricks/stone/griddle will determine baking time for each side of the cracker, so just follow the descriptions for baking above. If neither method works well, have a *Lavash* Baking Party with a friend who has a gas oven . . .

If making one's own bread and crackers is joy, eating one's own bread and crackers slathered with one's own fresh cheese is heaven. In Berkeley, I continued my experiments with cream cheese—I'd begun as a girl after reading *Heidi*. What tempted me were two memories: Heidi's Grandfather's mountain cheeses and the *Petit-suisse* from Paris.

When milk sours naturally—or when a culture, such as yogurt or buttermilk, is introduced to sour it—the milk clots and one can make a cheese of it. Naturally, fresh cheese made from soured milk tastes sour. As old as the ancients, that is the sort of cheese I made for years and years. But it wasn't sweet-tasting *Petit-suisse*. Although I'd known it before, it hadn't sunk in: rennet also clots milk. Sweet milk. Naturally, fresh cheese made from sweet milk tastes sweet! Then with rennet and help from John Ehle,* I have made cream cheese of which Heidi's Grandfather—and the gang at *Petit-suisse*, not to mention the gang at Gervais and Neufchâtel—would be proud.

A warning. Time in cheesemaking is quirky. If I tell you this cheese will take eight hours to clot, don't count on it. It could take sixteen. It has to do with the acid content of the milk, the temperature of the room, and, as with other mystical processes, the sun, the moon, the stars, and the seasons (milk is different in spring than in fall and winter—in spring, it makes less cheese, for one thing). "Patience" is a word one finds frequently in books on cheesemaking. But the reward of patience is great. *No* cream cheese will ever taste better.

This particular method adds more rennet than usual but also adds it at a lower temperature than some other fresh cheeses. After trying this, you can add half the rennet and add it to the milk at 86°F. Myself, I suspect the fluffiness and the remarkably French flavor of this cheese—sweet with just the merest hint of sour—comes from the cooler temperature, but I don't know that.

Do make an effort to find delicious milk for your cheese. Three times a week in Berkeley, our milkman Mike—running up our flight of stone steps, whistling all the way—brought us bottles of unhomogenized milk from cows that had dined on lush Marin County grass. Of course, these days very

---

*The Cheeses & Wines of England & France.

little milk is unhomogenized and in bottles and delivered. And delicious. Still there is usually one dairy in each part of the country that still respects God's cows.

As for God's goats, you can make fresh *chèvre* with this recipe, using goats' milk in place of cows'. It is marvelous and a fraction of the expense of store-bought—when you can buy it.

Petit-suisse is unsalted and at least twenty percent heavy cream, thus if you wish a richer cheese, use the *Petit-suisse* amounts in the list of ingredients. If you wish a leaner cheese, use low-fat or even non-fat milk and no heavy cream.

FROMAGE BLANC
Fresh cream cheese
[*Makes 1 3/4 pounds: 4 cups*]
The cheese will keep at least a week, tasting richer as it ripens.

4 quarts (Petit-suisse: *3 quarts plus 1 2/3 cups*) *fresh milk*
1 cup (Petit-suisse: *3 1/3 cups*) *heavy cream*
1/4 cup cultured buttermilk (add if the milk has been pasteurized, * *and add a splash more in spring)*

1/2 rennet tablet, † *finely crushed*
1/4 cup water, tepid
About 3/4 teaspoon non-iodized salt (none for Petit-suisse *or* fromage à la crème)
Nut or fruit leaves ‡ *(optional)*

Turn the milk and cream into a 2-gallon pot and bring it to 65°F—use a clean indoor-outdoor thermometer for the reading.§ If the milk has been pasteurized, also bring the buttermilk to 65°F and mix it in. Thoroughly dissolve the rennet in the water. Add it to the milk and stir constantly with a long-handled spoon for 4 minutes. Set the pot somewhere at 65°F (in a tub of 65°F water, if necessary). Cover the pot and do not disturb it. In 10 minutes, ripple the top of the milk with a spoon for 1 minute to help keep the cream from rising. In 30 minutes, ripple the top again and do it again 30 minutes after that. (Sometimes I forget to ripple altogether and the cheese is still creamy and fine.)

When the curd has set to the consistency of yogurt—8 or more hours (it won't harm the cheese if you don't catch it the moment it has set; you can leave it all day or all night, if need be), wring out a scrupulously clean cotton or linen cloth, set it in a large colander and turn the curd into it. Gather up all sides of the cloth and run strong string around it four times, then tie tightly. Hang from a hook or cupboard knob to drain, a bowl beneath it.

---

*This is called a "starter" and it adds helpful bacteria to replace bacteria killed in the pasteurizing process. Yogurt and sour cream may be used, but I prefer buttermilk's flavor.
†Or, according to package directions, enough rennet to clot 1 gallon of milk for fresh cheese.
‡Where do you find them? In the park or the right neighbor's garden . . .
§Droplets on the wrist feel almost as though they're not there.

When the stream of whey slows to a drip, in about half-an-hour, lift the bag into a large pot. Use a big spoon to scrape all the cheese adhering to the cloth, mixing it into the rest—this firmed cheese clogs the cloth and the whey can't drain. Do this every hour or so. After about 8 or 10 to 12 hours of dripping, when all the curd pulls away from the cloth as you open it, the cheese is ready to salt.* Stir in salt to taste.

Now you want to mold the cheese, but also to let it drain a little more. I line a shallow basket with a damp cloth—or nut leaves, in their season—smooth the cheese in it (about 2 inches thick), cover it with the cloth or leaves, set a plate on top, and set the cheese over a bowl in the refrigerator. The next morning, it's nicely firm but still fluffy. I leave it in the basket, if we're having guests; otherwise, I turn the cheese into a deep bowl, cover it with plastic film, then crimp foil around the rim and refrigerate.

Once you've eaten your fill of the fresh cheese on its own, you may want to experiment with enhancements, blended in after unmolding. (For a pretty presentation, you can turn the seasoned cheese back into a basket, with or without a lining of leaves.)

For savory cheese, if you're lucky enough to have pineapple sage in your garden, finely chopped, it adds delicious panache. As does watercress. And minced raw or sautéed mushrooms. For your own version of the herbal Boursin, with a light hand add minced shallots, chives, garlic, parsley, thyme, and freshly ground pepper. For Liptauer cheese spread (one of my mother's favorite hors d'oeuvres but I hate it), add minced capers, anchovies, scallions, caraway seeds, and paprika. Or mix the cheese equal parts with crumbled Roquefort or other blue cheese. And of course red salmon caviar is divine with cream cheese. Because it's so fluffy, think of this cheese not only for conventional cream cheese uses but also in the manner of sour cream. Over baked potatoes with chives, superb.

For sweet cheese, in summer the first thing to do is lightly sprinkle a portion (unmolded nicely from a small round or square or simply plopped on a flowered plate) with sugar and surround it with strawberries or raspberries. Or emblaze it with *Sauce Cardinal* (page 53). In winter, your best preserves or jellies—particularly red currant, strawberry, apricot, sour cherry, and quince—can be spooned over the cheese instead of sugar and fresh fruit. Or try a heap of warm buttery brandied apples (page 86), oh my.

With your last cupful of cheese, you must make the ephemeral *crémets d'Angers*, *fromage à la crème*, or *coeur à la crème*—same thing, different shapes.

---

*A friend tells me that the whey is full of vitamins and minerals and makes very light biscuits and scones, as on page 198.

CRÉMETS D'ANGERS . . . FROMAGE À LA CRÈME . . . COEUR À LA CRÈME

Lightened, sweetened, and molded cream cheese

[4 servings]

1 rounded cup (8 ounces) Fromage blanc
  *(recipe preceding)**

*½ cup heavy cream, cold, plus more for
  garnish (optional)*

*1 tablespoon sugar, plus more for garnish
  (optional)*

*2 extra large egg whites, at room
  temperature*

*Fresh berries or best preserves or jellies
  (optional)*

Press the cheese through a sieve. Beat the cream until stiff. Lightly but thoroughly fold half the cream into the cheese, then fold in the rest with the sugar. Beat the whites until stiff and fold them in.

Choose any mold you like—individual or large baskets or pottery molds or hearts pierced with holes for draining. Traditionally, the cheese is molded around 1½ inches thick. Line with a wrung-out cloth and smooth in the cheese. Cover with the cloth, lay a light plate on top, place over a bowl to catch the whey, and set in a cool place or the refrigerator for about 8 hours. Unmold gently.

Traditionally, again, sugar is sprinkled and thick cream poured over and around the unmolded cheese. For my taste, that's a bit much, and we simply garnish it with berries or preserves as described above.

Then early in 1959 we booked passage for three on the *Olympia*'s May crossing to Greece. Well, passage for three and four-ninths, really: our second child was due in September. Greece would be sunny and beautiful and, most important, cheap. When it came time to pack, we whittled what we couldn't live without for a year down to twenty-three suitcases, then flew to New York and what David called The Big Boat. Alice Vinegar came to send us off. It was to be the last time I would see her.

On board, we met a gracious woman who wore enough large green stones to make one think she was Ozma of Oz. She was introduced to us as the Duchess of Denver.† Someone said the stones were emeralds. Gene danced with her. Afterwards, he told me he was sure there was no such thing as a Duchess of Denver and that her jewels were as phony as her title.

Learning that we were going to Greece for a year, she said, "Don't! Go to Italy!" She told us she had recently bought one of the medieval towers of San Gimignano and offered it to us to live in for our year.

"Humor her," Gene whispered to me.

---

*Yes, of course you can make this with storebought cream cheese. But if you can buy it from a delicatessen that offers it without gum arabic gluing it together, do so.
†With help from Dorothy L. Sayers, the duchess's name has been changed.

We landed in Piraeus in the middle of the night. There sat our suitcases, the baby inside me was kicking up a storm, and David was asleep on his feet. Customs agents ahead of us were examining luggage in detail. When they saw our twenty-three suitcases, they looked at us warily.

Another philosopher friend in Berkeley had introduced us to a Greek friend teaching in the economics department that semester. His friend's father had recently been prime minister of Greece. The man was charming and generously offered us a letter of introduction, should we need it. Gene suddenly remembered the letter and thrust it at the customs inspectors impatiently. They looked startled, then one excused himself and took it to his superior. The man returned and proceeded to open every single one of our bags. How could we know that the former prime minister had just been jailed and that his son's name spelled nothing but trouble: Andreas Papandreou. Welcome to Greece.

From Athens to Rome to an Elizabethan Cottage on the Thames

In Athens that first sunlit evening, we drove down the coast to a tiny secluded bay aflutter with sailboats and studded with yachts. Terraced above it were half a dozen white stucco restaurants. Gene and I sat down at a table in one of them and David, our ever-patient, ever-gracious small David, perched himself between pots of geraniums at the edge of the patio, dangled his feet over the wall, and watched the boats. From time to time, two waiters carrying enormous laden trays rushed back and forth across the patio, ignoring us, although the restaurant was empty. Annoyed, we got up to leave. One of the waiters stopped us. Apologizing, he explained that the kitchen was just finishing an important order—he gestured toward a large white yacht anchored in the bay "—for Onassis." We went back to our table.

The meal we were served was one the ancients might have savored along those shores. The first course, garlanded with lemon, was simmered prawns in nature's full dress. They tasted as though they'd been pulled from the sea moments before. The main course was grilled *barbouni*—I still remember the name—that variety of red mullet both now and in ancient days one of the most prized fish in the Mediterranean. *Barbouni* is crimson, often yellow striped, with delicate white flesh and tiny bones.

Since then, we have grilled fish the Greek way a hundred times. On the Pacific Coast, the best fish we've tasted for grilling whole is rockfish of some three or four pounds.* From waters in other parts of the country, if you can

---

*Rockfish notes are on page 256.

find them whole and of an appropriate size, consider grouper, tilefish, red-fish, bluefish, black, sea, striped or rock bass, red snapper, whitefish, buffalo-fish, carp, catfish, ling cod, salmon, spotted sea or rainbow trout, pompano, or porgy.

WHOLE FISH GRILLED THE GREEK WAY
Best at room temperature, which means you can grill it an hour or two before serving.

Whole scaled and dressed fish; leave the heads and tails on; allow ¾ to 1 pound per serving
Light olive oil, plenty
Fresh lemon juice, about ½ lemon per serving
Salt, a bit
Freshly ground black pepper, to taste
Long sprigs of fresh rosemary, marjoram, dill, or thyme,* lots, if you have them; if not, use their dried leaves instead
Fresh lemons, in quarters, for garnish

Measure the fish crosswise at its thickest girth; plan to grill it a long 10 minutes to the inch. Fish like trout that are under 1-inch thick still want 5 minutes on each side. However, bear in mind that you're dealing with two unknown variables here: the fire and the fish. Some fish cook faster than others, some wood burns hotter than others, ditto some charcoal, so keep your eye on things.

Dry the fish thoroughly, then moisten well with olive oil, sprinkle lightly with lemon juice, and dash with salt† and pepper, inside and out (there will be more oil and lemon in the baste). If you have them, press a blanket of sprigs of an herb into the flesh of the fish lengthwise on both sides. Tie in place with thick cotton string, starting under the "neck," crossing over at the midsection, looping underneath and bringing the string up to tie in a bow over the tail. Or sprinkle the fish generously on both sides with dried leaves, crumbling them to release their oils. Let the dear thing loll about while the wood or coals are readied.

Build your fire of fruit or nut wood (or any wood except evergreens) or non-petroleum-based charcoal, making a solid firebed that will extend an inch or two on all sides of the fish. Set the grilling rack about 6 inches above the firebed. Light the fire. When the fire is glowing with just an occasional tongue of flame—you can hold your hand over the grilling rack 3 to 4 seconds—brush the rack with olive oil and lay the fish upon it. Cover with a tent of foil—shiny side in, extending several inches beyond the fish at either end. Don't mind the flames that flare up for a while. Frequently sprinkle the fish with a baste of something like four parts olive oil to one part lemon juice.

Halfway through your calculated grilling time, turn the fish over (two spatulas and another pair of hands helps), meanwhile quickly brushing the grill with more

---

*The more scented the herb—rosemary being foremost—the more its flavor will be imparted to the fish.
†If the grilling will be longer than 15 minutes, salt afterwards.

oil. When the fish flakes with a fork (120°F at the thickest part, if your meat thermometer goes that low), it is ready.

Let cool 10 to 15 minutes or until at room temperature. While it cools, occasionally spoon olive oil and lemon juice over the fish. Lay on a platter and garnish with lemon—in its sheath of herbs, it makes a beautiful presentation. A snip at the center X of the string will release it. Pass a plate for strings and herbs. Often fresh mayonnaise (page 249) is offered as an accompaniment and usually sliced cucumbers and tomatoes.

Boning and serving notes are on page 247.

If the fish is larger than 3 or 4 pounds, you'll have to protect the head and tail from frizzling up. I'm told that if you wrap the head and tail in oiled waxed paper, then in foil, then rest them on foil-covered pieces of wood, they'll be safe from burning.

[*At high altitude:* The fish might take longer than 10 minutes to the inch—figure something like 12.]

With our *barbounia* we drank *retsina*, the tingling resinated wine of Greece (the flavor of a pinecone in my glass, I confess, took getting used to, but my Hellenophile husband loved it straightaway). For dessert, we had a plate of *anthotyro*, goat's cheese from Crete, surrounded by a cascade of purple grapes. It was the foretaste of a country full of superb food.

Giving our twenty-three suitcases into the care of American Express, we began househunting. Athens itself proved to be dusty and noisy. We would look on the islands nearby.

Poros, an island a few hours from Athens, was sunny, stony, and fairly flat. We told the island's real estate agent that we wanted a two-bedroom house. He asked, "What for?" We explained we needed a bedroom for us, one for the children, a living room, and a study for Gene. He laughed and said that was a four-room house. We understood when we walked through houses with people in them. Except for the kitchen, and sometimes then, beds and chairs and tables were scattered throughout the house—eating and sleeping and talking and reading and studying and playing cards and making lace were common to every room.

Then came the blow. Back in Berkeley, we'd read in a magazine that we could live cheaply in the south of Spain, but that Greece was even cheaper. Electricity and running water weren't mentioned. In Greece, the man on Poros said, rent was calculated by the room. Without running water and electricity, the rule rather than the exception, rooms were about $12 apiece. With electricity and running water, sometimes hot but not always, rooms were $25 apiece. That would be the same rent as we'd paid in Berkeley, but for one less room and no washing machine. I took Gene aside and told him I could manage beautifully without electricity and running water—hadn't generations of women in my family before me? Wasn't I made of the same stuff? He wouldn't discuss it. I argued passionately. I lost.

The article we'd read neglected something else in Greece that came as a surprise: a result of four hundred years of Turkish occupation.

Our second afternoon on Poros was beastly hot. While Gene went off to look at another house, I put David down for a nap in our hotel room, then, beneath his window on the quay, I ordered myself a *lemonada* at one of the café's outdoor tables. In time I realized that I was the only woman in sight. I also realized that I hadn't seen a woman since noon. There hadn't been any women except me in the *taverna* or the café the night before, either. From the glances of the men at neighboring tables sipping *ouzo* and strolling past me along the quay, I became painfully aware of the fact that I was not only a woman out in the street in the afternoon, but I was pregnant. That night, as much as I wanted to be with him, I told Gene I was tired and that he should go off to the café by himself. Almost always choosing to be with me, he so adored the singing and dancing and warmth of the Greek men in their cafés that he gratefully did go. I tried very hard not to let it bother me, but I realized that staying on Poros would almost be like living in *purdah*.

The third day, we found the perfect house—secluded, spacious, with rich flat land for a garden, and a view of the sea. Every surface of the kitchen was tiled in rosy earthenware and it had a domed oven built into the wall for baking bread. The grandmother of the family—*i yayà*—who was there that day, showed me how the oven worked. We told the man we would take the house. He said *i yayà* would be glad to have our company. Our company?! Then we learned that in Greece, there is often a grandmother who stays behind when the family moves, and her room is usually in the center of the house. When Gene explained we would not be comfortable in such a situation, the man was baffled, saying, "But my dear Mr. Thompson, it's a *five*-room house—you would have all the rooms you will need!"*

We looked at a couple of other small islands further from Athens, but I'm afraid I began to feel more and more ostracized and Gene was concerned about the distance from a hospital when the baby came. In Berkeley, we had corresponded about a house on Corfu. At the time, the large island close to Italy had seemed remote. Now, an Italian influence was very appealing to me. We decided to go there, and on our way, we would see some of ancient Greece.

---

*Just last night I discovered the reason for *i yayà*. A friend owns a house in Mykonos. He has tenants. He wants to sell his house but it's impossible to sell with people living in it. His tenants won't leave. By Greek law, our friend has discovered, the only way tenants may be forced to quit the premises is that they must be given a year's notice and then the owner must move back into his house. (Our friend, ablither in frustration, lives and works in Los Angeles.) So if a grandmother remains in residence, the family has technically never moved out and their tenants can be asked to leave at any time.

Late in the afternoon the next day, we left Athens and headed for Delphi, driving slowly because we were still breaking in our adorable Citroën *Deux Chevaux* (was it two horsepower really?).

Around nine o'clock, we found a *taverna* in the country and had our first experience with the Greek custom of being invited back into the kitchen to choose our dinner. On top of a big black swelteringly hot stove were golden-topped pans of *moussaka* (baked layers of eggplant and ground lamb bound with cream sauce), *pastitsio* (baked layers of macaroni and ground beef, also bound with cream sauce), and *spanakopita* (creamy spinach set in layers of *phyllo* pastry). At the back of the stove there was also a pot of *patsa* (tripe soup) and a big garlic-scented roast leg of lamb. I chose the *spanakopita*, and Gene, the *patsa* and a piece of lamb. David wasn't tempted by anything he saw.

"Excuse me," I said to the cook in my faltering Greek, "but have you any chicken? Our son is very tired and a little chicken would be wonderful." I'd hoped he had one roasting in the oven.

The cook's eyes brightened. He went flying out the back door and in a moment returned with a chicken. Live. He held it by the neck the way you'd hold a hammer and it was wriggling and squawking to beat hell. The cook bent down and held the chicken under David's nose. "Would you like some chicken, little one? It won't take any time at all." David gasped and flung himself into my skirts. Gene politely asked the cook not to trouble—it was late and we were tired and *pastitsio* would be lovely!

Shaking his head, the cook pinched David's bottom and said he would make something his own little boy liked to eat. He tossed together the Greek version of an Italian *frittata*—beaten eggs and shredded zucchini slowly cooked in a skillet, setting quietly into a cake, sprinkled with feta cheese and flat-leaved parsley and served in wedges. David loved it.*

Of course, you mustn't limit the flavoring possibilities to squash—any savory vegetable will do. But for an appealing purity of flavor, keep it to one type of vegetable, letting color come from a mix of yellow and green summer squashes, or perhaps yellow, green, and red sweet peppers.

And after the cake has cooled, it makes a fine addition to a picnic.

Avga kolokithakia
A Greek *frittata* with summer's squashes
[*2 main-dish or 4 side-dish servings*]
To be served hot, this is a last-minute dish, but the vegetables can be sautéed half an hour or so in advance.

---

*Reading this recipe after having eaten this dish for supper, a friend said, "It doesn't sound nearly as good as it tastes." I said I would quote her.

4 medium-sized (1 pound) zucchini, yellow
 crookneck or yellow straightneck, or 6
 patty pan squashes, or 1 pound of any
 favorite vegetable
1 large onion
3 tablespoons olive oil
1 tablespoon butter, preferably unsalted

A small handful of fresh chopped oregano
 (or any favorite) leaves, or 2 teaspoons
 dried
6 or 8 turns of the black pepper mill
 (½ teaspoon plus, medium grind)
4 extra large eggs, beaten
3 to 4 ounces feta cheese
A handful of chopped parsley, preferably
 Italian

Using the #3 disc on a Mouli-Julienne,* a ⅛-inch shredding blade on a food processor, or the ⅛-inch side of a grater, shred the squash (or other vegetable)† and the
onion.

In a large heavy skillet over medium-high heat, warm the olive oil, then sauté
the vegetables in it until tender-crisp, stirring frequently, about 6 minutes. Turn
off the heat. Lift the vegetables (beating any excess juices into the eggs) and drop a
lump of butter beneath them, rolling it around the skillet, then smooth the vegetables evenly in the skillet. Sprinkle with herbs and pepper.

Pour the eggs over the skillet, tilting it so they evenly cover the vegetables. Turn
the heat to low, cover the skillet, and cook until the eggs have just set, about 10
minutes. Crumble the feta over the top and sprinkle with parsley. Serve in wedges.

A few rounds of cooked sausage are a good cold-weather addition.

Gene pronounced his *patsa* One of the Great Soups.

Honeycomb tripe, so named because it has a lovely honeycombed texture
on one side, is the most delicate sort of tripe and the one to cook. Beef tripe is
a muscle, the stomach muscle, and being muscle, wants long slow cooking.
However, these days, tripe has already been thoroughly washed, scraped,
soaked, and partially cooked before you buy it, so the lengthy preparations
described in older cookbooks no longer apply. A couple of hours' simmering
is all it needs.

If you've never tasted tripe, it has a mildly peppery flavor and a delightfully
chewy texture. I've read about broiling tripe and frying it and covering it with
batter, but for my part, I think of tripe as I do pasta (it resembles cuts of pasta
when cooked): a vehicle for a splendid sauce or surrounding. As with pasta,
tripe ought never be bland, in fact, the more ardently seasoned—old Calvados in *tripes à la mode de Caen* or masses of buttery onions in *tripes à la Lyon-
naise*—the more satisfying.

Then to the tripe soup lovers' repertory of Mexican *menudo*, Genoese *sbira*,
Lombardian *busecca*, Turkish *iskembe corbasi*, and Philadelphia Pepper Pot,

---

*About which, page 250.
†Of course, some vegetables don't lend themselves to this shredding, in which case, cut them
in matchsticks or chop them as you like.

we'll add this creamy, lemony Greek *patsa*. The stroke of inspiration is the liaison of egg and lemon sauce, *avgolemono*. Before the *avgolemono*, the soup is marvelous. After it, it's an ohmygosh! sort of thing.

But fair warning. Some years later, a friend at table said he loved tripe but thought the tripe in my *patsa* too chewy. Turns out the only tripe he'd eaten was in canned Pepper Pot soup! But after all, the soup is for pleasure, not edification, so if you have a guest like that, be prepared to simmer his an hour or two longer.

This and the following two recipes had their inspiration in Robin Howe's delightful book, *Greek Cooking*.

PATSA
Tripe soup
[4 to 6 servings]

Although you should cook the tripe the day you bring it home, once cooked, you may keep the soup in the refrigerator several days. Add the *avgolemono* just before serving.

1 ½ pounds fresh* honeycomb tripe,† all fat removed, cut in 1-inch squares	*2 large garlic cloves, finely chopped*
1 large onion, chopped	*6 cups excellent chicken broth*
1 large tomato, finely chopped	*1 cup water, cold*
1 large leafy celery stalk, cut in half lengthwise then thinly sliced	*2 tablespoons fresh lemon juice*
1 unpeeled carrot, finely chopped	*½ bay leaf*
2 handfuls of parsley leaves, finely chopped	*At least 12 turns of the black pepper mill (1 teaspoon plus, medium grind)*
	Avgolemono *(recipe follows)*

Turn the tripe, onion, tomato, celery, carrot, parsley, garlic, broth, water, lemon juice, bay, and pepper into your soup pot. Bring to a simmer over medium heat. Turn heat to lowest, set the cover on askew, and simmer gently until the tripe is tender-chewy, 2 to 3 hours. Stir occasionally. Cool and refrigerate, if desired.

To serve, return to a simmer, then remove from the heat and whisk in the

AVGOLEMONO
Lemon and egg sauce
[Makes about 1 cup]

2 extra large eggs, well beaten	*1 or 2 ladlefuls of the hot broth‡*
¼ cup fresh lemon juice (1 large juicy lemon)	

---

*Tripe is also sent to market pickled, but that's not what you want.
†Despite the fact that tripe has been tenderized somewhat before coming to market, there are still recipes that suggest blanching it before cooking. I don't, but if you'd feel better about it, cover the whole thing with cold water and a decent amount of salt and bring very slowly to the boil. Drain, rinse under cold running water, pat dry, and then begin this recipe.
‡Another day, to make this as a sauce on its own, use chicken or a delicate vegetable broth.

To the eggs in a bowl, very slowly whisk in the lemon juice, then the broth. Remove the *patsa* from the heat and stir in this liaison—do not heat the soup further. Cover the pot and let set a few minutes until the eggs thicken. If you're not serving from the pot, heat a soup tureen or bowl and turn the *patsa* into it.

Serve with crusty rolls to sop up the broth.

After dinner, the road grew ever narrower, winding and rising high into the mountains. A full moon gave the landscape an eerie glow. On the shoulders of Mount Parnassus, we rounded a curve and there, on a hillock next to the road, our headlights startled a young shepherd surrounded by sheep. Caped in black and carrying a crook, the lad darted into the night, almost an apparition from the past.

We arrived in Delphi after three in the morning. The streets were empty and the town pitch dark. Luckily, we found a policeman, who got us a room. We awoke in the blaze of noon and when we stepped outside, we were thunderstruck by the view—shining mountains cradled the town and down the chasm where two mountains met past a green sweep of olive groves shimmered a blue Gulf of Corinth. Delphi, equidistant between Mount Parnassus and the sea, was the ancients' center of the world.

In a *taverna*, ignoring breakfast, we ordered *arni sto klephtes*, lamb with herbs and cheese roasted in parchment paper. The cook explained that during a revolt against the Turks, *klephtes* were guerrilla bands that roamed the mountains. When they cooked, to escape detection, the men wrapped their meat in oiled paper, stuffed the packets in earthen pots and set them in the embers of a fire. The meat inside these miniature ovens roasted slowly, delectably, for hours. This is what it tasted like.

Arni sto klephtes
Lamb roasted in parchment
[*6 servings*]
The packages may be arranged in the pan in the morning and kept in a cool place or the refrigerator until the evening's roasting.

2 ½ to 3 pounds boneless leg of lamb
2 very large sweet onions
About ¼ cup olive oil
6 garlic cloves, in slivers
About 2 tablespoons fresh lemon juice
A little salt
Lots of freshly ground black pepper

4 ounces mild melting cheese such as Gruyère
or jack (Greeks use Kasseri), cut in
6 bricks
6 generous sprigs of fresh rosemary, or 6 big
pinches dried leaves
6 generous sprigs of fresh marjoram, or 6 big
pinches dried leaves

You'll also need 6 large squares (18 × 18 inches) of cooking parchment.*

Cut the meat into 6 pieces of uniform size. The shape will determine the manner you cut—try to keep the pieces as equal as possible so that some portions won't overcook while others just reach tenderness. Cut three ¼-inch-thick slices from the center of each onion.

Brush the parchments with oil and place a slice of onion in the center of each, then a portion of lamb on the onion. Make small slashes in the lamb and bury slivers of garlic in each piece, the equivalent of 1 clove per portion. Brush the lamb with oil and sprinkle with lemon juice, salt, and pepper. Lay a brick of cheese on the lamb and top with the rosemary and marjoram. Gather the ends of the paper together, being careful not to dislodge the cheese, twist firmly, and tie securely with string, finishing with a bow. You want not one drop of juice to escape! Brush the packages with oil and arrange them in a small shallow baking pan so they all touch and there are no gaps—this is important.

Bake the packets uncovered in a preheated 325°F oven without disturbing for 3 or even 4 hours, if the pieces of lamb are especially chunky. This is not lamb in the pink French manner but in the melting Greek way, so if you're in any doubt, longer roasting won't hurt. Serve the packages just as they are, passing a tray to collect wrappings.

Another time, use only 6 ounces of lamb and add vegetables such as browned cubes of eggplant, diced tomato, and sweet pepper.

We spent the next few days in the Peloponnesus seeing Olympia, Mycenae, and Tiryns (I think Tiryns moved me most because I could stand in the stone-enclosed chambers of the ancients and pick grain which grew from grain they once had threshed). The pleasures of dining in Greece extended to the delights of roadside treats. Oranges plucked from groves near Agrinion were so incredibly huge and juicy and sweet that one of them, rolled into the California Chamber of Commerce, would cause as much discord as the apple Paris rolled to the feet of Aphrodite. Cups of Turkish coffee, dark as earth, brimming with froth, could be found at cafés in every village with a population over ten, and lasted warmingly for empty miles and miles. And at each inn, on small sweet breakfast rounds of bread, we spread honey as exotic and scented as must be sucked from the fields of Paradise.

And in every part of Greece, nibbles of salt-cured olives from noble groves that for centuries have provided most of the peasant's nourishment and much of the country's wealth. As in Spain, there is plenty of water surrounding the land in Greece but painfully little for the soil.

But Corfu was another matter. In the Ionian Sea a spit away from Albania and not seventy miles from Italy, the land had abundant water and everywhere

---

*Available at department stores' cookware sections and at fancy food and cookware shops.

there were lush groves of olives, oranges, lemons, figs, pears, and apples, and of course its fruits of the sea were incomparable. Under the rule of Romans, Venetians, Genoese, Neapolitans, and again Venetians until the nineteenth century, Corfu was more Italian than Greek.

On the exquisite cypress-lined bay of Paleokastritsa—on the westernmost edge of the island where, some say, Odysseus landed after his travels—sitting beneath a cool arbor of grapes, we ordered lobsters for lunch. A moment later, we watched a boy race down the beach. Lugging a crate up from the water, he plunged his arms into it then pulled out a lobster in each hand. He raced back and ran up to our table where he held the two wriggling creatures uncomfortably close for us to inspect. While the lobsters were cooking, we were served *dolmades*, stuffed grape leaves—leaves no doubt plucked from the arbor over our heads.

There are plenty of recipes for *dolmades* in other books, but enough friends have told me these were better than any they'd eaten—even in Greece—that I don't feel abashed about including them.

DOLMADES*
Cool rice-stuffed grape leaves
[*Makes about 80 small bundles*†]
Make *dolmades* a day or two in advance. They will keep admirably in a cool place a week.

THE RICE STUFFING‡

2 large ripe tomatoes	*³/₄ teaspoon salt*
About 2 cups excellent chicken broth	*About 15 turns of the white pepper mill*
About ¹/₂ cup olive oil	*(1 ¹/₄ teaspoons, medium grind)*
3 medium-large onions, finely chopped	*2 ¹/₂ tablespoons finely chopped fresh mint*
1 ²/₃ cups long grain rice	*leaves, or 2 ¹/₂ teaspoons dried*
3 tablespoons toasted pine nuts, chopped	*2 ¹/₂ tablespoons finely chopped fresh dill*
3 tablespoons currants, chopped	*leaves, or 2 ¹/₂ teaspoons dried dill weed*

Whiz the tomatoes in a food processor or blender or chop them to a puree. Pass the puree through the medium blade of the food mill or a coarse sieve into a quart measure. Add chicken broth to make 3 ¹/₃ cups; set aside.

In a heavy wide saucepan, heat the oil and sauté the onions over low heat, stirring frequently. In 10 minutes, blend in the rice and continue sautéing and stirring until the onions are soft, about 10 minutes more. Add the pine nuts, currants, salt,

---

*The *d* is pronounced with a soft *th* sound.
†If it's a party with lots of other hors d'oeuvres, figure 2 or 3 per person, and let people eat them with their fingers. As a first course, allow 4 to 6 for each person and serve them on plates with forks.
‡The recipe makes about 6 cups.

pepper, and tomato-flavored broth. Cover, bring to a simmer, then turn the heat to its lowest and simmer until the rice is just tender, about 20 minutes. Stir in the mint and dill, turn off the heat, set the lid on askew, and cool.

THE LEAVES AND THE BAKING

16 ounces, in jars or cans, of preserved grape leaves;* 8 ounces are about 48 leaves (California leaves are quite as good as Greek)
Olive oil for the dish

3 cups excellent chicken broth
1 cup excellent beef broth
¼ cup fresh lemon juice (1 large juicy lemon)
Cut lemons or clusters of grapes for garnish

Rinse the leaves briefly under hot running water, then snip off their stems. Spread the leaves out, glossy sides down, broad ends toward you; you'll need 80 to 82. Set aside the very largest, the very smallest, and the torn leaves. Place stuffing along the base of each leaf in the size and shape of a small link sausage; leave an inch margin on either side. Fold the margins in and roll up. The rolls should be about ⅝-inch thick.

Lightly brush a heavy 9 × 13 × 2-inch baking dish with oil and cover the bottom with some of the reserved leaves. Arrange 40 rolls snugly side by side, seams down, setting some along the sides to fill in gaps. Jiggle the dish so they are evenly arranged, but none too tight. Cover with reserved leaves, arrange the second layer crisscrossed over the first, then cover with all the remaining leaves.

Bring the two broths and lemon juice to a simmer, then pour over the *dolmades*— the liquid should come an inch below the rim. Cover with foil, crimping along the sides, then lay a smaller baking dish, or whatever you have, on top for a weight.

Set in a 325°F oven (no need to preheat) and bake 2 hours. Remove the weight and the foil, lay the foil over loosely,[†] and cool. Keep the *dolmades* covered and in the dish in a cool place until serving, then line a serving platter with the flat leaves and carefully set the *dolmades* upon them. Garnish with lemon or perhaps clusters of grapes. No sauce is needed or wanted.

This rice is wonderfully Greek and attuned to the delicate flavors of vegetables. Greeks are fond of stuffing vegetables with rice. They're also fond of cool dishes—Greece is HOT!—so cool cooked vegetables heaped with well-flavored rice are irresistible in summer. Garnishes, a strewing of fruits of vine and tree as well as herbs, lift what otherwise is just rice in heaps on a plate to a Mediterranean study in green, red, yellow, and black on rosy coral.

Serving portions, of course, depend upon the rest of the menu. To accompany a simple grilled or roast meat, fowl, or fish for four people, I've found

---

*Aren't the leaves beautifully wrapped and ingeniously set in their jar? You can find preserved grape leaves in most European or Middle Eastern delicatessens.
†Otherwise the acid in the lemon juice will etch lacework into the aluminum.

that a sampler platter composed of one each of zucchini, cucumber, oriental eggplant, and sweet pepper (divided in four), four artichoke hearts, and eight small tomatoes are just right.

LAHANIKA YEMISTA
Cool vegetables stuffed with rosy rice
[*4 to 24 servings*]
You can prepare these in the morning for dinner or the night before for luncheon. (Another plus for your entertaining menu is that the vegetable and the starch are combined in one.)

1 recipe Rice Stuffing, page 181
4 medium-sized artichokes, or 24 artichoke bottoms, or
6 medium-sized (7 inches) zucchini or other long summer squashes, cucumbers, or oriental eggplant, or

9 medium-sized sweet peppers, or
12 medium-sized tomatoes, or
48 small (1 1/2-ounce size) tomatoes, or any combination of the above*

THE GARNISHES (ALL ARE ESSENTIAL):

Edible blossoms or mint or parsley sprigs for the artichokes
2 juicy lemons, 1 juiced and 1 cut lengthwise in eighths
A drizzling of olive oil
A small handful of pine nuts
A small handful of plumped† currants

A small handful of chopped fresh mint leaves, or a sprinkling of dried
A small handful of chopped fresh sweet basil leaves, or a sprinkling of dried
A small handful of chopped parsley
A handful of black olives, preferably Greek

N.B.: When you steam the vegetables for stuffing, save the flesh you scoop out—the recipe on the next page has a way of turning it into a refreshing summer soup.

For stuffed artichokes, ANGINARES YEMISTES, snip off the thorns of the leaves and slice off 1/2 inch across the whole top. Steam or boil until tender, about 40 minutes; cool. Gently spread open the center and pull out the thin inner leaves to reveal the heart. Use the blunt tip of a spoon to scrape out the fuzzy covering on the heart (discard both center leaves and fuzz). Set the artichoke in a wide flat bowl (to catch the rice that spills). Gently pull down each leaf and, with a teaspoon, lightly tuck rice between the leaf and the globe. With a fork, lightly fill the center with stuffing, coming to about 1/2 inch from the top. Esthetically, the center rice should not be heaped higher than the rice filling the leaves or the whole thing will look, well, overstuffed. Crown with a blossom or sprig.

---

*Filling required for the above vegetables: medium-sized artichokes = 1 1/2 cups; medium-sized zucchini, cucumbers, and oriental eggplant in halves lengthwise = 1 cup; medium-sized sweet peppers in quarters = 2/3 cup; medium-sized tomatoes whole = 1/2 cup; artichoke bottoms = 1/4 cup; small whole tomatoes = 2 tablespoons.
†Unless they are already moist, steep in hot water 10 to 15 minutes, then drain and pat dry.

If artichokes are plentiful, after steaming them until tender, remove all the leaves (pile them in a bowl and serve them to the family with mayonnaise for supper), scrape away the fuzz, trim the bottom, even up the sides and heap with rice. Crown with a blossom or sprig.

To prepare stuffed zucchini (or other summer squash), cucumbers, and oriental eggplant (KOLOKITHAKIA and ANGOURIA YEMISTA, MELITZANES YEMISTES)—leave on an inch or so of stem, if there is one. Steam the vegetables whole until tender: eggplants, about 13 minutes, zucchini and cucumbers, about 18 minutes. Cool. Slice in half lengthwise and make shells by running a curved grapefruit knife or large spoon about ¼ inch from the edge—or leave as much flesh on the vegetable as you like. Use a fork to lightly heap on the rice, mounding it nicely. For a sampler plate, cut each half in half across the center.

For stuffed peppers (PIPERIES YEMISTES), steam whole until tender, about 13 minutes. Cool. Remove stem, cut in quarters top to bottom, cut out ribs with scissors, and remove seeds. Use a fork to lightly heap on the rice, mounding it nicely.

Stuffed tomatoes (DOMATES YEMISTES) are filled raw. For medium-sized, remove the blossom scar on top and cut the tomato in half from top to bottom. For small tomatoes, slice off a small lid and level the bottom. With both sizes, scoop out most of the flesh, leaving a thin wall. Use a fork to lightly heap in the rice, mounding it nicely—with small tomatoes, mound almost an inch high.

Arrange the stuffed vegetables on a serving platter, or it might be easier to arrange them on individual dishes. Sprinkle generously with lemon juice and drizzle a thread of olive oil over each piece. Lightly strew with pine nuts, currants, chopped mint, basil, and parsley, then distribute black olives and lemon wedges about for color. Cover and set in a cool place until ready to serve.

And now, make the hearts of the vegetables you steamed into something quenching and Middle Eastern. The flesh of all the vegetables mentioned in the recipe above are compatible and may be blended together. Don't limit this treat to times when you've just stuffed vegetables—steam them deliberately in hot weather for

A Refreshing Summer Soup
Cold soup of pureed vegetables and yogurt
[*Allow about 1 cup per serving*]
This keeps nicely several days in the refrigerator.

1 part puree* of steamed vegetables such as summer squash, eggplant, and sweet peppers, and steamed or raw cucumbers and tomatoes	*Equal measure of plain yogurt (we use nonfat)*

---

*Cooked vegetables (skins included, if you have them) whizzed in the food processor or blender until smooth or passed through the medium blade of the food mill or a coarse sieve.

For every 3 cups of puree/yogurt mixture
1 garlic clove, finely chopped
A drizzle of olive oil
About ½ cup water, iced
About 1 teaspoon lemon juice
A little salt
A few turns of the white pepper mill (¼ teaspoon, medium grind)

Chopped fresh dill, mint, and/or sweet   *Nasturtiums or marigolds (optional)*
   basil leaves, or a sprinkling of dried

Whisk the vegetable puree and yogurt together and measure. Whisk in the garlic and olive oil, thin to a pleasing consistency with water, then add lemon juice, salt, and pepper to taste. Cover with plastic film and refrigerate until serving.

Serve in flat soup bowls—glass is especially handsome—sprinkle with an herb or two and perhaps an edible blossom.

For dessert at Paleokastritsa, we were served the wild strawberries of Corfu, the largest no bigger than the tip of my little finger and as perfumed as violets. They suddenly made the *fraises de bois* I'd loved in Paris seem gargantuan by comparison.

Late that afternoon, when we returned to our hotel, we were introduced to a mustachioed Corfiot gentleman, the mayor of Corfu, and his redhead Irish wife. They graciously invited us to dinner, sending a young friend to stay with David. In a *taverna* in one of the oldest parts of town, we ate divinely for the second time that day.

Gene and I both ordered *spagheto me garithes saltsa*, spaghetti sauced with shrimps. The sauce's base of tomatoes and onions is the fresh, quickly made sort of thing that can be neglected in one's ardor to explore Great New Notions. The list of ingredients gives no hint of the dish's quality—the sauce tastes like the sea.

Spagheto me garithes saltsa

Thin pasta* sauced with shrimps
[*6 main-course or 10 first-course servings*]

For convenience, shell and devein the shrimps† in advance (it's all that takes time with this dish). The base for the sauce may be prepared a few hours in advance, but it's at its best fresh fresh fresh.

---

*Because the shrimps are modest in size, I think the proportions are best if the pasta is fine.
†Methods are on page 257. And save the shells for shrimp butter, page 257.

2 ¼ *pounds medium-sized raw unshelled*
shrimps
¼ *cup olive oil, plus a splash for the pasta*
water
2 *onions, chopped medium-fine*
6 *large (3 ¼ pounds) ripe tomatoes, peeled**
and coarsely chopped
4 *large garlic cloves, finely chopped*
2 *big handfuls of chopped parsley*
2 *generous tablespoons fresh chopped oregano*
leaves, or 2 teaspoons dried

4 *quarts water, boiling*
1 *pound thin pasta* (spaghettini,
vermicelli, capellini, favettine, *and*
so on)
About 1 *cup of the pasta cooking water*
About 3 *tablespoons fresh lemon juice*
(1 *lemon*)
About 1 *teaspoon salt, plus* 1 ½ *tablespoons*
for the pasta water
About 12 *turns of the black pepper mill*
(1 *teaspoon, medium grind*)

Use your largest heavy skillet, top-of-the-stove-proof *cazuela*, or Dutch oven. Over medium-high heat, warm the oil, then sauté the onions until softened but still crisp, stirring occasionally, 5 to 10 minutes. Add the tomatoes and sauté, stirring frequently, another 5 minutes. Stir in the garlic, parsley, and oregano. (If preparing in advance, cover and refrigerate, then warm up before continuing.) Add the shrimps and stir until they turn coral. Turn off the heat and cover if the sauce is ready before the pasta.

Meanwhile, add oil and salt to a big pot of boiling water over highest heat. Stir in the pasta and boil, stirring often, until tender-chewy, but with no graininess in the center†—because it's thin, be very careful not to overcook.

Turn the heat on beneath the sauce (if necessary) and ladle in enough pasta-cooking water to loosen it nicely. Drain the pasta into your serving bowl to heat it, dump out the water and turn in the pasta. To the sauce add lemon juice, salt, and pepper to taste and turn into the pasta. Toss quickly and serve with more pepper, but without cheese—the flavor of the shrimp is too delicate.

Once, using proportionately more tomatoes, onions, and garlic, I added sautéed button mushrooms and chunks of cooked chicken with the shrimp, almost a Creole sort of thing, delicious. And although I haven't seen spinach pasta in Greece, the colors and flavors of coral shrimp, rose tomato, and green pasta are something.

This is, of course, also splendid over rice.

Early the next morning, our friend the mayor called. He'd found us a house. It was in Kanoni, a few minutes from the town of Corfu and a stroll from the summer villa of the King and Queen of Greece (*Mon Repos*, where Prince Philip was born). To our astonishment, it was the house we'd been corresponding about from Berkeley. It had four rooms and a terrace over the sea—

*Easily done if you drop them into the pasta water when it boils then lift them out as their skins split.
†Pasta cooking details are on page 252.

in that climate, the terrace could have been my study. But unlike the earthen-tiled house in a stone field on Poros, this house could have overlooked any sea in Europe. It wasn't Greek. It wasn't even Italian. And the rent was far more than we wanted to pay.

So back to Athens we tootled, frequently, on stretches of country roads under the hot Greek sun, passing a man and a woman approaching a village. One rode a donkey, the other staggered beneath a load of hay. Guess who was riding the donkey and who was under the hay?

We had been in Greece most of a month. David was beginning to understand the language. We had looked at houses from Athens to Hydra to Olympia to Corfu and back again and everywhere we either kept bumping into *i yayà* in the middle or could find nothing between the bare necessities and extravagance. Gene would have stayed, but he knew I was miserable. I tried to hide it, but I was not only miserable, I was miserable about being miserable. My ancestresses had crossed plains, planted fields, made everything that was on their families' backs and in their bellies. How could something so trivial as culture shock do me in? It was, indeed, my comeuppance.

In an international edition of *Time*, we'd read an article about a group of artists living cheaply in Rome. "We both love Italy," Gene said. "We'll go to Rome."

We did. We never found the artists living cheaply. After looking in all the places where we wanted to live, we wearily took a *villino* on the outskirts of Rome. The house itself was pleasant, but we regretted the fact that it was in an international community of people in the diplomatic corps—no Italians. And it was unfurnished. When I say unfurnished, I mean there weren't even plates on the outlets—electrical wires stuck out of the wall. We combed the second-hand shops and flea markets and I bargained brilliantly and we bought what we had to. The surprise came in shopping for a *ghiacceria*, the kind of ice box Tina had used. People looked at me cross-eyed, seeming not to recognize the word. Then they said they hadn't seen an icebox in years. It had only been five! But the prize was our bed, a four-poster in swirls of chestnut that took six men to carry up the stairs. We fitted it with a straw mattress made by Mattress Maker to the Pope. Sleeping on it was like sleeping in a hayfield.

We settled into a routine, Gene working on his novel, I playing with David and thinking about what I would like to write. And marketing with abandon, chattering away to the shopkeepers in an Italian that came back in a rush. And cooking again!

The woman at the greengrocer's on the Via Cassia had grown up in Bologna, which, she said, everybody knew had the finest cuisine in Italy. She looked down her patrician nose at *la ruvidezza*, the coarseness, of Roman cooking. She gave me her recipe for "straw and hay," a lustrous Bolognese mix of green and golden pasta. As made in Bologna, it is rich! Thin or thinner ribbon noodles are sauced with peas or mushrooms, sausage, cream, and cheese. But *la fruttivendola*, after years in Rome in spite of herself, instead tossed the noodles with fresh tomatoes steeped in olive oil and garlic. Bolognese subtlety combined with Roman warmth.

PAGLIA E FIENO COI POMODORI CRUDI
Straw and hay—spinach and egg ribbon noodles—with raw tomatoes
[*4 to 6 servings*]

The sauce is made well in advance to let the flavors marry, so when your pasta is cooked, the dish is ready. Choose a pasta no more than ¼-inch wide, whether it's called *tagliatelle*, *tagliolini* (Bolognese), or *fettucine* (Roman). If the pasta should be freshly made, *com'è bella!*

3 huge (1 ½ pounds) ripe tomatoes, peeled, seeded,* and coarsely chopped
3 garlic cloves, finely chopped
2 handfuls of parsley, chopped
2 to 3 sprigs of fresh mint or sweet basil, finely chopped, or if out of season, rub in a couple of pinches of dried leaves
⅓ cup olive oil, plus 2 splashes for the pasta pots
4 quarts water, boiling—divided between 2 big pots

8 ounces fresh or 6 ounces dry spinach tagliatelle, tagliolini, or fettucine
8 ounces fresh or 6 ounces dry egg tagliatelle, tagliolini, or fettucine
A couple of pinches of salt, plus 1 ½ tablespoons divided between the pasta pots
A dozen turns of the black pepper mill (1 teaspoon, medium grind)
Grated Romano and Parmesan cheese, half and half (optional)

In a bowl, gently mix the tomatoes, garlic, parsley, mint, and olive oil. Cover and set in a cool place half a day (or in the morning for the evening, if you'll be away). Stir once or twice, if you're there. You can, of course, also do this at the last minute.

When ready to serve, add ¾ tablespoon salt and a splash of oil to each pot of boiling water over highest heat.† Stir in the noodles and boil, stirring often, until tender-chewy, but with no graininess in the center. Freshly made pasta will be ready almost as soon as the water returns to a boil—do not overcook! Drain into your serving bowl to heat it, dump out the water, and turn the pasta into the bowl. Toss the pasta with the tomatoes, salt, and pepper, then serve at once, with or without cheese.

There is another way of making this dish that is done practically in an instant—a lot faster than a TV dinner, almost as fast as heating up something

---

*Peeling and seeding notes are on page 259.
†Spinach pasta cooks faster than egg, so they must cook separately. Notes on cooking pasta are on page 252.

from a can, and worlds more satisfying to the palate and the spirit. When it's been a long day and I have neither the time nor inclination to cook, or when I need to make something special on the spur of the moment and I haven't anything special on hand (I always have tomatoes, they are my security blanket), I make

PASTA COI POMODORI CRUDI ISTANTE
Pasta with raw tomatoes in an instant
[For each person]

2½ to 3* ounces pasta (shape isn't important)	1 large garlic clove
	A drizzle of olive oil
A big pot of salted and oiled water, boiling†	A sprinkling of salt
1 large ripe tomato	Lots of freshly ground black pepper
½ dried red chili pepper (optional)‡	A handful of pine nuts (optional)
A small handful of fresh basil, oregano, or marjoram leaves, chopped, or a hefty pinch of dried	

Stir the pasta into the boiling water over highest heat. Drop in the tomato, then lift it out after a minute and peel it. Chop it coarsely and turn into a small bowl. Remember to stir the pasta occasionally. Crumble the chili pepper and herbs into the bowl. Finely chop the garlic and mix it in. By now, the pasta should be tender-chewy, but with no graininess in the center. Drain into your serving bowl to heat it, dump out the water, and turn the pasta into the bowl. Add the tomatoes, oil, salt, and pepper. Toss quickly and serve sprinkled with pine nuts, if you have them.

As the days passed, dear Gene grew increasingly sad. I couldn't imagine what was wrong. Then one night at dinner he mentioned Shaw's line about entering a drawing room in Paris where everyone was speaking French: "And there I stood, my bow broken in my hands." Gene had never lived anywhere where he didn't know the language. He was picking up Italian, but because everyone around us spoke English, it was coming slowly. I told him in that case, we ought to go to England. It was no fairer for me to be the only happy one in Italy than it was for him to be the only happy one in Greece. He argued. This time *I* won. So two weeks after we moved in, we called the people from the secondhand shops and flea markets and sold everything back and, in the middle of August, piled David once again in the back seat of the *Deux Chevaux* and headed for England.

In Rapallo, we dined with Orsina, a brief but happy reunion as I intro-

---

*Although a trencherman wants 4 . . .
†Pasta cooking notes are on page 252.
‡To me, the chili isn't really optional—it gives a wonderful zip.

duced her to my husband and son. The next morning, we followed *La Route bleue* up to Paris. We stopped in Paris just long enough for the Louvre and for drinks at Deux Magots (had we only known that one day we would sit there and proudly look down the block at the window of the Gallimard book shop, resplendent with copies of the French edition of one of Gene's novels).

In England, we found a dream of a house, an Elizabethan cottage on six acres on the Thames: Lodge Hill Cottage, Medmenham, Marlow, Buckinghamshire! Hardly what we'd expected when we set out from Berkeley, but finally, we were home. How many times have I closed my eyes and felt (I can all but touch it) that I am once again in the timbered drawing room of Lodge Hill Cottage, the room that had been the kitchen of the cottage four hundred years before? In my mind's eye, I always seem to be draped languorously across the overstuffed sofa before the huge walk-in fireplace, my fingers smoothing the rust velvet cushions or straightening the rust silk shade of the lamp above my head. Odd that I should picture myself at my ease, because the summer and winter that we lived there, I did nothing but scrub and wash, market and cook, write articles, begin a book, and have a baby.

The garden consisted of an acre of lawn, three or four acres of meadow, and an acre of apple trees down to the Thames. A creamy sweep of Michaelmas daisies finished the bottom of the garden, and to the left were the vegetables, which the gardener had already planted—cold frames for cucumbers, marrows (which the English refused to think of as zucchini, picked three weeks too late and cooked three times too long, but that was years ago), spinach, lettuces, carrots, and the inevitable patch of cabbages.

I think of everything I loved about our life in Medmenham (*Med*'n'em), I most loved the way we got our food. The incomparable milk, eggs, and cream were delivered every other day by Green's Dairyman. The first time I tried the double-cream, I held the bottle at the customary angle, expecting to pour a slosh over some plums. After a moment, I felt silly because nothing happened. Then I gingerly turned the bottle upside down. Still nothing. Gently, I shook it. Ve-ry slowly, the incredibly thick cream came glopping down. It was so gorgeous it made me laugh.

Another who came around with good things was the fishmonger. He'd open the rear doors of his little van to a shimmer of crushed ice and sea creatures. I learned that scallops came with a lick of coral in their shells. I learned to leave the liver in red mullet when I cooked it. I learned about plaice—a fish so generously given to English waters, it was disprized. The fishmonger agreed with me that were plaice rare instead of plentiful and cheap, it would be as cherished as Dover sole.

For basic provisions, I climbed into the *Deux Chevaux* (incredible in the snow: I'd just brush off the pile from the windshield and hood, get in the car, pull out the starter, and the engine would burst into a warm melodic thrumming) and turn right for Marlow. At W. R. Clark, Butcher (high marble counters, sawdust on the floor), I learned the difference between English and Scottish beef, between English and New Zealand lamb, and that there were a dozen sorts of fresh sausages to choose from. Across the street at the baker's, there were six sorts of "wheatmeal" and eight sorts of bread from refined flours. Down the block at Brown's Grocer's (every good thing one could think of stacked on shelves ceiling to floor), more choices, more to learn.

The first time I asked for "—and a box of tea, please . . ."

"China or India, Madam?" came the reply. I didn't know. I asked the young man to explain the difference and tried to remember what he told me. Another day I asked for brown sugar. "Crystals, refined golden or dark, Demerara, Barbados, castor, or loaf, Madam?" Gulp. A tin of pepper, please. "Black or white peppercorns, Java or Malabar, mignonette, or cayenne, Mrs. Thompson?" It took time, but eventually I learned to ask for Ceylon tea, Demerara sugar, and Malabar Black peppercorns as well as white, please.

Choices were one of the joys of marketing in England. Our butter was from Denmark, our creamy cheeses and *pâtés* were from France, our pasta was from Italy, our oranges (blood oranges again!) were from Algeria or Israel, and once the best apples in the shop were McIntosh from Washington State.

Next I would tool past Lodge Hill Cottage on the Henley-Marlow road and go into Henley-on-Thames to Frenchs' Greengrocer. Mr. Frenchs was charming and seemed pleased to have an American customer who appreciated his produce. He would handpick his choicest morsels for me, sometimes taking me behind the curtain into the back of the shop to pull out new crates of goodies that had just come in. And for David's Halloween jack-o-lantern, Mr. Frenchs special-ordered a pumpkin (apparently the good people of Henley didn't eat them). I'll never forget the telephone call: "Your squash has arrived from London, madam. When will you be coming to pick it up?"

And when I needed just one or two things for the kitchen, at the post office down Ferry Lane, two sisters kept a small grocery (at the end of Ferry lane, in busier times, you could catch a ferry and cross the Thames). David and I would stroll past the churchyard and turn right down the road canopied with trees, past the abbey once inhabited by the Mad Monks of Medmenham. At the grocery I would buy whatever we needed and always a bottle of Ribena black currant syrup to make a purply cold crush for my young man's tea.

Then, just before the autumnal equinox, another young man entered our lives. After sloshing along through Greece, Italy, France, and England under cover, in nearby Oxford's Nuffield Maternity Home, our Achilles, Benjamin Stuart, finally emerged.

The morning after, I was ravenous. Matron carried in my breakfast tray.

Now we had eaten dozens of the best breakfasts we'd ever eaten anywhere in the world in English bed and breakfasts while looking for our house. Enormous halves of grapefruits. Porridges of every texture and grain. Piles of excellent sausages and bacon and ham. Eggs so fresh they quivered. Stacks of every sort of toast from the thinnest slices of wheat to great slabs of country white. Marmalades, jellies, and preserves that melted in your mouth. I couldn't wait. I lifted the big silvery bell with a flourish—and burst out laughing. There was one piece of fried bread in the center of the plate. No parsley, no bacon, no egg, no nothing. That was it. One of the memorable gustatory moments of my life.

David was introduced to his brother at Miss Bond's. Miss Emily Bond's bed and breakfast was on Wytham Street in Oxford. It had turned out to be our home away from home and Miss Bond was our fairy godmother. She was in her seventies and had cornflower blue eyes. When we arrived, she led us into the kitchen and, gesturing at her mother seated cozily by the stove, cried out proudly, "Ninety-two! *Nine-ty-two!*"

Miss Bond served only breakfast to her other guests, but for us, she made wonderful English suppers. Her table was quintessentially English and I discovered many new treats. I first ate steak and kidney pie and then steak and kidney pudding there—mad about the pie, ambivalent about the pudding. And my first pork and apple pie.

To my taste, some of the most delectable culinary marriages are the flavors of rich meat or poultry with tart-sweet fruits: French duckling with oranges or cherries, Danish chicken with apples and prunes, Greek lamb or beef with quinces, Hawaiian anything with pineapple, and English pork and apple pie. It is a pie of longstanding. "To make a Chefshire pork-pie" was first published in 1747 in Hannah Glasse's *The Art of Cookery, Made Plain and Easy*. I've made one from a 1788 copy borrowed from the UCLA library. Why did that pie have peculiar magic?

Once, making it, I had some boiled potatoes on hand. Feeling that others just like me have added their own touch to traditional recipes—whether out of necessity or invention—I layered in the potatoes. The potatoes not only added their homely texture but bridged the flavors of sweet apples and savory pork. Miss Bond, of course, made hers without potato. Make it both ways and see what you think.

The final splash of white wine or hard cider traditionally called for is a matter of choice. Wine adds an underlying sprightliness, but I feel cider belongs. If cider, hard cider must be used. Sweet cider would throw the balance toward sweetness, which the English embrace but Americans find cloying. If you intend to serve this at room temperature for a picnic or such, omit the cider or wine because the extra liquid will sog the crust. Eaten hot, however, the juices are delicious spooned over each serving.

ENGLISH PORK, APPLE, AND PERHAPS POTATO PIE
[*8 servings*]
The pie may be served hot from the oven, at room temperature, or carefully reheated.

This pastry is wonderfully short and melt-in-the-mouth.

THE SAVORY SHORTCRUST PASTRY*
This pastry may be made the day before and kept in the refrigerator, or frozen. Bring to malleable temperature before rolling.

2 ½ cups all-purpose flour, plus more for the board
½ teaspoon salt

1 cup (8 ounces) lard, chilled, cut in ½-inch chips; vegetable shortening may be substituted
½ cup plus ½ tablespoon water, iced

Make the pastry, following the method for Perfect Pie Pastry on page 8. In place of the water/egg/vinegar mixture, just add the ice water. The finished dough will be slightly sticky.

THE FILLING AND THE BAKING

1 recipe Savory Shortcrust Pastry (recipe preceding)
3 medium-large (1 pound) boiling† potatoes
2 ½ pounds boneless lean pork shoulder or loin
1 onion, chopped
Generous 1 tablespoon fresh chopped sage leaves, or generous 1 teaspoon dried
1 teaspoon salt, plus a little more for the potatoes
About 12 turns of the white pepper mill, plus a little more for the potatoes (1 teaspoon plus, medium grind)

About 1 ½ tablespoons light brown sugar
About 2 teaspoons fresh lemon juice
1 very large (8 ounces) sweet-tart cooking apple, cored, peeled, and sliced ⅛ inch thick‡
4 large strips of uncooked lean bacon, chopped
2 tablespoons butter, cold, plus 1 tablespoon for the shell, softened
¾ cup hard cider or dry white wine (optional)
1 egg, beaten

Divide the pastry dough into 2 parts, one slightly larger than the other. Wrap and refrigerate about 20 minutes, then roll the pieces ⅛-inch thick: The larger round should be 15 inches in diameter and the smaller round 13 inches. Line a 9½ × 2-inch glass pie dish with the larger round (leaving a ½-inch margin at the edges) and

---

*The recipe makes enough for a 9½-inch double crust.
†Thin-skinned, new, and waxy as opposed to baking potatoes that are thicker-skinned, have been in storage, and are fluffy or mealy when cooked.
‡Pages 235–236 have a guide of cooking apples for all seasons.

brush the surface with softened butter. Slip the other round on its rolling-out towel onto a baking sheet and keep both in a cool place while you finish the preparations.

Boil the potatoes* until a fine skewer goes through without much resistance but they're not altogether tender, 10 to 15 minutes. Peel and cool, then slice into ⅛-inch-thick rounds. Meanwhile, trim fat and sinew from the pork, leaving about one-quarter of the fat on the meat for juiciness. Send the meat once through the coarse blade of a meat grinder or chop medium-fine in the food processor or with a sharp chef's knife or cleaver. Turn into a mixing bowl and with your hands, blend in the onion, sage, salt, and pepper. In another bowl, also use your hands to gently mix sugar and lemon juice into the apple (for the amount of each, be guided by the apple's sweetness).

Heat the oven to 375°F. Divide the pork, potatoes, and bacon in thirds and the apple slices in half. Cover the bottom of the pie shell with one portion of pork, lightly packed. Next, make a layer of potatoes, season very lightly with salt and a grinding of pepper, then sprinkle with bacon. Apple slices come next. Layer everything flat, not the usual heaping in the center, but build straight up. Continue in this manner, finishing with bacon. Dot with flakes of butter and sprinkle over the cider or wine, if you're using it.

Brush the rim of the pastry with beaten egg and lay on the pastry lid. Trim the lid to a margin ½ inch beyond the bottom rim, then tuck the top underneath the bottom. Flute the border with the tip of a little finger, pressing the edges together to seal. If you break the dough as you flute, daub with egg and gently but firmly press in a patch of dough. Cut a 3-inch circle out of the center of the lid—this venting takes the pressure off the edges. You can cut narrow apple leaves from leftover dough and set them decoratively around the top. Brush all over with beaten egg.

Bake 45 minutes, then carefully turn the dish halfway around for even baking, checking for breaks in the pastry that need patching. Bake until everything tests tender with a thin skewer and the crust is a gorgeous golden brown, about 45 minutes more. Serve warm, not hot: cool on a rack about 1 hour. Or cool completely and serve at room temperature the next day, *or* reheat at 375°F for a long hour.

Miss Bond's garden in the back was filled with rows and rows of enormous cabbages and Brussels sprouts, fountains of raspberries, sprays of gooseberries, patches of strawberries, and a fine young plum tree in the center. Miss Bond's plum jam was richly flavored and wonderfully straightforward—the fruit was neither peeled nor pitted. There's charm in its naturalness—you'll come across a clump of plum on your toast, just as it came off the tree. (If you give a jar to someone who might be caught unaware by the pits, for heaven's sake, warn them!) Any sweet-tart plum such as Santa Rosas would be fine for Miss Bond's jam, but if you can use Blue Damsons, golden Mirabelles, or Greengages, lucky you.

---

*Cut them in half crosswise—but not lengthwise—for faster cooking. Cover with cold water, cover the pot, and bring to a boil over medium-high heat.

ENGLISH PLUM JAM
[Makes about sixteen 8-ounce jars]

6 pounds unpitted sweet-tart firm-ripe juicy   14¼ cups (6 pounds) sugar
* plums, rinsed and stemmed*
2⅓ cups water, cool (a little more, if some of
* the plums are underripe)*

Gently simmer the plums and water very briefly, just until the skins soften—the plums mustn't cook to a mush. Turn half the plums-and-juice and half the sugar into your preserving kettle.* Stir over medium heat until the sugar has dissolved. Bring to a boil and skim off all the pits that rise to the surface. Boil rapidly uncovered, stirring frequently, until a bit of cooled syrup held between thumb and index finger still stays connected by peaky threads when the fingers are opened. Test after 10 minutes. Remove from the heat. When the jam has settled down, skim off any foam. Let the jam settle a few more minutes, then pack, seal, and store according to directions on pages 242 to 244.

A felicitous mix of fruits and a great discovery was Miss Bond's Summer Pudding, which she made especially for David. Classically, the pudding is made of raspberries and red currants, but Miss Bond added tart red cherries, which gave a beautiful lift.

Some of America's sour cherries are Early Richmond, Montmorency, and Meteor (amarelle types: yellow flesh, clear juice) and English Morello and North Star (morello types: red flesh and juice). But if your garden is fresh out of red currants and sour cherries, summer pudding of pure raspberries is no punishment.†

AN OXFORD SUMMER PUDDING
Molded soft fruits
[6 servings]

This should be refrigerated 12 hours before serving so the juices can saturate the bread (turning it rosy scarlet) and the fruit can set for unmolding. You might squeak by with 9 hours—or make it 24 hours in advance. And of course I needn't say to use only fresh fruit . . .

A 20-ounce loaf of homemade-quality   2 cups (8 ounces) raspberries
* white bread, 1 to 2 days old, cut into   1½ cups (8 ounces§) sour red cherries, pitted*
* ⅜-inch-thick slices, crusts removed‡*

---

*If you have one of the enormous French copper preserving pans (about which, see the footnote on page 70), you can make this all in one batch.
†Once I hadn't enough raspberries, so I added small perfumed strawberries—sublime. Any of the blackberry family would have been lovely, too.
‡Dry the crusts and trimmings in a slow oven until crisp then roll into breadcrumbs for another day.
§Purchase, not pitted, weight.

Scant 1 cup (4 ounces) red currants
½ cup sugar

Cold heavy cream or whipped cream, or
light custard sauce (recipe follows,
optional)

Find a deep quart-size mold—something like a rounded pudding-steaming bowl or a soufflé dish. Cut a piece of heavy cardboard to just fit inside the top and wrap it in foil.

Cut and fit the slices of bread together to snugly line the mold. Carefully plug any cracks and holes.

In a medium-sized heavy skillet over medium heat, gently stir the raspberries, cherries, red currants, and sugar together with a wooden spoon just until the juices flow and the sugar dissolves, 2 to 3 minutes. Spoon the fruit and juice into the bread-lined mold, gently shaking the bowl to settle the fruit. If there is more juice than will fit, reserve it. Cover the fruit neatly with a lid of bread that fits inside the other pieces. Lay on a piece of plastic film. Set the cardboard on top of the pudding and on that, a 3-pound weight. Refrigerate 12 hours.

To serve, remove weight and coverings and run a thin knife all the way down the sides of the mold, lay a rimmed serving dish on top, then invert and let the pudding drop down. Pour any reserved juice around the bottom. Cut in wedges and serve plain or with cream, lightly whipped cream, or custard sauce.

At Miss Bond's table I also first tasted what she called pour custard, that ineffable creamy gilding known as custard sauce or, being English, *crème anglaise*. I have published another recipe for it, but since then, I've learned to make it more simply. And less sweetly: the traditional rule calls for at least twice this amount of sugar, but less means more of the inherent sweetness of the milk and egg shine through.

RULE-OF-1 CUSTARD SAUCE
[*Makes 1¼ cups: 5 or 6 servings*]
This keeps several days in the refrigerator.

1 extra large egg
1 cup milk, preferably rich*

1 heaping tablespoon sugar
1 teaspoon vanilla extract

In a small heavy saucepan, lightly whisk the egg, then whisk in the milk and sugar. Stir with a wooden spoon over medium heat just until the sauce thickens and coats the spoon—one bubble will pop up or small bubbles will sizzle around the edges. Remove from the heat. (If you've overcooked the sauce and little curds have formed, turn into a bowl and whisk like crazy until they come out.)

---

*A little half-and-half or heavy cream in the bottom of the measuring cup, then fill it with regular or low-fat or non-fat milk.

Stir in the vanilla and pour through a strainer into a serving pitcher or bowl. The sauce will thicken as it cools. Plastic film laid directly on the custard keeps a skin from forming. Refrigerate until cold, about 4 hours.

Soon it was Christmas. I unpacked cherished bits of the holiday we would celebrate far from home, including the mold for my grandmother's carrot pudding. But I'd forgotten to pack the recipe. I knew it was one cup of everything except one ingredient, which was half-a-cup, but I couldn't remember which. The day before Christmas, I made the pudding—everything one cup. Well, I thought, we'll just have to see. I steamed and unmolded it. The pudding stood tall and proud—I wanted to dash to the phone and call my grandmother. But then it gave a tiny shudder. And then another. And another. And then suddenly, the whole thing sank to its knees, oozing rivulets of butter. Butter! *That* was the half-a-cup! After it had rid itself of the excess butter, I spooned everything back into the mold and set it in the larder. The next day, I steamed the pudding and unmolded it again and it was splendid.

We'd invited old friends in London to join us in the country for Christmas dinner. I wanted to roast a pheasant, so I'd gone to the poulterer's in nearby Hambleden. I'd never tasted pheasant. Entering the shop, I realized that all sorts of furred and feathered shapes were hanging about upside down. I tried to look firmly at the poulterer while we discussed my purchase.

I learned that aging wild birds is an art few understood. Pheasant must be hung in a cool, dark, preferably earthen-floored shed for precisely five days, with plenty of circulating air—if the weather is right. If the weather is too warm or too cool, the hanging time is tricky. The meat must be a delicate cross between game and chicken, neither too high nor too bland. I took a bird home, making sure David wouldn't see it—the beautiful pheasants that lived in our meadow were David's friends ("I'm talking to my friend, Mommy"). And then I roasted it (the pheasant was a good size for the cottage's sixteen-inch-wide oven heated with two electric bars on either side; at Thanksgiving, the sixteen-pound turkey I'd automatically chosen had to be delicately balanced first on one wing, then the other, and it was roasted the entire time with the door half-open—Americans never learn to think small). I sauced the pheasant with white wine and garnished it with white grapes. Even though it might have been related to some of David's friends, it was a treat.

In fact the whole dinner, I noted in my journal, was divine. "For once in my life, everything pleased me. I couldn't find fault with one dish . . ."

David turned three in January and we managed to find three little boys to celebrate with him. I made a chocolate birthday cake in the shape of a horse (not one child noticed—I've always thought children's parties most intimidating of all to plan). Benjamin was pure joy (twenty-three dimples!) and would lie still for hours, listening to music on the BBC Home Service. At day's end, after a bath from Papa in the big tub (Gene would wrap David in a towel, then turn him upside down and exclaim, "Darling, I've been cheated! This boy has no head!" as David giggled helplessly), David played on the indigo rug before the fire with the Dinky cars Norah sent him from Switzerland and I sat at my study table at the end of the long room nursing Benje. We all listened to Papa as, leaning against a slipper chair, he read the day's pages of his novel. I, too, was writing happily. Our lives were in order.

I cooked simply. The big treat was saved for Sunday breakfast, when I made Irish scones. I was given the recipe by a neighbor, a woman from Cork in her eighties who called on us with scones in a basket when she heard we had a new baby in the house. Hold one in the palm of your hand—a feather!

Handle this dough gently—none of the usual kneading, rerolling, or bashing about.

IRISH SOURED MILK SCONES
(or Buttermilk Biscuits)
[*Makes 12 scones*]
These are best straight from the oven—but the prepared scones can wait 2 hours in a cool place or the refrigerator before baking.

2 cups all-purpose flour, plus more for the
    board
2 teaspoons sugar
2 teaspoons baking powder
1/2 teaspoon baking soda
1/2 teaspoon salt
1/4 cup (2 ounces) lard, cold, in 1/2-inch
    chips

1/2 stick butter, cold, in 1/2-inch chips
1 cup soured milk* or buttermilk, cold†
A handful of currants or golden raisins
    (optional)‡
1 egg, beaten (a small egg will do)

In a mixing or food processor bowl, blend the flour, sugar, baking powder, baking soda, and salt together. Drop in the lard and butter.

Hand method (preferable, because the dough is so soft): With your fingertips, rub the fat into the flour until the texture of breadcrumbs. Add the milk and mix with a fork just until the flour is moistened. The dough will be very soft.

Food processor method: Whiz until the largest pieces of fat are the size of small peas, about 6 seconds; stop. Pour the milk evenly over the flour and process just until the

---

*Use milk that has naturally soured in the refrigerator, or sour sweet milk by putting 1 tablespoon lemon juice or cider vinegar or white vinegar in a 1-cup measure and fill to the top with milk.

†As footnoted in the fresh cheese recipe on page 169, I'm told whey also makes light scones. I will try it.

‡Although the addition of currants, raisins, or even candied peel is traditional, curiously I've found that children—ever the purists—carefully pick them out, and so I've always made these scones plain.

dough masses together and revolves around the blade once. The dough will be very soft.

With a fork, lightly blend in the currants or raisins, if you're using them. Turn onto a floured board, dust the top of the dough with flour, and pat a generous ³/₄-inch thick, handling the dough as little as possible. Dip a glass or a cutter around 2½ inches wide in flour and cut out the scones, setting them a good inch apart on an unbuttered baking sheet. Press the remaining scraps of dough together for the last scone or two. Brush the scones all over with beaten egg.

When ready to bake, heat the oven to 450°F. Bake until crisp and golden, about 12 minutes. Serve at once, then split and spread with butter and what-you-will (English plum jam, page 195, is superb).

For supper, my most popular dish according to Gene and David was something that took three minutes to make. Not only did the library of Lodge Hill Cottage include the complete twenty-one-volume set of *The Oxford English Dictionary*, which I coveted, but it had an old copy of *Mrs. Beeton's Household Management*. Fortunately, I didn't have to covet that, too, because my mother had handed hers on to me.

WELSH RAREBIT, AFTER MRS. BEETON'S
[*4 servings*]

¼ *stick butter*
2 *cups grated* (*8 ounces*) *Cheshire or sharp Cheddar cheese*
¼ *cup ale or beer*

2 *teaspoons prepared mustard, preferably a good mellow brown sort*
A few turns of the white pepper mill (*a pinch*)
4 *pieces of hot buttered toast* (*white is traditional, rye is super*)

In a heavy saucepan over medium-low heat, melt the butter, add the cheese, and stir with a wooden spoon until melted, then gradually add the ale, mustard, and pepper. Pour over the toast and serve as hot as possible.

And Welsh Rarebit over steamed broccoli or cauliflower makes a marvelous light supper.

One morning a few days before we were to go back to California, Gene brought in the London *Times*, opened it and, staring at it, said, "Oh, my God!" There on the page was a picture of the Queen cutting a ribbon and declaring a children's hospital open. At her side was a woman whose face was only too familiar, identified by a caption as "Her Grace, the Duchess of Denver."

" 'Humor her!' " I said.

His answer is unprintable.

...And Here and There...

I am a wholehearted traveler. When I'm in a place that speaks to me, it's not long before I imagine myself living there. A few years ago in the Burgundian hilltop town of Vézelay, we happened to stroll past a small stone house perched on the town's northern edge. The house, perhaps hundreds of years old, was empty and open because it was in process of being remodeled. As I stood in the gate to the garden that flowed in terraces below my feet, the unbroken prospect was of rolling hills stippled with vineyards, checkered with villages, brilliant with mustard (it was May). The tiny garden held one venerable apple tree, a heap of strawberries, and bursts of artichoke, fennel, and chard. From the moment we had arrived, Romanesque Vézelay had a peculiar pull on me. The longer I stood in that garden gate, the more I became convinced that that stone house was being readied for Gene and me. My head began spinning and I began making plans for the rest of my life in Vézelay.

But the more I come to know myself, the more I realize that, like the banana trees at The Garden of Allah, I cannot be transplanted. I am a Californian. More, I am a Southern Californian, which, as you probably know, is Another Breed of Cat. Looking back on it, it was inevitable that we would again live in Southern California. We did, but the way wound through four years and as many houses.

From England, we flew to Los Angeles because my father was ill. By chance, the apartment mirroring my parents' was vacant, Mother and Daddy urged us to take it, and so we moved next door. Benjamin was such a treat I couldn't stand it, and so in December 1960, our Athena, Dinah Vaughn, was born. Meanwhile, my father recovered his health, the four of us became even closer friends, and the boys whizzed happily back and forth between parents and grandparents.

Then Gene decided to go back to advertising in San Francisco. We bought our first house, the carriage house of an old Berkeley estate. We could afford such a mansion because the once-quiet one-lane road outside was now the fastest route between Berkeley and Oakland—vroomvroomvroom! Gene still worked nights and weekends writing fiction and I was finishing my first cookbook. But the house began taking its toll. My mother had a way of phoning the first of every month when the bills came in. I'd chat cheerily for a minute or two, then have to leave the phone, in tears. Thank heaven we unloaded the Millstone and rented a reasonable house on Belvedere, a small island in the Bay.

Knowing that everything was going to be all right, knowing that Dinah would want a sister, I managed it so that in July 1962, with Gene for the fourth time holding my hand and charming me through it, our Euterpe, Amanda Greenleaf, arrived.

Then we bought another house, also across the Golden Gate. It was an exquisite redwood Victorian restored in a Japanese mood. By now, Gene was in Los Angeles most of the time producing commercials. It got to the point that I would dump the laundry from the dryer onto our bed and defiantly sleep beneath the heap, since there was nobody in the house who cared about folded laundry.

But there were the comforts of my children, my work, and my friends. M. F. once arrived with a basket of persimmons from her bountiful tree in St. Helena. Those which we didn't eat out of hand with squirts of lemon and a spoon, we lined up along the redwood ledge beneath the mitered glass windows in the corner of the kitchen—matte orange orbs glowing in the sun with crimson fuchsias in the windowbox behind them.

M. F. no longer lives beside that venerable tree but other friends are generous with their persimmons. And when we can eat no more and those at the bottom of the basket threaten to melt into persimmon-colored pools, I bake cakes of their puckery sweet meat for Christmas.* The recipe, which couldn't be easier, was inspired by one of James Beard's.† I've called them "tea" cakes because a slice is the perfect accompaniment to a cup of China tea.

Brandied Persimmon Tea Cakes
[*Makes 4 loaves, about 16 slices each*]
These keep in the refrigerator 2 or 3 weeks, in the freezer 3 or 4 months. The recipe may be doubled.

3½ cups all-purpose flour, plus more for the molds	*½ cup (firmly packed) light brown sugar*
1 cup sugar	*½ tablespoon baking soda*
	1 teaspoon nutmeg

---

*Drop ripe persimmons whole into the freezer, then thaw to use for Christmas baking.
†*Beard on Bread.*

4 large or 6 to 8 small unpeeled soft-ripe
   persimmons
2 sticks butter, preferably unsalted, melted,
   plus a little for the molds, softened
4 extra large eggs, at room temperature*

*²/₃ cup brandy
2 cups golden raisins, plumped a few
   minutes in hot water, if very dry
1¼ cups chopped toasted walnuts or pecans
A little sifted confectioner's sugar*

Choose four pretty 3-cup baking molds—or any selection adding up to 12 cups. Brush with butter and dust with flour. Heat the oven to 350°F. In a large bowl, mix the flour, granulated and brown sugars, baking soda, and nutmeg.

Food processor method: Puree the persimmons in your work bowl. You'll need 2 cups. Return the puree to the bowl and add the butter, eggs, and brandy; whiz just until blended.

Hand method: Puree the persimmons through a food mill or sieve into another large bowl. You'll need 2 cups. To the puree add the butter, eggs, and brandy and beat with a wooden spoon until blended.

Turn the puree mixture into the flour mixture and beat with a wooden spoon until smooth. Stir in the raisins and nuts, then divide the batter among the molds, filling them ¾ full and smoothing the tops. Rap gently on the counter to knock out any air bubbles.

Bake until a thin skewer, thrust in the center, comes out clean and the top springs back when lightly tapped with a forefinger, from 45 to 60 minutes (depending on the material, size, and shape of the mold). Cool in the pans 5 minutes, then turn out onto a cake rack right or wrong sides up, to cool. Dust with confectioner's sugar before serving or wrapping as a gift. Slice thinly.

In Hollywood, Gene was casting a commercial for a well-known beverage. It featured a sultry woman in a white-spangled sheath. He spent days looking for the right girl. Finding an unknown, he filmed the commercial and took it to the client.

The client said, "She's selling her package more than she's selling mine."

"That girl is going to be a star," Gene said.

Silence.

Some time went by. Suddenly the client called Gene, saying, "Okay, put it on the air."

"I can't. Our option has expired."

"The hell with the option. Get that girl back."

"I can't. That girl is Raquel Welch."

Gene came home and said to me, "Let's pack." The time had come. So we sold the house, put cats, dog, and children into the station wagon, and moved back to Southern California. To the Malibu I'd loved as a child.

---

*But don't forget to look for and remove the seeds before pureeing.

Malibu

WELLCOME!!!
glad you could come
    ALLMOST all the food was done
by
CHILDREN so please say thank you to any
child you see.
        BY
          AMANDA
            A CHILD

Nearly thirty years after helping my mother with hers, I made a *rijsttafel* of my own. But instead of having one little girl to help, I had my children's band of cooks—eight in all. As the first guests arrived, I discovered the note above on the front door. It was typewritten on blue paper and stuck to the wood with two gummed hearts left over from Valentine's Day. Amanda was ten.

We lived in a horseshoe-shaped canyon half a mile from the sea. The canyon, a community of about fifty families, was a small secluded world in which we all watched out for one another. Our house was a sprawling California ranch house on a bluff, with walls of glass and adobe tile floors, a stone's throw from a creek below that emptied into a lagoon beside the ocean. The children fished for trout in the creek when they weren't catching turtles in Turtle Swamp or playing baseball down the road at the MacKenzies'. From the deck of the house we looked across chaparral and mustard to see an occasional rider streaking across the meadows and an occasional great blue heron standing on one leg in the lagoon's bird sanctuary. And beyond that, a brilliant patchwork of scarlet, cerise, orange, and flame—fields of geraniums grown for their seeds.

Gene was off at the studio, and, having found a lovely young thing to help out and with the children in school all day, I began cooking and writing with a vengeance.

My *rijsttafel* was, in fact, a menu I was testing for an article. (Dinah once asked wearily, sitting down to a meal, "Is this testing or is it dinner?" Dinah was a great one for *bon mots*, also once asking, "What is this, Mommy?" "Veal, darling." "No, I mean, what *was* it?") I couldn't have put the party together without the children. I had come to depend on them just as my mother had depended on me. It wasn't until I began entertaining that I realized something extraordinary had been happening to me while buttering all those orange rolls, stuffing all those candles into sconces, arranging all those flowers as a child. I was absorbing a wealth of knowledge about how to entertain, which gave me a self-assurance that only comes with practice. So ever since our children could stand up, they in their turn, and any of their friends who happened through, were asked to help prepare for our guests. For my part, in time I learned four rules for entertaining with the aid of children.

First, make a list. Children get a sinking feeling and turn cranky when they think the work is open-ended. So I tacked up a list of all the things I needed done and each child initialed the jobs he would be responsible for. When they quarreled over who would do what, I disappeared. I've learned that children solve their problems better than I.

Second rule is really the cardinal rule of living with children: a child will give back what he senses is expected of him. I've found that children are magically able to do many more things, and do them well, than I would have thought. If they sense my confidence, they'll knock themselves out to get it done.

Third rule is praise, praise, praise. Children want to be thanked for every job, which is really just good manners. And they like a remark about the quality of their work, which proves you've seen what they've done and appreciate it—"I really wasn't sure there was any *silver* under all that black!" Then, at day's end, a trip to the ice cream parlor is a nice thank-you. For devotion above and beyond the call of kindness, mash notes are in order.

And the fourth rule is obvious but wants stating: suit the child to the task.

David, a remarkably structured young man, did the bar. He lined up glasses in geometric designs, ranged bottles like short, medium, and tall soldiers, pyramided pickled onions and swirled cocktail napkins. Benjamin, with his uncommon eye, lit the garden (often with *luminaria*, votive candles in paper bags weighted with sand) and composed the centerpieces. For the *rijsttafel*, Benje loaned me the brightly painted model of a motorcycle he'd made (a "chopped hog"), tying a nosegay of yellow daisies to its green tailpipe with thin red ribbon.

Unlike her mother, Dinah is *organized*. In a fit of frenzied cooking, I depended on Dinah to rescue me from myself and she always did. Dinah and I have burned many a midnight candle when I bought too many flats of straw-berries for preserves, too many boxes of quinces for Paradise jelly. And since Dinah loved things ordered, I armed her with spray can and rags and she whoosshted and wiped her way through the house until the rooms had a lemon-scented glow.

The morning of the party, Amanda, Miss Green Thumb, snipped her way through the canyon, bringing home matilija poppies, black-eyed susans, ni-cotianas, coreopsis, and pale shoots of eucalyptus. Then she distributed her arrangements in crocks and pitchers and vases through the house, with al-ways something herbal for the kitchen.

The balance of my children's band were friends. For the *rijsttafel*, young Fred, a budding chef, sliced ginger, mashed garlic, shredded chicken, and ar-ranged the candy dishes (outlining a peace symbol in lemon drops). Michelle and Jenni beautifully prepared all the fruits and vegetables for cooking, and Keri and Kristi made scallion and radish flowers before helping set the table.

Taken at its best, a dinner party is giving of oneself so that others may have pleasure. Children are good at that.

A couple of months after the *rijsttafel*, I began preparations for my moth-er's seventieth birthday party (sixty of her most intimate friends). Wanting something amusing, surefire delicious, yet easy enough to serve to so many, I made *tostadas*. They were smashing. I think that's because *tostadas* as this house has come to do them—Mexican with a certain California abundance—are not only sensational eating, but festive. The table is laden. I've always aimed for the Russian ideal of a table: you shouldn't be able to see the cloth. And there's a feeling of sumptuousness about piling your plate with so many beautiful colors until it rises into a sparkling mountain. Another virtue of *tos-tadas* is that it's every course in one—meat, vegetables, salad, cheese, you-name-it.

For the birthday girl, I made a tub of sponge cake in two developing pans from my father's old darkroom and glazed it with bittersweet chocolate (page 91). For a non-birthday party, offer scoops of the darkest chocolate ice cream you can buy, sauced with orange-flavored burnt sugar sauce (page 210), very Mexican.

To begin such a feast, all you want with drinks are non-rich, non-filling nibbles. Plates of peeled jícama, the slices to be picked up with fingers and squeezed with lime or orange juice,* are set here and there among baskets of roasted nuts, pumpkin seeds, and unhulled strawberries. These, and the prospect of what's happening on the buffet, are plenty. Just garnish every-thing with hot-colored flowers.

---

*If you can't buy jícama—the tropical tuber with the texture and flavor resembling water chestnuts—have perky radishes with their leafy tops left on.

TOSTADA DINNER

WITH MARGARITAS

Thin slices of jícama with wedges of lime
Roasted pumpkin seeds
Roasted almonds or peanuts
Unhulled strawberries

THE BUFFET

Tostada shells
Hot refried beans
Coarsely shredded turkey
Thinly sliced tomatoes
Shredded lettuce
Sliced black olives
Whole scallion rings
Sliced radishes
Grated jack cheese
Guacamole
Sour cream
Salsa cruda
Chopped cilantro

TO DRINK WITH DINNER

Cold Mexican beer
and a quaffing white wine (for diehard wine drinkers)

DESSERT

Chocolate ice cream with Cointreau burnt sugar sauce
Coffee

Learning what I planned to serve, my mother said, "My friends can't eat that! It's much too spicy for them at their age. Besides, they're all on diets."

Knowing better, I served it anyway and there was barely enough left over for my children's band of cooks. The only spicy elements in the dinner are the refried beans (and only if you add chili powder) and the *salsa cruda*, which non-spicy types can ignore (put a up sign: *Hot!*).

The recipes that follow are for a *tostada* dinner for twelve (but everything can be multiplied or divided). Amounts for accompaniments to the following recipes are on pages 259–260.

Thin and delicate large flour tortillas fry up divinely and make a generous foundation for the heap. Buy them 10 inches wide. Better, make them yourself. If you've ever rolled out pastry, you can make incomparable flour tortillas with their characteristic sweet grain flavor, slightly chewy texture, and speckled creamy color.

Tortillas de harina*
Flour tortillas
[Makes fifteen 10-inch tortillas]
Although best when fresh, tortillas keep well in a plastic bag, refrigerated (several days) or frozen (a month or two).

3 3/4 cups flour, preferably unbleached, plus more for the board
2 1/2 tablespoons lard or vegetable shortening, at room temperature

Slightly rounded 1/2 teaspoon salt
1/2 cup plus 2 tablespoons water, hot
1/2 cup plus 2 tablespoons milk, cold

In a bowl, rub the flour and fat together with your fingertips until mixture has the texture of cornmeal. Drop the salt into a measuring cup, add the hot water, then the cold milk. Stir the liquid into the flour with a fork, then knead the dough until smooth and silky on a floured surface, about 3 minutes. Cover with plastic film and let rest at room temperature, 15 minutes to 2 hours.

Divide the dough into fifteen equal parts and pat into balls. With a heavy rolling pin (preferably stockinette-covered†) on a lightly floured cloth, roll out into rounds that are so thin you can see the weave of the towel beneath and are a full 10 inches in diameter. Roll as you do pie pastry, from the center out, turning the round occasionally to keep it even. Stack one on top of the other. Once you've got the knack, they'll take less than a minute each to roll.

Heat a dry heavy 10-inch griddle or skillet, preferably cast iron, over medium-high heat until it begins to smoke. Lay in a tortilla and bake until the bottom is speckled golden brown, about 20 seconds. Turn and bake until the bottom again is speckled, using a corner of your spatula to pierce the bubbles on top. Do not over-bake—they should remain soft. Stack as they bake. When cool, turn into a heavy plastic bag and refrigerate or freeze.

But the tortilla maker must have a treat even beyond the pleasure of turning out such handsome Mexican bread. Before you put them all away, make yourself one or two

Quesadillas‡
Tortilla melted-cheese turnovers
[For each serving]
Set a dry cast iron skillet over medium-high heat. When hot, lay in a tortilla (flour or corn).§ As it softens, lay some thinly sliced or grated melting cheese‖ over one

---

*The *h* is silent in *harina*.
†Details about the sleeve on page 254.
‡Kay-sah-*DEE*-ya, as in tor-*TEE*-ya.
§It can be straight from the freezer: just hold it down until it thaws on one side, turn it over and repeat, then fill.
‖Melting cheese notes, page 244.

side. That's all you need do, unless you want to throw in a few chopped chilies from a jar or spoon over some *salsa—cruda* (page 209) or otherwise. Fold over the top and turn the *quesadilla* over, toasting it just until the cheese melts, a long minute. Eat hot out of hand and expect to want another.

Think of *quesadillas* also as hors d'oeuvres—make the tortillas palm-size. And hot flour tortillas are the beginnings of BURRITOS—slather hot refried beans and grated melting cheese inside, fold in the ends, roll up, and eat out of hand doused with *salsa*.

Now to make the edible plates for your party.

Tostada Shells
Crisp fried tortillas
These may be prepared the day before serving, but be sure to stash them where they won't get broken.

Fry the tortillas one by one in ½-inch-deep hot oil or lard in a large heavy skillet over medium-high heat until puffed, cracker-crisp, and the top is a rich brown. Turn with tongs and brown the other side. Lift onto brown paper, stacking the *tostadas* between paper towels. When cool, set out of harm's way (they are fragile!). If your air is damp, you may have to crispen them in a moderate oven before serving, but they needn't be warm for the buffet.

The only thing hot on the *tostada* buffet, in terms of temperature, are the refried beans. And they are the only thing, besides the olives, that come from a can. FRIJOLES REFRITOS made from fresh beans are lovely, but they don't taste a greal deal different from top-quality canned refried beans. The major criticism we have of canned food is that it's overcooked, but that's not a problem with refried beans—*frijoles refritos* literally means "well-fried beans." And for a party like this, the time saved is welcome. I refresh the beans by heating them in a little melted lard* with softened chopped onion, garlic, and chili powder.† Their consistency, when hot, should be gloppy, and the flavor of the onions, garlic, and chili should be present but unobtrusive. Once this is done, they can be covered and put away until time for reheating, which you do in their covered casserole in a moderate oven for a long half hour.

Guacamole was once called *mantequilla de pobre*, poor man's butter. With so many other flavors in the *tostada*, a modest mash of avocados is just right.‡

---

*Or olive oil, should you prefer it.
†For each pound of refried beans: 2 tablespoons lard, ¼ finely chopped onion, 1 finely chopped garlic clove, and 1 tablespoon chili powder. For 12 servings, have 3 pounds of refried beans.
‡For a dip on its own, fancy up this *guacamole* with finely chopped onion, peeled and seeded tomatoes, chopped fresh chilies, and cilantro to taste.

GUACAMOLE
Poor man's butter of avocados
[*12 servings*]
Best made at the last minute, but it may be held an hour or two without darkening, if closely covered.

6 medium-sized (2¼ pounds) ripe
   avocados, cut in half, pits discarded
About 2¼ tablespoons fresh lemon juice
   (1 juicy lemon)

About ¾ teaspoon salt
A little juice from a fresh tomato, if
   necessary

Run a dessert spoon between avocado's skin and flesh, dropping the flesh into a bowl. Mash with a fork—no large lumps but not perfectly smooth either. Mix in lemon juice and salt to taste. You may wish to loosen the consistency with fresh tomato juice. Cover with plastic film and keep cool.

This *salsa cruda* is the sauce you'll find on your table in a good Mexican restaurant. Its freshness and sprightliness add to everything it touches. It is inspired by Diana Kennedy's recipe.*

Cilantro, the soul of this sauce, is an acquired taste. If it's new to you and you think you don't like it, just keep eating. Once you become accustomed to cilantro, you'll understand why others are mad about it.

SALSA CRUDA
Piquant fresh tomato and onion sauce
[*Makes a scant 4 cups: 12* tostada *servings*]
Ideally served within moments of making, but for a complicated party, the sauce may be prepared in the morning and chilled.

To preserve the sauce's characteristic handmade appearance, don't use the food processor here—the chopping won't take that long and the texture will be right.

And there are no substitutes for fresh cilantro (nix on parsley) or fresh chilies (nothing canned) in this sauce.

4 tomatoes (1 pound), finely chopped
½ large onion, finely chopped
2 handfuls of fresh cilantro† leaves, finely
   chopped

1 to 2 fresh small yellow or other medium-
   hot to hot chilies,‡ seeds included, finely
   chopped
⅔ to 1 cup water, cold
½ teaspoon salt

N.B.: When handling chilies—fresh, canned, or dried—do not touch your face, especially your eyes, until you've washed your hands and scrubbed beneath your

---

*The Cuisines of Mexico.
†Also called fresh coriander and Chinese parsley, and available in Latin American, Chinese, and other exotic markets.
‡Available in markets wherever there is a Mexican community.

nails with hot soapy water—some of these babies burn painfully. If the chilies are fiery, best to use rubber gloves or your fingertips will tingle for awhile.

In a bowl, stir the tomatoes, onion, cilantro, and chilies together. Loosen to a sauce consistency with water* and season with salt. Cover and keep cool.

For dessert, the Cointreau in the recipe title is generic. When it comes to which orange liqueur to use in the sauce, unless you can compare their flavors side by side, it's easiest just to choose which suits your purse. The finest are Grand Marnier (based on cognac)† and Cointreau (best-quality triple sec). Curaçao (flavored with the dried peel of green oranges) and triple sec (a white curaçao, flavored with both bitter and sweet peels) are a step below in quality, but lovely. Mandarine (tangerine, on a brandy base), is another fine thought.

COINTREAU BURNT SUGAR SAUCE
[Makes about 2 cups: 12 servings]
Strained of the zest, tightly covered and refrigerated, this keeps indefinitely— ideal for unexpected company. To serve, replace the zest and taste to see whether a bit more liqueur might be in order.

1 2/3 cups sugar
11 fluid ounces water, cool

2 tablespoons orange-flavored liqueur (see
above), or to taste
The zest of 1 large orange, finely shredded

In a heavy saucepan, moisten the sugar with ¼ cup of the water. Set over lowest heat and stir constantly until the sugar has completely dissolved. Use a brush dipped in cold water to frequently wash down the sides (helps prevent crystals forming‡). Raise heat to high and boil the syrup without stirring until it has turned amber. Stir at this point to evenly blend the caramel. Meanwhile, bring the remaining water to a boil.

Watch closely because suddenly the syrup will boil up furiously, turn a rich deep caramel, and begin to smell burned. Remove from the heat, add the water—very carefully, because it sputters wildly—and stir until blended. Cool, then stir in the liqueur and zest. Serve at room temperature.

For this occasion, ladle over scoops of dark chocolate ice cream (3 quarts for 12 servings) and sprinkle with chopped toasted pistachios or almonds (about 1¼ cups). (The ice cream can be scooped into balls ahead of time, bagged airtight in heavy plastic, and kept in the freezer until serving.) This sauce is suited to many

---

*Some like a thin *salsa*, some like it thick. For spooning over a mountain of a *tostada*, thinner is more practical.

†I have read about aurum, also based on brandy, but I haven't been able to find it.

‡Sometimes, despite precautions, the sugar crystallizes anyway. Not to worry. By the time the syrup has finished, the crystals will dissolve away.

other flavors of ice cream and ices and you might even prefer one of them to choco-late: vanilla, coffee, pistachio, almond, strawberry, raspberry, cherry, peach, or-ange, and tangerine. Top with chopped toasted pistachios, hazelnuts, or almonds.

I loved the whirl of dinner parties—it never occurred to me that everything wouldn't be wonderful. But early on in the Malibu years I was faced with a dinner party that, not since the Lobster Absinthe, had me so undone.

The evening was in honor of a food editor visiting from New York. At her request, we invited a man who had collaborated on several classic cookbooks and a publisher well known for his cookbook list. Among them, our guests had probably cooked and eaten everything I'd ever thought of making in my life. I asked my mother for ideas. She was as baroque as ever. "I once read a rec-ipe I've always wanted to do: boned duck stuffed with boned chicken stuffed with boned squab stuffed with an orange. It was called Panamanian Duck." All she remembered of the recipe was that this fantasy was roasted. I thought, Mother is right. Of course I should make them something unique.

After a morning with the boning knife, I fashioned a Panamanian duck. Everyone seemed delighted. Except me. Slicing it, I suddenly felt embar-rassed. It was so *silly*. Gene gets cross when I say this—he thought it was great fun. Nonetheless, I decided then and there that no matter whether the com-mittee from Michelin or a reincarnated Carême himself appeared at my door, I'd serve roast chicken—perfect, mind you, succulent and sweet, but noth-ing out of the ordinary.

Ahem. That was true until the day I put together my charcoal-grilled gal-antine of chicken. A playwright and his wife were coming to dinner. Amus-ing people, they were passionate New Yorkers who didn't mind telling you how provincial they thought everything was "out here on the Coast" (once, at our table, they said this to Christopher Isherwood, who had lived in Santa Monica forty years). This time, we'd just see.

Technically, a boned, stuffed, and rolled chicken served at room temper-ature is called a galantine; if it's served hot, it's a ballottine. Although this meat is delectable straight from the grill, like most complex matters it's even better a day or two after, cold or at room temperature. For that reason, I've called it a galantine.

The charcoaled slices are speckled with fresh tomatoes and green chilies, accompanied by black beans and yellow rice, and decorated with avocado and orange slices. The colors, the flavors, are pure Southwest. Provincial.

GRILLED GALANTINE OF CHICKEN
[*Makes about 26 thin slices: 12 or more servings*]
If well-wrapped and refrigerated afterward, the galantine may be grilled 2 or 3 days in advance.

*1 pound mushrooms, evenly sliced cap to
   stem*
*1/2 stick butter plus about 1/2 stick more for
   basting, melted*
*5 walnut-sized (3 ounces) shallots, peeled
   and finely chopped*
2 ounces fresh jalapeño or other hot green
   chilies, seeds included, finely chopped†*
*6 medium-large (1 1/2 pounds) ripe
   tomatoes, peeled, seeded,‡ and finely
   chopped*
*12 ounces ground turkey or, if unavailable,
   buy 1 1/2 pounds unboned breast of turkey
   or chicken, then skin, bone,§ and grind
   or finely chop*

2 extra large eggs, beaten
*1 tablespoon chopped fresh marjoram leaves,
   or 1 teaspoon dried*
2 teaspoons fresh lemon juice
1 teaspoon salt
1/2 teaspoon ground cumin
*One 4 1/4-pound best-quality frying chicken,
   boned‖*
A little light oil for the grill

You'll also need 4 or 5 thin skewers, good cotton (no synthetics) string, a sharp darning needle with an eye large enough for the string, and, to be on the safe side, 8 to 10 pounds of mesquite or other non-petroleum-based charcoal.

In a large heavy skillet over medium heat, sauté the mushrooms in the butter just until they turn from beige to khaki, stirring frequently—they should still be slightly firm. Lift out with a slotted spoon, chop finely, and turn into a large bowl.# Add the shallots and chilies to the juices in the skillet and sauté over medium heat just until the shallots soften. Add to the mushrooms. Sauté the tomatoes in the skillet over high heat until their juices have evaporated, stirring frequently. Turn them into the bowl, then also add the ground turkey or chicken, the eggs, marjoram, lemon juice, salt, and cumin. Use your hands to blend the mixture thoroughly. Cook a spoonful in a small dry skillet over low heat to taste for seasoning.

Now for the wrassle. Spread out the boned chicken and evenly spread the force-meat over it. Fold long sides to meet at the center, pulling up excess skin so that flesh meets flesh at the seam. Secure this seam with a thin skewer through the excess skin—where the skin is thin, double it and secure through two thicknesses. Work your way along with the skewers, finally tipping the bird on end to fasten the bottom closed. Now sew the seam with needle and string, removing the skewers. Take a stitch or two through the wing and leg folds so they won't pop open. Tightly tie crosswise** in 6 or 7 or 8 places, knotting and cutting each time, with the aim of pulling the bobbling mass into an even sausage-shaped roll. Now run string the

---

*Weigh them at the market—hot peppers vary so in size.
†Please refer to the note about working with chilies on page 209.
‡Tomato peeling and seeding notes are on page 259.
§Skinning and boning chicken breast notes are on page 238.
‖Whole chicken boning notes are on page 238.
#If you chopped the mushrooms finely and then sautéed them, you'd end up with a bit of a
moosh—this way, the mushrooms retain their texture.
**Remember that a double loop holds twice as tightly when you pull.

long way, looping it around every cross tie; pull tightly. If it bulges where the legs are, run needle and string beneath the stitches there, to anchor it, and pull tightly. Don't be discouraged when you've done all you can—the roll will compact nicely as it roasts.

You can wrap the bird in plastic film and refrigerate it all day or overnight, if that would be helpful. Remove to room temperature an hour before continuing.

In grilling a large oblong shape that takes time, fashion a shallow drip pan of heavy-duty foil a little longer and a little wider than the meat and set it in the center of the coal rack. Arrange coals on either side (the long sides) of the pan, banked about 3 inches high and 4 inches wide. The meat rack should be about 6 inches above the heat. For poultry, the fire should be medium-hot: when you hold your hand next to the meat rack, 3 seconds is all you can bear. When the fire is at that stage, brush the grill over the drip pan with oil, then set the chicken there. If you have an open fire, set a tent of heavy foil (shiny side toward the meat) over the roll; if you have a covered grill, omit the tent and set on the cover.

Every 10 to 15 minutes, baste the roll all over with melted butter and use a spray bottle or bulb baster to spritz out flames that flare up. Every 30 minutes, give the roll a quarter-turn using tongs, not a fork, then add 3 lumps of coal on either side, directly on top of hot coals, spacing them evenly. Grill until a good meat thermometer* registers 180°F in the center of the roll; start testing after an hour, then every 15 minutes. The roll will take about 2 hours, but there are many variable factors in timing, so trust the thermometer. Remove the meat from the grill. If planning to serve hot, cover with foil and let it rest 30 minutes before slicing. Otherwise wrap loosely in foil and refrigerate, then wrap tightly once cold. Bring to room temperature before slicing and serving.

I haven't done it yet, but a small turkey prepared this way would be marvelous for a big party.

Black beans and rice—red, white, yellow, and otherwise—are a Latin American staple. I borrowed the combination for our dinner. They were stunning.

MEXICAN BLACK BEANS
[8 servings]
These may be prepared days in advance, to advantage.

1 pound black beans, rinsed and carefully inspected for stones	*12 turns of the black pepper mill (1 teaspoon, medium grind)*
18 cups water	*A splash of olive oil*
1 onion, chopped	*About 2 teaspoons salt*
2 garlic cloves, finely chopped	

Cover the beans with 9 cups of cool water, bring to a boil, and boil 2 minutes. Pour off the water (hard to do, I know, but it helps the digestive situation). Cover with 9

*About which, page 250.

cups of boiling water,* add the onion, garlic, pepper, and oil. Bring to a simmer, cover, and simmer 3 to 4 hours, stirring occasionally so the beans won't stick. The beans must be very tender and the broth should have cooked down to a thick liquor. Now add salt to taste. Heat a serving bowl. Lift the beans with a slotted spoon into the bowl. There will be about 4 cups of bean broth left for a soup.

Yellow rice is compatible with every cuisine from Latin to Mediterranean to oriental. I love its pulsing color and the delicacy of the turmeric—the spice doesn't compete with anything the rice accompanies. That wouldn't be true of saffron or curry powder, so don't substitute them unless you know the flavors will be compatible. Buy a premium grade of turmeric bottled in glass (mine comes from Madras) and keep it in the refrigerator.

YELLOW RICE
[*4 to 5 servings*]
Although at its best when fresh, the rice may be cooked even a day in advance and reheated over very low heat.

1 cup long-grain rice　　　　　　　*2 ½ cups excellent chicken broth, simmering*
2 tablespoons olive oil　　　　　　*Salt, only if the broth is unsalted*
1 teaspoon turmeric

In a heavy saucepan over low heat, stir the rice in the oil, about 3 minutes. Stir in the turmeric, then the broth. Cover, turn heat to lowest, and cook until the rice is tender and the broth has been absorbed, about 20 minutes. Taste for salt and serve.
　　A small chopped fresh tomato makes a colorful addition.

For dessert for our New York friends, I made what I consider perhaps my finest invention, a dazzling display of California bounty: a wheel of a tart set with a myriad of jams, jellies, and preserves. I called it Stained Glass Window because it looks like one.

　I've never made this pastry with precisely the same fillings simply because the same selection isn't always available. I begin with what I've got, then go to the market and fill in the gaps, holding each jar up to the light to see its hue. As in real stained glass windows, I aim for a balance not only of colors but of textures. And, of course, I consider a balance of flavors as well. Everything must be of premium quality—thick, not runny, and wonderfully bright. You'll only need a spoonful or two from each jar, an extravagance, and of course you can use a more modest selection, but part of the charm of this pas-

---

*When changing water with beans, you always want to maintain the water's temperature.

try lies in its glorious richness of tints and flavors. Just keep the jars in the refrigerator and make lots of popovers Sunday mornings.

The pastry, a rich dough that is beautiful for any sweet pastry, was inspired by the brilliant Paula Peck.*

STAINED GLASS WINDOW
A tart with assorted jellies, jams, preserves, and marmalades
[*About 12 servings*]
Although it's still gorgeous the next day, try to serve the tart the day of baking.

THE WINDOW FRAMES: NE PLUS ULTRA ALMOND PASTRY†
The dough may be prepared a day in advance if wrapped in foil and refrigerated. Freeze any left over.

1 cup (loosely packed; 3 ounces) finely ground toasted unblanched almonds	*1 extra large egg*
1²/₃ cups all-purpose flour	*2 extra large egg yolks*
¼ cup sugar	*1½ teaspoons of French‡ orange flower water*
A rounded ¼ teaspoon cinnamon	*⅓ cup (a scant 4 ounces) almond paste,*
A pinch of salt	*at room temperature, in small bits*
The zest of 1 large lemon, finely shredded	*1½ sticks unsalted butter, cool but*
The zest of 1 small orange, finely shredded	*malleable, in ½-inch chips*

In a mixing bowl or food processor work bowl, use a fork to blend the ground almonds, flour, sugar, cinnamon, salt, and lemon and orange zests. In a separate bowl, blend the egg, yolks, and orange flower water.

Traditional method: Heap the flour mixture on your work surface and make a well in the center. Into it put the almond paste, the butter, and the egg mixture. Lightly, with your fingertips, make a paste of these center ingredients, working out lumps in the butter. Gradually pull in the flour mixture, wiping down your fingers frequently. Press the dough together until blended; do not overwork.

Food processor method: Over the flour mixture, evenly distribute the almond paste, the butter, and the egg mixture. Process until the dough has pulled together and revolves around the blade just once.

Mixer method: Make a well in the center of the flour mixture. Into it put the almond paste, the butter, and the egg mixture. Mix at low speed, pushing flour from

---

*The Art of Fine Baking.

†The recipe makes about 1½ pounds, ample for the Stained Glass Window or two 11 × 1-inch tarts. For tarts or tartlets, roll out chilled dough ⅛-inch thick. In warm weather, the dough might fall apart when you lift it over the mold, but you can patch until it's perfect without harm. Chill thoroughly before baking—directions are on pages 253–256. This pastry doesn't need pie weights. It may be fully baked up to a week before filling if wrapped in foil and refrigerated.

‡From other sources, the quality can be iffy.

sides to center with a rubber spatula. Stop when the flour is incorporated and the dough is smooth, about 30 seconds.

Pat into an inch-thick round, wrap in foil, and chill until firm enough to roll out as directed.

THE STAINED GLASS

To fill the panes—choose at least half a dozen, the more the merrier:
  Apple or crabapple jelly
  Apricot preserves
  Blackberry jam, seedless
  Black raspberry jelly
  Blueberry preserves
  Concord grape jelly
  Lemon or lime marmalade
  Mint jelly (essential)
  Orange or tangerine marmalade
  Peach or nectarine preserves

Quince or guava jelly
Raspberry jam, seedless
Red currant jelly (essential)
Red plum jam
Sour cherry preserves
Strawberry jelly
1 recipe Ne Plus Ultra Almond Pastry,
  chilled, recipe preceding
A little flour for rolling
A little butter for the paper

Lay out your selection of fillings, grouping the light golds, the rich ambers, the ripe reds, and the deep purples together. Set the preserves from each group in front—bumps of blueberries, rounds of cherries, and mounds of apricots filling angles here and there give unexpected dimension (the bigger the pieces of fruit, the better) and the sheen of jelly, the opacity of jam, and the texture of marmalades and preserves give the stained glass window warmth. You will inevitably have the same colors adjacent in places, so make them different values—quince jelly next to orange marmalade rather than lookalike apple jelly, for example. The first thing to place is the mint jelly for its emerald—somewhere just off center is where I like it. Next place the red currant for its brilliance—not too far from the emerald, perhaps? Now balance the ambers, next to the reds, and finally lay in the accents of purple. A map is prudent.

Lay the dough on a lightly floured tea towel. With a stockinette sleeve* on your rolling pin or waxed paper over the dough, roll the dough out in a circle just a shade under ¼-inch thick.† Cut into a perfect 13-inch round. Butter a 14-inch square of cooking parchment or brown paper and lay it over the pastry, then lay a pizza pan or large baking sheet over the paper. Slide your hand under the cloth and invert the pastry onto the paper-covered pan.

Using a ruler as a guide and cutting with a pizza cutter, if you have one, cut the remaining pastry into ½-inch wide strips, only rerolling once or twice—this dough patches successfully. Picking up the strips with a long spatula, make a raised border for the tart by laying a strip flat around the rim, the edge of the strip even with the edge of the pastry, gently pressing the ends of strips together as needed to patch. Place 1 strip down the center, then run 2 more strips on either side of it with

---

*Where and why to find one, page 254.
†Mark a toothpick at ¼-inch and use it as a depth measure.

their edges a shade over 1½ inches apart—5 evenly spaced vertical lines. Give the round only a quarter turn (so the lattice will be diamonds, not squares) and repeat with 5 more strips spaced the same way, making a lattice of 26 diamonds (some on the border will just be dots).

Use a teaspoon to gently break up any lumps in jelly, to spread the filling to fill the space, and to tuck it into every corner. Use only enough filling to make it level with the surrounding pastry strips—jelly will melt in the oven, and you don't want it to overflow its borders. Fill every diamond, even the tiny dots.

When you've only 3 or 4 spaces to go, heat the oven to 400°F. Bake the pastry 10 minutes, then turn the sheet around, reduce the temperature to 350°F, and bake until the pastry is pale nut brown and the jellies have melted, about 10 minutes more. Gently pull the tart by the paper onto a cooling rack. After 10 minutes, slide a long spatula under the tart and pull away the paper. When completely cool, slip onto a serving platter. Cut in wedges to serve.*

The conversation that evening was delicious. The playwright and his wife said not one word about the dinner. (Perhaps my expecting them to was just one more example of Californians being provincial . . .)

About this time, a rough jewel came into my life. Her name was Alma. We had had great luck with the young women who lived with us—few of them were much older than our children, most of them were related to one another, and we were handed on from cousin to cousin. All were willing cooks and each had her specialty. Maria Luisa made perfect *enchiladas*, her cousin Luz whipped up poetry in mashed potatoes, Gloria made a fascinating *sopa de fideo* (a "dry soup" with vermicelli), and her cousin Bertil made *chiles rellenos* that put me away.

Alma, a roly-poly woman of a certain age, was a superb cook. I knew I would be mad about her the day after she arrived. I found her outside beneath the big pittosporum by the fence, vigorously ringing a bell. She had seen a swarm of bees overhead and was calling them down, she explained. To my amazement and delight, Alma's bees settled in a hollow of the fence. The colony stayed there as long as we lived in the house.

Alma did especially nice things with cheese. Viz.:

ALMA'S CORN ON THE COB
Corn with grated cheese
[*For each serving*]
Grate about an ounce of Cheddar cheese (rounded ¼ cup, loosely packed, medium-grated). After buttering the cooked ear of corn, sprinkle over the cheese as you eat it. The hotter the corn, the better the cheese sticks to it—the cheese will even melt a little, if you eat slowly.

---

*A pretty variation for another night is just a circle of the pastry with a pinched border spread with your favorite preserves—or make individual tartlets of different textures and colors.

And here is Alma's way with fish. It is quickly made, delicate, the onions are slightly crunchy, the tomato still fresh, and if you have a fresh green chili on hand, sprinkle it over an assertively flavored fish. Serve with yellow rice (page 214) or a baked potato for the juices, and bright green peas—¡*que linda*!

PESCADO CON QUESO*
Fish fillets with melted cheese
[*2 servings*]
Everything can be prepared for cooking well in advance.

About 3 tablespoons chicken broth (or fish stock, dry vermouth, or white wine)
4 thin fillets (about 12 ounces) of any fish you like
½ smallish onion, finely chopped
1 fresh serrano or jalapeño chili, finely chopped (optional)

About 1 cup (3 to 4 ounces) Cheddar or jack or other melting cheese, medium-grated
2 tomatoes, thinly sliced
A sprinkling of ground cumin

In a large heavy skillet over medium-high heat, heat enough broth to lightly cover the bottom. When piping hot, remove from the heat and lay in the fish. Cover with the onion (and chili), cheese, and tomato, and sprinkle with cumin. Return to the heat, bring to a simmer, cover, and cook without turning until the fish is milky white and the cheese has melted—3 to 4 minutes if the fillets are very thin, a bit longer if they are thicker.

The Malibu years flew by. All at once our little David was out of UCLA and celebrating his twenty-first birthday. Impossible. There had been so many adventures together, culinary and otherwise.

All the mussel-gathering we did, for example. Not five minutes from our house were sea rocks with a blueblack veneer of mussels sparkling in the sun. Once, visiting a friend who lived beside them, I asked if she had ever gathered any of the mussels. She looked startled. "Can you *eat* them?" she asked. The next day, a marine biologist whose specialty was the Santa Monica Bay assured me that yes indeed, the mussels off Old Malibu Road were safe to eat[†]— but only between November and April. The red tide that blooms on warm ocean waters between May and October doesn't bother the bivalves themselves—they filter it through their systems—but it kills anyone who eats the mussels. It was February. I ran screaming for the buckets and the children.

Armed with prying knives (I lost the tips of more good knives on those

---

*If you live somewhere where good fresh fish is a sometime thing, this is an excellent way to handle the often oily aftertaste of frozen fish.
†Sadly, those days are past. But unpolluted waters—and mussels on their rocks—still ebb and flow over less populated beaches on the Pacific Coast.

rocks), we gathered mussels, choosing small ones, dropping them gently into pails of seawater as we went. And, as we went, gathering after gathering, year after year, we gathered know-how about picking mussels as well. We took them at low tide from the farthest-out spot on the rocks—those submerged most of the time taste freshest. We picked from the sides, not the tops, of the rocks—those mussels would be cleanest, rinsed free of sand and barnacles by the splash and fall of waves. We never took any that were open— they were goners—nor any extra-heavy ones—they were filled only with sand. (And we knew, were we to go mussel gathering in other places, not to take them from copper-bound wrecks nor off the pilings of wharves, and certainly never from polluted waters.)

The children never complained about our forays, not even of the tedious job of cleaning the mussels when we got home. They, too, were mytilophiles. Of course I introduced them to mussels with Giancarlo's birthday treat of *muscoli alla marinara*. Then there were *moules au gratin*, mussels on the half-shell sprinkled with minced parsley (mussels and parsley are like chicken and tarragon, sole and dill, lamb and mint), garlic, breadcrumbs, and melted butter, browned beneath the broiler, served with lemon. And, since all of us were writers (genes will out), I made Alexandre Dumas's Mussel Soup: one part rich bouillon, one part puree of tomatoes and white onions, one part mussels and their liquor, finished at the end with a speck of browned garlic. And there were lots of *moules à la bourguignonne*—better known for snails, creamed unsalted butter flavored with finely chopped shallots, garlic, parsley, salt, and pepper, spread on raw mussels on the half-shell, then roasted until bubbly.

A footnote. Although Indians were dining on native mussels in Malibu waters in prehistoric times (I have dug in ancient Chumash sites, in kitchen middens spangled with mussel shells),* the choicest mussels—the ones I told the children to look out for, the ones which grew in patchy colonies here and there amongst the others—were parvenus, in these waters only four hundred years.† They had been stowaways, attached perhaps to the hulls of Cabrillo's *San Salvador* and *Victoria* from Mediterranean harbors or to Drake's *Golden Hind* from English Channel ports. Once here, the mussels dropped off and anchored themselves to our rocks. So what I enjoyed in my dish in Malibu were the mussels I adored in Portofino!

And there were the gatherings of the olives.

In 1970, we had a fire in Malibu. There were fires nearly every year along

---

Mytilus californianus: longish thickish dull-greyish rounded shells, the meat apricot.
†*Mytilus edulis*: squat thin shiny blueblack flat shells, the meat peach.

the coast (my mother remembers fires in all the canyons every summer of her childhood and is always surprised when others are surprised when Southern California canyons burn). But in 1970, it was disastrous. That November afternoon, it came sweeping down into our canyon and we lost thirty-three of fifty-one houses. Ours, incredibly, was saved.

Up the road from us on a sloped lot where a less lucky house had been were half a dozen olive trees. I hadn't noticed them before because the house had hidden them from view. The first year after the fire, I watched the olives ripening and waited for the owners to come and harvest them. They never came. The next year, I waited until the fruit could wait no longer, then I got the children to help me pick. With black-stained fingers, we lugged home a bushel basket of plump ripe olives. A Greek friend told me what to do with them.

If there are olive trees in your part of the world, in late October or early November, you can probably harvest their fruit for the asking.

OLIVES CURED THE ANCIENT WAY
We ate our last Malibu olive five years after we'd picked it.

Pick the olives when they are soft and fully ripe, resembling black cherries, and handle them gently, as you would cherries. Smaller olives are more successful than large ones, which can become too soft. Rinse the olives only if they're dusty. Find a large wooden box with narrow slats—the produce man at the market can probably come up with one. Set the box on a surface that won't be marred by the brown tannin that will seep from the box—it stains.

Make a single layer of olives in the bottom of the box, then cover with a layer of rock salt (ice cream salt is the cheapest). Layer all your olives with salt this way. Cover the box. Let set 24 hours, then, with your hands, gently but thoroughly mix olives and salt.* Mix thoroughly every day for about 1 month, when the salt will have absorbed most of the tannin and the olives will no longer be acrid—your taste will tell you when they're ready. Remove the olives and brush off excess salt. Pack in jars and cover with olive oil (they'll also keep simply coated with oil, but I take no chances). Store in a cool place.

The one catch is that you *must* be faithful about mixing the olives daily, otherwise you'll lose them. Ask how I know.

Then there was my health food period. I had discovered Chico—the batter for blossoms on page 135 was his. Chico Bucaro owned an organic farm across from Zuma Beach (about ten minutes up the coast from where we lived). Chico was a small strong man in his sixties who spoke broken English with a Sicilian accent. He was, in fact, illiterate, but he was immensely clever, especially with growing things, a quality he doubtless inherited from his fa-

*If you have any cuts on your hands, the salt is painful—rubber gloves are a good idea.

ther, who had been herbalist to the King of Naples. Chico showed me a citrus fruit he said his father had created: it was fresh and plump, bright green on one end, bright yellow on the other, a lemon-lime. Chico sliced it in half. Sure enough. I seem to remember a faint scar around the center—these were in the days before I knew about grafting. I wonder . . .

Chico grew another curiosity, an herb. Gene was with me one morning and the two men chatted. Gene must have looked tired, Chico must have remarked on it, and Gene must have said he wasn't sleeping well. Chico put a hand on Gene's arm and said, "You gonna sleep tonight, kid." He took us to a small bush that looked and smelled like bay. Chico said he'd brought the plant from Italy, that it was invaluable. He called it *adaghiro*. He pulled off a handful of leaves, wrapped them in a napkin, and instructed me to make a tea of a few leaves for Gene at bedtime. That night, I made a pale tea with two of the *adaghiro* leaves. Gene slept fourteen hours and when he finally woke up, felt woozy the rest of the day. "That stuff could have killed me!" he cried. I said at least it had worked—I'd make a milder tea next time—but Gene made me throw the rest of the *adaghiro* out. To this day, I've no idea what it was.

Chico's olives, however, Gene loved. After I bought a jar, Chico told me how he made them. They are to be eaten with forks, as part of an antipasto.

SICILIAN OLIVES
Green olives with celery and garlic
[*6 to 8 servings*]
These keep forever.

1 pound small whole unpitted green olives, drained
½ bunch of Italian parsley, finely chopped
A small leafy celery heart, cut in thin crescents

A small head of garlic, the cloves peeled and very finely chopped
About 1¼ cups olive oil

Gently press the flat blade of your chopping knife or cleaver down on the olives one by one until the skin breaks. In a bowl, mix parsley, celery, and garlic. Layer the olives and herbery in a clean quart jar, then top with oil. Cover and keep in a cool place or the refrigerator a day or two before serving. To serve, bring to room temperature and scoop the olives and greens into a dish, leaving the oil behind. The same oil can be used to preserve batch after batch—refresh the herbery now and then.

Chico's farm was on the road to the junior high school, which made it very convenient. After picking up Dinah one afternoon, we dropped in. Chico had a red wine he'd made and wanted us to taste. We went into his big cooler and he pulled down a gallon jug from the top shelf. The shelf was heavy with jugs filled with Chico's tomato sauce (thickened and sweetened with figs), honey from his bees (Chico loved to cover his face and head with bees and have his picture taken), salad dressing, Sicilian olives, and other organic concoctions. He opened the jar and poured dark red into a dusty glass for Dinah. Obligingly, she took a swallow, then choked and blew it all out. "Good grief!" she exclaimed, "What was *that?*" Chico smelled the jar then hit his head. "Oh boy, Dine, I'm sorry. You got the jar with my hair tonic!"

My organic period ended with a whimper. Jonathan Norton Leonard came to town researching his book on the food of the West* for the Time-Life series on American cooking. He was sent to me so I could cook him a Southern California dinner. I knew immediately what I would make. I'd roast a couple of chickens (see?) and surround them with a Della Robbia wreath of vegetables. Jon arrived early so he could shop with me. I learned he was an avid gardener, but I didn't want to unnerve him with the quixotic air at Chico's, so we drove into Hollywood to a market that I'd heard carried the finest organic produce in Los Angeles.

I was pleased about the quality of the vegetables we found there because, on our drive as I waxed *exaltée* over the organic produce I fed my family, Jon had been polite but reserved. He quietly remarked that, before he wrote about food, he had been a science editor on *Time*. What he was saying was that his opinions about growing things had both a theoretical and practical foundation.

The cure came with cauliflower. A perfect, unblemished, creamy cauliflower. Picking up one cauliflower after another from the bin, Jon held them upside down. "You see this stalk, Sylvia?" he said, pointing. "It hasn't a hole in it. Now I've grown cauliflowers for years without sprays and it's impossible to grow one without a little worm, harmless though it may be, getting into the stalk. If there's no hole in the cauliflower stalk, it's been dusted or sprayed."

Common sense told me he was right. I was particularly anguished because Gene had been asking me from the beginning, "How do you *know* it's organic?" "The box *says* . . ."

At least I knew Chico's things were honest. His ears of corn had so many worms in them, half the kernels were gone. Chico complained that it was because all the kids who came to work for him kept making love in the cornfield instead of pinching out worms. Who can blame them?†

American Cooking: The Great West.
†Chico wanted a book written about his organic theories and practices and asked if I wouldn't do it with him. I was complimented but not free. Happily, David Wallechinsky set Chico down on paper. Their collaboration, *Chico's Organic Gardening and Natural Living*, is delightful.

As one by one the children grew up and left home for the university, fate again made it possible for Gene to make a change. He came home to his book-lined study to write only novels.

A couple of years later, when Gene's French publisher and her husband and Gene's French agent all came to Los Angeles for a book fair, in planning a dinner party for them, I obviously couldn't do something French—or Italian, Indian, or Greek. Then inspiration struck. I'd give them something Californiano, something they'd probably never tasted. *Si. ¡Tostadas!* They were a great success.

But for the most part, we entertained less and less. The emptier the nest became, the more Gene and I hunkered down to our work. Whenever we'd have a birthday or celebration, we'd surround ourselves with the children, their close friends, and my mother and father, our favorite company.

But the big celebrations we did have, we had *con brio*.

I think the dearest of all, which we inherited from Norah, was Easter breakfast. Except in our house, it isn't really Easter, it's a celebration of spring. The spring Gene and I were engaged, Norah invited us to a midday feast in her Berkeley garden. She had roast turkey and fresh strawberries and asparagus and a rich Russian cheese called *paskha* and the moving voices of Bach's *Actus Tragicus* wafting through the open windows onto the terrace. We were entranced and kept the custom.

In Malibu, our house was ideal for dining out of doors. The big deck, floating in the trees and facing the sea, held an umbrella table and chairs, and on the small rectangular deck in front, in Mr. Yamashiro's Japanese garden, were two banks of built-in benches. We usually had twenty or thirty for Easter breakfast, all ages. My children's band of cooks helped, then came to eat what they had made, and there were always a few close friends and their children from town. Everyone arrived between eleven and twelve, we had the traditional Easter egg hunt (Papa hid the eggs in the tubs of roses on the deck), then came the buffet. Afterward, we'd stroll around the canyon or up to Connelly's Hill with its view—all of Santa Monica Bay from Point Dume to Palos Verdes. It was almost dark before everyone reluctantly went home.

Our menu, evolved after so many Easters, contains uncommon traditional dishes as well as new inventions. The colors and shapes are splendid—the breakfast is much a feast to the eye as to the palate. The *pâté*, *paskha*, and cake are complex, but everything else is simple. It's all fork food and everything is at room temperature so there's no worrying about when people will arrive or when they'll be ready to eat or whether the food in chafing dishes is dying. And there are enough familiar foods for skittish children to enjoy.

The recipes are for twenty, an easy number to multiply or divide.

EASTER BREAKFAST
ON THE BEVERAGE TABLE
Bowle
Fresh orange juice*
THE BUFFET
Basket of Easter eggs
(a dyed egg inscribed for each person)
Pâté primavera
with Fresh tomato aspic the color of Rosé
Salad of new red potatoes and watercress
Basket of skinny raw asparagus
Homemade mayonnaise
Fromage blanc avec caviar noir
Paskha
Basket of big fat unhulled strawberries
French bread
Crisp sweet pastries
THE CENTERPIECE AND DESSERT
The Paschal lamb
(Cornish currant and ginger cake
with Coconut icing)
TO DRINK WITH BREAKFAST
California *Blanc de Pinot Noir*†
Coffee or Tea‡

Gene learned to make *bowle* in Heidelberg from a Greek friend. It has always been our punch at Easter. But fair warning, *bowle* sneaks up on you.

BOWLE
Greek champagne punch
[*About thirty-eight 4-ounce glasses: allow at least 2 per person*]

*1 large ripe pineapple, peeled, cored, and
cut in bite-size pieces*
2 cups triple sec
2 cups maraschino liqueur
2 cups brandy

2 or 3 large chunks of ice§
2 fifths dry champagne, chilled
2 fifths dry white wine, chilled

In a large bowl in a cool place, steep the pineapple pieces overnight in the triple sec, maraschino, and brandy. Just before serving, set the ice in your punch bowl, add the pineapple-and-spirits and stir in the champagne and white wine. Ladle up, including pineapple.

---

*You'll need 30 to 40 oranges, depending on how juicy they are.
†Four ounces constitutes a serving. After the *bowle*, most people will only want one glass.
‡Calculate ½ ounce (2 tablespoons) ground coffee or ⅛ ounce (1 teaspoon) tea leaves per cup.
§Gene feels one big block of ice gets in the way of the ladle.

I have long been taken with the delightful *Cima alla genovese*—breast of veal stuffed with a forcemeat of veal, sweetbreads, brains, fresh peas, and artichoke hearts. Since veal is a luxury, but chicken is not, I adapted the *cima* to make a *pâté* enfolded in chicken breasts. Because it can only be made in springtime, I've called it

PÂTÉ PRIMAVERA
A springtime pâté molded in chicken breasts
[*Makes about 20 to 26 slices, 20 or more servings*]
For best flavor, make the *pâté* 3 or 4 days before serving; it will keep a long week in the refrigerator.

8 chicken breasts: 5 pounds bone-in,* or
   3 pounds boneless
½ stick unsalted butter, plus more for the
   mold, softened
6 ounces chicken livers, patted dry
2 large artichokes, stems removed
½ lemon
1 pound fresh peas in the pod
6 ounces best quality lean ham steak, skin
   removed
1 medium-large onion, finely chopped
2 garlic cloves, finely chopped

8 extra large eggs
⅓ cup (about 1 ounce) grated Parmesan
   cheese
Rounded ¼ cup of fresh marjoram leaves,
   chopped, or 1½ tablespoons dried
8 turns of the black pepper mill (rounded
   ½ teaspoon, medium grind)
12 ounces lean boneless pork, chopped
   medium-fine
12 ounces fresh pork fat, chopped medium-
   fine
Fresh Tomato Aspic (recipe follows)

As each ingredient is prepared, cover and set aside.

Remove all skin, sinew, and fat from the boned breasts; trim ragged edges. Slice the breasts ⅜-inch thick, then with a meat pounder or sturdy dinner plate pound them down between sheets of plastic film, to ⅛-inch thickness. Chop the trimmings from the breasts medium-fine. Cover and reserve. In a heavy skillet over medium heat, melt ¼ stick of butter and sauté the chicken livers until they stiffen, stirring frequently. Remove from the heat.

Turn the artichokes tip-down on your work surface and press hard with the heel of your hand to loosen the leaves. Snap off all the leaves (steam them for supper), then use a teaspoon to scrape the thistle from the heart. Trim off green stubs left from the leaves down to the creamy yellow heart; rub the hearts with the lemon to keep them from darkening. Shell the peas. Cut ham in dice the size of the largest peas.

In a small heavy skillet over medium heat, soften the onion in the remaining ¼ stick of butter, stirring frequently, then add the garlic and stir until it softens. Cool. In a large bowl, whisk the eggs, Parmesan, marjoram, and pepper together until blended. Add the pork, the fat, the chopped chicken, and the onions, and blend this forcemeat thoroughly.

*Better buys and it takes only minutes to bone one; the method is on page 238.

Cut the artichoke hearts in slightly smaller dice than the ham and blend with the ham and peas into the forcemeat. Cut the chicken livers in pea-sized pieces and add with their butter to the mixture, blending gently with your hands so as not to mash them. Taste for seasoning by cooking a small amount. Cover and keep this forcemeat cool.

Butter a 9×3-inch springform cake pan.* Choose the 7 handsomest chicken breasts. Arrange them on the bottom and up the sides of the pan in a star shape, spreading the fillets to their fullest width, overlapping their tips and sides in the same direction—spaces between the fillets will be bare. Trim the fillets neatly from their edges to their points as needed. Finely chop the trimmings and mix into the forcemeat.

Heat the oven to 325°F. Smooth the forcemeat into the mold. Cover with heavy foil and tightly crimp around the edges. Set the mold in a large square of heavy foil, fold up and pleat the sides (a springform pan leaks). Lift into a larger pan and fill the pan with hot water up two-thirds of the side of the mold.

Set on the bottom rack of the oven and bake until a meat thermometer thrust in the center (through the foil) measures 160°F, about 3 hours. Lift the mold from the water, set on a large plate, put an 8-inch plate on top, and add a 2-pound weight. Refrigerate overnight, at least. Keep refrigerated in the mold until ready to serve.

To unmold the *pâté*, scrape off any fat, then run a knife around the inside edge of the pan, lay a large serving platter on top, flip the two over, and lift off the pan. Surround the bottom and heap the top of the *pâté* with diced tomato aspic. To serve, slice across the *pâté*, dividing the largest slices into 2 or 3 portions.

FRESH TOMATO ASPIC THE COLOR OF ROSÉ

[*Makes about 6 cups; as garnish, allow ¼ cup per serving*]
Well wrapped and refrigerated, the aspic will keep fresh as long as the *pâté* it's meant to garnish.

6 tablespoons unflavored gelatin
3½ cups excellent beef broth, all fat removed

1¾ cups dry white wine
6 tomatoes (1½ pounds), ripe but firm

In a saucepan or vessel for the microwave, sprinkle the gelatin over 1½ cups of the broth. Stir to blend and let soak 5 to 10 minutes. Heat just until the gelatin has thoroughly dissolved, then stir in the remaining broth and the wine.

Cut tomatoes in half through the center. Juice on a reamer or juice as you would oranges. Strain through a medium sieve, then press the puree through a very fine sieve into a measuring pitcher. Blend ¾ cup of this puree into the gelatin mixture and stir well. Pour into a wet mold around ½-inch thick—an 11 × 17-inch baking pan is about right. Cover and chill until stiff (it sets quickly), then, just before serving, cut it into ½-inch dice. (Another time, it is beautiful whipped with a fork into a zillion prisms.)

---

*This is the perfect size and shape; if you haven't one, choose another deepish mold with a 4-quart capacity.

The whole red potatoes for the buffet are banded down the center with a lemon zester or the tip of a vegetable peeler, steamed until tender, mixed with a goodly amount of watercress leaves, and lightly dressed with olive oil, lemon juice, and a little salt and white pepper. Nutty raw asparagus give crunch and an interesting form to the composition—just trim their stems and keep them in a pitcher of water until serving. And the way to make your own mayonnaise is on page 249. (Allow 1 smallish potato, a handful of watercress leaves, 4 or 5 skinny asparagus, and 1 tablespoon of mayonnaise per serving.)

Fromage blanc is on page 168—one-and-one-half times the recipe would probably leave some for yourself. Smooth the cheese on a flattish decorative plate and heap as much black caviar in the center as you can afford (a costly grade is not necessary). The black-and-white of this composition lends sparkle to the table and makes a savory contrast to the *paskha*.

Paskha means "Easter" in Russian. The traditional Russian *paskha* mold is made of five pieces of wood, a tall four-sided pyramid—I've never seen one, but a tall narrow cloth-lined flowerpot makes an excellent mold. If you are fresh out of flowerpots, you could pierce a pleasingly shaped tin can and use it as a mold—tall and slender is the thing.

Paskha is so rich—and unfamiliar—that most people will only take a dab (guests who have been at your Easter table before will take more). But it keeps at least a week so you can dreamily spoon up any leftover for yourself. This, the best in thirty years, was inspired by a recipe in *Russian Cookery*.

PASKHA
Russian sweet cheese for Easter
[Makes about 2 1/2 pounds—plenty for 20 people]
This absolutely must be made *at least* 48 hours before unmolding so it will have time to drain and firm up.* Then it will be fresh for at least 4 or 5 days after that.

2 pounds ricotta cheese	*1/4 cup currants, plumped a few minutes in*
1 1/3 cups sugar	*hot water, if very dry*
2 extra large egg yolks	*1 teaspoon finely shredded lemon zest*
1/2 cup heavy cream	*1/4 cup finely chopped roasted almonds*
1 vanilla bean, split	*Decoration of fresh flowers or blanched*
1 1/2 sticks unsalted butter, softened	*almonds or candied peel, as you like*

You'll also need a 6-cup draining mold (a flower pot measuring 6 1/2 inches at top, 4 1/2 inches at bottom and 5 inches tall is perfect) and a 16-inch square of clean cloth.

If at all moist, drain the ricotta in a bag of the dampened cloth overnight. Next day, in the quart-size top part of a double boiler, beat 1/3 cup of the sugar with the

---

*If your ricotta is *very* moist, then begin 3 days ahead and drain the ricotta 24 hours. Use method for *fromage blanc*, pages 168–169.

yolks until thick and pale. Stir in the cream, scrape in the vanilla bean's seeds, then add the pieces of bean itself. Stir the custard over boiling water over medium-high heat until thickened (you can see the bottom of the pot when you stir). Strain into a large mixing bowl* and add the butter in small bits, whisking until smooth. Whisk in the ricotta, then add the remaining 1 cup sugar. Add the currants, lemon zest, and almonds, and mix thoroughly.

Rinse the draining cloth and line the mold with it, making neat, even folds (the folds will be impressed into the cheese). Smooth in the *paskha*, fold the cloth over the top, cover with plastic film (to keep out refrigerator flavors), lay on a dish that just fits inside, and top with a 3-pound weight (a tall can of fruit juice). Set on a rack over something to catch the drips and refrigerate.

Just before serving, pull back the cloth, unmold onto a pretty dish and decorate as suits your fancy—I like a wreath of spring flowers at the base and a posy on top, but it's traditional to make a cross with almonds or peel.

For your buffet, people will only take one or two big fat strawberries, so buy with that in mind. Just buy the best. Slice the French bread thinly (2 loaves should be more than enough)—it's lovely covered with the *pâté*. The sweet pastries should be small and not rich or gooey—something crispy like *palmiers* made of Danish pastry is ideal. Buy one or two for each guest.

The lamb cake is usually sliced after we've come back from our walk and eaten out of hand. David, I suppose feeling his eldest son-ness and being appallingly macho at times, has traditionally beheaded the lamb with a flourish.

For many years, I made the lamb of pound cake. It was lovely but nothing wildly sensational. Now my mother is mad for ginger and has begged me to make a *panettone* with ginger in it for Easter. I can't bring myself to do that, but when I found a cake from Cornwall with candied ginger in it, I thought, That's what I'll do for the lamb! Now the cake is wildly sensational.

For ginger lovers, this cake from Penzance, where the Pirates live, is a not-sweet light-colored cake drenched with currants and candied ginger—a bit like a fruitcake. First, reading the recipe, I couldn't imagine what dried black currants were doing with ginger and I considered leaving them out. But the combination proved to be superb—a subtle blend of moist tartness with spicy heat. For all other days but Easter, bake the cake in a loaf or deep layer pan and serve dusted with confectioner's sugar—a sprightly slice for tea. For the Paschal lamb, it will be iced and coconuted. Inspired by a recipe in *British Cookery*.

---

*At some point, dry the vanilla bean pieces and return them to your vanilla sugar jar (page 258).

CORNISH CURRANT AND CANDIED GINGER CAKE

[*16 or more servings*]

Like most dense fruited cakes, this is good a day after baking but better a week or two later. Tightly wrapped in an airtight heavy plastic bag, it keeps in the refrigerator for weeks. It also freezes well.

1 ½ cups (½ pound) currants
¼ cup rum
1 ¾ cups all-purpose flour, plus a little for the mold
1 cup less 2 tablespoons sugar
1 teaspoon cinnamon
½ stick unsalted butter, plus more for the mold, softened

½ cup milk, lukewarm
3 extra large eggs, at room temperature
1 ¾ cups (½ pound) candied ginger, chopped (pieces may range from grains of rice to small peas)
Sifted confectioner's sugar or Rum Butter Icing (recipe follows)

Toss the currants and rum together and let the currants soak at least 2 hours. Generously brush the inside of your mold (whether a two-part lamb mold or a 4- to 6-cup loaf or cake pan) with butter. Dust with flour, knocking out excess. When ready to bake, heat the oven to 325°F.

In a mixing bowl, combine the flour, sugar, cinnamon, butter, and milk. Blend well, then beat at medium speed on the mixer or with a wooden spoon until smooth, scraping the bowl and beaters or spoon once. Add the eggs one at a time, beating until smooth after each. Thoroughly blend in the ginger and the currants (and any rum in the bottom of the bowl). Beat 2 minutes. *For the lamb cake, continue with directions on page 230.* Smooth the batter into the mold. Rap gently on the counter to knock out any air bubbles. Bake until a thin skewer thrust in the center comes out clean, about 1 hour. Cool 10 minutes on a rack, then unmold, top side up. Cool thoroughly, then wrap tightly until needed.

Either dust with sifted confectioner's sugar or frost with

RUM BUTTER ICING

[*Makes 2 cups**]

This may be prepared a day in advance, covered tightly, and refrigerated. Bring to room temperature before spreading.

4 cups confectioner's sugar, and perhaps a bit more
1 stick unsalted butter, softened

¼ cup rum (light rum, for the lamb)
A little milk, if needed for thinning

In a bowl with the mixer on low speed or a wooden spoon, beat the confectioner's sugar, butter, and rum together until smooth and creamy. For the lamb, it should be thick enough to hold its shape; if it isn't, beat in a little more sugar. For icing other cakes and pastries, you may want the icing thinner; add a little milk. Cover until needed.

---

*This amount is for the lamb cake. To ice the top of a loaf or round, halve the recipe.

PASCHAL LAMB CAKE
[20 *small but rich slices*]

1 recipe Cornish Currant and Candied
   Ginger Cake (previous page)
1 recipe Rum Butter Icing (recipe preceding)
14 ounces shredded coconut*
A dot of red food coloring
A dot of blue food coloring or tiny blue or
   purple flowers

A few drops of green food coloring
Some small fresh, dried, or silk flowers such
   as forget-me-nots, yellow marshmallow
   chickens; speckled jelly beans; small foil-
   covered chocolate eggs, and so forth to
   decorate the platter
Scant yard narrow pink[†] silk ribbon

You'll also need a lamb mold, whether an old one of cast iron or a newer one of aluminum[‡] and a few toothpicks.

Make the batter for the currant and ginger cake, following the recipe until directed to move to this page. Set the front half of the lamb mold nose-down on a baking sheet. Smooth all the cake batter into it, filling the ears nicely and moving a chopstick or thin knife up and down in the nose to make sure there are no air pockets. Unless your mold is the old-fashioned cast iron lamb, the batter will be higher than the sides; smooth it evenly, sloping it slightly away from the sides. Lay a toothpick along the center of each ear and set one straight down into the muzzle for support. Rap gently on the counter to knock out any air bubbles. Fit on the top, set on a baking sheet and slide into the oven.

Bake 1 hour, then thrust a thin skewer in a vent in the top; if it comes out clean, the cake is done. If there isn't a vent (some molds don't have them), give the cake 5 minutes more and assume it's done. Set the unopened lamb on its nose on a cooling rack 15 minutes, then lift off the top. Run a knife gently all around the sides. Turn the cake onto its back on the rack and lift away the mold. Cool completely, then brush off any crumbs. Make the icing.

With a table knife, smooth icing over the bottom of the lamb and stand it on your prettiest serving platter. Slather the rest of the icing over the lamb, vaguely following the contours of the mold—lots of whirls and swirls. Make the bridge of its nose smooth and flat, narrowing the nose to the mouth. With a flip of the knife, shape a curl upon its brow. Press in coconut all over its body except on the face from the curl down—coconut goes under the jaw, however. Put a dot of icing in each of two small dishes. Dip a toothpick in red coloring and mix with icing to make shell pink. With the tip of the toothpick, draw a line of a pink mouth—I make a rather smug little smile (she knows she's beautiful—he knows he's handsome—and this *is* her/his day!). Dip another toothpick in blue food coloring and mix with the other icing to make sky blue. With the tip of the toothpick, draw the eyes—I make two downward half-circles so the eyes are demurely downcast. Don't hesitate to lift off anything you draw, erase the traces with white icing and do it again until it's right.

---

*Fresh and dried coconut notes are on page 16.
†Of course, if your lamb is a lad, make it blue.
‡Available from fancy cookware shops, especially at Eastertime. Or write to the Maid of Scandinavia Co. (address, page 256, under Rice paper).

Shake the remaining coconut in a jar with a few drops of green food coloring and distribute the grass around the lamb on the platter. Tuck flowers in the grass and stick a bit of one jauntily out of a corner of the lamb's mouth—if the flowers are fresh, place them at the last minute. Arrange the marshmallow chickens here and there, then the jelly beans, and foil-covered eggs. Finally, tie a silk ribbon around its neck with a bow and set your dearie in the center of your Easter table.

Well. Amanda, who had been suffering life as an only child for a couple of years ("What am I doing on a Saturday night sitting and having dinner alone with my PARENTS!*#?"), was mercifully admitted to Berkeley. The day she left, we put the Malibu house on the market. It was, after all, a seven-person house with two people in it—Alma had long since left for a protracted visit with her family, and Gene and I had come to the point that we preferred the house to ourselves. We also preferred to give our waking hours to our work rather than to sweeping eucalyptus leaves, skimming the pool, and cleaning up after visits from the children and their friends when they left in a dash and didn't quite have time to put things back to rights. The children said they understood our giving up the house but it gave them pain. The house sold in early December and we all had one last Christmas in it together.

And then, in January, the Mover Men, as the children used to call them, packed us up and said they would meet us the next day. We had bought a magnificent piece of property in the mountains two-and-a-half hours from our family, and Gene had asked me if I wouldn't design a chalet for us. We would see.

We went through the beautiful big house one last time. Sixteen years. We locked the front door and walked out the front gate. We stood at the top of the stairs in the driveway in the dark, put our hands over the switch, and together turned out the garden lights for the last time.

Then off we went. Just the two of us again. A whole new mountain world awaited us.

On the Mountain

To my astonishment, I did pull a house out of my hat for the two of us. Pinned to a granite boulder, it has a prospect of a wooded valley set in a bowl of mountains rising to eleven thousand feet above the desert floor. From their summit, you can see the ocean. The house is a chalet of redwood and cedar, with a river rock chimney three storeys high. People tell me it looks as though it has always been here. Just what I'd hoped for.

We live with a myriad of birds and absolute tranquility, enjoying our morning walks with our black Lab Sam, the change of seasons, the garden (classical herbs, old roses, and heritage vegetables—lots of European yellow potatoes), and on our slopes of decomposed granite, a small young orchard of apples, apricots, peaches, pears, European plums, cherry plums, Japanese persimmons, sour cherries, quinces, medlars, red, black, and yellow currants, elderberries, raspberries, gooseberries, blackberries, blueberries, huckleberries, strawberries, and a dozen other sorts of berries, which often the wild things get to before we do. And, in front, Gene's pride and joy, his pocket handkerchief of a lawn on which we keep meaning to play croquet. The week's rounds include visits to our Hospice patients, guests for dinner or a rented movie Saturday night, and my chiefest pleasure, our Great-but-how-come-you-have-eleven-cards-in-your-hand-Gene? poker game with half a dozen friends. Family and old friends come for the weekend, which makes for more satisfying visits than catch-up conversations over dinner. Our four children have become eight—and have given us children of their own. Bliss.

We eat simply. And, heaven bless me, Gene does at least half the cooking. He makes breakfast, lunch, and, a couple of nights a week, marvelous dinners. After I dine on his thresher shark grilled with garlic-lemon-butter (from the waist-high kitchen fireplace I copied from an English book), I tell God He can take me, I am ready. Once a month or so, when we go to Los Angeles, we bring home fresh fish and chickens from Sonoma County raised free-ranging (a match for the *poulets de grain* we loved in France). When we entertain, we like to grill, or Chinese tea-and-spice-smoke something in our smoker, a new toy.

My favorite entrée for guests these days is tenderloin of pork, an extraordinary cut of meat I've just discovered. Tenderloin of pork, like tenderloin of beef (page 97), has no fat, no bones, and is the tenderest of the tender, as well as being endowed with the sweet subtle flavor of pork. I do nothing to it. It's gorgeous and it's foolproof.

GRILLED TENDERLOIN OF PORK
[5 servings]

2 ³/₄-pounds tenderloins of pork—they will probably come packaged as 1 ¹/₂ pounds and fitted together, at room temperature

A little olive or peanut oil for basting

You'll also need 3 or 4 pieces of fruitwood* or 2 to 3 dozen lumps of mesquite or other non–petroleum-based charcoal.

Trim any fat or fiber from around the meat.

Have the meat rack 5 to 6 inches above the surface of the fire. Build the wood fire or lay the bed of coals mirroring the pieces of meat (set an inch or so apart), plus a 1 to 2-inch margin on all sides. When the coals are covered with ash and the fire is medium-hot—so that you can only hold your hand over the grill for 3 seconds— it's ready.

Brush the grill with oil and brush the tenderloins with oil all over. Lay them on the grill and cover with a tent of foil, shiny side in—the tent should extend several inches beyond the meat at either end. Grill 15 minutes, basting occasionally, then turn with tongs. Continue basting while you grill the other side until a good meat thermometer thrust in the center of both pieces registers 140°F (pink but safe) to 160°F, 12 to 15 minutes longer. Remove and let the juices settle 5 to 10 minutes. Or serve at room temperature. Superb.

Cut the meat across the grain on a slant, about ¹/₂-inch thick (the way we like it) or thinner.

We serve the pork with mushroom risotto or yellow rice (page 214), broccoli or another green vegetable in season, and pear chutney (page 163).

What could be simpler or better?

Indeed. Lucky me. Story of my life.

---

*Or nutwood or oak or . . . Just avoid resinous woods like pine.

Appendix

Here are terms and phrases referred to elsewhere in this book as well as scraps of information that might be useful.

APPLES
. . . keeping.
Wrap blemish-free apples in newspaper or tissue, turn into a plastic food bag, force out the air (submerge all but one corner of the opening in a pot of water), and close tight. Refrigerate or keep in a cellar as close to (but no lower than) 32°F as you can. Every 2 to 3 weeks, feel the apples and remove any that are softening. Long-keeping varieties will last through winter this way.
. . . varieties for cooking.
Here are a baker's dozen perfect apples for pie and most cooking uses. As surely as there are inventive pomologists in this world, more fine apples will be added to the list.

Do remember that the apples you see in the market between the end of October and the end of July are storage apples. Some apples keep beautifully (these are noted) and you can cook with them until March or April. But in May, June, and July, switch to summer fruits as they come into season.

LATE SUMMER
Gravenstein. Fine-grained, firm, juicy, aromatic, and slightly tart. *Red Gravenstein*: Ripened Gravensteins and even more delectable. Buy only when fresh.

EARLY AUTUMN
Jonathan. Fine-grained, firm, juicy, slightly tart, with a rich appley flavor. Buy only when fresh.
McIntosh. Tender, juicy, aromatic, and slightly tart. Buy only when they've been grown in cold climates (ask to see the box) and only when fresh.
Cortland. Firmer than McIntosh, as juicy, aromatic, and sweet-tart—some think better than McIntosh on all counts. Buy only when fresh.

Rhode Island Greening. Firm, juicy, rich, and pleasantly tart.

LATE AUTUMN

Baldwin. Firm, juicy, and sweet to sweet-tart

Golden Delicious. Fine-grained, firm, juicy, aromatic, and sweet. Under ideal conditions, can keep until March. (Not sprightly enough for pie but lovely for sautéing and for tarts.)

Rome (or Red Rome) Beauty. Firm, juicy, and mildly tart. Every other cooking apple will have more flavor. Buy only when fresh.

Winesap. Firm, very juicy, aromatic, and sweet-tart.

York Imperial. Firm, aromatic, and mildly tart.

Northern Spy. Fine-grained, tender, firm, very juicy, sprightly, and slightly tart. Keeps until February and is remarkable for its freshness after long storage.

EARLY WINTER

Newtown (Albemarle or Yellow) Pippin—usually simply "Pippin." Firm, moderately fine-grained, aromatic, and tart. Keeps until March and April, becoming richer and sweeter.

(By a twist of fate, this great early American apple—a favorite of Benjamin Franklin—is now little grown in the East but flourishes in orchards in Washington, Oregon, and California, where it is primarily available. Helps to make up for Westerners' painful lack of Northern Spys, Greenings, Baldwins, Cortlands, and York Imperials. . . .)

Granny Smith. Firm, juicy, and mildly tart. Keeps until spring, becoming sweeter.

Mutsu. Firm, juicy, mildly tart to sweet. A Japanese cross between Indo and Golden Delicious that promises to upstage its famous Golden parent for its excellent keeping, eating, cooking, and baking qualities.

You'll note the emphasis in several varieties on only using the apples when fresh. How can you tell when apples are fresh? First, apply the usual common-sense rules for choosing any fresh fruit or vegetables: a characteristic bright color (and I don't mean the sheen the lamentable wax dip gives, I mean an inner glow), flesh that is firm and tight beneath the skin, and no soft spots or bruises. Then, the surest way to know if an apple is right for your pie or cobbler is to rub it on your sleeve and take a bite. Try a number, if necessary, but drop the rejects into a bag for the check-out stand so you'll keep your good name at the market. Big apples tend to mature and turn mushy or mealy more rapidly than small ones, so bear that in mind.

You may also note there is one more apple on the list than a baker's dozen. That's because I've just made a pie with Mutsu apples for the first time. They are superb.

. . . a good corer.

The best I have ever used is made by a firm named Bethany. The handle is bright red, but, curiously, the name isn't marked on it. See if you can find one.

BAIN MARIE

Merely a deepish vessel of hot water in which a smaller vessel is placed. In a *bain marie*, hot water surrounds the food in the smaller vessel as compared with a double boiler in which hot water is simply underneath it.

BEAN SPROUTS

. . . growing.

Sprinkle a small amount of mung seeds (available from health food stores) in a clean widemouth jar, any size from a quart up. Turn the jar on its side and sprinkle a veil of seeds along the "bottom." Cover with cool water and soak 8 hours. Cover the mouth of the jar with cheesecloth (secure with its canning ring or a rubber band) and drain, then shake the jar, distributing the seeds as widely and evenly as possible. Set in dim light. Rinse well 3 or 4 times a day with fresh water—this is important. After 2 or 3 days, set the jar in sunlight. The sprouts are ready in 3 or 4 days from the beginning. Turn into something transparent and keep in the refrigerator, then start a new batch so you won't run out.

Soybean, lentil, sunflower, and alfalfa seeds are sprouted the same way. Soybean, lentil, and sunflower sprouts are best when ¼-inch long, alfalfa when 2 inches long—all are ready after 3 or 4 days.

BEEF

. . . cutting your own petits filets.

Buy well-marbled porterhouse steaks at least 1½ inches thick, choosing them for the round nuggets of tenderloin to one side of the bone: they should be about 3 inches in diameter. Try to buy steaks without the chewy "tail," which is from the flank. Trim out the bones with a long sharp knife. Viola! The nuggets, which should weigh from 5 to 7 ounces, are your *petits filets*, and the others are New York steaks for the freezer. Who needs a butcher?

BEETS

. . . cooking fresh.

Choose firm beets, and, for company, have them all the same size so they will cook uniformly and look handsome. (When you must buy in bunches, if your greengrocer ties together baseball-sized beets with babies, you'll have to take an extra bunch or two and eat buttered beets a couple of nights before the party.)

Scrub gently and do not peel. Cut off the stems 1 to 2 inches above the beet, but don't trim the root (the greens, I'm sure you know, are even more valuable nutritionally than the roots—cook them like spinach, page 258). In a pot, bring enough water to cover the beets to a boil. Drop in the beets, reduce the heat to maintain a simmer, and cook uncovered until tender when pierced with a thin skewer—30 minutes for small young beets (less, if they're from your garden), longer for older fellows. Lift out to a bowl of cold water, then slip off the skins. A nudge from your thumb should remove stems and rootlets, then trim the scars with a paring knife. Proceed with your recipe or simply add butter, a few drops of lemon juice, salt, white pepper, and chopped dill or parsley.

BONING

Poultry meat, after removing skin, bones, and fat, comes down to about half its purchased weight. Turkey loses a little less than chicken because the larger the bird, the more meat there is proportionate to bones.

. . . chicken or turkey breasts.

Start with a sharp knife at the tip of the breast and run it around the edges, then follow the span of the breast, freeing the meat from the bone. It's that simple.

. . . chicken or turkey, whole.

Keep your soup pot at hand and toss everything you remove from the bird into it.

Begin by removing the first two joints of the wings; poultry shears or a cleaver are easiest, but a sharp knife works, too. Cut off the knobs of the drumsticks. For the boning, use a small sharp knife, the thinner the better. As you work, be careful not to pierce the skin, if you're going to be using it.

Turn the bird breast down. Run the tip of the knife the length of the back, down to the bone. Slip the knife over to a wing and cut the wing free from the shoulder at the joint. Working from the inside toward the outside, bone out the wing by following along the bone with the knife, scraping the meat free, pulling up the bone as you go—soon it will come out, turning the wing inside out. Repeat with the other wing. Use the same technique with the thigh and leg bones, cutting the two bones apart at the joint when you've boned out the thigh bone. The legs will also finish inside out. Now, beginning at the seam you've cut on top and working down the ribs, just move the knife along close to the bones while you scrape the meat free. It's a good idea to sharpen your knife frequently as you work.

When the bird is completely boned, be meticulous about removing—

scraping the meat from, then pulling out—every tendon from the legs, a te-dious but necessary job. Catch any bits of bone your knife may have missed, and remove the tail and all deposits of fat. For a galantine (or ballottine), straighten the skin—the shape will be that of an upside down V—and ar-range the pieces of flesh as evenly over it as you can. Cover with plastic film and roll up, then wrap the roll in plastic and refrigerate until ready to stuff. Cover your bones and bits in the soup pot with water, add savory vegetables, and make yourself a broth.

Brandy
. . . warming for flaming.
Do this *ve-ry* carefully. Turn the brandy into a small covered pot and warm over lowest heat a long minute or in the microwave for 30 seconds. Hold the brandy away from you and not underneath anything flammable when you set the match to it.

Breadcrumbs
. . . fine dry.
Toast slices of bread (crusts included) in a 300°F oven until bone dry. Finely crush beneath a rolling pin or in the blender. About 6 medium slices of bread yield 1 cup.

Bread dough
. . . detailed instructions
MAKING THE DOUGH
In a warm mixing bowl, stir the yeast into the warm liquid and let proof until dissolved, about 5 minutes. Stir in the salt, any fat and eggs, and then half the flour. (If the flour is stored in a cold bin, warm it slightly in the oven for a few minutes but do not overheat. If the flour is very cold it will slow down the pro-cess, not ruin it.) Beat until there are no more lumps, 2 minutes—this step is important. Beat in the remaining flour by the half-cupful—beating until smooth after each addition—until the dough is soft but firm enough to knead—it should clean the sides of the bowl as you beat. (The softer the dough, the lighter the finished crumb.) Let rest 5 minutes so the flour can ab-sorb the liquid—also important.
KNEADING BY HAND
Sprinkle about ¼ cup of flour on your work surface—marble is more efficient than wood at keeping the dough from sticking to it. Knead by folding the top edge of the dough down to the bottom edge, firmly pressing the edges to-gether with the heels of your hands, then giving the dough a quarter turn and repeating the folding-pressing-quarter-turning rhythmically. Don't be

gentle with the dough—your aim is to develop the gluten in the flour, and a few slam! bang! whams! onto the work surface will only better develop the gluten. Always use as little flour as possible in kneading, and when you rub your hands together to clean them of sticky dough, drop the bits to one side—they're too tough to return to your increasingly smooth and tender dough. Knead until the dough is silky, there are tiny bubbles under the surface, it no longer sticks to the board, and it bounces back when tapped smartly with a finger—generally speaking, about 8 minutes for doughs with butter and eggs, 10 minutes for plainer doughs.

KNEADING BY MIXER

If you have a mixer with a powerful motor and a dough hook, you will use less flour and have lighter bread if you use it. Out of superstition, I suppose, I always knead 10 minutes by machine, regardless of the dough.

KNEADING BY FOOD PROCESSOR

A standard food processor can handle 2 to 3 cups of flour; if your recipe has more, you must divide up the dough. Turn the dough into the work bowl and process until the dough cleans the sides of the bowl and forms a smooth ball that turns around the blade; now count 25 turns. Turn out the dough, let it rest 1 to 2 minutes, then return it to the bowl, bottom now on top. Process 25 more turns around the blade. *So* easy.

RISING

Measure the dough in a measuring pitcher, then mark a vessel at double that amount. Butter or oil the vessel well, add the dough, then turn it over so the top is buttered. Pat flat and cover with plastic film and a towel wrung out of warm water.

If the house is chilly, wrap the vessel in a warm blanket and set to rise out of a draft, ideally somewhere around 70°F; 75°F is acceptable, but I try not to let the dough rise at temperatures higher than that—I find the texture and flavor will coarsen. I know it's wasteful of energy, but I find my microwave oven with the light on and the door closed makes a perfect 70°F bread-proofing box in winter.

When the shoulders of the dough hit the mark, usually about 1 to 2 hours, turn it onto your work surface, punch down, and knead a few times to expel any air bubbles. If the recipe directs a second rising, butter or oil the vessel again, add the dough, turn over, cover, and let it rise as before. Again knead out any bubbles, then cover and let rest 5 to 10 minutes—it will be easier to shape if it has plumped with air a bit.

N.B. In a light dough of mostly white flour that has been enriched with butter and eggs, the second rising improves the texture of the bread, but can be omitted if time is short. For plain unenriched, and particularly whole grain doughs, a second rising is essential.

SHAPING

Lightly flour your work surface and shape the loaf according to directions. Do not knead or fold the dough too many strokes at this point because the dough no longer will stick back together and the result of too much folding and manipulating might be gaps in the baked bread. Arrange the dough on a well-oiled baking sheet or in a well-oiled mold—it should fill the mold two-thirds full. Generously brush all exposed surfaces with oil or melted butter, cover lightly with the dampened towel, and return to the 70°F place to rise again until doubled (or in the case of French bread, tripled) in bulk. *The dough is ready to be baked when you poke the tip of a little finger into a corner and the dimple doesn't push back.* Heat your oven about 10 minutes before you expect the dough to be ready for baking.

BURRIDA

. . . fish, molluscs, and crustaceans—and their American counterparts—commonly used are:

ANGLER (OR MONK OR GOOSE) FISH: (From New England waters) *Rospo*, its Adriatic name, means toad (the fish has been variously described as exceedingly ugly, hideous, and grotesque). Its firm, sweet succulent meat is reminiscent of lobster, and it's my first choice of fish for soup. Pacific Coast fishes with qualities similar to angler are cabezon and rockfish (rules for selecting which are on page 256). All are available throughout the year.

CONGER EEL: Although congers and morays (some consider morays the finest of all Mediterranean fish) abound in coastal and inland waters of the north Atlantic and in the Mississippi River and its tributaries, I suspect that it's usually the common eel that comes to market—and then, usually only around the holidays and *then* only in Italian, Greek, or Portuguese neighborhoods. For eel, I substitute another fish with dark fat flesh, one of the tunas or mackerels. One kind or another is always available.

SMOOTH HOUND SHARK: It feeds on crabs and lobsters, thus giving its flesh a delicate savor, and DOGFISH, another shark. Both are also native to North American Atlantic waters. If you can't find them, substitute thresher, leopard, or any other tasty shark. In my opinion, shark is one of the stars of *burrida*. Its lean meaty flesh remains succulent when cooked, which is an invaluable quality in soup (nothing worse than having a lump of fish stick in your throat as the broth goes skimming down). And shark's sweet flavor is just flavorful enough. Lacking shark, use swordfish. All are available all year.

OCTOPUS: You'll have to pound hell out of it before you cook it and then boil it for hours before you can put it in your soup. And CUTTLEFISH, a middling size fellow in the octopus family (whose internal shell is the "bone" cherished by pet birds for sharpening their beaks). For either, substitute squid.

IN ADDITION TO THOSE ABOVE, other sea creatures from American waters good for soup are blue-mouth (related to the incomparable *rascasse*, and also ugly as sin but with the flavor and texture of lobster), John Dory (also lobster-like), striped and black mullet, cod, catfish, carp, turbot, drum (corbina on the west coast), grouper, haddock, porgy, ling cod, ray or skate, crayfish/crawfish, and spiny lobster.

And a passel of small whole fish—anchovies, herrings, and smelts—add charming texture to any fish soup.

CAKES

. . . when they're done.

A fine skewer thrust into the center comes out clean, the cake springs back when tapped lightly with a finger, and the cake has *begun* to pull away from the sides of the pan.

CANNING

. . . jars.

After many years of using paraffin to seal all sorts of preserves, jams, and jellies in all sorts of jars, I've thrown away my bars of wax and now only use sterilized canning jars. This isn't much more trouble than melting paraffin (getting hardened paraffin out of the pot can take forever). And spoilage in properly sealed sterilized canning jars is unheard of.

Using canning jars also saves face. We've received paraffin-sealed jellies and preserves that had turned moldy or even fermented. Of course we could never tell our friends, who gave the gifts with pride. Paraffin works better with the smooth surface of jelly than with the uneven forms of preserves, but paraffin will not reliably preserve good things in hot, humid, or dusty places. So instead of collecting every pretty jar and glass and crock I come across, these days I use 8-, 12-, or 16-ounce canning jars with 2-piece lids, which these days are made quite prettily.

And canning jars are the only choice if the preserves are going to travel. Of course homemade goodies make splendid remembrances for far-flung friends, and I like to give houseguests a jar of something to take home in their suitcase—heaven forfend it should leak!

Canning jars must have no nicks or cracks, sealing rings must not be rusty or bent, the sealing compound on lids must have no indentation from a previous canning. In other words, healthy jars and rings may be processed many times, but lids get only one turn.

. . . sterilizing jars.

This is a bore but cheap spoilage insurance. Unless the canning process itself will be longer than the sterilizing time (or unless you're pressure canning), sterilize.

Wash and rinse canning jars and sealing rings in hot soapy water; no need to dry. Put rings aside. Set a trivet, cake rack, or folded towel in the bottom of your largest kettle—boiling water should circulate beneath the jars and they might break if they rattle around on bare metal. Fill the kettle half-full with hot water and set it over medium-high heat. Fill the jars with hot water and set them in the kettle so they won't touch one another or the sides of the kettle. (If you're going to do much of this, invest in a canning kettle with a rack because it gives every jar a proper place to set.) When all the jars are in, add hot water to cover them by 1 inch. Cover the kettle, raise the heat to highest, and bring to a rolling boil. Time 15 minutes from when the water boils. Turn off the heat and leave the jars in the kettle until needed.

[*At high altitude:* Add 1 minute boiling time for every 1,000 feet above sea level.

Meanwhile, pour boiling water over the lids in a bowl to soften the sealing compound.

. . . *"pack . . . ."*

Lift out the sterilized jars using a jar lifter or tongs, empty them, and shake out excess water (don't touch the inside). Ladle in preserves or chutney or similar preparations up to $\frac{1}{4}$ inch from the top. (Some foods need $\frac{1}{2}$-inch margin—the recipe will tell you.) A wide-mouth canning funnel makes the job neater and easier. Run a table knife down through the jar to force out any bubbles. Wipe the rims clean with a damp cloth, lay on the lids, and screw on the rings as tightly as you comfortably can; do not force them.

The water in your kettle should be hot, but not boiling. Place the jars in the kettle, setting them, as before, so they won't touch one another or the kettle's sides. When all the jars are in, add hot water to cover by 1 inch. Cover the kettle, raise the heat to highest, and bring to a rolling boil. Time from the moment the water boils, according to the recipe. For preserves, chutneys, jams, and jellies, boil 10 minutes.

[*At high altitude:* Add 1 minute boiling time for every 1,000 feet above sea level.]

Turn off the heat, lift out the jars, and set them on a folded towel out of a draft, leaving room between them for air to circulate.

. . . *"seal . . . ."*

As the jars cool, you will hear the music of their sealing—plink! plink! plink!—the pleasing sound of the metal lids contracting as the vacuum forms inside the jar. Do not disturb until they are cold. When the jars are cold, press down in the center of the lids. They shouldn't budge. If any pops back up, it hasn't sealed and you have to boil the jar again—*have to*. Or keep the jar in the refrigerator and use it as though you had just opened it.

. . . "and store . . . ."

Store in the proverbial cool dark dry place. Your preserves will be good for at least one year, if nobody finds them.

CHEESE

. . . ". . . melting" cheeses.

Simply the Cheddars, jacks, Swiss/Gruyères, mozzarellas, and such of this world that, generally speaking, are those that slice rather than crumble.

CHICKEN

. . . cutting it up the French way.

Trying to make pieces as equal and as equally shaped for uniform cooking as possible, disjoint the chicken with a sharp knife thus:

Laying the chicken on one side, pull back the leg. With your fingers, find the joint connecting the thigh to the body. Following the round contours of the thigh, cut through the thigh and the joint to release it. Find the joint connecting the leg to the thigh. Cut through it. (This next is optional: you may like the little knob on the drumstick.) With a heavy chef's knife or cleaver, cut off the nubbin at the end of the leg. Push down the flesh so the remaining bone will show.

Use the tip of the knife to find the joint connecting the wing to the body. Cut through the wing joint, bringing the knife down to the breast section and including a generous length of breast meat above the ribs with the wing— this gives a much fairer portion to the Wing Person. Trim off the tip of the wing at the joint and save it for soup. Turn the chicken on its other side and do the same with the other leg and wing.

Free the cartilaginous breast bone from the carcass at one end and cut through the joints connecting the breast meat at the other end. If you've taken quite a bit of breast meat for the wings, you can keep this piece intact and have 1 generous breast piece. Or, if it seems too big, you can cut it in half *crosswise* and have 2 chunky pieces.

. . . trussing.

Trim away the wingtips at the joint. For a 3- to 5-pound chicken, cut a piece of good cotton string (no synthetics) about 2 arm's lengths. Lay the bird on its back and slip the string underneath, in the middle of the wings; pull up both ends of the string so they'll be even. Cross the strings over the breast (thus pinning the wings to the sides) and flip the bird over, tail over neck. Cross the strings again over the lower back, then turn the bird over again. Cross the legs and push the legs toward the breast to make the bird compact. Cross the strings over the legs, flip the bird over again, and tie securely (a double loop holds best), making a knot just above the tail. Trim any extra string. After roasting, one flick of the carving knife releases the string.

CREAM
. . . *whipping.*
If possible, chill the heavy cream, beaters, and bowl (preferably metal) a couple of hours in the refrigerator before beating. Turn the cream into the bowl and set it in a larger bowl of ice. The cream will mount wonderfully quickly. Beat only until the cream looks like the "stiff but not dry" stage of beaten egg whites.

If you wish to beat the cream in advance of serving, beat it a little beyond this point—but not much—and turn it into a strainer. Set the strainer over a bowl, cover tightly with plastic film, and refrigerate; the excess liquid will drain out and the cream will hold its form nicely at least 3 or 4 hours.

DEGLAZE
To scrape up every jot and tittle of browned bits in a pan by first loosening them with liquid.

EELS
. . . *cooking.*
This is how Ada Boni suggests you treat conger eel before it goes into your *burrida*:*

> Clean the eel but do not remove the head. Rinse it several times in running water and wipe dry. Starting from the head, roll the eel round and round like the springs of a clock and place it in a non-metallic casserole just large enough to hold it. [Cover with water,] cover the casserole, and bring to the boil slowly, then lower the heat and simmer.

One hour sees the eel tender, so simmer it only half an hour because it has that much more to cook in the soup.

EGGPLANT
. . . *salting.*
Allowing 1 tablespoon of salt for 2 pounds of eggplant, sprinkle it over the cubes or slices, weight slightly with a dish, and let drain for about 1 hour. Rinse and dry thoroughly. The same method is used for summer squashes.

---
*Italian Regional Cooking.

EGGS

. . . hard cooking.

Ideally, the eggs should be a few days old (no problem for most of us super-market egg buyers)—the shells of fresh eggs simply will not come away without crumbling into a thousand teeny bits. Best insurance of all against cracked shells is Jacques Pepin's notion of tapping two eggs together next to your ear: sound eggs "clink" and cracked eggs "clunk"—and if anyone walks in while you're listening intently to the timbre of two eggs, well, whoever said good cooks weren't eccentric?

Pierce the large end of each egg with a clean pushpin. Set the eggs in a pot, and add cool water to cover by an inch and about 1½ teaspoons salt per quart of water (salt slightly toughens the shells). Set over high heat, bring to a boil, immediately cover, and remove from the heat. I usually just leave them there until they are cool enough to handle but you're supposed to time 7 minutes, then plunge the eggs into cold water until cool.

[*At high altitude:* Add 1 minute in hot water for every 1,000 feet over sea level.]

When the eggs are cold, crack them on the counter all over so the shell is in a hundred dozen bits. To shell, begin at the large end (there's supposed to be a remnant of an air pocket there, which makes starting the peeling easier). Peel under cold running water. Wrap the eggs airtight and refrigerate. They will keep up to 1 week.

. . . poaching.

This technique sounds fussy but it's not. It's the classic method and if you've never poached an egg this way, you've never tasted a perfect poached egg—a silky thing of beauty—and once you do, you'll never go back to those tinny little scoops set in a frame over hot water. As contrasted to eggs that will be hard cooked, eggs for poaching must be very fresh.

While it's comforting to know that you can poach eggs as much as 2 or 3 days in advance (short of a celebration such as a huge wedding breakfast, I can't imagine why you would want to), it's of course best to poach them closer to serving time.

Have a fresh dish towel folded beside the stove. *If the eggs are to be served immediately*, have a bowl of hot water there, too. *If the eggs are being poached in advance*, have a bowl of cold water ready.

In a wide deep heavy pot, bring 2 inches of water and a splash of mild vinegar to a simmer. Crack the egg sharply, and, holding it over the water, just pull the shell apart and let the egg glide in. (If you drop the first next to the handle, you can keep track of them.) Run a slotted spatula or spoon beneath the egg to keep it from sticking. Time 3 minutes. Drop in the remaining eggs, noting the time between entries. Maintain the water at a tremble.

When the timer rings, lift the first egg with the slotted spoon. The white should be just set and the yolk, when lightly tapped with a finger, should be soft. Slip the egg into the bowl of water to rinse off the vinegar and stop the cooking, then lift it onto the towel to drain. Quickly trim any ragged edges with the edge of the spatula or spoon. Continue with the remaining eggs, when they are ready.

If the poached eggs are to be served later, now slip them into a bowl of fresh cold water to cover. Refrigerate the bowl *uncovered*.

To reheat, slip the eggs into a saucepan of barely simmering water. Time 1 minute; if the eggs are chilled, add a few seconds more. Drain again on the towel.

To set the poached egg in place, lift the towel enough to tip it back onto the spatula or spoon (this is not so tricky an operation as it may seem, as the white and yolk are amply cooked to bear the stress) then set the egg in place.

FISH
. . . *"dressed."*
Head and tail intact, entrails removed, gills may or may not be removed.
. . . *how to tell if it's fresh.*
First, look at the eyes. They must be clear and perky, not in the least bit dull and sunken (however, the eyes of some deep water fish, such as rockfish, might be cloudy as a result of having been brought up suddenly from the vasty deep). If there are no eyes to look upon, then press a forefinger into the flesh. It must spring back and leave no impression. The gills should be bright crimson. The scales must be shiny. If there are no gills and no scales, sniff the fish. It must smell sweet and of the sea, with no "fishiness" about it. The flesh of fish steaks should look bright and shiny—bright and shiny are key words in buying fresh fish. You can almost always distinguish thawed frozen fish in the case by its dull pasty appearance.
. . . *keeping it fresh.*
Buy a special fish the day you're going to cook it, and family fish no more than the day before. Place it in a plastic bag, set the bag in a pan covered lightly with ice in the coldest part of the refrigerator. Drain off the melted ice and add more as needed.
. . . *serving (or eating) a whole unboned fish.*
Run the tip of a fish knife, spatula, or table knife lengthwise down the center of the top of the fish (usually there's a grain line there), cutting down to the bone.

For a one-serving-size fish like trout or catfish, slip the knife down the center line—flatly this time, freeing the flesh from the bones on one side. Flip this flesh over onto the plate. Repeat on the other side. The skeleton will be completely exposed. Hold down the fish beneath the skeleton with the knife then gingerly lift the skeleton up and away. Have a platter ready to receive it.

For a large fish like salmon, beginning at the shoulders, cut slices crosswise, again cutting to the bone, then lift with the fish knife (the slices will be half the width of the fish). When you've finished with the top, use the knife and a fork to pull the skeleton up and away—have a platter ready to receive it. Serve the bottom of the fish as you did the top.

. . . *serving a chunk of fish.*

Slice down in pieces the size you want until you feel the bone, then lift and serve them. Lift away the bone once you've finished the top—have a plate ready to receive it—and repeat on the bottom half.

. . . *some all-purpose fish—flavorful, firm-fleshed, not too fat.*

angler, bass (rock, sea, and striped), cabezon, carp (best flavor, October through March), catfish, cod, corbina, croaker, drum, flounder (fluke and plaice), grouper, haddock, halibut, John Dory, lingcod, mullet, orange roughy, pompano, redfish, red snapper, rockfish, salmon, shark, sole, tilefish, trout, turbot, whitefish, and whiting.

FLOWERS

. . . *poisonous.*

(Years ago, in my young womanhood, I decorated a friend's birthday cake with vibrant scarlet blossoms from a bush on an empty lot next door. I knew it was oleander, but I didn't know it was lethal. My friend—still my friend—has managed not to let me forget it . . .)

This is only a partial list. Consult your county agricultural inspector if in any doubt:

Autumn crocus, bleeding heart, castor bean, daffodil, daphne, foxglove, hydrangea, lantana, larkspur, lily-of-the-valley, meadow saffron, mistletoe, monkshood, narcissus, oleander, poinsettia, rhododendron, sweet pea, and wisteria.

FOOD MILL

If you lack a food mill—you shouldn't—puree your food in the food processor, blender, or pass it through a sieve. *Then* buy a top quality food mill. They're not expensive and they hold up forever (mine is already twenty-nine years old and I keep thinking of it as my new food mill) and they're invaluable. See Moulin-legume, page 250.

GARLIC

. . . *peeling.*

Set the clove beneath the broad blade of a chef's knife or cleaver laid over it.

Press the blade down gently but firmly with the heel of your hand, thereby crushing the clove. This pops the skin and makes it easy to pull off.

. . . chopping.

Why not use a garlic press? Certainly there are times when you'll want just the presence of garlic with no tell-tale bits, and then the press is called for. But most times, when you want garlic, you want garlic, and if you use the press, you'll notice that you leave behind some of its flesh and consequently no small amount of its inner being. Wasteful.

After peeling, cut the clove lengthwise into very thin strips, then make fine cuts crosswise, and you'll about have it finely chopped.

LAMB

. . . carving the leg.

Wrap a napkin around the shank bone and hold it with your non-dexterous hand. Set the leg on a carving board or piece of heavy foil. If the joint is tippy, turn it over and slice a piece or two off the bony side, so the leg will lie flat, then turn it back again, meaty side up. Make slices, as thick or as thin as you like, vertically all along the leg, cutting down to the bone. Now run the knife along the bone the length of the leg, freeing the slices. Turn the leg over and repeat. There will be chunks of meat still attached to either side of the bone, and you can again run your knife along the bones to free this meat. Slice it like the rest.

LEEKS

. . . flushing (cleaning).

Trim off the root and any discolored or raggedy leaves. Slice the leek lengthwise and flush out any grit or mud caught between the layers under cold running water. Pat dry.

MAYONNAISE

. . . homemade . . . handmade.

This is a luxurious light sauce, not an everyday slathering-over-bread spread.

[*Makes 1 cup: up to 10 servings*]
Mayonnaise keeps fresh 4 to 5 days in the refrigerator.

1 egg yolk
A rounded ½ teaspoon Dijon
  mustard
A good pinch of salt
1 tablespoon fresh lemon juice

¾ cup plus 2 tablespoons best
  quality light olive oil
2 or 3 turns of the white pepper
  mill (¼ teaspoon, medium
  grind)

Everything, including the bowl, must be at room temperature.

In a small mixing bowl, whisk the yolk, mustard, salt, and lemon juice until blended. Let rest a few minutes. Now, drop by drop, whisk in about ¼ cup of the olive oil. When the mixture has thickened somewhat, whisk in the remaining oil in a slow steady fine fine drizzle, always making sure the sauce has absorbed all the oil before adding more. When finished, add the pepper, turn into a jar, cover, and refrigerate.

Should the mixture threaten to curdle, whisk in a teaspoon or two of boiling water. If that doesn't restore the texture, drop an egg yolk into a fresh bowl and whisk your mayonnaise into the yolk as slowly as you did the olive oil into the mayonnaise. That'll do it.

. . . *machine made.*

Once you get the feel for making mayonnaise by hand, you can confidently drop a whole egg into the food processor or blender with the mustard, salt, and lemon juice, turn on the motor, and very slowly drizzle in olive oil ad lib until the mayonnaise is the consistency you like. But somehow this lacks the fineness of the handmade sauce. (Machines need the volume of a whole egg, otherwise the sauce would become too thick even before you added any oil; adding an extra yolk to the food processor is even better still.)

MEAT THERMOMETER

Use the thinnest meat thermometer you can buy (to avoid gouging the flesh) and one that doesn't stay in the roast while it's roasting. Before taking your measure, judge in your mind's eye where the bone is and then spot a place in the thickest part of the meat halfway between the bone and the surface—or with poultry, the fleshiest part of the thigh, away from the bone and close to the body. Place the thermometer with the tip at that point, pinch your fingers where the surface of the meat will be, then gently thrust in the thermometer, stopping at your fingertips. In a boneless roast, just plunge it into the very center.

MOULI-JULIENNE

A handy metal device with interchangeable disks and a red-knobbed turning-stick that, before the days of food processors with shredding attachments, performed this task beautifully—still does. Available at fancy cookware shops.

MOULIN-LÉGUME

A food mill. Made by the same people in France as Mouli-Julienne, this is a handy metal device with interchangeable disks and a red-knobbed turning-stick that, before the days of food processors, pureed food beautifully—still does; in some situations, more efficiently than the machine. Also available at fancy cookware shops.

MUSHROOMS
. . . keeping.
In an open paper bag in the refrigerator, lightly covered with a damp paper towel.

MUSSELS
. . . cleaning.
If your mussels need cleaning, do it just before cooking because their keeping quality deteriorates once submitted to all that scrubbing. (Remember, if any are not tightly closed or do not close when prodded, discard them.) Pull off the filaments, then scrape and scrub the mussels with a stiff non-metal brush under cold running water until squeaky clean.
. . . keeping.
Keep mussels in the refrigerator with a damp cloth covering them, or if you've gathered them, in clear water to cover (they will "self-clean"). Cook within 24 hours.

OCTOPUS
. . . precooking. From Ada Boni:*

> Turn out the inside bag of the octopus and empty it. Remove and discard the eye and "beak," which is at the bottom of the bag. Wash the octopus well and beat it vigorously with a cutlet bat to tenderize it. Put it into a large pan—it should fill about two-thirds of the pan—and cover with water. If living near the sea, this should be three parts seawater to one part fresh water. Bring to the boil slowly and simmer for 2 hours, or until tender. If using small octopus, they will require less "tenderizing" and be cooked in a much shorter time.

OLIVE OIL
Not until Elizabeth David remarked on the beauties of "fruity" olive oil did I understand that all olive oil mustn't be light light light. On the contrary, there are occasions when you want the spirit of the olive to shimmer through,

---

*Italian Regional Cooking.

and on those occasions, a roistering Greek or dark green Italian olive oil is heaven. But always buy *virgin* olive oil. You don't want somebody's cast-off beauty. And extra virgin is for those special moments . . .

PASTA
. . . cooking.

For every pound of dry pasta, which will serve 4 to 8, depending on menu and appetite: Add 4 generous quarts of water and a splash of olive oil to your spaghetti pot, set it over highest heat, cover it, and bring the water to the boil. Drop in 1½ heaping tablespoons salt and after the water fizzles and resumes boiling, drop in the pasta all at once. Give the pasta a vigorous swishing thorough stir with something long-handled to keep the pieces from sticking together, then clap on the lid. When the water boils again, remove the lid, stir the pasta vigorously again and set the timer for 5 minutes—the water should boil with determination but not spit and hiss threateningly. When the timer rings, pull up a strand of pasta and take a bite. Every minute or half-minute thereafter, fish out a strand and bite into it.

When the pasta is tender but still a little chewy in the center—not to be confused with gritty—it will be *al dente*, "firm to the bite." It can take 6 or 7 minutes for *spaghettini*, longer for thicker pastas. The timing depends upon the quality of the flour, the age of the pasta, the water, the pot, the heat, the sun, the moon, the stars, and, yes, the altitude.

Have a colander in the sink over your serving bowl (assuming it's heatproof). The instant the pasta tests *al dente*, rush the pot to the colander and carefully pour the contents through it (the boiling water heats your bowl). Give the colander a few firm shakes back and forth and sideways to shake out excess water. Dump out the water and turn the pasta into the bowl.

N.B.: Some sauces, such as *pesto*, want a little of the pasta water to thin them out, so it may be prudent to first pour a little of the water into a pitcher, then dump out the rest and turn your pasta into its bowl.

PEPPERCORNS
Black peppercorns are fruit picked green from the vine (*piper nigrum*) and dried in the sun. Black pepper is usually more aromatic than white. There is a beautiful range of flavors of black peppercorns available—Malabar (hotsy-totsy: of these four, the most intense and among the finest of all peppercorns), Lampong (a toasty Malabar), Tellicherry (a milder Malabar), and Brazil (a pale Malabar) being a few.

(These, as well as white and green peppercorns, may be purchased through the mail from Freed Teller & Freed's, venerable San Francisco purveyors of coffees, teas, herbs, and spices: P.O. Box 640189, San Francisco, California 94164-0189.)

White peppercorns are the same fruit as black except they have been picked fully ripe and their outer husk has been removed (just as nutmeg is the kernel of the nut in which mace is the lacy outer covering). I've heard people say they thought white pepper an affectation, but the difference is more than cosmetic. White pepper has a warmer more pungent flavor than black and I find I reach for the white pepper mill more often than not.

In France, a mixture of white peppercorns for heat and black peppercorns for snap is called *mignonette*. Why not *mignonette* your own?

Green peppercorns, by the way, are black peppercorns that have not been dried, a flavor and aroma, to quote Elizabeth David, "pungent and at the same time very fresh and clean."

PIE PASTRY
An English friend once gave me three golden rules for making pastry: keep it cool, handle it lightly, and bake it in a quick oven.
. . . *mixing the dough.*
In blending the fat into the flour, you want to finish with flour-coated pieces in three sizes: baby peas, raw oats, and breadcrumbs, in roughly even proportions. This mix of fat particles in the dough contributes to the short and flaky texture of the pastry. Lard, shortening, and butter have different consistencies, and they will cut just this way.

In my experience, the food processor makes the surest pastry because the dough is handled least. If you're temporarily out of machines, rubbing the fat into the flour with your fingertips also makes tender pastry.
. . . *resting the dough.*
The finest pastry cooks disagree radically as to its necessity. Some argue persuasively that a period of resting before rolling gives the flour time to absorb the liquid and gives the gluten in the flour—which has been somewhat developed by all that bashing about—time to relax. These cooks insist that the dough rest anywhere from two to eight hours. There are equally fine pastry cooks who recommend that the dough be chilled in the refrigerator a quarter-to-half-an-hour simply because it will be easier to roll. Still others feel that if the dough's ingredients and proportions are correct and the dough has not been overworked, the finished pastry will be quite lovely, thank you, if rolled out at once. I have done it all ways, and always found my pastry splendid.
. . . *the pan.*
On the one hand, too shallow a pie seems skimpy and the pie doesn't say, Eat Me! But too generous a pie, I find, can be unaesthetic. After trying all sorts of sizes, shapes, and materials in pans, for most pies I feel the proportions of

the heatproof glass 9 × 1 ½-inch dish *with a rim* is just right. (More and more dishes seem to be rimless, which gives the lovely fluted border, hallmark of pies, nowhere to go—although you can perch it above the rim, it's not the same. If necessary, look for a rimmed pie dish in garage sales, swap meets, or thrift shops, treasure troves of disappearing cookware.) Glass bakes pastry beautifully with any fuel, the amount of filling is in balance, and the dish itself is esthetic as slices of pie are removed.

. . . rolling out.

Use a large smooth heavy cotton or linen tea towel—an enormous improvement over any other floured surface. Rub in an even veil of flour—a fair amount for sticky pastries, a sprinkling for dry ones—and roll out the pastry upon it. When you're finished, unless the cloth is blistered with dough, fold it up and keep it for another day.

. . . a stockinette sleeve.

The companion to the tea towel for rolling pins. It keeps the pin from sticking to the dough. After each use, I usually brush off excess flour and scrape off flecks of dough. If the sleeve is tacky, I wash it under the faucet and let it dry. The sleeve will last for years and is invaluable. Available in most department store cookware sections and fancy cookware shops. Lacking the sleeve, dust the dough with flour and lay waxed paper over it.

. . . rolling from the center outward.

Do so, and dust with more flour only when necessary. Roll evenly, and unless otherwise noted, ⅛-inch thick for both bottom and top pastries.

. . . the bottom pastry—the shell.

Use the cloth to lift the dough and curl it over the rolling pin, then slide the pie dish underneath and center the dough over the dish. Uncurl the pin, dropping the dough evenly into the dish. Be careful not to stretch the dough. Push the dough down toward the center until it snugly lines the dish. Work out any pleats and push out any air bubbles. Press any tears together and patch where necessary (just press the dough until it holds, but don't use water). Trim as directed with scissors or a knife.

Brush the inside of the shell with softened butter (sog protection).

For a one-crust pie, trim a scant ½-inch beyond the edge of the dish, then tuck the margin of dough under itself, flush with the rim; flute the edge (suggestions follow).

For a lattice-topped or *two-crust pie*, trim the dough a little beyond the edge and leave it for now.

. . . partially baking a shell.

Chill the shell at least ½ hour before baking. Heat the oven to 425°F and set the rack in the upper third of the oven. Press a square of foil firmly against the pastry, folding it carefully over the border and crimping it against the outside—this helps keep the sides from slumping. Fill the shell half-full with dry beans or pebbles or pie weights, pushing them up against the sides. Bake 12 minutes, then gingerly remove the foil and weights; cool thoroughly in the dish on a rack before filling.

. . . *completely baking a shell (baking "blind").*

After removing the foil and weights (above), return the shell to the oven. Check in a few minutes—if the bottom puffs up, prick with a fork to release the steam; check again in a few minutes and prick again, if necessary. Bake until the pastry is crisp, dry, and golden brown, 6 to 8 more minutes—do not underbake. Cool thoroughly in its dish on a rack before filling.

For a tart shell of *pâte sucrée* or almond pastry, remove from the mold immediately and cool on a rack.

. . . *the top pastry—resting.*

After rolling out the top, whether a lid or strips for a lattice, since the edge of the top pastry isn't trimmed until in place over the filling, slide a large inverted plate beneath the cloth under the dough, cover the dough with plastic film, and set in a cool place. Do not refrigerate because the pastry will become brittle and break when you handle it.

. . . *the top pastry—a lid.*

Fill the shell and brush the bottom rim with cold water or egg yolk. Curl the pastry lid onto your rolling pin—don't stretch it—and slide the pie dish beneath, centering it. Uncurl the pastry over the pie. Smooth the lid over the filling, avoiding folds. If anything pierces the pastry, patch the tear carefully, or juices will be lost. Trim the pastry ½-inch beyond the rim of the dish. To ensure a seal, tuck this margin under the bottom pastry, making the edge flush with the rim. Flute the edge. For a juicy pie, the best insurance against juices bubbling over is to cut a hole the size of a silver dollar in the center (you can decoratively arrange pastry leaves or other fancies around it).

. . . *the top pastry—a lattice.*

Cut the round into ½-inch-wide strips—a pizza cutter against a ruler does the best job. When ready to bake, smooth the filling evenly into the unbaked shell. Brush the bottom rim with cold water or egg yolk. Lay on the pastry strips in a diamond lattice (or squares, if you prefer), setting them a scant ½ inch apart (or any distance you like), and centering the strips so their tails are evenly spaced at each side. When all the strips are in place, trim the tails a scant ½-inch beyond the bottom shell. Tuck each tail under the bottom, making the edge flush with the rim. Flute the edge.

. . . *fluting.*

Whether for the bottom shell alone or for the lid and bottom shell together: Press a forefinger, chopstick, or the tip of a handle slantwise around the rim while your opposite forefinger presses against its side. Do this all around the edge, shaping the fluting as high as you can. You can make your flutes straight on instead of slanted and broad instead of narrow and ruffled instead of swirled. Just don't use fork tines because it looks like the borders machines make for store-bought pies.

. . . *before you make a fine* JAM TURNOVER
with any pastry scraps for The Baker or an Object of the Baker's Affection, best wait until the pie has nearly baked—there may be patching to be done, either during the finishing touches or in the oven. Then press the scraps together, roll into a thin round, drop a spoonful of jam or jelly in the center, moisten the rim, fold over, press the seam together with a fork, prick the top, slip onto a small baking sheet or a couple of layers of foil, and bake until lightly browned, 15 to 20 minutes.

RICE PAPER, EDIBLE
Calissons d'Aix are traditionally spread on a very thin paper made of rice. The paper not only keeps the candy from sticking, but gives a pleasing finish to the bottom of the confection. Rice paper is available from bakers' supplies (look in the yellow pages) or from Maid of Scandinavia Co., 3244 Raleigh Avenue, Minneapolis, Minnesota 55416. Ask for "wafer paper." Because you'll use them so seldom, a bundle of the papers will last for years (I've had mine going on ten).

ROCKFISH
(Also sold as rock cod, red, or Pacific snapper.)
. . . *selecting.*
The rules are: If you can see the whole fish, choose the deeper-bodied species, which usually are firmer fleshed and fuller flavored than the more elongated species. If you can't see the whole fish, price will be an indication of the qualities you want—when you can, buy the most expensive. A good place to shop for rockfish is a Chinese market, since Chinese cuisine appreciates its fineness.

RULER
Look in the drafting section of a stationery or art supply store for an 18- by 4-inch clear plastic ruler with the inches marked down the length of the ruler as well as along the width—a great help in cutting pastry strips and such.

"SET THE LID ON ASKEW . . ."
That's called for for one of two reasons. The first is that, when you're simmering, if the lid is on tight, chances are the pot will roil and bubble and sputter and make a terrible mess; if the lid is on askew, enough steam can escape to handle the energy inside.

The second reason is that, when you're cooling something, you want cold air to be able to reach the food—circulation is important. Otherwise you'd be trapping all the bacteria and potential bad guys inside and the food might spoil before morning. *Always* cool a covered pot with its lid askew.

SHRIMPS

. . . BUTTER

Pulverize the shells in a blender or food processor and melt with an equal weight of unsalted butter. In a heavy saucepan over low heat, bring to a simmer. Remove from the heat and let cool a little, then strain through a damp cloth lining a sieve into an appropriately sized vessel. Cover well and refrigerate up to 1 week or freeze for several months. If any whey separates from the butter, discard it.

The soft shells of prawns, crayfish, crabs, and lobsters can be used in the same way.

. . . *buying.*

Even when we were on the Gulf of Mexico, shrimps in the market were frozen. All things being equal, quick-frozen-last-minute-thawed shrimps are probably the freshest tasting.

If you can buy them fresh, as with all fish, shrimps must *smell* sweet (give the fish man the fish-eye right back if he's snippy when you ask to sniff his wares). If they are in a plastic-wrapped tray, buy them, then open and smell them on the spot. If the raw shrimps have been frozen, try to buy them still in a block, then thaw in the refrigerator or if in a hurry, in cold water. If the fish dealer insists on thawing the shrimps before you can buy them (this just happened to me), ideally you should go back the day you'll be cooking them. If that's impractical, turn the thawed shrimps into a plastic bag and keep over or under crushed ice in the coldest part of the refrigerator no more than 1 day.

. . . *shelling.*

Do not wash (flavor goes, and anyway, all the shrimp's covering is going to be removed). Holding firmly by the fan of the tail with one hand, slip the thumb of your other hand beneath the "legs" and the shell and lift off several of the sections, then pull off the remaining sections of shell. For some presentations, you'll want to leave the fan on the tail, for others, you'll want to nip it off with your thumbnail. Shelling (and deveining) may be done a few hours in advance of cooking; just return the shrimps to the refrigerator.

. . . *deveining.*

It used to be that deveining shrimps was a matter of esthetics. But my daughter Dinah, knowledgeable about the sea, points out that shrimps are bottom feeders and there are plenty of impurities that have settled to the bottom of our oceans. The "vein," then, becomes the repository of those impurities in the shrimp—therefore deveining is highly recommended.

After shelling, hold the shrimp by its thickest end and, with the tip of a small knife, peel away the thin layer of flesh over the center of the back, then simply lift up or pull away the black thread.

SPINACH, FRESH—AND ALL OTHER LEAFY GREENS

. . . *rinsing.*

Swish in a sinkful of warm water (warm water causes the leaves to relax and release sand faster than does cold water). Drain the water and repeat until there is no more sand at the bottom of the sink. Shake excess moisture off the leaves. For most company dishes, pinch off and discard the stems; leave them in place for the family. (Chard and other fleshy stems are cut like celery and cooked either separately or along with the leaves.)

. . . *cooking.*

Use the leaves with just the moisture left on them from rinsing. Turn into a broad heavy skillet (the more surface, the more evenly the vegetable will cook, and if you cook the leaves in an iron skillet, you'll pick up a little extra iron). Cover and cook gently over low to medium heat, stirring occasionally, just until the leaves are limp, 3 to 4 minutes. Continue with your recipe, or chop and serve with lots of butter and a little lemon juice, salt, and pepper.

SQUID

. . . *cleaning.*

Under cool running water, pull the tentacled body from the hood, then rub off all the hood's speckled membrane. Pull out and discard the insides of the hood; rinse it clean—this is mainly what you'll cook. Cut the tentacles from the body and use them as the recipe directs. Discard everything else.

SUGAR

. . . *coarse crystals.*

When you see sugar of coarse crystals on sweet breads and cookies at a bakery, ask to buy a couple of pounds of the sugar. It keeps forever in a tightly covered jar and makes such a difference in the looks of baked goods. Sometimes you can buy sugar in a swirl of pretty colors. Great for Christmas, but for most baking, you want the shimmering white crystals.

. . . *vanilla.*

Granulated sugar in a jar with as many vanilla beans as you can muster buried in it. The bean can be whole or in pieces, pristine or recycled—bits of bean used in flavoring may be returned to the jar over and over until they have spent their vanilla scent, at which time, replace them.

SWEET PEPPERS

. . . peeling.

Set the whole peppers directly on the flame of a gas burner or under a hot broiler. Turn with tongs until as much of the skin as possible is charred. At once turn into a damp paper bag and twist the end tight—this creates a little steam, to help loosen the skin. When cool enough to handle, scrape the peel off with a knife blade. Do not wash—you'll lose flavor. In most dishes, a little of the charred skin not only won't hurt, but will add a tad of flavor. This is the technique used for peeling chili peppers as well, only remember to keep your hands away from your face and to wear rubber gloves if the peppers are fiery.

TOMATOES

. . . keeping.

In the butter compartment of the refrigerator (if it's between 50°F and 60°F) or at room temperature, out of the sun.

. . . peeling.

Drop them in boiling water or set them directly on the gas burner and turn with tongs just until the skin splits. Slip off the skin—you may have to use a small sharp knife to begin the peeling, if the tomatoes aren't qute ripe.

. . . seeding.

Cut tomatoes in half through the middle (like an orange for juicing). Then, over a strainer set over a bowl, run the tip of a finger into each chamber and nip out the seeds; often they'll come out in a bundle. Press the contents of the strainer to extract their juice and use the juice in the bowl in cooking.

TOSTADA DINNER FOR 12

. . . amounts for accompaniments to the recipes.

Please use these figures as guidelines, taking into consideration the appetites of your guests. My feeling is that it's better to have too much rather than too little . . .

JÍCAMA

1 pound, peeled and thinly sliced

FOR SERVING WITH THE JÍCAMA

2 limes or 1 orange; either cut in thin wedges

PUMPKIN OR SUNFLOWER SEEDS

8 ounces; toast them

ALMONDS OR PEANUTS

8 ounces; toast them

STRAWBERRIES

about 18 big fat ones; unhulled

TURKEY

6 to 7 pounds bone-in; poached or roasted, then skinned, boned, and coarsely shredded

TOMATOES

3 pounds; thinly sliced

ICEBERG LETTUCE

2 small heads; shredded

SLICED BLACK OLIVES

3 small cans; well drained

SCALLIONS

2 whole bunches; cut in thin rings

RADISHES

2 bunches; thinly sliced

JACK CHEESE

about 1⅔ pounds; medium-grated

SOUR CREAM

about 1½ pints

CILANTRO

2 small bunches; the leaves chopped

BEER AND WINE

On average, 18 bottles of beer and a 1.5 liter bottle of wine

WHISK

My flat stainless steel whisk (it looks like a small old-fashioned rug beater) is the tool I use most in the kitchen. For some reason, a flat whisk is hard to find—balloon whisks abound. But I think the flat shape is the best for everything from mixing clumps of frozen juices at breakfast to staving off lumps in a sauce for dinner.

WOODEN SPATULA

Years ago from France, M. F. sent me something made of olivewood in the size and shape of a large rubber spatula with dime-size holes in the working end. The tool's chiefest virtue is that it has a broad flat end, which makes it marvelous for stirring sauces or other viscid mixtures that threaten to stick to the bottom of the pot. Highly recommended. I see versions of them all the time now in cookware shops.

"WRAP IT . . ."

Although I don't fancy plastic in the kitchen, I do use plastic film for wrapping when wrapping is called for. Alas, plastic film is most efficient, unless it's a matter of conducting a temperature, such as dough that's refrigerated—

in that case, aluminum foil conducts the cold to the package better. But we all managed beautifully with waxed paper B.P.F., so you can do that, too, if you prefer.

YEAST

If you're going to be baking frequently, buy active dry yeast in bulk at the health food store and keep it tightly wrapped in the refrigerator. You'll save a fortune over a hundred little packets.

Bibliography

More than anything else, books have been my teachers. Listing all the ones I care about would take pages, so in the interest of brevity, here are the books mentioned in this work:

Alexandre Dumas' Dictionary of Cuisine by Alexandre Dumas. Edited, abridged, and translated by Louis Colman. New York: An Avon book, 1958.

Alexis Lichine's Guide to the Wines and Vineyards of France by Alexis Lichine. New York: Alfred A. Knopf, 1979.

The Alice B. Toklas Cook Book by Alice B. Toklas. New York: Harper & Brothers, 1954.

American Cooking: The Great West by Jonathan Norton Leonard and the Editors of Time-Life Books. New York: Time-Life Books, 1971.

America's Cook Book compiled by The Home Institute of The New York Herald Tribune. New York: Charles Scribner's Sons, 1947.

The Art of Cookery, Made Plain and Easy by Hannah Glasse. London: J. Rivington and Sons, 1788.

The Art of Eating by M. F. K. Fisher. Cleveland and New York: The World Publishing Company, 1954.

The Art of Fine Baking by Paula Peck. New York: Simon and Schuster, 1961.

Beard on Bread by James Beard. New York: Alfred A. Knopf, 1975.

British Cookery. Edited by Lizzie Boyd. London: Croom Helm Ltd., 1977.

The Cheeses & Wines of England & France by John Ehle. New York: Harper & Row, Publishers, 1972.

Chico's Organic Gardening and Natural Living by Frank (Chico) Bucaro and David Wallechinsky. New York: J. B. Lippincott Company, 1972.

The Cooking of South-West France by Paula Wolfert. New York: Doubleday & Company, Inc., 1983.

Crumbs from Everybody's Table, publisher, place, and date unknown.

La Cuisine by Raymond Oliver. New York: Tudor Publishing Company, 1969.

La cuisine moderne by *Une réunion de cuisiniers*, Aristide Quillet, editor. Paris: Librairie Commerciale, 1907.

La cuisinière Provençale by J.-B. Reboul. Seventeenth edition. Marseille: Tacussel, n.d.

Cuisines et vins de France by Curnonsky (Maurice-Edmond Sailland). Paris: Librairie Larousse, 1953.

The Cuisines of Mexico by Diana Kennedy. New York: Harper & Row, Publishers, 1972.

The Escoffier Cook Book by A. Escoffier. New York: Crown Publishers, 1941.

Food by Waverley Root. New York: Simon and Schuster, 1980.

French Provincial Cooking by Elizabeth David. Harmondsworth, Middlesex: Penguin Books Ltd., 1964.

From Julia Child's Kitchen. New York: Alfred A. Knopf, 1975.

Gastronomie bretonne by Simone Morand. Paris: Flammarion, 1965.

Greek Cooking by Robin Howe. London: André Deutsch, 1960.

Italian Regional Cooking by Ada Boni. Translated by Maria Langdale and Ursula Whyte. New York: Bonanza Books, 1969.

The Joy of Cooking by Irma S. Rombauer. New York: The Bobbs-Merrill Company, 1946.

Larousse gastronomique by Prosper Montagné. New York: Crown Publishers, Inc., 1961.

Leaves from Our Tuscan Kitchen by Janet Ross and Michael Waterfield. New York: Vintage Books, 1975.

Martha Washington's Booke of Cookery transcribed by Karen Hess. New York: Columbia University Press, 1981.

Mrs. Beeton's Household Management. London: Ward, Lock & Co., Limited, n.d.

Mrs Rorer's New Cook Book by Sarah Tyson Rorer. Philadelphia: Arnold and Company, 1902.

Russian Cookery by Nina Petrova. Harmondsworth, Middlesex: Penguin Books Ltd., 1970.

Il Talismano della Felicità by Ada Boni. Twenty-third edition. Rome: Casa Editrice Carlo Colombo, n.d.

The Times Cook Book No. 4. Los Angeles: The Times-Mirror Co., 1911.

The Vegetable Garden by Mm. Vilmorin-Andrieux. Berkeley: Ten Speed Press, 1981.

Index

An asterisk indicates the entry is an outline for a dish in the text, rather than a recipe.

†Any fish you bring home will find recipes here, since fish is prepared by shape.

braised, with fresh peas 60
braising time 59–60
test for doneness, *see* chicken
garlic
 chopping 249
 with green olives and celery in a Sicilian relish
  221
 in melted butter and lemon juice over grilled
  fish* 232
 peeling 248
Gastronomical Me, The 101
Gastronomie bretonne 29
Gâteau breton
 aux abricots * 41
  secs * 41
 aux brugnons * 41
 aux cerises * 41
 aux coings * 41
 aux confitures * 41
 aux framboises * 41
  et groseilles * 41
 aux groseilles vertes * 41
 aux mûres * 41
 aux pêches * 41
  sèches * 41
 aux petits machins bleus * 41
 aux poires * 41
  sèches * 41
 aux pommes 39
 de pruneaux * 41
 aux prunes * 41
 de rhubarbe et fraises * 41
Gâteau de pain 32
Gigot à la bretonne classique 50
ginger
 candied, with currants in a Cornish cake
  229
 fresh:
  cake 152
  keeping 151fn
  no need to peel 152fn
  in pear chutney 163
  substituting ground 152fn
Glaçage au chocolat 91
Glace royale 96
glazes, *see* frostings and glazes
Gnocchi verdi squisiti 118

goose
 fat:
  browning and braising in 64fn
  rendering and using 64
 in Kirschwasser aspic 62
 liver for *pâté* * 64
 oven-poached 62
 stock 63
 test for doneness, *see* chicken
gooseberries
 in brandied fruit conserve 72
 filling a Breton sweet pastry* 41
 in fresh fruits with maraschino 122
 molded in an English pudding 195
 under or over pastry 23
goosefish, *see* angler
Goose in the Kirschwasser Aspic, The 62
graham crackers, number to make crumbs 80fn
Graham Torte, After Abby's 80
Grandmother's Carrot Pudding, My 24
Granita di melone 120
grape
 Concord jelly, in a tart of almond pastry 216, 217fn
 leaves, in *dolmades* 181
gratins
 bay shrimp and buttery onions, Breton 47
 mussels* 219
 scallops and buttery onions, Breton 46
Greek Cooking 178
greens, cooked like spinach 258
Grilled Galantine of Chicken 211
Grilled Kid 109
Grilled Tenderloin of Pork 233
grilling (over coals or wood)
 chicken (or turkey*), galantine 211
 fish:
  steaks* 232
  whole 173
 kid 109
 lamb, leg 51
 pork, tenderloin 233
 setting the drip pan 51fn
grouper
 an all-purpose fish 248
 good in soup 242
 grilled the Greek way 173
 also see fish